Functional Features
in Language and Space

Functional Features in Language and Space: Insights from Perception, Categorization, and Development

Edited by

LAURA CARLSON *and*
EMILE VAN DER ZEE

OXFORD
UNIVERSITY PRESS

*This book has been printed digitally and produced in a standard specification
in order to ensure its continuing availability*

OXFORD
UNIVERSITY PRESS

Great Clarendon Street, Oxford OX2 6DP

Oxford University Press is a department of the University of Oxford.
It furthers the University's objective of excellence in research, scholarship,
and education by publishing worldwide in

Oxford New York

Auckland Cape Town Dar es Salaam Hong Kong Karachi
Kuala Lumpur Madrid Melbourne Mexico City Nairobi
New Delhi Shanghai Taipei Toronto
With offices in
Argentina Austria Brazil Chile Czech Republic France Greece
Guatemala Hungary Italy Japan South Korea Poland Portugal
Singapore Switzerland Thailand Turkey Ukraine Vietnam

Oxford is a registered trade mark of Oxford University Press
in the UK and in certain other countries

Published in the United States
by Oxford University Press Inc., New York

ISBN 0-19-926432-5

Printed and bound by CPI Antony Rowe, Eastbourne

Contents

PART THREE—FEATURES THAT ARE FUNCTIONAL:
CATEGORIZATION, LEARNING, AND LANGUAGE

Preface

This volume is based on edited papers presented at the Language and Space Workshop: Defining Functional and Spatial Features, held at the University of Notre Dame, South Bend, IN in June 2001. As we discuss in the introductory chapter, the goal of the conference was to examine how the concepts of 'feature' and 'function' and 'functional feature' are defined across the domain of cognitive science (including development, categorization, perception, and spatial language), and to assess the applicability of these definitions for defining features in language and space. The Notre Dame workshop was the second in a series, preceded by the 'Defining Direction in Language and Space: Axes and Vector Representations', held in Lincoln, UK in 2000, and followed by 'Defining Granularity in Language and Space', held in Bielefeld, Germany, 2002. We thank the Graduate School, the Institute for Scholarship in the Liberal Arts, the Department of Psychology, and the College of Arts and Letters Dean's office, all at the University of Notre Dame, for funding for the conference. We thank John Davey, editor at Oxford University Press for his support and guidance during the editing process.

Laura Carlson
Emile van der Zee

List of Contributors

LAWRENCE BARSALOU is on the faculty of Psychology at Emory University (USA). He performs research on human knowledge from the perspectives of cognitive psychology, cognitive science, and cognitive neuroscience.

LAURA CARLSON is associate professor of psychology at the University of Notre Dame. Her research interests are in spatial language, spatial cognition, and visual perception.

SERGIO CHAIGNEAU is on the faculty of Psychology at the University of Tarapaca (Chile). He performs research on human knowledge from the perspectives of cognitive psychology and cognitive science.

BRYCE CORRIGAN is a graduate student in statistics at Carnegie-Mellon University. His research interests are in statistical modeling in the social sciences.

EDWIN COVELL is a graduate student in the Department of Psychology at the University of Notre Dame. His research interests are in visual perception.

KENNY COVENTRY is Reader in the Centre for Thinking and Language, Department of Psychology, University of Plymouth, United Kingdom.

MANUEL DE VEGA is a professor of Psychology at the University of La Laguna, Spain. His research interests are the interface between language and spatial knowledge, and how situation models are built and updated during text comprehension.

CAROLA ESCHENBACH is a senior researcher at the Department for Informatics at the University of Hamburg, Germany. She works on formal ontology and formal approaches to the semantics of natural language.

SIMON GARROD is Professor of Psychology in the Human Communication Research Centre, Department of Psychology, University of Glasgow, Scotland. His research interests are in text comprehension, psychological approaches to semantics, and language processing in dialogue.

ARTHUR GLENBERG is on the faculty of the Psychology Department at the University of Wisconsin—Madison. His research interests are memory and language comprehension.

ROBERT GOLDSTONE is a professor at Indiana University. His research interests include concept learning, perceptual learning, computational modeling, and comparison processes.

CHRISTOPHER HABEL is Professor of Computer Science and Linguistics at the University of Hamburg. His research topics include the interaction of semantics and spatial cognition from a cognitive as well as from a mathematical point of view.

MICHAEL KASCHAK is on the Faculty of the Psychology Department at Florida State University. His research interests are in the role of experience and context in shaping language acquisition and comprehension.

RAJESH KASTURIRANGAN is a graduate student in the Department of Brain and Cognitive Science at MIT. His research interests include computational models of spatial cognition, and the interface of spatial knowledge with other cognitive systems such as language.

KELLY MADOLE is an Associate Professor of Psychology at Western Kentucky University. Her research has focused on infants' understanding of functional properties of objects and how they use those properties to categorize as well as on how children come to construct social categories such as race and gender.

URPO NIKANNE is a Professor of Finnish at Åbo Akademi University in Finland. His research interests are the structure of the Finnish language and the theory of conceptual semantics.

LISA OAKES is an Associate Professor of Psychology at the University of Iowa. Her research has focused on the development of causal perception, categorization, and attention allocation in infancy. Her most recent work has been aimed at understanding the processes through which infants form categories.

PAUL C. QUINN is a Professor of Psychology at the University of Delaware. He is interested in early cognitive development with a focus on the abilities of young infants to represent information about objects and space.

SANDEEP PRASADA is an Associate Professor of Psychology in the Department of Psychology at Hunter College, CUNY. His research interests are conceptual representation, lexical and conceptual development, and the interaction of linguistic and conceptual structure.

TERRY REGIER is associate professor of psychology at the University of Chicago. His research interests are in computational modeling of the interaction of language and thought, with a focus on word-learning.

LYNN RICHARDS is a Lecuturer in Human Sciences, Peninsula Medical School, Plymouth, United Kingdom. Her research interests are in the development of spatial cognition and spatial language.

MARÍA J. RODRIGO is a professor of Developmental Psychology at the University of La Laguna, Spain. Her research interests are the early development of verbal and gestural deixis and the role of maternal input.

BRIAN ROGOSKY is developing cognitive modeling software at Discovery Machine, Inc. His interests include knowledge representation and applied cognitive science.

STEVEN SLOMAN is on the faculty of Cognitive and Linguistic Sciences at Brown University (USA). He performs research on human reasoning from the perspectives of cognitive psychology and cognitive science.

LINDA B. SMITH is a Chancellor's Professor of Psychology and Cognitive Science at Indiana University—Bloomington. Her research is directed to understanding developmental processes especially at it applies to cognition and early word learning. Her current work seeks to understand how word learning changes processes fundamental to word learning itself—including attention and object perception.

BARBARA TVERSKY is a professor in the Department of Psychology at Stanford University. Her research interests include spatial language and thinking, memory, categorization, including eyewitness testimony, diagrammatic reasoning, human–computer interaction, design, and influences of language on thought.

CLAUDE VANDELOISE is a professor in the Department of French Studies at Louisiana State University. His main interests are in cognitive semantics and in the linguistic description of space in French.

EMILE van der ZEE is a principal lecturer at the Department of Psychology at the University of Lincoln (UK). His main research interest is the representation of spatial information in language and its interfaces.

RANXIAO FRANCES WANG is an assistant professor in the Department of Psychology at the University of Illinois at Urbana-Champaign. Her research interests are in visual perception and spatial memory.

MATT WATSON is a graduate student at the University of Edinburgh. His main research interests are the communication of object location in dialogue, and the structure and access of semantic memory.

1

Functional Features in Language and Space

LAURA A. CARLSON and EMILE VAN DER ZEE

> If the only tool you have is a hammer, you tend to see every problem as a nail.
>
> Abraham Maslow

This book examines the role of *functional features* in language and space. Let us start by exploring what functional features might be, and then examine why such features might play a role in spatial language. Consider the above quote about hammers. A paraphrase of that quote could be that having a hammer encourages one to view other objects in light of their potential interactions with the hammer. For example, if a spider were crawling across the floor, you might think of a squashing function that involves the head of the hammer. In contrast, if a lid were stuck on a jar, you might think of a prying function that involves the claw of the hammer. In this way, various perceptual features or affordances of the object (hammer) in conjunction with the goal of the user (kill the spider, open the lid) dictate the type of interaction between the objects. The concept of functional features thereby contains the following elements: perceptual properties or affordances of the objects (features); the functions or uses that such features enable (functions); and the means by which such features are used in the context of satisfying a goal (features that are functional).

One may wonder what the notions of 'feature' and 'function' have to do with spatial language. *Spatial language* refers to the total set of linguistic expressions that denote aspects of space. Within this broad definition, spatial language includes not only prepositions that refer to the location of an entity in relation to another entity (e.g. 'John is in front of the house'), but also adverbs that refer to the perceived deformation of an entity (e.g. 'The road runs straight'), verbs that refer to the perceived movement of an entity through space (e.g. 'John ran home'), adjectives that refer to perceived spatial properties of entities (e.g. 'John is tall'), and nouns that refer to perceived parts of entities (e.g., 'John's nose'). Figure 1.1 illustrates the domain of space–time, and from it, the derived formal/cognitive representation of this domain. The research area of *Language and Space*

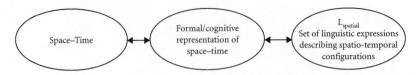

FIG. 1.1. The mappings or interfaces that are studied in the area of language and space. Functional features may reside in the formal/cognitive domain, in $L_{spatial}$, but also in the mapping relation between both domains.

examines how expressions in spatial language ($L_{spatial}$) obtain their meaning as a function of the set of formal or cognitive representations of space–time (see also Peterson, Nadel, Bloom, and Garrett, 1996; van der Zee and Slack, 2003).

Formally, functional features are derived features that result from a formal or cognitive operation on space–time entities. As such, functional features do not occupy the space–time domain in Fig. 1.1, but rather are situated within the formal or cognitive domain representing space–time, within $L_{spatial}$, within both, or within their mapping. This is consistent with the assertion that the meaning of spatial expressions is influenced by the identities and functions of the objects, their interaction, and the context in which they occur, and is supported on theoretical grounds (Herskovits, 1986, 1998; Vandeloise, 1991, 1994) and by empirical studies (Carlson-Radvansky, Covey, and Lattanzi, 1999; Carlson-Radvansky and Radvansky, 1996; Carlson-Radvansky and Tang, 2000; Coventry, Carmichael, and Garrod, 1994; Coventry, Prat-Sala, and Richards, 2001; for an excellent review, see Coventry and Garrod, 2004). Functional features thus impact spatial language, and a complete understanding of spatial language therefore requires an understanding of these features.

Viewed as derived features, our bias is that an understanding of functional features in spatial language may begin with an understanding of how the key elements of this concept are defined in closely related subdisciplines of cognitive science, including perception, categorization, and development. This is especially important, because each of the elements of this concept ('features', 'function', and 'features that are functional for a given purpose') are not always consistently defined across authors and disciplines. A central goal of the current book is to give an overview of existing definitions of the elements of the concept 'functional feature', thus contributing to a better understanding of how these elements are put to use within the cognitive representations serving spatial language. To assist in this endeavor, we have asked each author to supply a definition at the outset of their chapter that conveys for the reader the way in which 'features', 'function', 'functional features', or a highly related concept is defined within their research domain. As will become clear over the course of reading the chapters in this book, these terms are highly polysemous. As such, these definitions provide the reader with a guide, not only for interpreting the work within the context of a given chapter, but also for fitting ideas together across chapters.

The integration across chapters is also assisted by organizing the book around clusters of definitions that tend to focus on similar aspects. Specifically, Part One is organized around features that are derived from perception, action, and embodiment, with a focus on the situation in which language is embedded. The chapters in this section focus on how features are used in context and sometimes offer definitions of 'function' that can be transferred into any one of several theoretical frameworks in the language and space area. In this sense the definitions may be generalizable across domains. The second part is organized around defining function from the perspective of more specific theoretical frameworks, and illustrates approaches for assessing the impact of such features within spatial language. While the two parts differ, the common elements in both parts reflect the idea that this book focuses on features of objects pertaining to their function, a particular linguistic reference situation, and the particular goal espoused by the interlocutors, all of which are derived from perception, action, and embodiment. The third part is organized around features that are functional for particular cognitive tasks, including learning, categorization, and language. The fourth part offers a convincing portrait of the pervasiveness of functional features throughout various research domains within the research area of language and space, and serves to highlight some of the central points emerging out of the previous sections. We prefer this organization over a more traditional organization built around the various subdisciplines (perception, categorization, development, psycholinguistics, linguistics) because it stresses the interdisciplinary use of these elements, and, we hope, will further encourage collaborative work across these areas. While a uniform understanding of each of these elements is far from being achieved, the similarities and differences in treatments of these elements both within and across domains may lead to insights as to the best way to define and examine 'features', and 'function', for language and space.

In the remaining sections of this chapter, we will briefly characterize the chapters within each section of the book, discussing how each chapter addresses the ideas of 'feature', 'function', and 'features that are functional', and its potential impact for spatial language.

1.1 Part One—Features: Derived from Perception, Action, and Embodiement

The chapters in this section all focus on features that are derived from the perceptual characteristics of the objects in a given setting, and how they interact with a person and the environment. Glenberg and Kaschak (Ch. 2) offer the *Indexical Hypothesis*, according to which language is to be understood in terms of action. Within this perspective, meaning is not based on abstract, amodal, and arbitrary symbols, but is grounded in the goals, context, and action surrounding the situation described by the language. This approach questions the assumption that a set of features can be defined in the abstract. According to Glenberg and Kaschak functional features correspond to *affordances*—the way in which an animal with a particular type of body can interact with a particular type of object. The use of syntax is one mechanism by which affordances can be expressed via language. Functional features are thus both an integral part of the general cognitive system, as well of the language system

The next three chapters take a similar approach but make the additional point that the impact of features may be task-dependent. For example, de Vega and Rodrigo (Ch. 3) contrast two spatial communicative tasks to examine directional terms such *as front* and *left*, one based on language (describing) and one based on action (pointing). They find a different pattern of performance within each task, suggesting that features that are salient within one are not necessarily salient in the other. In addition, they espouse an approach similar to Glenberg and Kaschak (Ch. 2) in interpreting functional features as features emerging from an interaction between an animate agent and their environment. This means that functional features underlying directional term use are more remotely tied to bodily action—hence second-order embodiment—than functional features emerging from direct action (first-order embodiment). The work of de Vega and Rodrigo thus points to distinctive manifestations of functional features at different levels of cognitive processing. Similarly, Wang (Ch. 4) questions whether a feature (i.e. an imagined spatial perspective) that is central to functioning within a particular domain (i.e. a verbal-based system) is necessarily central within a different cognitive domain (i.e. an action-based system). Finally, Kasturirangan (Ch. 5) focuses on the representation of spatial relations within language and perception, and presents a framework in which certain spatial features (i.e. *coordinate frames* and *topological structures*) are common to language and perception whereas others (i.e. metric structures) are specific to one system. This approach thus echoes the issue raised by Wang and deVega and Rodrigo as to whether features within one domain are functional in other domains.

The remaining chapters in this section postulate the use of different types of features, and seek to characterize these sets and their relations. Eschenbach (Ch. 6) takes a linguistic approach in examining a collection of German projective terms (including prepositions, postpositions, adverbs, and adjectives) in order to identify similarities between different items, and map them to common semantic components or syntactic regularities. Within her approach, the geometric components and the functional components are combined in the semantics of the lexemes, and contextual influences are represented within the argument structure of the lexemes and the free variables occurring in the semantic form. Habel (Ch. 7) focuses on changes in orientation, examining the characteristics of the object being oriented, as well as on the orientation movement itself, and how they influence the particular expressions that are used to describe these spatial changes. With 'functional concepts' Habel also refers to those concepts that cannot completely be described in a geometric framework. As in Eschenbach's chapter, Habel's concepts are lexical entities. Taking a more narrow focus on a particular spatial term, van der Zee and Watson (Ch. 8) present an in-depth analysis of *between,* identifying several kinds of features that may specify its meaning, and assess their relative contributions. They conclude that the lexical specification of *between* is mainly based on spatial features, but must also allow for context effects based on *visual functional features* (visual features playing a role in object categorization), *linguistic functional features* (lexical features of other words inviting a particular object categorization), *general functional features* (features contributed by cognitive processes found across cognitive systems), and *dynamic–kinematic features* (features directly specifying actual or potential interaction between physical entities). This work thus considers how the influence of geometric and extra-geometric features from several cognitive domains may be integrated by the lexicon to account for the contextual meaning of *between.*

With respect to research in language and space, all chapters in this part of the book make the point that spatial language cannot be examined in isolation but must be interpreted within a situational context (see also Clark, 1996). This means not only that the salient features of a object that is being described may vary across tasks, but also that a variety of features, defined from across different domains (perceptual, geometric, affordances, extra-geometric) and across different levels of analysis, may apply, emphasizing the necessity of studying their relationship.

1.2   Part Two—Function: Definitions and Influence

Part Two is devoted to defining function and assessing its influence. It opens with Barsalou, Sloman, and Chaigneau's (Ch. 9) presentation of a new theoretical framework for defining function. According to their *HIPE theory,* function is a complex relational concept that draws on the domains of history, intentional perspective, the physical environment, and event sequences for its content. Moreover, echoing the idea from Part One that features are not fixed, different senses of the function of a particular entity can be constructed that depend on the conceptualizer's current goal, setting, and personal history.

Coventry and Garrod (Ch. 10) present a classification of extra-geometric features, dichotomizing them into dynamic–kinematic aspects of scenes, and knowledge of the functions of objects and their typical interaction, outlining evidence in favor of each, and the conditions under which such features may operate. Richards and Coventry (Ch. 11) adopt a developmental approach, examining the emergence of the extra-geometric factor of *location control* and its influence on spatial language use. Location control is a force dynamic relationship whereby the position of the located object is determined over time by the position of the reference object. They show that children from age 3 to 4 modify their spatial expressions under the influence of location control manipulations.

The next pair of chapters uses a particular functional effect—that participants are likely to define a given spatial relation with respect to a functional part of an object (Carlson-Radvansky, Covey, and Lattanzi, 1999)—as a starting point, defining function with respect to the objects being spatially related. Specifically, Carlson and Covell (Ch. 12) seek to associate variability in this functional effect with various features of the reference object. Regier, Carlson, and Corrigan (Ch. 13) start with the original *attention-vector sum model* or *AVS* (Regier and Carlson, 2001) that offers an account of spatial language, and modify it to include a functional component that takes into account the parts of the reference object and its interaction with the located object, thereby accommodating both geometric and functional features.

Prasada (Ch. 14) examines functional properties in terms of our conceptions of different kinds of objects, drawing a distinction between construals of entities as objects and as stuff. Such construals impose an explanatory structure on entities, specifying a particular way of thinking about the entities and their geometric properties. In this manner, construals operate to combine the geometric and extra-geometric properties discussed by Coventry and Garrod (Ch. 10) and Regier, Carlson, and Corrigan (Ch. 13).

Finally, Vandeloise (Ch. 15) focuses on the function of containment, and its role in the development of the spatial uses of the preposition *in*. Specifically, he defines *in* with respect to the kinetic and dynamic properties, with properties representing envelopment and concavity treated as consequences of the function of containment. His in-depth analysis of this particular function gives insight into the level of description that may be required for applying 'function' to spatial language.

With respect to research on language and space, the work in this section of the book offers potentially rich characterizations of function (e.g. a relational concept, a construal). It also documents a variety of influences related to the interaction between the objects on the interpretation of spatial language. The next step is a systematic comparison across the definitions, and a more formal characterization of the influences and their relationship, with a goal of rallying around a terminology that can be uniformly applied across the domain of spatial language research.

1.3   Part Three—Features that are Functional: Categorization, Learning, and Language

This section of the book focuses on features that are functional within categorization, learning, and language, emphasizing the role that features play in accomplishing a given cognitive task. Smith (Ch. 16) focuses on features defining sameness with respect to shape, a necessary component to object recognition. She argues that perception of object shape is a product of category learning, achieved through actions on objects. Within this view, features are not prespecified but are built from experience. In a similar vein, Rogosky and Goldstone (Ch. 17) argue against a classic view of features as entities that do not change over time, presenting an alternative view in which features are created and adapted according to the immediate goals and context of tasks, and over longer time periods in terms of perceptual and conceptual learning, and development. In this sense, features are 'functional' because they play a functional role in cognitive processing, such as the act of including (or excluding) the stimulus as a member of a category.

Madole and Oakes (Ch. 18) offer a developmental approach to defining features that begins with an attentional focus on the structural properties of objects, then to a focus on both the structural and functional properties of the object, and finally to a focus on the correlation between structural and functional properties. In a similar vein, Quinn (Ch. 19) examines how features can be used to construct a category representation for a given spatial relation. He suggests that the acquisition of underlying features tied to the spatial relations are not dependent upon the objects themselves, but that infants learn to generalize their category representations from the specific objects depicting the relations to different objects.

Finally, Nikanne (Ch. 20) examines features that are functional in licensing particular mappings of meanings across languages. Specifically, he presents a comparison of Swedish and Finnish with respect to path expressions that convey a goal-direction through the repeated use of a preposition (or locative case) without using the coordinating conjunction 'and' (e.g. *John ran from home to the supermarket to the bank*). This syntactic form is interesting because it maps onto different meanings in the two languages. Nikanne shows that these syntactic-to-conceptual mappings are not part of the normal productive mapping system, but must be explained in terms of constructions. *Constructions* specify particular conditions under which nonproductive mappings are licensed. Nikanne interprets the features that are part of such conditions as functional features, since these features function to license mappings that are otherwise not allowed.

The work in this section is important to research in language and space because it emphasizes the point that the features that are derived, whether they be perceptual, linguistic, spatial, extra-geometric, or functional, are derived precisely because they are functional in the sense of accomplishing a particular goal. This interpretation of 'functional' is arguably as critically important to an understanding of spatial language as the interpretation of function is tied to the use of a particular object as espoused in Part Two of this volume. It thus echoes one of the points raised in Part One that emphasized the importance of the goal and context in which the language occurs.

1.4   Part Four—Overview of Research in Space and Language

Tversky (Ch. 21) presents an overview chapter on the current state of research in space and language, ranging across a myriad of paradigms and approaches. By tackling the issue from such a broad perspective, Tversky is able to pull together a central theme of the book, arising in various places in the preceding chapters: that definitions of 'features', 'function' and 'features that are functional' are not fixed but dependent upon goal, situations, and context.

Thus, the problem posed for researchers of spatial language is really the same problem as that posed to researchers of language more generally, or of action, categorization, perception, and development: that is, characterizing cognition as a function of experience, context, and current goals. While this book cannot offer such a characterization, its contribution is in bringing together researchers actively working on this problem across the various domains, thereby facilitating the detection of common features that may ultimately be applied to language and space.

Part One

Features: Derived from Perception, Action, and Embodiment

2

Language is Grounded in Action

ARTHUR GLENBERG and MICHAEL KASCHAK

Abstract

We describe what appear to be insurmountable theoretical and empirical problems with the current standard psychological approach to meaning based on abstract, amodal, and arbitrary symbols. In its stead, we offer a theory of meaning grounded in human action, and the Indexical Hypothesis, which describes how language is understood in terms of action. We review some of our recent research supporting the hypothesis, including the Action-sentence Compatibility Effect, an effect that shows that the mere understanding of a sentence can interfere with taking an action in a direction contrary to that implied by the sentence. This direct link between understanding and action is difficult for abstract symbol theory to accommodate, whereas it provides strong support for the Indexical Hypothesis.

Functional features

Affordances, that is, how an animal with a particular type of body can interact with a particular type of object. Language works by using syntax to direct the combination of affordances to accomplish goals.

2.1   Theories of Meaning

We speak and write to communicate meaning. But, how is it that language comes to mean something to us? Here we review several recent studies from our laboratory, and describe a new result that supports a radical hypothesis of linguistic meaning, namely, that meaning is rooted in action. The new result is the *Action-sentence Compatibility Effect* (ACE): when a sentence implies a particular action, understanding the sentence can interfere with real actions that are opposite to those implied by the sentence.

This work was supported by a grant from the University of Wisconsin to the first author, and by National Science Foundation grants to the first and second authors.

We begin the chapter with a discussion of extant theories of cognition, and the assumptions these theories make with regard to meaning. The conclusion reached from this discussion is that theories based on abstract, amodal symbols (i.e. virtually all computational or information processing models) cannot capture meaning. This conclusion sets the groundwork for the introduction of an alternative account of meaning, the Indexical Hypothesis (IH), and an overview of recent research consistent with the hypothesis. Finally, we discuss several experiments demonstrating the ACE and argue why this effect cannot be accommodated by abstract symbol accounts of meaning, but provides strong support for the IH.

2.1.1   Abstract symbol theory

Virtually all formal theories of meaning are based on abstract, amodal, arbitrary symbols. These symbols are elements such as nodes, links, and features encoded as numbers. The symbols are abstract in that the same type of node may be used to represent, say, a kitchen chair, regardless of whether that chair is metal or plastic or wood. The symbol is amodal in that the same symbol may be used whether the information is conveyed by sight, language, or touch. Most importantly, the symbol has an arbitrary relation to what it is supposed to represent. That is, the theorist may select the feature code 11011101 to represent the kitchen chair, but that sequence of numbers has no intrinsic relation to actual chairs, and the theorist could have used pretty much any other sequence of numbers. This arbitrariness is important for several reasons. First, by using arbitrary numbers the theorist is assured that only the information related to the theory is included in the encoding: there is no excess information (such as the size or fuzziness of a perceptual image) that could interfere with symbol manipulation or inference. Second, the arbitrariness is an important condition that underlies the information processing view of thinking, reasoning, and meaning. According to this view, all meaning arises from the relations among the symbols, and all reasoning and thinking results from the manipulation of symbols. This is the Physical Symbol System Hypothesis of Newell (1980). If thinking is symbol manipulation, and symbol manipulation is to be the same in all thinking machines (human and not so), then the symbols cannot depend on the particular physical or perceptual characteristics of the machine: they must be arbitrary from the point of view of the particular machine. Thus the thinking (symbol manipulations) works the same from machine to machine because it depends only on the relations among the abstract symbols, and those relations are the same from machine to machine.

This account of symbols and thinking may not seem to correspond to our rich intuitions about memory (e.g. that it includes images), or our rich intuitions about thinking (e.g. that we often think in particulars, not in the abstract symbols of logic). These intuitions notwithstanding, theories of memory, meaning, and cognition are formulated using abstract, amodal, arbitrary symbols. For example, Hintzman's MINERVA II (Hintzman, 1986) uses a vector of numbers to encode memories. That vector is nothing other than an abstract, amodal, arbitrary symbol. Masson's (1995) connectionist theory of semantic memory makes use of 80-place vectors to represent concepts. These vectors are abstract, amodal, arbitrary symbols, as are all the representations in all connectionist networks of memory with which we are familiar. High dimensional space theories of meaning (Burgess and Lund, 1997; Landauer and Dumais, 1997) make use of very large vectors of numbers, but remain abstract symbols. All theories based on propositions (e.g. Kintsch, 1998) make use of abstract, amodal, arbitrary symbols.

Semantic networks may appear different because the nodes (which are prototypical abstract, amodal, arbitrary symbols) are labeled with words. The difference is an illusion. The point of these networks is to provide the meaning of the words, that is, to define them, and that definition is supposed to arise from the system of relations to other nodes. The labels are there only for the convenience of the reader, so that the reader knows what the theorist intends a given node to stand for. The illusion arises because the label allows the reader to impart to the node his or her knowledge of the meaning of the word. Similarly, theories based on propositions may look different, but they are not. A proposition is like a miniature semantic network. There is a relational term (which is itself an abstract symbol) and several arguments that are being related. Each argument is an abstract, amodal, arbitrary symbol. Hence, a proposition meant to correspond to the idea 'the chair is on the floor' may be set in type as 'Rel:On (Arg1: chair; Arg2: floor)'. In fact, however, the words are a convenience and an illusion. Within the theory, the proposition is much closer to 'Rel:001001 (Arg1:100011; Arg2:110000)'.

2.1.2   Problems with abstract symbol theories

Abstract symbol theories of meaning and memory have become so commonplace that we accept them uncritically. But, closer analysis reveals a host of problems that are briefly described here and that are discussed more completely in Barsalou (1993, 1999). Where could those symbols have come from? There is no evolutionary story that culminates in a brain with abstract, amodal, arbitrary symbols. There are no convincing cognitive development stories that describe how the specific, modal, and analogical sensory representations of the newborn and toddler get transformed into abstract symbols. When one looks into the brain, all one sees are neurons that are modal; that is, the neurons are influenced by the perceptual and motor processes many synapses down- and up-stream. How many dimensions (e.g. elements in the vector) and which dimensions (color? angle?) contribute to the abstract symbol, and how are those dimensions learned? Do the dimensions of encoding stay constant (as is required for the mathematics of the theories to work) throughout the lifespan even though what is important to an individual changes over the lifespan? Abstract symbol theories provide no satisfactory answers.

In addition, the symbol grounding problem (Glenberg and Robertson, 2000; Harnad, 1990; Searle, 1980) is a major stumbling block for abstract symbol theories. The problem is revealed by Harnad's version of Searle's Chinese Room argument. Harnad suggests that we imagine landing at the airport in a country (perhaps China) whose language we do not speak. We are equipped solely with a dictionary written in that language. We see a sign composed of logograms and wish to translate it. We look up the first logogram (an abstract, amodal, arbitrary symbol) in our dictionary to find out its meaning. The definition of that logogram is a list of other abstract symbols. So, we look up the meaning of the first logogram in the definition to find that it is defined in terms of still other abstract symbols. The point is that we will never be able to discover the meaning of any of the logograms simply from their relations to other logograms. Contrary to the Physical Symbol System Hypothesis, meaning cannot arise simply from symbol manipulation; instead the symbols must be grounded, that is, they must make contact with something outside of the system, such as objects in the world.

But how is that grounding to be achieved? Lakoff (1987) reviews data and arguments about the impossibility of grounding arbitrary symbols. An important component of Lakoff's review is an argument developed by Putnam (1981). Putnam begins with a set of abstract symbols that are related to one another, much like a series of algebraic equations that relate variables. He then demonstrates that the set of relations is insufficient to uniquely identify the set of corresponding objects in the world. That is, any set of relations among symbols, no matter how complex, can be put into correspondence with a variety of objects sharing the same relations, much like a series of algebraic equations can be used to describe many different objects. In short, if we thought in terms of abstract symbols, we could never be certain what we were thinking about.

Several forms of empirical evidence also question the hegemony of abstract symbol theories. For example, the difficulty in understanding negated sentences (e.g. 'The star is not above the cross') has long been used as critical support for abstract symbol theories of reasoning about negated sentences (e.g. Carpenter and Just, 1975). As reported in Glenberg, Robertson, Jansen, and Johnson-Glenberg (1999), however, the difficulty with negated sentences is artifactual; it is only found when negated sentences are used outside of the proper pragmatic context. When used appropriately, negated sentences are no harder to comprehend than the corresponding positive sentences. Another type of evidence strongly questioning abstract symbol theory comes from experiments conducted in Barsalou's laboratory, and reviewed in Barsalou, Solomon, and Wu (1999). These simple but powerful experiments demonstrate that concepts have perceptual components. For example, when asked to list the features of a watermelon, people might say *green*, *striped*, and *sweet*. But, when asked to list the features of half a watermelon (that logically has the same features as a watermelon except that it is smaller), people say *red*, *seedy*, and *sweet*. Apparently, people are not consulting a list of abstract features. Instead, the features seem to arise from simulating what one perceives when faced with a whole or half watermelon. Finally, Stanfield and Zwaan (2001) demonstrated how sentence understanding may generate analogical symbols. The participants in their experiment judged whether or not a pictured object (e.g. a pencil) was referred to in a sentence. When the pictured object was in the same orientation (e.g. horizontal) as that implied by the sentence (e.g. *He stuck the pencil behind his ear*) responding was faster than when the two orientations mismatched.

2.1.3   An alternative: embodied meaning and the Indexical Hypothesis

An embodied approach to meaning and cognition is being developed in several fields and multiple laboratories. To name just a few of the investigators, in computer science, there is the work of Brooks (1987); in linguistics, Lakoff (1987), Langacker (1987), and Tomasello (1998); in philosophy, Newton (1996); in developmental psychology, Mandler (1992), MacWhinney (1998), and Thelen and Smith (1994); and in cognitive psychology, Barsalou (1999), Glenberg (1997), Rieser, Garing, and Young (1994), and Schwartz and Black (1999). Although there is much theoretical variability, there are several common themes. First, thinking is more a matter of biology and interaction with the environment than computation. Second, thinking and cognition must reflect the operation of the bodies (including the perceptual systems) of the thinkers.

Our own approach to embodied cognition (Glenberg, 1997; Glenberg and Robertson, 1999, 2000; Kaschak and Glenberg, 2000) begins with the premise that cognition evolved because it contributes to survival and reproductive success. Furthermore, that contribution can only be through effective action that takes into account the body. For example, consider an animal (e.g. a bird) faced with a predator (e.g. a snake). Effective action for the bird includes flapping its wings and flying away. If the animal were a mole, then effective action might include diving into a hole. But, if the mole tried to flap its wings, or the bird tried to dive into a hole, it would be dead and unable to contribute to the gene pool. Similarly for humans: our actions must take into account the capabilities of our bodies, or we will not contribute to the gene pool.

If cognition evolved to control action, then it is natural to speculate about a close connection between action and meaning. Thus, we propose the following definition:

The meaning of a situation to an individual is the set of actions available to that individual in that situation. The set of actions results from the mesh of affordances, action-based knowledge, and action-based goals.

Consider this definition one component at a time. Affordances (Gibson, 1979*a*) are interactive qualities: how an organism, with its type of body and perceptual apparatus, can interact with an object or environment. For example, what makes a chair a chair (to someone with a human body) is that the chair affords sitting. This is in contrast to an abstract symbol representation of chair as a set of features, such as back, seat, legs, etc. Of course, an ordinary chair also affords many other actions: standing, lifting, throwing, and so on. All of these affordances depend on the type of body interacting with the chair, however. The chair does not afford sitting for an elephant. Although the chair may well afford sitting for a toddler, the ordinary chair does not afford, for the toddler, lifting and throwing.

The meaning of the situation (e.g. a situation including a chair) also depends on action-based knowledge from memory. If we know that we recently glued the rickety legs in place, we must be able to use that knowledge to block the affordance of sitting or standing on the chair. Or, if we know that the person who vacated the chair did so only temporarily, then my knowledge of social norms prevents me from sitting in the chair. Finally, the meaning of a situation depends on action-based goals: do we want to rest, change the bulb in a ceiling fixture, or protect ourselves from a snarling dog?

These components of meaning must be combined into a coherent conceptualization that can be used to guide action. The combination is possible, because all of the components of knowledge are action-based. The process of combining affordances, knowledge, and goals is *mesh*. Unlike association formation or construction of propositions, mesh is a process that respects intrinsic constraints of physics and biology. That is, when the components can be combined so that smooth and doable action results, the components mesh. Not all affordances can be combined to accomplish goals, however. For example, I can sit in a chair and eat at a table, but I cannot sit in a chair while jumping rope. The actions of sitting and jumping do not mesh.

The Indexical Hypothesis (IH, Glenberg and Robertson, 1999, 2000; Kaschak and Glenberg, 2000) applies the theory of embodied cognition to language. The hypothesis is needed because words are abstract, amodal, arbitrary symbols. For example, the word *chair* is the same whether we are talking about a big chair or a little chair, whether the chair is seen or felt, and the form of the word is arbitrary (as is demonstrated by the change in form, but not meaning, across languages). If manipulation of abstract arbitrary symbols cannot produce meaning (as argued above), then how do we understand language? According to the IH, there are three steps. First, words and phrases are indexed or mapped onto real objects or their perceptual symbols (Glenberg and Robertson, 1999). Second, affordances are derived from the objects or perceptual symbols (Glenberg and Robertson, 2000). Perceptual symbols (Barsalou, 1999) are based on the neural representations underlying the perception of objects. Perceptual symbols are not mere copies of experience, however, in that they only preserve information that has been selectively attended. Barsalou also describes how perceptual symbol systems can represent a range of concepts that are not generally thought of as deriving from action and perception, such as 'and', 'truth', and 'exclusive-or'. Third, the affordances are meshed as directed by syntax but under the intrinsic constraints of physics and biology (Kaschak and Glenberg, 2000). These processes are described in more detail in the next section.

2.2   Testing the Indexical Hypothesis

We have published a series of studies that support the IH and question most standard accounts of language processing. Here we review three series of studies investigating learning, understanding language about novel situations, and understanding linguistic innovations.

2.2.1   Learning

In Glenberg and Robertson (1999), participants learned to use a device that was unfamiliar to them: a compass. The experiment was meant to be an analog to a typical real world experience, such as trying to put together a bookshelf from written instructions. At first such instructions seem uninterpretable, and terms such as *back, front, top,* and *bottom* do not seem to clearly map on to anything in the situation. However, after manipulating the boards and screws of the bookshelf, one is able to index the terms to particular components, and the meaning of the instructions (e.g. how to align boards) becomes clear.

In Glenberg and Robertson (1999), participants began the experiment by taking a pre-test on their knowledge of the compass. Then participants were given basic information about the compass in one of four conditions:

(1) *Read:* Read instructions about how to use the compass.
(2) *Listen:* Listen to instructions about how to use the compass.
(3) *Listen and Read:* Listen to instructions about how to use the compass, while reading the instructions at the same time.
(4) *Listen and Index:* Listen to the instructions while an actor pointed to (i.e. indexed) the aspects of the compass that were being discussed by the speaker.

A post-test showed that participants in the various conditions gained an equal amount of knowledge about components of the compass (e.g. that the *direction of travel arrows* are imprinted on the base plate of the compass). Next, participants were given further instructions on how to use a compass and a map together to identify objects in the environment. For example, one instruction could be paraphrased as *Hold the compass so that the direction of travel arrows point at the object you need to identify.* In this task, the participants in the *Listen and Index* condition out-performed participants in the other conditions. That is, the participants in the *Listen and Index* condition were able to hold and point the compass more appropriately more quickly. Why should this be the case? By virtue of having indexed the words, *direction of travel arrows* to the appropriate part of the actual object (the arrows on the base of the compass), participants in the *Listen and Index* condition were able to derive the affordances of the *direction of travel arrows* and thus knew how those objects could be pointed by holding the compass flat in the palm of the hand and orienting the fingers toward the object to be identified. Participants in the other conditions, although knowing about direction of travel arrows abstractly, could not use that type of knowledge to understand the instruction *Hold the compass so that the direction of travel arrows point at the object* well enough to actually do it (much like you might know, in the abstract, about the top and bottom of a shelf and yet be unable to execute the directions for building a bookcase). Apparently, understanding sentences to the point where they can guide action requires a consideration of the affordances of the objects indexed by the words in the sentences. Note that this result cannot be a simple levels of processing effect because the participants in the various groups did equally well on the verbal post-test. The difference in learning was revealed when participants needed to demonstrate learning and not just rote memory.

2.2.2   Comprehension of novel situations

Consider the following scenario, adapted from Glenberg and Robertson (2000), and its continuations (*Afforded*, and *Non-afforded*):

Phil was trying to get a barbecue going early in the morning for a tailgater. He got dizzy from blowing on the coals, but they still weren't burning well.

Afforded: Phil grabbed a map and used it to fan the fire.

Non-afforded: Phil grabbed a rock and used it to fan the fire.

The *Afforded* continuation appears to make sense, whereas the *Non-afforded* continuation does not. But, from the point of view of abstract symbol theory, both sentences should make sense: both are perfectly grammatical, both satisfy 'semantic' constraints with regard to argument roles of the verb (i.e. the agent is animate, the instrument is an object, etc.), both are easy to break into propositions, and so on. One might propose that 'world knowledge' is used to discriminate between sensible continuations and nonsense continuations. In some way that must be correct, but the world knowledge based on abstract symbols is not sufficient to discriminate between the sentences. That is, often world knowledge is conceptualized as propositions or facts such as 'bellows are used to fan fires', 'maps are used to find your way', and 'rocks are heavy'. Here are three reasons why this sort of world knowledge does not help for these examples. First, in making up the scenarios, the experimenters intentionally tried to come up with novel situations in which people would not have had relevant specific experience (world knowledge). For example, in one scenario, a character uses an upright vacuum cleaner as a coat rack (*Afforded*) or an electrical outlet as a coat rack (*Non-afforded*), and in another scenario a character stands on a tractor to be able to reach the top of a wall he is painting (*Afforded*) or stands on a hammer (*Non-afforded*). It is unlikely that any one reader has done or learned about these activities; nonetheless, the *Afforded* sentences were rated as much more sensible than the *Non-afforded* sentences. Second, Glenberg and Robertson (2000) demonstrated (using LSA; Landauer and Dumais, 1997) that the content words (e.g. *fire, rock, map*) in both the *Afforded* and *Non-afforded* sentences occurred rarely in similar contexts. Thus, reading-dependent background knowledge is not a likely source for the knowledge that distinguishes between the two sentences. Third, in another experiment, it was shown that participants were equally fast at reading *Afforded* sentences as at reading sentences that used objects specifically designed to accomplish the goals (e.g. *Phil grabbed a bellows and used it to fan the fire*). Given the equivalent reading times, it is unlikely that participants needed to make complex inferences from propositional knowledge (e.g. *Maps are often made of paper; paper can be folded; folded paper can be stiff and easy to hold; things that are stiff and easy to hold can be used as fans*) to understand the *Afforded* sentences.

It appears that the way people discriminate between the 'map' and 'rock' versions of the sentence is that they imaginatively simulate the situation using perceptual symbols, and they note that the affordances of a map can be meshed with the goals of fanning the fire, whereas the affordances of a rock cannot. This sort of simulation is exactly what cannot be done when abstract symbols are arbitrarily related to their referents. The reason is that information encoded by abstract symbols is stripped of its perceptual/action qualities. If a function or property is not specifically encoded (or derivable through a chain of logic-based inferences), it cannot be generated. Because the scenarios used in Glenberg and Robertson (2000) required properties based on the unique interaction of people (how they can hold things or stand on things), objects, and goals, the needed properties were almost certainly not already stored. In conclusion, people discriminate between *Afforded* and *Non-afforded* sentences using background knowledge. But, that background knowledge cannot be in the form of abstract, amodal, arbitrary symbols.

2.2.3   Mesh of affordances guided by grammatical constructions

Deriving affordances is not the end of language comprehension. According to the IH, the affordances need to be meshed under the guidance of the syntax of the sentence. Kaschak and Glenberg (2000) proposed that a particular type of grammatical information, grammatical constructions (e.g. Goldberg, 1995), provide the information that guides mesh. According to Goldberg, constructions are form-meaning pairs. Thus, words are constructions that pair an abstract symbol (e.g. *chair*) with a meaning (a thing you can sit in). Furthermore,

Goldberg (1995) claims that basic sentence structures are also form-meaning pairings, carrying meanings beyond those contributed by the lexical items in the sentence frame. Consider, for example, transitive sentences such as:

Mike hit/threw/sent the feather.

Goldberg proposes that the transitive form (subject–verb–object) carries the meaning *act on*, and that our understanding of this sentence develops in part from meaning conveyed by the construction.

Another example of a construction is the double object construction, subject–verb–object1–object2. Goldberg suggests that the meaning of this construction is *transfer*. For example consider the sentence:

Mike hit/threw/sent David the feather.

Thus, the subject (*Mike*) transfers the second object (*the feather*) to the first object (*David*). The double object construction seems to force verbs to take on a transfer meaning, even when the verbs don't normally have such a meaning. Consider, for example, *Mike blew David the feather*, or even, *Mike sneezed David the feather*. The fact that the last sentence is sensible is quite remarkable given that *to sneeze* is generally taken to be an intransitive verb that cannot take an object (let alone two). Put another way, the dictionary meaning of the verb *to sneeze* has nothing to do with transfer. But, the double object construction coerces that meaning from the verb.

Kaschak and Glenberg (2000) took Goldberg's ideas one step further. They proposed that the meaning conveyed by the construction provides the goal that guides the derivation and mesh of affordances. Consider again the sentence *Mike sneezed David the feather*. A limitless variety of affordances can be derived from the perceptual symbols for *Mike, David,* and *feather* and those affordances can be meshed in an equally limitless fashion. When put into a double object construction, however, the meshing process is constrained to produce a conceptualization in which transfer of a particular sort takes place: Mike has to start out with the feather and David has to end up with it.

We tested this idea using innovative denominal verbs (e.g. Clark and Clark, 1979). Denominal verbs are verbs based on nouns (e.g. *to bicycle, to bottle*). Innovative denominal verbs are made up (and understood) on the fly. For example:

Mike crutched David the toy to help him out.

We used innovative denominal verbs in the experiment because these verbs have no conventional meaning: any meaning that is derived must come from the interaction of the verb and the syntax. When the innovative denominal verbs were placed in the double object construction (as above), the participants in our experiments overwhelmingly interpreted the innovative denominal verb as implying a type of transfer in which the noun (e.g. *a crutch*) is used to effect the transfer. We also placed innovative denominal verbs in transitive constructions such as:

Mike crutched the toy to help David out.

In this case, people overwhelmingly interpreted the innovative denominal verb as implying *act upon* in which the noun (e.g. *a crutch*) is used to act on the toy, but people did not interpret the sentence as implying transfer. Thus, meaning of the innovative verb *to crutch* is determined by the construction in which it appears. This supports the notion that particular sentence frames are independently existing, meaning-bearing linguistic entities (see Kaschak and Glenberg, 2000, for more detailed arguments).

Importantly, Kaschak and Glenberg (2000) also demonstrated that syntax alone cannot generate sensible meaning. Instead, the affordances of the noun underlying the denominal verb must be such that they can be used to accomplish the goals conveyed by the scene. Thus, people have a hard time understanding sentences such as, *Mike egg-shelled David the toy to help him out*, because egg shells do not have the proper affordances to effect the transfer of a toy. In short, language comprehension requires the combination of affordances into patterns of action needed to accomplish goals specified by grammatical constructions.

2.3. The Action-sentence Compatibility Effect

The research described so far has been consistent with the IH in that the research demonstrates that meaning, understanding, and sensibility are often related to our conceptions of what are doable actions. But the work has yet to show that these ideas should be treated as anything more than metaphor. Is understanding really in terms of action, or is that just a way of describing the results? If understanding is in terms of action, how can we understand abstract ideas that may not have any actionable components? Similarly, if understanding requires derivation of affordances from perceptible objects, how can we understand language about the non-perceptible? The research paradigm described next is a tool for investigating these sorts of questions.

In the basic paradigm (Glenberg and Kaschak, 2002), participants judged the sensibility of sentences, half of which were intended to be sensible and half not. Responses were made using a specially constructed button box approximately 18 cm × 28 cm × 6 cm. The box was held in the lap, with the longest dimension projected outward from the body. Three response buttons were arrayed on the top surface. Visual presentation of a sentence was initiated by pressing the middle button with the index finger of the right hand. After a short delay, the sentence was presented in the center of a screen controlled by a computer. The sentence remained on the screen until the button was no longer pressed. In the *Yes-is-far* condition, to respond *yes, the sentence is sensible* participants moved from the middle button to one that was farther away from the body. These participants responded *no* by moving from the middle button to one closer to the body. Participants in the *Yes-is-near* condition had the reverse assignment of buttons. That is, they moved to the button closer to the body to respond *yes.*

A second variable was the type of sentence presented: Toward, Away, or Nonsense. Toward sentences, such as *Scratch your head* or *Wipe the sweat off your brow,* implied action toward the reader. Away sentences, such as *Scratch your cat* and *Wipe the sweat off your bench,* implied action away from the reader. The Nonsense sentences were meant to describe actions that were difficult to envision, such as *Open the plate.*

According to the IH, meaning is action-based, that is, understanding of sentences is grounded in the actions which underlie them. Suppose that those actions are computed by the same processes that compute, enable, and guide real action in the environment. In that case, the mere understanding of a sentence implying action in one direction (e.g. toward the reader) would interfere with the ability to take real action in the opposite direction (e.g. *Yes-is-far*). Thus, the prediction derived from the IH is for an interaction: when the direction of responding necessary to say *yes* is consistent with the implied direction in the sentence, reaction/reading time will be faster than when the two directions conflict. This is the *Action-sentence Compatibility Effect,* or ACE.

The prediction was confirmed (see Fig. 2.1). When the *yes* response required a movement toward the body, the mean time to read and respond to sentences implying a movement toward the body was 1,298 msec, whereas the time to read and respond to sentences implying a movement away from the body was

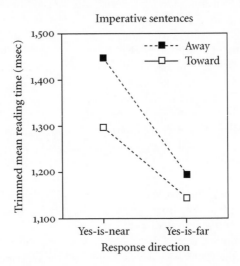

Fig. 2.1. The Action-sentence Compatibility Effect for imperative sentences (Experiment 1).

1,447 msec, for a difference of 149 msec. When the *yes* response required a movement away from the body, the difference (1,193−1,149) was 44 msec. The ACE interaction was highly significant.

At first blush, theories of language based on abstract symbols will have a difficult time explaining the ACE. That is, if meaning is based on having the right symbols in the correct relations to one another, then whether one responds *yes* by moving toward or away from the body would appear to be irrelevant. However, there is a way in which abstract symbol theories can accommodate this result post hoc. We call this the post-understanding translation hypothesis. Abstract symbol theories might claim that understanding has little to do with action, but that people do use language to coordinate action in the world. Once a sentence is understood (by arranging the symbols correctly), the linguistic propositions are translated into a motor code for dealing with the world. On this account, the observed interference between the implied direction of the sentence and the actual direction of the response arises from this post-understanding translation.

We tested this alternative in a second experiment. In this experiment, each participant judged the sensibility of 160 sentences, half of which were intended to be sensible and half of which were intended to be nonsense. The 80 sensible sentences were based on 80 Toward/Away pairs, and 40 of those pairs were the imperative sentences from Experiment 1. An additional 20 pairs described a transfer of a concrete object between *you* and another person. Ten of those pairs used the double-object construction (e.g. *Courtney handed you the notebook/You handed Courtney the notebook*) and ten used the variant dative form (e.g. *Andy delivered the pizza to you/You delivered the Pizza to Andy*). Another 20 pairs described transfer of something abstract. Examples are *Liz told you the story/You told Liz the story* and *The policeman radioed the message to you/You radioed the message to the policeman.*

The ACE was significant (Fig. 2.2) for the three types of sentences (Imperative, Concrete Transfer, and Abstract Transfer). These results demonstrate that the

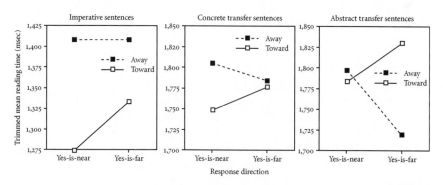

Fig. 2.2. The Action-sentence Compatibility Effect for three types of sentences: imperatives, concrete transfer, and abstract transfer (Experiment 2).

effect can be found for constructions other than the imperative which are closely associated with action. Importantly, observing the ACE for the abstract transfer sentences rules out the post-understanding translation hypothesis. Consider, for example, what it would mean to translate a sentence such as *You told Liz the story* into a motor code. Such a code involves moving the articulators (e.g. lips), and there is no reason to expect that moving the lips would differentially interfere with *Yes-is-near* or *Yes-is-far* responding.

Instead of a post-understanding translation, the data imply that the meaning of transfer, even the transfer of abstract entities such as information, seems to be embodied as action. Why should this be? We think that it is related to the learning of the double-object construction that carries the general meaning of transfer. It is likely that young children learn the actions associated with frequently heard verbs, such as *to give*. Thus, toddlers correctly respond to commands such as *Give me the bottle*. The actions then become associated with the double object construction because of the frequent conjunction of the verb *to give* and the double object construction as in *You give Liz the toy*. Through this sort of guided experience, the double object construction comes to be treated as an instruction to mesh affordances of the referents of *you*, *Liz*, and *toy* in order to accomplish the goal of giving, that is, transfer. Over development, the double-object instructions for meshing are applied to other sorts of actions that can effect transfer, such as *to hand*, *to send*, *to bicycle*, and so on. The final step is to apply the instructions for mesh to accomplish transfer when the transfer is not of a physical object, but of information, as in *You told Liz the story*. That is, we come to understand the sentence as a equivalent to physical movement from *you* to *Liz*. The important point is that even the understanding of abstract notions such as communication appears to be grounded in action.

2.4 Conclusions

We began by discussing the many serious problems, both theoretical (e.g. symbol grounding) and empirical (e.g. Barsalou *et al.*, 1999), associated with abstract symbol theories of meaning. In its place, we offered an embodied theory that relates human meaning to human actions, and we described the IH as an account of how the abstract symbols of language can be used to create embodied meaning. This hypothesis gives us the power to understand two forms of linguistic creativity, how we can understand language about novel situations, and how we can understand linguistic innovations such as innovated denominal verbs. Finally, we demonstrated that understanding in terms of action is not simply metaphorical. Instead, it appears that real action underlies the understanding of language, even language about abstract events.

3

The Bicycle Pedal is in Front of the Table. Why some Objects do not Fit into some Spatial Relations

MANUEL DE VEGA and MARÍA J. RODRIGO

Abstract

We studied the meaning of locative sentences involving directional terms such as 'in front of', 'behind', 'right of', etc. First, we contrasted two spatial communication tasks: pointing to objects in a layout and telling their direction. We observed that after imagining a body rotation, pointing was considerably impaired with respect to a physical body rotation, whereas performance in the verbal location task was similar under imaginary and physical rotation. We propose that producing locative sentences, unlike pointing to objects, involves a second-order embodiment. That is, language spatial relations are represented and updated into a mental framework that is detached from body proprioceptive information, but still preserves spatial relations analogically. Second, we described a corpus-based study of locative sentences that demonstrated that some features of the figure and the ground are associated with the direction or dimension tagged by the preposition. For instance, partitive entities (e.g. parts of bodies or machines) were more frequently associated to vertical directions, whereas animate entities were more frequently associated to horizontal terms. This fit between object information (provided by nouns) and spatial information (provided by prepositions), is compatible with an integration or meshing hypothesis.

Functional features

Features emerging from the interaction between animate agents and objects in the world. The term 'functional' necessarily involves an animate and intentional individual. Purely geometric and physical features such as size, shape, or solidity

The preparation of this chapter was supported by the grant PB98-0431, by the Ministerio de Ciencia y Tecnología (Spain).

are not functional themselves. However, their combination with a layout can determine the emergence of functional features for a given organism. For instance, the relative size of figure–ground is functional for describing spatial relations that are informative, a horizontal and solid ground determines functional support relations, object and body parts are functional as they involve specific motor programs, etc.

3.1 Introduction

Most languages have a repertoire of locative terms used to describe the position of one object (figure) in relation to another object (ground), as in the sentences 'The book *is to the right* of the window', or 'The girl is *in front of* the mirror'. Understanding the spatial meaning of this kind of sentence, requires interfacing between at least two different codes: language and the spatial representation system. Comprehenders receive the linear code of the sentence and they must elaborate a representation of a spatial layout including two objects with a certain directional relation between them. We do not understand yet the details of this interface, which probably involve mapping functions between the different codes (e.g. Jackendoff, 1996a), but we can make some progress by trying to describe how mental representations are derived from locative sentences or, in other words, by understanding the nature of their meaning.

This paper will develop two issues concerning the meaning of sentences with directional terms. First, we analyzed to what extent their meaning is embodied. With this aim, we contrasted how people represent and update imaginary environments under two tasks: one verbal (using directional labels) and one non-verbal (pointing to object locations). The results clearly suggest that language forces speakers to encode spatial information in a different way than pointing. Thus, we established a distinction between *first-order* embodiment which relies on the current sensory-motor information, and is proper of non-verbal tasks like pointing, and *second-order* embodiment, which operates in a representational space detached from the current sensory-motor information, and is characteristic of verbal communication. Second-order embodiment requires, in addition, the computation of a *figure-to-ground* relation within a mental framework.[1]

The second issue of this paper concerns the hypothesis that the meaning of directional sentences is a multiple constraint process in which the features of the figure and the ground, and the direction tagged by the preposition must fit into

[1] First-order embodiment grossly corresponds to 'basic relations' (e.g. Garnham, 1989), whereas second-order embodiment corresponds to both 'deictic relations' and 'intrinsic relations' (see Logan and Sadler, 1996, for a review of terminology). We did not adopt these labels, because the term 'deictic' is ambiguous, as it is also used in some contexts to refer to the pointing gesture, as well as to demonstratives (this/that), and adverbs (here/there) which are conceptually closer to basic relations.

a coherent pattern. To support this hypothesis, we sampled sentences with directional terms from corpora of written narratives, and we analyzed the sensory-motor and functional features of their nouns (figure and ground). Finally, we tried to establish how these features were associated with the particular direction or dimension denoted by the directional prepositions.

3.2   Meaning as Embodied Representation

How is spatial meaning derived from locative sentences? One interesting possibility is that meaning involves embodied representations, not very different from those we build when we interact with real perceptual environments (e.g. Lakoff, 1987; Glenberg, 1997; Barsalou, 1999). There is abundant empirical support for the embodied nature of meaning derived from spatial language. People are able to form sophisticated spatial simulations when they read or learn verbal descriptions of environments. For instance, they can imagine that they reorient their point of view in an imaginary layout, and accurately locate object positions from each imaginary reorientation (Franklin and Tversky, 1990; de Vega, 1994; Maki and Marek, 1997), they can also take 'mental walks' using a protagonist's perspective described by a text (Morrow, Greenspan, and Bower, 1987; Rinck and Bower, 1995; de Vega, 1995), and they can mentally scan a previously described map, by moving an imaginary spot at a remarkably constant speed (Denis and Cocude, 1992). In some cases, the implicit perspective taken in the imaginary environment governs the accessibility of entities. Thus, imaginary objects placed 'in front' or 'behind' can be more accessible than those placed at the 'right' or the 'left' (Franklin and Tversky, 1990; Bryant, Tversky, and Franklin, 1992; de Vega, 1994), or objects placed in the goal room of a moving character can be more accessible than objects placed in the source room or in the path room (Morrow *et al.*, 1987; Rinck and Bower, 1995; de Vega 1995).

However, the notion of embodied meaning requires some elaboration. To what extent are language-based representations of environments perceptual-like? The most obvious difference is that perception and action are much richer and detailed than representations derived from language. But it is also possible that understanding locative sentences involves some specific processing of spatial information, that is usually absent in our ordinary experience with real environments. In particular, we postulate that the meaning of locative sentences involves a *framing* process that consists of establishing an *explicit* spatial relation between a figure object and a ground object used as a reference frame.

Sensitivity to spatial relations is not exclusive of locative language. It has also been reported in the literature on visual search tasks (e.g. Chun and Jian, 1998; Chun, 2000). Thus, contextual cueing involves a facilitation of visual search performance, when the target repeatedly appears in a given spatial configuration. This sensitivity to spatial context occurs in spite of the fact that the visual search task is not mediated by language. However, contextual cueing is an implicit learning of global spatial configurations. Instead, language-based framing, even when it refers to the current environment, is an explicit process of segregating a single figure–ground spatial relation from the cluster of spatial relations available in the layout. We also provide evidence that figure–ground relations are computed in a purely representational framework, that allows the speaker and addressee to detach their spatial representation from the current sensory-motor information of the environment or their own bodies.

To explore the cognitive demands of framing, we analyzed how people locate objects in imaginary environments under two task conditions: by pointing to them or by using the directional labels 'front', 'back', 'right', and 'left' (de Vega, Rodrigo, and Zimmer, 1996; de Vega, Cocude, Denis, Rodrigo, and Zimmer, 2001; de Vega and Rodrigo, 2001). The nonverbal task of pointing may serve thus as a base-line to reveal the specific demands of verbal communication. In some of the experiments, participants were asked to periodically reorient themselves either by turning physically their bodies to face a given object (physical rotation), or by imagining themselves as turning to face an object while their body remained still (imaginary rotation). In each new reorientation all participants had to locate the position of several imaginary objects either by pointing or labeling their direction. The results showed a striking difference between pointing and verbal labeling. As Fig. 3.1 shows, pointing was very efficient under physical rotation,

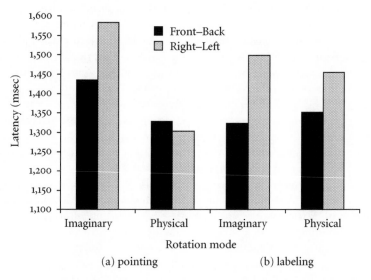

FIG. 3.1. Latency of response as a function of Dimensions and Mode of rotation in the pointing (a) and the labeling task (b).

Source: de Vega and Rodrigo, 2001.

and both front–back and right–left dimensions were equally accessible. However, performance dramatically decreased under imaginary rotation, and the pattern of accessibility changed: front–back was faster than right–left. By contrast, labeling always involved the standard accessibility pattern (front–back faster than right–left), and it was equally efficient under physical and imaginary rotation.

We suggest that pointing relies on a first-order embodiment that involves a low-cost sensory-motor updating of an object's position governed by proprioceptive information of the body (de Vega and Rodrigo, 2001). This might explain the advantage of pointing under physical rotation, and the equally fast access to all directions. In contrast, pointing under mental rotation was difficult, because participants have to neglect the proprioceptive cues of their bodies, and determine the new point of view in a representational space that conflicts with their own body position.

Using verbal labels, instead, involves a second-order embodiment, by which objects and the body are routinely represented as entities in a mental space, detached from the current sensory-motor information. This might explain the insensitivity of the verbal location task to the mode of rotation. Indeed, the accessibility pattern in regard to the dimensions suggests that language-based spatial representations are still 'embodied' rather than, for instance, propositional. Objects in the front and the back were located fast, because these directions are mapped into the morphological and functional asymmetries of the body, whereas objects in the right and the left are slowly located, because both sides of the body are symmetric and therefore less distinctive (Franklin and Tversky, 1990). An advantage of verbal communication is its flexibility: People can describe not only the current perceptual environment, but also a memory-based or a fictitious environment; they can communicate layouts to an implicit or physically absent addressee; and they can choose a ground (the speaker's own body, other person's body, or an object) with respect to which the referent position is expressed.

Using a quite different experimental setting, Wang (this volume, Ch. 4) has shown convergent evidence that pointing performance is dramatically impaired under imaginary rotation, whereas verbal estimations of an object's angular position was similar under both imaginary and physical rotation. One possible interpretation discussed by Wang is that the action system (responsible for pointing) and the verbal system are guided by separate representations. This interpretation is compatible with our first-order/second-order embodiment distinction.

3.3 Figures and Grounds

Consider a familiar situation. You are seated in your office and you want to describe the position of a given book to your interlocutor (avoiding pointing or deixis). You have to chose a particular ground object as a framework, but you have many potential grounds available such as the table, the telephone, the computer, the window, the addressee, yourself, etc. Your choice of one of these options does not seem arbitrary, it might depend on assessing several geometric, functional, and informational features of the ground that make it easy for the addressee to locate the figure. For instance, it has been suggested that grounds are usually more static, larger and more salient than figures (e.g. Talmy, 1983; Herskovits, 1985; Landau and Jackendoff, 1993). Consequently, it seems more acceptable to say 'the child is in front of the bank' than 'the bank is in front of the child'. However, other features in addition to those aforementioned may differ systematically between figures and grounds. For example, figure and ground features may be closely associated with the particular direction or dimension tagged by locative prepositions (front, back, above, below, right, left). Unfortunately not much effort has been focused on systematically exploring the figure and ground features that may be related to the spatial terms used in locative sentences.

3.3.1   The schematization hypothesis

The relative neglect in the literature of an empirical analysis of figure and ground features, is probably related to the frequent assumption of the schematization hypothesis. According to the schematization hypothesis the meaning of locative expressions (directional expressions included) is only represented in terms of abstract and schematic features of spatial information. The use of a spatial preposition would be independent of any particular geometric feature of the figure and the ground, such as their shape, or size. Instead, the ground is considered as a system of geometric axes in which the figure is located as a point. Thus, an utterance involving a directional preposition would be neutral with respect to the shape, the size, the mobility, the substance, or any functional feature of the figure and the ground. Consequently, spatial prepositions seem to convey an 'ideal' meaning, and the figure and the ground are considered either as empty symbols or as minimal geometric entities (e.g. Talmy, 1983; Landau and Jackendoff, 1993; Regier, 1996).

In their modular version of the schematization hypothesis, Landau and Jackendoff (1993) propose that spatial prepositions 'filter' object descriptions, removing much of the details of object shape and preserving only certain schematic properties such as boundedness, surface, or axial structure. Understanding the nouns of locative sentences (the figure and the ground), relies on the 'what' system which independently processes the visual features of the corresponding objects. However, it is not clear how language users deal separately with the 'what' and 'where' information provided by a sentence. Such functional dissociation seems psychologically strange, and Landau and Jackendoff propose a sort of 'link' or 'co-indexing' between the two sources of information, although they do not elaborate upon this idea. We explicitly propose that the spatial information and the object information are integrated into a single representation when locative sentences are produced and understood.

3.3.2   The integration hypothesis

According to our integration hypothesis, locative sentences, in order to be sensible or coherent, require a fit between spatial information (provided by prepositions) and object information (provided by nouns). We can conceive integration as a multiple-constraint process which depends on: (a) the locative construction, (b) the directional preposition, and (c) the sensory-motor features of the objects. Constructions with the format [NOUN 1–VERB–LOCATIVE PREPOSITION–NOUN 2] provide the general guidelines to simulate a spatial layout. Namely, the NOUN 1 phrase takes the role of figure, the NOUN 2 phrase takes the role of ground, and the preposition indicates the spatial relation between them. The meaning of the locative construction is not a simple addition of the meanings of the nouns, the verb, and the preposition. Instead, the meanings of these components have to fit into a coherent pattern. Thus, the sensory-motor features of the objects (e.g. animacy, solidity, part–whole, size, etc.) are retrieved from memory, they are placed into the slots for figure and ground, provided by the grammar, and then the simulation of the layout marked by the directional preposition is run. The simulation proposed here is similar to the notion described by Barsalou (1999), who claims that 'As selective attention focuses on spoken and written words, schematic memories extracted from perceptual states become integrated into simulators that later produce simulations of these words in recognition, imagination, and production' (p. 592).

The success of the simulation depends on how well the direction tagged by the preposition and the properties of the figure and the ground fit together. The integration hypothesis is akin to Glenberg's and collaborators' indexical hypothesis of meaning that considers syntactic constructions as general guidelines to meshing the properties of entities (affordances) into a coherent pattern (Glenberg and Robertson, 2000; Kaschak and Glenberg, 2000). However, unlike the indexical hypothesis, we focus on the geometrical and functional features of objects rather than on their affordances for action. In addition, we extend the notion of construction-based meaning to prepositional clauses.

3.4   A Study on Locative Sentences

In a corpus-based study we analyzed the meaning of directional sentences rather than isolated prepositions (de Vega, Rodrigo, Ato, Dehn and Barquero, 2002). We expected to find evidence for the integration hypothesis, exploring whether figures and grounds differ in their features, depending on the direction or dimension denoted by prepositions. Several semantic features of figures and grounds were analyzed in the study: animacy, part–whole, countability, mobility, and solidity. Other parameters referred to the interaction between figure and ground in the layout, such as the relative size of figure–ground, the support relation, and the speaker's projected point of view. The semantic parameters were coded binarily, and their descriptions together with the reasons for including them in our analysis are given below.

Animacy of the figure or the ground

The categorization of objects as animate or inanimate entities develops very early in preverbal children (e.g. Mandler, 1992). That is, young children distinguish between animate objects (being moved by themselves, with irregular paths, responding to other objects from a distance, etc.) and inanimate objects (moved by others, with linear paths, etc.). Animacy, besides, becomes a very important feature in language, as most grammatical subjects involve animate agents (e.g. Bock, Loebell, and Morey, 1992). We encoded each noun as animate or inanimate.

Part–whole of the figure or the ground

Many objects have parts that are strongly associated to particular functions, such as the wheels of vehicles or the different body parts (Tversky, 1989). Given the salience of functional parts speakers may be interested in using an object part either as figure or ground in a spatial layout. Carlson-Radvansky, Covey, and Lattanzi (1999) reported that the spatial relation between a figure and a ground is sometimes biased towards a functional part of the ground rather than towards its center-of-mass. We encoded each noun as being a part or a whole.

Countability of the figure or the ground

Some entities in our lexicon have well-defined boundaries and can be easily enumerated or counted (e.g. stones, persons, rivers, etc.). Other entities are unbounded substances or aggregates which are uncountable (e.g. water, sand, crowd, etc.). This semantic feature is sometimes labeled as the mass/count distinction (Talmy, 1987; Jackendoff, 1996*a*), or the thing/stuff distinction (see Prasada, this volume, Ch. 14). Many languages require different quantity adjectives for the two categories (e.g. many/few for countable objects and much/little for uncountable objects). We encoded each noun as countable or uncountable.

Solidity of the figure or the ground

Preverbal children as young as three–four months, who are still unable to interact with objects, are sensitive to the solidity or non-solidity of material objects (Spelke, Breinlinger, Macomber, and Jacobson, 1992). The perceptual experience of rigidity, opacity, and impenetrability seems to be sufficient for an initial conceptualization of object solidity. In later development, the solidity of objects becomes critical to develop specific sensory-motor programs for interacting with objects. We encoded each noun as solid or non-solid.

Mobility of the figure or the ground

Mobile objects are those that do not have a fixed position in the environment either because they move by themselves (a person or most animals) or they are frequently moved by an external agent (a pencil, a car, or a chair). By contrast, non-mobile or stable objects have a fixed position in the environment or are seldom moved (houses, trees, windows, etc.). Infants are very early sensitive to the degree and kind of mobility of objects and as we have mentioned above, they use motion cues to acquire the category of animacy (Mandler, 1992).

Support relation

Because of gravity, objects arranged in the vertical dimension tend to be supported by other objects. This supporting relationship usually involves a surface contact between the supporting and the supported object. Six-month-old infants are sensitive to object–support relationships in perceptual events (Baillargeon and Hanko-Summers, 1990). We encoded each locative expression as describing a layout with a support or non-support relationship.

Relative size between figure and ground

Infants are sensitive to the relative size of objects, as demonstrated in some experiments. For instance, they show surprise when they are exposed to a videotape showing a large object entering a small container. Concerning locative sentences, some authors propose that grounds tend to be larger than figures (Talmy, 1983; Herskovits, 1985; Landau and Jackendoff, 1993), although their claim seems to rely on intuitive observations rather than on a systematic investigation. We encoded the relative size as normative (figure < ground) or non-normative (figure > = ground).

Speakers' projected point of view in the layout (herein: Projective view)

If the ground object has no intrinsic directions (e.g. a sphere, a rock or a mountain), people tend to rely on a deictic or observer-centered frame of reference. This sort of reference frame involves a projection of an implicit speaker in the described layout (Landau and Jackendoff, 1993; Levelt, 1996). For instance, the sentence 'The cow is in front of the rock', may be interpreted as the cow being somewhere between the speaker and the rock. This should hold because the rock has no intrinsic 'front'. We encoded a sentence as 'projective view' when the ground object had no intrinsic directions.

Sentences with literal meanings were selected for analysis that included any Spanish or German directional term and two noun phrases as figure and ground, respectively. Those sentences were taken from two 1-million-words corpora, one in Spanish and one in German. The two corpora included paragraphs from contemporary narratives, originally written in their respective language. The final sample consisted of 2,122 sentences in Spanish and 2,069 in German. The proportion of locative sentences for each of the six direction categories was similar in Spanish and German, respectively: Above or Over (48 percent and 37 percent), Below or Under (17.7 percent and 18 percent), In front of (22.8 percent and 30.5 percent), Behind (9.5 percent and 12 percent), Right of (0.9 percent and 0.9 percent), and Left of (0.6 percent and 1 percent). The data for Left and Right sentences were discarded from the analysis because of their small number of occurrences.

Several logistic regression analyses were carried out for each language, using the semantic features as predictors for pairs of dimensions (e.g. 0 = vertical; 1 = horizontal), or for pairs of directions (e.g. 0 = front, 1 = behind). Table 3.1 shows the features that distinguish the vertical and the horizontal dimension, in both Spanish and German.

The results showed a remarkable convergence across languages. In both languages, sentences with horizontal prepositions are more likely to involve figures and grounds that are solid, countable, and animate, and they are more likely to

TABLE 3.1. *Global contrast between dimensions <Above–Below> vs. <Front–Behind>, indicating convergent and unique features across languages*

Convergent features	Unique features
Above–below	*Above–below*
Figure partitive	Figure mobility (German)
Support relation	
Figure < Ground	
Front–behind	*Front–behind*
Figure animate	Ground mobility (Spanish)
Figure solid	
Ground animate	
Ground countable	
Ground solid	
Projective view	

Note: Spanish sample: the overall model predicts 95% of the responses correctly (Max-rescaled $R^2 = 0.76$; Model chi-square statistic = 1647.5, df = 10, $p < .01$). German sample: the overall model predicts 88.5% of the responses correctly (Max-rescaled $R^2 = 0.57$; Model chi-square statistic = 1133.675, df = 10; $p < .01$).

Source: de Vega, Rodrigo, Ato, Dehn, and Barquero, 2002.

contain a projective view. By contrast, sentences that include vertical prepositions are more likely to involve partitive figures which are smaller than their grounds, and a support relation between them.

Some of the distinctive features identified in the analyses are rather intuitive. For instance, the high frequency of figure–ground support relations in sentences that refer to the vertical dimension is a consequence of the effects of gravity on solid objects. In the same vein the overwhelming frequency of a projective view in the horizontal dimension is a consequence of the fact that some objects used as grounds, such as mountains or rocks, do not have an intrinsic 'front' nor 'behind'. Consequently, speakers assign the 'front' and 'behind' depending on whether, from their own perspective, the figure is visible or occluded by the ground. A projective view is usually unnecessary in the vertical dimension, as most grounds have an 'above' and 'below' marked by the gravity, or by morphological and functional differences (e.g. even mountains and rocks have an intrinsic 'top' and 'bottom').

There are other less obvious distinctive features, such as the abundance of partitive figures in sentences that contain 'above' or 'below'. An inspection of the corpora showed that, in many cases, sentences with vertical prepositions refer to small-scale layouts, typically in the peripersonal space, in which body parts or functional parts of objects are under attentional focus. For instance, 'He put his hand over her shoulder'; or 'She left the bicycle pedal under the table'. Instead, partitive figures are much less frequently associated with horizontal small-scale layouts. Thus, sentences such as 'He put his hand behind her shoulder', or 'She left the bicycle pedal in front of the table' are rather odd. One possible reason for this, is that approaching functional parts of objects (e.g. with a manipulative purpose) probably involves a vertical contact in most cases.

The fact that the animacy of figures and animacy of grounds are distinctive features in sentences with 'front' and 'behind', indicates that people, animals, and plants are more frequently used as figures and as reference points in the horizontal than in the vertical dimension. For instance, some typical horizontal scenes involve social interactions, in which a character is described as placed in front or behind another character. Finally, the pattern 'figure smaller than ground' seems to be a distinctive feature of the vertical dimension, because supporting grounds are usually larger than supported figures. As opposed to this, the figures and grounds do not generally differ in size in sentences with a horizontal preposition. These sentences frequently describe, as we mentioned above, the position of a person in the ground of another person ('John sat behind Mary').

To sum up, the corpus study demonstrated that the combination of some features of figures and grounds fits better the vertical dimension, whereas a different set of features is more appropriate for the horizontal dimension. These results go beyond the classical figure–ground asymmetry at least in two ways. First, the number of features explored was larger than in previous studies, and the analysis with samples of natural language was a more empirical approach.

Second, our findings suggest that the figure–ground asymmetry is modulated by the particular direction or dimension tagged by the preposition. For instance, the 'figure smaller than ground' feature was distinctive for the vertical dimension, but not for the horizontal dimension. We suggest that the results are compatible with the integration hypothesis. On the speaker side, the choice of a ground is not independent of the figure features, nor the choice of a directional preposition is independent of the figure and ground features. On the addressee side, the syntactic construction provides the roles of figure and ground for the noun phrases, and the addressee may flesh out their implicit features and, if they are appropriate for that direction, to arrange an integrated representation of the layout.

3.5   Concluding Remarks

In this chapter we elaborated the notion of embodied meaning applied to locative sentences. We share with other authors the idea that understanding and producing these sentences does not rely on the activation of arbitrary, amodal symbols, but involves embodied representations of the layout. However, we provided some evidence that the meaning of locative sentences differs from peripheral sensory-motor experience, in some important respect. Specifically, whereas locating objects by means of the pointing gesture is directly governed by the proprioceptive information of our body (first-order embodiment), communicating objects' position by means of language is based on a mental framework which is detached from the body. We think that language-based spatial meaning can be characterized as a second-order embodiment, because it involves a simulation of figure–ground relations in a represented layout or mental framework. This second-order embodiment might occur even when we speak about the current perceptual layout and use our own body as framework. The advantages of building spatial meaning in a mental framework are that it preserves spatial information and, at the same time, gives the speakers and addressees flexibility and autonomy in the production and comprehension of spatial sentences. Particularly, representing spatial relations in a mental framework liberates us from the rigid control of peripheral information, that governs our navigation and manipulation of the environment. One problem, however, is that representing language-based spatial relations and updating them requires much more cognitive effort than keeping track of spatial relations in our interaction with the environment.

Second-order embodiment involves some specific computations that are not necessary in perception and action on real environments. In particular, the location of the figure has to be expressed in relation to a reference frame or ground object. This involves an important decision process on the speaker's side. From the cluster of spatial relations available to the perceptual system the speaker has to select a single ground that is particularly informative to the addressee. This choice is not random, as our corpus-based study suggests. Some features of figure and grounds are systematically related to the directions and dimensions denoted by prepositions. Therefore, the semantic analysis of isolated prepositions does not grasp entirely how the meaning of locative sentences is built in a constructive and integrative manner.

4

Dissociation between Verbal and Pointing Responding in Perspective Change Problems

RANXIAO FRANCES WANG

Abstract

Predicting the outcome of spatial transformations, such as viewpoint changes, is very important in everyday life. It has been shown that it is very difficult to point to where an object would be as if one is facing a different direction (perspective change problem). These difficulties are often attributed to the imagination process, that is mentally rotating oneself or the object array. The current chapter investigates this hypothesis by varying the 'imagination time' before the target is given. In two experiments I show that when using a pointing task, there is no improvement in performance even when the participants are allowed to complete the 'imagination' process first. In contrast, when using a verbal reporting task, participants are able to describe the egocentric angles of the imagined target location as quickly as the no-imagination control condition. These results suggest that participants are able to transform and maintain a representation of the new perspective, but this representation is accessible to a verbal system that subserves the verbal response task, but not to an action system that subserves the pointing task. Thus, functional features defined with respect to one cognitive system may not generalize to another cognitive system.

Functional features

Properties of the environment the cognitive systems represent and operate on. For example, an object is at certain distance from the viewer. This distance is a functional feature of the object if the cognitive system contains this information

Thanks to Elizabeth Spelke for discussions, and to Elizabeth Hennessey for help in collecting some of the data. Supported in part by a University of Illinois Institutional Research Board Grant to R. F. Wang.

and operates accordingly. According to the definition, functional features may vary depending on the specific cognitive systems involved. This chapter will investigate the hypothesis that functional features differ for different cognitive systems using a spatial reasoning task.

4.1   Introduction

4.1.1   Spatial reasoning and transformation of spatial representations

Transformation or manipulation of spatial relationships is an important spatial ability in everyday life. For example, we often need to take another person's perspective, and predict what he or she sees in order to give directions or coordinate actions. This ability is often studied using spatial reasoning tasks that require one to make inferences about spatial relationships from different viewpoints relative to a test display. For example, one type of spatial reasoning task, that is perspective change task, requires one to imagine him- or herself turning to face a different orientation or translating to a different location, and report a target's egocentric direction from the imagined perspective. As an advanced form of spatial processing, spatial reasoning problems have received a great deal of attention in research on human spatial abilities, mechanisms of spatial processing, and the nature of spatial representations (e.g. Brockmole and Wang, 2003; Easton and Sholl, 1995; Farrell and Robertson, 1998; Franklin, and Tversky, 1990; Franklin, Tversky, and Coon, 1992; Huttenlocher and Presson, 1973, 1979; Newcombe and Huttenlocher, 1992; Piaget and Inhelder, 1956; Presson, 1980, 1982; Rieser, 1989; Rieser, Garing, and Young, 1994; Sholl and Nolin, 1997; Wraga, Creem, and Proffitt, 1999, 2000; Zacks, Rypma, Gabrieli, Tversky, and Glover, 1999). Furthermore, various research in related areas uses the spatial reasoning paradigm to address issues in scene memory, reference frame selection, and navigation, using both real and virtual environments (Amorim and Stucchi, 1997; Bryant and Tversky, 1992; Bryant, Tversky, and Franklin, 1992; Christou and Bülthoff, 1999; Presson and Montello, 1994; Roskos-Ewoldsen, McNamara, Shelton, and Carr, 1998; Shelton and McNamara, 1997, 2000; Simons and Wang, 1998; Wang and Simons, 1999; Werner and Schmidt, 1999).

Based on the findings of the extensive research on spatial reasoning problems in the past thirty years, important conclusions have been drawn regarding the nature of one's representations of the environment, the reference frames used to encode spatial locations, and the transformations of spatial representations. For example, Rieser (1989; also see Easton and Sholl, 1995; Shelton and McNamara, 1997; Wraga *et al.*, 2000) showed that when participants were asked to imagine themselves turning to face a different orientation and 'point to object **X** as if you were facing object **Y**', errors and reaction times significantly increased as the imagined heading deviated farther and farther away from their actual heading.

These results were usually interpreted as due to a mental rotation type of process. Assuming that imagining oneself turning takes time, then the more one has to 'rotate' the longer it takes, and the less accurate the rotation may be.

The second major finding in spatial reasoning research concerns the difference between imagined self-rotation vs. imagined self-translation. Rieser (1989; also see Easton and Sholl, 1995; May, 2000) showed that imagined self-rotations were slower and performance decreased as the imagined rotation angle increased. In contrast, imagined self-translation was easy and fast, and remained relatively constant. The difference between imagined rotation and imagined translation was considered to support a representation that specified object-to-object relationships, rather than the self-to-object relationships. The logic was, according to Rieser (1989), that a representation of object-to-object relationship directly specifies where other objects are relative to a given object, thus allowing easy imagined translation to that object but not imagined rotation. In contrast, a representation of self-to-object relationships specifies directions of objects relative to one's current position, thus should allow easy rotation but not translation.

The third major finding concerns the difference between imagined self-rotation and imagined target-rotation. Wraga *et al.* (2000) showed that when participants were asked to imagine themselves or some targets rotating, and to name the target in a specified direction, imagined self-rotation was easier than imagined target-rotation, an effect they referred to as the 'viewer advantage'. Wraga *et al.* (2000) interpreted their results as the relative ease of transforming an egocentric reference frame than an object or array-based reference frame. Huttenlocher and Presson (1973, 1979; Presson, 1982) argued that the spatial reasoning task was hard whenever the array had to be mentally moved relative to the environment, and was relatively easy when that relationship remained constant. This finding suggested, they further argued, that both the self and the objects must be encoded individually relative to the stable environment, and this made the array rotation harder because of the large number of items that need to be mentally 'transformed'. In support of this view, Wraga *et al.* (2000) showed that imagined array or object rotation became easier when the targets were more 'integrated' or coherent.

4.1.2   The responding processes and accessibility of spatial representations

There is a potential issue in spatial reasoning tasks that has often been overlooked in the previous research. A typical perspective change task, for example, involves imagining oneself turning to face a different direction and pointing to where a target would be relative to that imagined perspective. Such a task includes two potentially independent processes, namely an imagination process (imagine oneself turning and form a representation of the world from the new perspective) and a responding process (make a response according to the new representation) (e.g. Tversky, Kim, and Cohen, 1999). In other words, in order to perform a spatial reasoning task, one has to perform at least two subtasks, if he or she follows the instruction literally. First, one has to perform the 'imagination task', mentally rotate or translate oneself or the targets. Second, one has to make a response, either a judgment task (such as a recognition task or an 'item question') or an action task (typically pointing). Most studies focus on questions about the first process, that is how spatial representations are transformed. However, the second process may be equally, or even more important, for two reasons. First, behavioral measures are affected by both processes, therefore without knowing the source of the effects observed, it is virtually impossible to investigate the first process alone. Second, understanding the second process, that is how transformed representations are accessed by various cognitive systems, can shed light on the underlying mechanisms of spatial processing.

Research on perception and action has suggested the possibility that a representation may be transformed, but may not be accessible to various cognitive systems. Various studies have shown that a veridical representation of an object's size, distance, and orientation may be used to guide actions, but does not enter perceptual awareness (e.g. Bridgeman and Huemer, 1998; Creem and Proffitt, 1998; Goodale and Milner, 1992; Loomis, Da Silva, Philbeck, and Fukusima, 1996; Proffitt, Bhalla, Gossweiler, and Midgett, 1995; also see De Vega and Rodrigo, 2001; Ch. 3). For example, Loomis and colleagues asked participants to adjust the sagittal distance (in depth) between two objects so that it perceptually matches a standard frontoparallel interval. The sagittal distance was vastly compressed perceptually compared to that of the frontoparallel one. This distortion of perceptual space in depth, however, did not seem to manifest itself when the participants were asked to estimate the intervals by walking to the first target and then to the second (Loomis *et al.* 1996). As another example, the dissociation between a perceptual task and an action task has also been shown in the estimation of orientation (slant). Proffitt, Bhalla, Gossweiler, and Midgett (1995; Creem and Proffitt, 1998) found that verbal judgments of the incline of hills were greatly overestimated but motoric (haptic) adjustments were much more accurate. More interestingly, in judging slant from memory following a brief or extended time delay, away from the hill, short-term visual guidance memory no longer persisted, and both motor and verbal responses were driven by an explicit representation and both were less accurate. Finally, physiological evidence also showed that the neural substrates underlying visual perception may be quite distinct from those underlying the visual control of actions. For example, Goodale and Milner (1992) proposed that the ventral stream of projections from the striate cortex to the inferotemporal cortex plays a major role in the perceptual identification of objects, while the dorsal stream projecting from the striate cortex to the posterior parietal region mediates the required sensorimotor transformations for visually guided actions.

The current study provides a complementary example for the dissociation between perceptual/linguistic systems and action systems. In the examples cited above, superior performance has been found when using an action task, and it was argued that action systems are less prone to these perceptual illusions. This special characteristic of the action system may be due to the fundamental importance of action to an organism's survival. Here I look at the opposite side of the coin: representations that may be useful and accessible to a perceptual/ verbal system, but not to an action system. In a spatial reasoning task, one may transform a spatial representation to cognitively examine the spatial aspects that are not obvious in the current representations, but one might expect such flexible transformations to serve the function of acquiring cognitive knowledge and communication only, and these imaginations should not be readily executed as an action in the real world. As a consequence, these representations may be inaccessible to an action system.

The experiments reported here investigate whether the transformed spatial representations are universally available to all systems (e.g. perceptual system/ linguistic system, action system) or only accessible to a subset of systems. In order to examine the responding processes involving different cognitive systems, a critical modification had to be made to the standard spatial reasoning task to separate the imagination and responding processes. The standard instruction used in most spatial reasoning tasks asks the participants 'where is **Y** if you were facing **X**?' Because the imagination target (**X**) is given after the responding target (**Y**), participants cannot start the transformation processes until the name of the imagination target is given. This procedure ensures that the reaction time gives a clean measure of the entire process, and is unaffected by the length of the target names. The disadvantage is that the RT reflects a combination of both imagination and responding processes. The current procedure attempted to disentangle the two processes by giving the imagination target first, and a delay to allow the imagination process to complete. However, before making this change in procedure, the effects of such a change need to be examined. Thus, Experiment 1 compared spatial reasoning performance in a control condition (no imagination), imagination condition without delay (similar to the standard procedure), and the imagination condition with delay (new procedure).

4.2 Experiment 1

4.2.1 Methods

Apparatus

Participants were tested individually in a rectangular room (3.8 m × 2.4 m), as illustrated in Fig. 4.1. Five targets—a closet, a door, a VCR, a poster, and a computer—were placed around the participants. The overhead image of the room and the participants' responses were recorded with a VCR that was

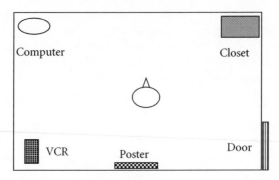

Fig. 4.1. An overhead view of the rectangular room with five targets for Experiment 1.

connected to a small video camera mounted on the ceiling just above the swivel chair where the participants sat. A Gateway PC4200 desktop computer randomized the order of the targets for each participant and controlled the timing for the imagination stage, as described below.

Design

Eight undergraduate students from the University of Illinois participated in the experiment in exchange for course credit. Each participant was tested in three conditions: a no-imagination control condition, an imagination-without-delay condition, and an imagination-with-delay condition. The test perspectives (i.e. egocentric response directions) were matched in the three conditions, in the following way, in order to eliminate any potential differences between different perspectives (e.g. Shelton and McNamara, 2001). In each of the two imagination conditions, all participants physically faced the computer, and then imagined facing each of the four remaining targets once (thus yielding four trials per condition). In the control condition, two participants faced each of the four targets (which were the to-be-imagined facing targets in the imagination conditions). Overall, across all participants, each object (except for the computer) served as the imagined heading target twice in each imagination condition, and as the actual heading target twice, for a complete match. The control condition always came first, followed by the two imagination conditions, the order of which was counterbalanced across participants.

The purpose of this experiment was twofold. First, the comparison between the two imagination conditions examined whether the cost observed in the perspective change tasks continued to exist after extended time was given to complete the imagination process. Second, an estimate of how long the 'imagination' process would take, at least subjectively, was obtained by asking the participants to give an overt response whenever they thought they had completed the 'imagining' process.

Procedure

Each participant sat in the swivel chair, and was allowed to study the target array for as long as she or he needed, turning his or her head and seat as desired. When the participants claimed they were ready, they were blindfolded and turned to face the assigned heading. They pointed to the actual target locations (except for the one they were physically facing) in a random order, once each for a total of four trials (control condition). Then they turned to face the computer and were tested in the two imagination conditions, four trials each. Before each condition, they were told whether there would be a delay, determined by themselves, or no delay. In each trial, they were asked to 'imagine turning to face X', followed by a delay until the participant responded 'ready' if in the delay-condition. There was no delay in the No-delay condition. Then they were asked to point to 'where's Y?' Participants responded by pointing using whichever hand was more convenient, as quickly and accurately as possible, to the target as if they were at the imagined perspective.

Coding and data analysis

The directions of the targets and the pointing responses were measured from the TV monitor after the testing was completed, by superimposing a transparent radial grid on the monitor, which had $10°$ units. The response latencies (RT) were measured from the ending of the target name to the completion of the pointing response, indicated by the stabilization of the hand. The angular error for each response was calculated as the small angle (i.e. $\leq 180°$, unsigned) between the correct direction and the actual pointing direction. Both reaction time and response error were then averaged across all pointing responses within a condition for each participant.

4.2.2 Results and discussion

Comparisons between the two imagination conditions revealed little difference in performance, either in terms of reaction time (paired $t(7) = .14$, $p = .90$) or response accuracy (paired $t(7) = .94$, $p = .38$), as shown in Fig. 4.2. Both imagination conditions were significantly worse than the control condition, in both the RT measure (paired $ts(7) > 3.5$, $ps < .01$) and the error measure (paired $ts(7) > 8.0$, $ps < .001$).

The subjective report of imagination time ranged from 2.2 s to 8.4 s, with a mean of 4.3 s. Despite this additional time to 'imagine' themselves turning, the participants didn't respond any faster or more accurately. Furthermore, compared to the control condition, performance was significantly worse even when participants were allowed extra time to do the 'imagination', and the only requirement was to make a pointing response according to the transformed representation. These results suggest that either the participants were not able to

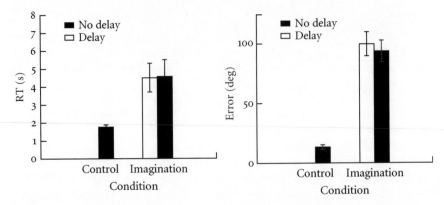

FIG. 4.2. The results of Experiment 1. The left panel shows RT in the three conditions (no-imagination control, imagination without delay, and imagination with a self-determined delay). The right panel shows response errors in degrees. The error bars are standard errors.

form a representation of the new perspective, or they were not able to make a pointing response according to that representation. Was there a transformed representation of the imagined perspective at all, which may be unavailable to the specific responding system, but may be used for other types of systems? In the second experiment, the action response (pointing) was contrasted with a verbal response to examine whether participants were able to transform and maintain spatial representations, and whether these representations were differentially accessible to different cognitive systems.

4.3   Experiment 2

In this experiment, participants imagined themselves turning in place to face a given object, and after an extended time to complete this imagination process, they either pointed to another object (pointing task) or verbally reported the egocentric direction as angles, as if they had turned to face the imagined direction (verbal task). The pointing task served as a comparison for the verbal task, and also as a replication of the basic findings of Experiment 1 using a slightly different procedure, a differently shaped room, a different number and arrangement of targets, and a slightly longer, fixed imagination delay.

4.3.1   Methods

Apparatus

Participants were tested in a square room (1.9 m × 1.9 m × 2.0 m) with six small objects (toy car, stool, poster, toy bear, plate, basket) randomly placed by the

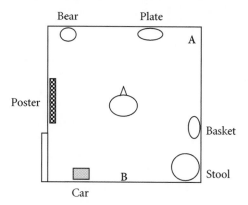

Fig. 4.3. An overhead view of the square room with six targets for Experiment 2.

walls, as shown in Fig. 4.3. A video camera mounted at the center of the ceiling took the overhead image of the room and recorded the entire session for further data analysis. A swivel chair was fixed on the ground in the middle of the room; participants sat in the chair, and made their responses. The names of the targets were recorded on an audiotape in advance, and were played back through a portable tape recorder.

Design

To compare the accessibility of a transformed representation to different cognitive systems, sufficient time was given to the participants to complete the imagination process. According to the subjective reports in Experiment 1, and the results of previous studies (typical reaction times for an imagined self-rotation task were about 5 s or less, e.g. Rieser, 1989), a 10 s imagination period should be sufficient to complete the imagination process. If so, then when the target names were given after the 10 s delay, participants simply had to respond according to the results of the imagination process. Therefore the reaction times in the current study should reflect the responding process, that is how readily available the information is to the specific responding system.

The critical comparison is between performance using an action response (i.e. pointing) and that using a verbal response. To make the two tasks as comparable as possible, both tasks need to retrieve the same spatial information. Because a pointing task is generally believed to require information about the egocentric directions of targets, the same information was probed in the verbal task. Thus, if participants were able to verbally report the egocentric directions of a target from the imagined perspective but were not able to make a pointing response, then one can conclude that the verbal system must have access to a representation of egocentric directions from the imagined perspective but the action system does not.

Eight undergraduate students at the Cornell University from a psychology class participated for course credits. Each participant was tested in two tasks, a pointing task and a verbal task. For each task, there were two conditions: a control condition, in which the participants simply reported the actual direction of the target either by pointing or verbal description, and an imagination condition, in which they imagined facing a different direction and then after a 10 s delay reported the egocentric directions of the remaining targets. The test perspectives (i.e. actual facing directions and imagined facing directions), and the order of tasks were counterbalanced across participants. Thus, half of the participants had the pointing task first and the other half had the verbal task first. For each task, half of the participants physically faced a corner (i.e. A) and imagined facing the *poster*, as in Fig. 4.1, and the other half physically faced the middle of a wall (i.e. B) and imagined facing the *bear*. In both cases, the imagined rotation was about 135°, which was sufficiently large to demonstrate the effects of imagined perspective changes (e.g. May, 1996; Rieser, 1989; Wraga *et al.*, 2000).

Procedure

Participants first learned the six targets while sitting in the middle of the room, either turning their head or the chair, until they claimed they were ready. Then they were blindfolded and turned to face a predetermined orientation according to the condition they were assigned to. Each participant was asked to point to the targets as quickly and accurately as they could, using whichever hand was convenient, according to the names announced by the experimenter. All six targets were tested for each participant in a random order. This condition served as the no-imagination control.

After the control condition, the participants were instructed that next they were to imagine themselves turning to face a different direction, and then pointing to where the targets would be if they were facing that way (pointing task). In the verbal task, they were told that straight ahead was 0°, straight left or right would be 90° left or right, and straight back would be 180°, and they were asked to report the angles in the form of 'n° left/right', as accurately as they could. For example, the participants may say the stool is '40° to my left', or the poster is '75° to my right'. After the participants were clear about the instructions, they were told to 'imagine that you are facing **X**'. After 10 s delay, during which they were allowed to do the imagination, a random sequence of five targets (the one they imagined facing was not tested) were announced one by one and they responded accordingly (*imagination condition*).

After the first task, the blindfold was removed and the participants relearned the target locations. Then the procedure was repeated for the second task.

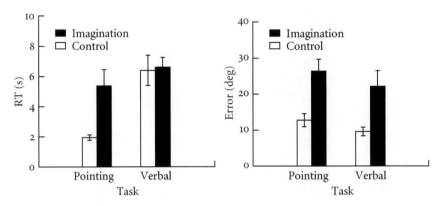

FIG. 4.4. The results of Experiment 2. The left panel shows RT in the control and imagination conditions in the pointing task and the verbal report task. The right panel shows response errors in degrees. The error bars are standard errors.

Coding and data analysis

The response time and errors were coded as in Experiment 1. The response latencies for the verbal task were measured from the ending of the target name to the end of the verbal response.[1] Both reaction time and response error were averaged across all responses within a condition for each participant (six for the control conditions, five for the imagination conditions).

The primary measure of interest was the reaction time (RT), which indicates the availability of the information for the particular task without further processing. The errors were also measured to indicate possible speed–accuracy tradeoff.

4.3.2   Results

In the pointing task, the results essentially replicated Experiment 1 despite changes in the imagination delay, the number of targets, the imagined rotation angle, and the shape of the room. Even with the extended time provided for imagination, participants showed significant increase in response latency in the imagination condition compared to the control condition (see Fig. 4.4). Mean reaction time increased from 1.95 s to 5.36 s (paired $t(7) = 3.9$, $p = .006$). These data suggest that the information needed to make a pointing response after an imagined viewpoint change was not readily available, and some additional

---

[1] The RTs reported here were measured as the end of the verbal response to ensure the completion of the response. The pattern of the results was the same when measured as the starting of the verbal response.

processing was needed. On the contrary, the reaction time in the verbal task did not differ significantly in the imagination condition compared to the control condition (paired $t(7) = .21$, $p = .84$), and there was a significant interaction between task and condition (F$(1, 7) = 9.2$, $p = .02$). These results suggest that the participants did not need extra time in the imagination condition to make a response, thus information about the egocentric angles after the perspective change was more or less readily available for verbal reporting.

The mean response errors increased in the imagination conditions for both tasks (paired $ts(7) < 3.2$, $ps < .02$), and there was no significant interaction (F$(1, 7) = .06$, $p = .82$), suggesting the difference in RT was not a result of speed–accuracy tradeoff.

4.3.3   Discussion

The results of this experiment showed that pointing to objects from the imagined perspective was much slower than pointing to their actual positions, but verbally reporting the egocentric direction of a target from the imagined perspective was as fast as verbally reporting its actual position.[2] This contrast indicates that a transformed representation of the new spatial relationships can be constructed and maintained, but it seems to directly support only the verbal assessment of the egocentric angles but not pointing responses. Thus, additional processing seems to be needed for a pointing response.

4.4   General Discussion

In two experiments I examined whether transformations of spatial representations can be accessed by different cognitive systems equally or differentially, using a variant of the classical perspective-taking task. Participants imagined themselves facing a different direction, and reported where targets would be relative to that perspective. By giving the imagination target in advance and allowing sufficient time to perform any possible transformations of the spatial representations, the reaction time should reflect how well different responding systems are able to make use of these transformed representations. The imagination process seemed to take about 4–5 s to perform, according to the subjective reports. However, even allowing 10 s to complete the imagination process, pointing responses still took significantly longer in the imagination condition than in the control condition. On the contrary, in the verbal reporting task RT did not differ significantly in the imagination condition than in the control condition. These

---

[2] The main effect in RT between the two tasks is not surprising, because verbal responding involves an extra process of converting the angles to numbers, and the vocal response itself is slower than moving the hand.

results suggest that transformed spatial representations may be readily used for verbal reporting, but not for pointing responses.

It was puzzling that the participants knew where a target would be relative to themselves if they were facing a different direction, but they apparently didn't know how to move their hands to point in that egocentric direction. The information necessary to make such a pointing response was clearly there, but somehow the pointing system failed to use that information. Why should such an imagined representation allow verbal descriptions readily but fail to guide the pointing task? Both tasks measure the same information, namely the metric direction of a target relative to one's body in an imagined orientation. The only difference is that one involves an action while the other involves judgments or verbal communications. What aspects of the two types of tasks may be responsible for the dissociation?

The first possibility is that action and verbal communications are guided by separate representations, through different pathways and neural connections (e.g. Goodale and Milner, 1992). Thus, if spatial transformations or 'imaginations' are operated by the verbal system, while the action systems maintain a representation of the physical reality and are not connected with those imaginary representations, then one would expect that extra cognitive effort and special strategies will be needed to overcome those natural limitations in the action system when the task requires a connection between the action system and representations in the verbal system. It is also conceivable that interference may play a role in the responding stage, if the action system is tightly connected to a representation of physical reality. For example, one may have to inhibit those automatic activations leading one's hands to point to a target's actual location instead of the imaginary direction. Several researchers have proposed similar interference theories (e.g. May, 1996; Newcombe and Huttenlocher, 1992; Presson, 1982).

A related alternative is that the transformed representation may be 'farther away' from the action system but 'closer' to the verbal system. If one assumes that a flexible transformation of spatial representations is essential to verbal communication, the processes may occur within the verbal system. Thus, the verbal system can access such information readily and as quickly as the original representations. On the other hand, an action system is farther away from these representations and thus takes longer to access the transformed representations than the original ones. If this hypothesis is true, then one might expect to see highly similar error patterns because both action responses and verbal responses are based on the same representation.

There is, however, a different possibility. Studies have shown that linguistic systems are very flexible in reference frame use (e.g. Carlson-Radvansky and Irwin, 1993; Carlson-Radvansky and Jiang, 1998; Levinson, 1996), while action systems rely exclusively on egocentric reference frames anchored on the physical body. Thus, in order to estimate the egocentric directions from the imagined perspective, the linguistic system may impose a reference frame on the imagined 'self', and select between the reference frames anchored either on the imagined self or the physical self freely. For an action system, however, such free selection may not be possible, because the arms' positions may only be represented in the reference frame anchored at the physical body.

The dissociation between the action system and the linguistic system suggests that functional features of the environment differ for different cognitive systems. For example, the egocentric direction of an object takes a fixed value in the action system, and this value determines how the actions are carried out with respect to the target object, and thus constitutes a functional feature of the object for the action system. On the contrary, the linguistic system does not commit to the specific values of the egocentric directions, and does not necessarily respond according to that value. In that sense egocentric direction is not a functional feature for the linguistic system. Because different cognitive systems represent different features of the environment, cautions should be raised in defining functional features of objects and environments, especially when generalizing to different cognitive systems.

5

An Ecological Approach to the Interface between Language and Vision

RAJESH KASTURIRANGAN

Abstract

Spatial relations are represented in language as well as in perception. On the surface, the relationship between these forms of spatial representation is problematic. Language is schematic and context-sensitive while perception is detailed. Nevertheless, both spatial language and perception occur in a common ecological context. A computational characterization of the ecological context, based on the mathematical notions of co-dimension and invariance shows that spatial features are organized in the form of a hierarchical structure consisting of three qualitatively different categories: Coordinate Frames, Topological Structures, and Metric Structures. Coordinate Frames and Topological Structures are present in language as well as in perception, while Metric Structures are present only in perception. I argue that language and perception are neither disjoint, nor are they isomorphic. They share a core set of representations—the coordinate frame and topological representations. This core set interfaces with other representations that may be language or perception specific.

Feature

A discrete property of an organism's environment, including its own physical attributes as well as its goals and beliefs that can be inferred reliably from perceptual input.

5.1 Introduction

Inquiries about the relationship between spatial language and perception have usually been motivated by the question: 'How do we talk about what we see?'

I want to thank Whitman Richards for many comments and suggestions.

For human beings, talking about the perceptual world seems effortless. Naive phenomenology—also called the canonical model (Herskovits, 1986)—suggests that there is an objective world outside our senses that we 'see' and 'talk' about. According to the canonical model, the task of the linguist is to show the correspondence between spatial language and objective reality.[1] However, the relationship between spatial language and the external world is complicated. Linguistic representations are *schematic* and *context sensitive* (Lakoff, 1987; Jackendoff, 1990), two properties that are hard to reconcile with a fixed, objective external world as embodied in the canonical model. The canonical model is implicitly accepted in most computational modeling of perception (Marr, 1982). Computational theories of perception have been strongly guided by the idea that the goal of perception is:

To know what is where by looking. In other words, vision is the process of discovering from images what is present in the world, and where it is (Marr, 1982).

According to the canonical model, the final goal of (visual) perception is to recover the three-dimensional structure of the world, culminating in a three-dimensional 'object centered' model of the world. Influential accounts of the language–perception interface (e.g. Jackendoff, 1996a) have assumed that spatial language interfaces with a perceptual system obeying the constraints of the canonical model. However, it is possible that one of the impediments to understanding the language–perception interface is the canonical model itself. Instead of taking the canonical model for granted, we could ask 'What are the ecological conditions under which perception takes place?' Therefore, the question 'What can we talk about?' should precede 'How do we talk about what we see?' The goal of this chapter is to undertake an ecological analysis of spatial language and perception within the framework of a computational ecological approach, where by computational ecology, I mean a formal analysis of the spatial environment of a human being. Computational ecology is a way of formalizing notions of embodiment, such as neural and psychological (Glenberg and Kaschak, this volume, Ch. 2; Barsalou, Sloman, and Chaigneau, this volume, Ch. 9) and therefore it is complementary to these approaches. The main goal of computational ecology is to uncover the computational principles constraining embodied structures. One consequence of performing an ecological analysis of spatial representation is that properties of spatial language such as schematization and context sensitivity that appear *ad hoc* are shown to be consequences of common ecological constraints.

In this chapter, I argue that there are common constraints on language and perception. In particular, I make four claims about the language–perception interface.

---

[1] Or more generally, how spatial language is in one–one correspondence with a subset of objective reality.

(1) The visual representation of spatial relations shares a common computational scaffolding, a *structure lattice*—with the linguistic representation of prepositions. The structure lattice has a formal hierarchy with three levels that are qualitatively different from a computational perspective: coordinate frame, topological structure, and metric structure. These three qualitative levels are reflected in language as well as perception, although metric structure is mostly absent in language.

(2) Each qualitative level consists of two major kinds of computational structures: *geometric states* and *geometric routines*. Geometric states characterize the geometric properties relevant to a task at that moment. Geometric routines are transformations that need to be performed on geometric states in order to solve a particular task.

(3) The levels and their representations are organized hierarchically according to their invariance with respect to a group of geometric transformations.

(4) The probability of a visual state or routine in language is proportional to its invariance under perturbations (e.g. metric structure is least invariant under perturbation, but is also 'least' probable to surface in language). This implies that coordinate frame representations (which embody the universal structures of our three-dimensional world such as a vertical gravitational force) are largely preserved in language; furthermore, topological structures (which consist of features invariant under the transformations allowed in the world defined by the coordinate frames) less so, and that metric structures are not represented in language.

The rest of the chapter is organized as follows. In Section 5.2, I give a brief introduction to the problems posed by schematization and context sensitivity. Section 5.3 presents a model of the Language–Perception interface and develops an ecological analysis of spatial representations. Section 5.4 provides some predictions derived from this ecological analysis, after which Section 5.5 draws some conclusions about the contribution of such an analysis.

5.2   Schematization and Context Sensitivity

To elaborate upon the comments in the introduction, I begin by focusing on two properties of spatial language—schematization and context sensitivity—that I find particularly salient. Linguistic representations are schematic because they are highly impoverished, as is seen in the following sentences:

(1) The *village* is on the other side of the river.
(2) *John* lives in *Chicago*.

In the first sentence, the term 'village' is plausibly conceptualized as a point. In the second sentence, the preposition *in* does not identify an exact spatio-temporal location, only a certain region of space. Furthermore, Chicago does not have a definite shape either. In both of these sentences, spatial language represents only a tiny fraction of the spatial information available about Chicago or villages. Even though schematization destroys all hope of a one–one correspondence between language and the external world, it is still compatible with the canonical model. For example, one could postulate that spatial language is determined by the canonical model after being filtered through a mechanism that removes unnecessary information. If so, linguistic expressions would map onto a fixed list of schematized geometric quantities. However this naive 'Schematization' hypothesis is patently false. For example, consider the preposition *on*. A provisional definition of *on* is:

Definition 1. *on* (X, Y) if and only if CONTACT(X, Y) as in

(3)   The painting is on the wall.

However Definition 1 does not capture the meaning of *on*. For example, *on* in the sentence

(4)   The black book is on the table (see Fig. 5.1a).

is not compatible with Definition 1; rather, Sentence (4) suggests an alternative definition of *on*:

Definition 2. *on* (X, Y) if and only if SUPPORT(X, Y) AND CONTACT(X, Y).

However, Definition 2 is also inadequate because Sentence (4) is also an appropriate description of Fig. 5.1b, where CONTACT(Book, Table) does not hold.

Sentences (3) and (4) show that the meaning of prepositions is *context sensitive*, that is there is no fixed map from spatial language to geometric properties of the canonical world. Within the framework of the canonical model, schematization and context sensitivity force us to conclude that there are no general principles guiding the interface. I claim that the canonical model blinds us to the underlying structure of the spatial language–perception interface. I argue that schematization and context sensitivity are consequences of the ecological

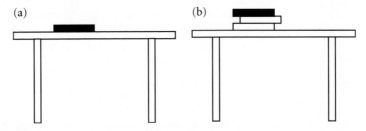

(a)   (b)

FIG. 5.1. Generativity of prepositions.

constraints on an organism in a spatial environment. Ecological theories have a distinguished history in perceptual science (Gibson, 1979a, see also Marr, 1982 and W. Richards, 1988). In general, an ecological analysis consists of taking the following three steps:

(1) statement of the ecological boundary conditions, that is relevant facts about our bodies and our environments, in the form of computational constraints;
(2) derivation of a representational framework that embodies the above computational constraints;
(3) empirical testing of the validity of this representational framework.

The purpose of this chapter is to offer a principled explanation of schematization and context sensitivity by performing an ecological analysis of the language–perception interface.

5.3   A Model of the Language–Perception Interface

In the previous two sections, I have argued that spatial representations for language are intrinsically biased towards highly invariant representations. I believe that schematization and context-sensitivity are common to language and perception. Schematization is a description of a scene using the top few levels in the lattice structure. Similarly, context sensitivity is a consequence of the many–many nature of spatial tasks. Context sensitivity can be understood using geometric states and geometric routines. By combining Topological Structure and Coordinate Frame states and routines we may be able to model a significant subset of linguistic representations of spatial structure. On the other hand, spatial language is used in non-spatial situations that involve abstract uses of language as well as social/emotional uses of language, as shown in sentences 5 and 6 below:

(5)   John is on my graduate committee.
(6)   John fell in love with Mary.

Similarly, the perceptual representation of spatial relations contains spatial detail that is not represented in language. One is forced to conclude that language and perception are neither disjoint nor are they isomorphic. A better way of looking at the language–perception relationship may be that of two overlapping systems. They share a core set of representations, namely, the coordinate frame and topological representations.

5.3.1   Ecological analysis I

In this section, I derive the computational constraints on spatial representations in the context of the interface between language and perception. The most important step in the ecological analysis of a system is the formalization of the systems' constraints, that is the boundary conditions that have to be satisfied by the system. The formal constraints constitute the *competence* of the system. A theory of spatial representation has to satisfy the following boundary conditions:

(1) It should be rich enough to account for recognition, categorization, and navigation.
(2) It should represent spatial relations that are needed for spatial reasoning.
(3) It should be reliably inferable from sensory stimuli from various modalities such as vision and touch.
(4) It should interface with language.
(5) It should be task minimal, that is a given task is performed using the (computationally) least expensive set of representations.

In this chapter, I will focus on spatial representations for navigation along with constraints (2)–(5). In the canonical model, the goal of spatial representation is to recover the three-dimensional structure of objects in the world, which consists of objects with (more or less) fixed shape in a three-dimensional environment. Perhaps, the canonical model is the appropriate representation for recognition and categorization. However, navigation and spatial reasoning should not be predicated on the fine structure of the objects in an organism's environment (why not?). A better model for navigation and spatial reasoning is that of an organism with sensors—of finite spatio-temporal resolution—moving in a gravitational environment consisting of surfaces. We can model the environment as follows:

(a) The ground plane can be modeled as an infinite flat plane. Surfaces (of objects) can be modeled as smooth two-dimensional manifolds distributed over the ground plane. Because the scene is always viewed by an observer, we also have one coordinate frame in which the observer occupies the origin of the ground plane, though this is not necessary in all coordinate frames. Formally:

(i)   The ground plane, **GP** = The upper half space = $(x,y,z): z \geq 0$.
(ii)   World surfaces form a collection of smooth manifolds S_i.
(iii) In some cases, the observer, **O**, maps onto the origin $(0,0,0)$.

(b) Since organisms move constantly, the sensible portion of the environment is a dynamic entity. For simplicity, let us assume that all objects in the spatial environment are rigid. Then, transformations of the environment can be divided into two types:

(i)   transformations due to rotation in depth;
(ii)   transformations due to translation.

Rotation in depth is caused by changes in the observers' viewpoint and also by rotating objects. Translation is caused by moving toward or away from an object or by an object moving toward or away from the observer. We can model rotations and translations in the following manner:

Environmental transformations are parametrized by the space of affine transformations—$\mathbf{T_{aff}}$—of the ground plane. $\mathbf{T_{aff}}$ splits into rigid rotations around the Z axis and into translations along the ground plane.

(c) The spatial environment is intrinsically gravitational with a universal downward direction and a ground plane that supports objects. Therefore, the problem of spatial representation is not a purely geometric problem, but also a physical one, with gravitational notions such as support entering into spatial representation from the beginning. Formally, there is a designated direction vector $\mathbf{v_g}$ given by the positive Z axis.

Summing (a)–(c) above, we can define the spatial environment as

$$E = \mathbf{GP} \,\&\, \mathbf{T_{aff}} \,\&\, \mathbf{O} \,\&\, \mathbf{v_g} \,\&\, \mathbf{S_i}. \tag{1}$$

There are two more constraints that are important for our investigation: *task-context sensitivity* and *local environment*. Task-context sensitivity captures the intuition that spatial tasks are inherently context sensitive. For example, consider the three visual tasks in Fig. 5.2. Each one of the tasks is consistent with the stimulus given in Fig. 5.2. One can imagine that the number of tasks that are commensurable with a given image is extremely large if not infinite. On the other hand, most tasks can be carried out in an infinite number of visual environments; we can pick up a book on a table irrespective of the other objects on that table. Consequently, there cannot be any fixed set of world features acting as referents of spatial representations. Instead, it is likely that spatial representations are compositional and that they can be divided into two types of constituents: geometric states and geometric routines. Geometric states consist of the geometric structures relevant to a task at that moment. Geometric routines are the actions that need to be performed on geometric states in order to solve a particular task. Let us use task 1 from Fig. 5.2 to understand geometric states and

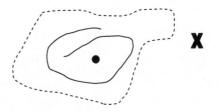

1. Is the Dot inside the dashed curve?
2. Is the Dot inside the solid curve?
3. Can the dot move to the position marked with an X?

FIG. 5.2. Generativity of visual tasks.

routines. In task 1, the geometric state at the beginning of the task is the set of dashes. In order to perform task 1, we have to check if the dashed curve contains the dot. A plausible first step consists of filling in the dotted curve by connecting the dots. This is the first geometric routine invoked for this task, and it outputs a closed curve. It is important to note that the closed curve is not present in the stimulus itself.

At any given time, an organism can sense only a small subset of the world. I call the directly sensible portion of the world the local environment. For human visual perception, the local environment is to the front of the human being and consists of objects larger than the visual resolution threshold. The local environment consists of human sized objects, their spatial relationships, and the spatial context surrounding the objects. The local environment for visual perception does not include the structure of much larger spaces such as the structure of a city or of a country. On the other hand, there is no local environment for language because we are able to talk about things that we do not see.

Therefore, the most plausible assumption about the local environment of language is that it is an empty set. So far, we have seen that the structure of the spatial environment—E—differs from the structure of the canonical model. However, spatial representation is not entirely determined by the external environment. The representations in the observer's mind need to be understood as well. World properties that are represented in an observer's mind have to be reliably inferable from images. Furthermore, not all world properties are necessary to perform a given task. The tasks in Fig. 5.2 do not require the representation of the exact shape of the curves. It is computationally unnecessary (and possibly counter to the organism's survival) to extract the detailed structure of the environment before performing a task. Therefore, it is reasonable to assume that the set of representations used in a particular task is the minimal number that is required for performing the task. One measure of reliable inference is given by the notion of a *key feature* (Jepson and Richards, 1993; Lowe, 1985). A key feature is a feature in an image that is unlikely to happen by accident and, as a consequence, can be used to infer world properties reliably. More formally, one can define key features as follows (Richards, Jepson, and Feldman, 1996):

A feature F, with resolution parameter r is said to be a key feature for property P if:

$R_{likelihood} = p(F|P)/p(F|\text{not } P)$ is unbounded as $r \to 0$ and
$R_{prior} = p(P)/p(\text{not } P)$ remains bounded away from zero as $r \to 0$, $\qquad(2)$
where $R_{likelihood}$ and R_{prior} are the Bayesian likelihood and prior ratios respectively and $p(X|Y)$ is the probability of X given Y.

Therefore, reliable inference is a function of the properties, features, and their relationship. So what is this relationship between properties and features, and how are they represented in our minds? According to equation (2), R_{prior} must be nonzero for reliable inference to occur. In fact, the prior distribution must be highly peaked. Otherwise, for any given hypothesis P, $p(\text{not } P) \gg p(P)$, which in turn implies that R_{prior} is close to 0.

According to equation (2), a world property P is represented if it projects to a key feature. Let us call these world properties Key Properties. In the E model, changes in the image come from changes in the location or the viewpoint of the observer and from motions of objects. In both cases, changes in the image can be attributed to a transformation that belongs to T_{aff}. Key properties project to image features that are highly invariant with respect to T_{aff}. For key properties, the minimality constraint implies that a task should be performed using the most invariant representations possible. As a consequence, we have to characterize environmental properties in terms of their invariance with respect to the transformations T_{aff}. In the next section, I show that imposing the key property and minimality constraints on E leads to a hierarchical lattice of spatial properties and relations.

5.3.2   Ecological analysis II

The second step in performing an ecological analysis, namely deriving a representational framework, can be divided into two parts, classifying the geometric state space and classifying geometric routines. I first classify the geometric state space according to invariance under transformations. Then I show how the same technique can be used for the classification of geometric routines. Mathematical tools from topology, based on the mathematical ideas of *co-dimension* and *invariance* can be used to classify E (Poston and Stewart, 1978). The basic intuitions behind co-dimension and invariance are simple. Co-dimension is defined as follows:

Definition. Let **M** be a n-dimensional manifold and let **S** be a m-dimensional sub-manifold of **M**. Then we say that **S** has co-dimension m-n.

Now suppose that a group **G** of transformations acts on **M**. We can then classify sub-manifolds of **M** by looking at the action of **G** on the sub-manifolds. In particular, given a sub-manifold **S**, an important set is the subset of transformations G_S of **G** that leave **S** invariant, that is takes points of **S** to points of **S**. Formally,

Definition: $g \in G_S$ if and only if $g(s) \in S, \forall s \in S$.

Then one can define an ordering, $\gg$, on the space of sub-manifolds, Σ_M, in the following way:

Definition: $S \angle T$ if and only if $G_S \subseteq G_T$.

It is easy to verify that $\angle$ is a partial ordering on Σ_M and consequently, $\angle$ defines a partially ordered lattice L_M on Σ_M. I call L_M the *Structure Lattice*. Going up the structure lattice is equivalent to finding sub-manifolds that are more invariant with respect to G_M. Let us take a concrete example in order to understand $\angle$. Consider the space of triangles **T**. This space is a three-dimensional manifold,

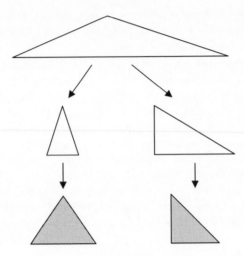

FIG. 5.3. Space of triangles.

with each point corresponding to a triangle (Fig. 5.3). Picking a triangle at random almost always implies (with probability 1) that none of the sides of the triangle will have the same length. The space of isosceles triangles—T_{iso}—forms a two-dimensional sub-manifold of T. Therefore, T_{iso} has co-dimension 1. The space of right-angled triangles—T_{right}—is also two dimensional, and therefore, has co-dimension 1. Finally, the space of equilateral triangles as well as the space of right-angled isosceles triangles—T_{equi}, $T_{r\text{-}iso}$—are 1-dimensional sub-manifolds and consequently have co-dimension 2. Now consider the group of transformations given by linear shears and dilations, where a shear is a transformation that consists of moving a vertex along a predetermined direction.

T is invariant under all of these transformations. T_{iso} is invariant under all dilations as well as those shears that are based on the vertex between the two equal sides and in a direction perpendicular to the bisector. T_{equi} is invariant only under dilations. Therefore the following relation holds:

$$T_{equi} \angle T_{iso} \angle T \qquad (3)$$

The above techniques can also be applied to E. Classifying environmental properties according to their invariance with respect to T_{aff} leads to subdivision of E into three broad categories: Coordinate frames, Topological Structure, and Metric Structure. Coordinate frame and topological structure are qualitative features of E while metric structure is a quantitative feature of E. Coordinate frame, topological structure, and metric structure satisfy the following relationships.

Metric Structure $\angle$ Coordinate Frame
Metric Structure $\angle$ Topological Structure

Coordinate frame, topological structure, and metric structure are complex representations with the following sub-representations:

(1) *Coordinate Frame Representations*: In order of decreasing invariance, we have four Coordinate frame representations—Gravitational Frame, Blob-location, Principal Axis-location and Minor Axis-location. Gravitational Frame (GF) is the universal vertical frame defined by gravitation. It is a global coordinate frame since it is valid at all spatial locations. Blob-location (BL) represents a Blob at a particular location. Similarly, Principal Axis-Location (PA) represents a principal axis of an object at a given location while Minor Axis-Location (MA) represents a Minor Axis at a given location.

(2) *Topological Structure Representations*: Blobs (B), are undifferentiated spatial representations, with no internal structure. Therefore, they are the most invariant representation of an object. Dimension (D) gives the inherent dimension of an object, that is whether it is 0, 1, 2, or 3 dimensional. Generic spatial invariants (GI) are those spatial invariants that do not change when the stimulus is perturbed slightly. For example, Containment and Closure are generic invariants. Non-generic invariants (NGI) are those spatial invariants that change when perturbed along a certain direction. However, non-generic invariants are still topological invariants because they do not depend on metric properties of surfaces. Contact is a good example of a non-generic invariant. Higher Topological Invariants are topological invariants such as Sphere-like and Torus-like that involve computing a global topological property of the stimulus.

(3) *Metric Structure Representations*: While the previous two categories were both qualitative since they do not involve numerical quantities, Metric Structure captures the quantitative structure of the environment. Global Properties (GP) are quantitative properties—such as Area and Diameter—that are properties of an object as a whole. The Part Structure Hierarchy (PSH) contains the decomposition of the object into parts.[2] Furthermore, by looking at the major and minor axes one can classify a part as convex or concave. This classification in terms of convexity gives rise to the Convexity Hierarchy (CH). Why is this a hierarchy, and not simply a distinction? Finally, Riemannian Structure (RS) captures the detailed surface structure of objects. This is the level that is often called the 2.5 D sketch (Marr, 1982).

When classified according to invariance, Coordinate Frame, Topological Structure and Metric Structure can be further decomposed into the partially

---

[2] The part structure can be derived by looking at curvature minima at various scales (Hoffman–Richards, 1984).

ordered lattices given below:

Coordinate Frame: MA ∠ PA ∠ BL ∠ GF.
Topological Structure: HTI ∠ NGI ∠ GI ∠ D ∠ B.
Metric Structure: RS ∠ CH, PSH ∠ GP.

The structure lattice of **E** is the collection of all the partially ordered sequences given above. Co-dimension and invariance can also be used to classify the structure lattice of geometric routines. Recall that a geometric routine is an action performed on a geometric state (Ullman, 1997). Consequently, one can model a geometric routine as follows:

Definition. A geometric routine is a transformation $T: S_1 \rightarrow S_2$ where S_1 and S_2 are geometric states.

We can assume that a geometric routine maps a geometric state S_1 into a geometric state S_2 that is at the same level in the structure lattice. Then, the space of routines acquires a structure lattice that parallels the structure lattice of the geometric state space. A list of prominent geometric routines is given below (see Fig. 5.4):

(1) Coordinate Frame routines such as Move focus to a Blob location or a Principal axis location or a Minor axis location.
(2) Topological Structure Routines such as (a) Trace a curve/surface and (b) Fill in a curve/surface.
(3) Metric Structure routines such as: Draw a generalized cylinder around a given point/curve/surface.

So far, we have seen that the classification of environmental variables according to invariance gives rise to structure lattices for geometric states and geometric routines respectively. The structure lattices can be used to make strong empirical

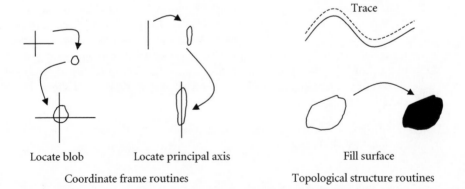

Trace

Locate blob   Locate principal axis   Fill surface
        Coordinate frame routines   Topological structure routines

FIG. 5.4. Routines.

predictions. In the next section, I discuss two predictions: the 'Structure Lattice Hypothesis' and the 'Linguistic Routine Hypothesis'.

5.4   Predictions

Ecological arguments suggest that spatial representations for navigation and spatial reasoning should represent the upper levels of the structure lattice since they are more invariant than the lower levels of the structure lattice. Therefore, upper level properties such as blobs and major axes are represented before lower level properties such as the Riemannian structure of surfaces. Furthermore, language and vision should represent different properties since the local environments for perception and language are different. Perception has access to the entire visual field while language does not contain the notion of a local environment. Formally, we can assume that the local environment for language satisfies

$$p(I) = 0 \text{ for all images I, where } p(X) \text{ is the prior probability of a given image feature X.} \tag{4}$$

Combining equation (4) with equation (2), we derive the following formula for a property to be represented in language:

A feature P is represented in language if and only if $p(P) = 1$.

Therefore, we should make the following prediction:

Structure Lattice Hypothesis: Perceptual representations for navigation and spatial reasoning should go from representing top-level structures to representing the lowest level structures. Linguistic Representations should be highly biased toward representing only the top-level structures.

Experiments on animals with relatively primitive visual systems—such as ants and frogs—have demonstrated their ability to use coordinate frames and topological structures (Gallistel, 1990). Frogs snap at all moving blobs irrespective of the detailed shape of the blob (Lettvin, Maturana, McCollough, and Pitts, 1959). Frogs can also detect if a curve is closed or open, suggesting that topological information is of importance to frogs. The primacy of topological structure and coordinate frames is not restricted to simpler visual systems. In humans, the detection of topological and coordinate frame information is effortless and immediate (Ullman, 1997). Every one of the three tasks in Fig. 5.2 can be performed by computing a series of topological structures and coordinate frames using operations such as coloring and curve tracing (Ullman, 1997). Topological categories are often considered natural categories for classifying a range of visual stimuli (Feldman, 1997).

The Structure Lattice hypothesis can also be tested by looking at the geometric meaning of prepositions. For simplicity, let us assume that each preposition has a default, geometric meaning. For example, the default meaning of *in* is 'containment' which is a generic topological relation. A classification of geometric features associated with the default meaning of prepositions, based on an (informal) corpus analysis of the *New York Times* is given in Tables 5.1 and 5.2. The attributes used in this classification provide a set of spatial features used in language. While this classification does not provide an exhaustive account of the meaning of prepositions, since physical and functional features are not taken into account, it serves to demonstrate that metric features are not part of the meaning of prepositions. Even seemingly metric prepositions such as 'near' are ordinal and not truly metric. Ordinal relations are topological because they are invariant under all geometric transformations such as dilations, stretches, etc.

None of the prepositions have any metric structure whatsoever. Therefore, it seems plausible that language represents only those aspects of spatial relations that are almost always present, independent of the actual shapes and sizes of the objects. From a communicative point of view, the preponderance of Generic Invariant and Gravitational Frame features makes sense; presumably a listener only wants to know the approximate spatial relationship between objects of interest, since the details can be supplied online by perception. On the other hand, communicating too little information is not of much use at all, which provides an explanation for why Blobs are not common. Furthermore, the Structure Lattice hypothesis implies that language and perception should converge when neither have access to environmental input. Indeed, this prediction is true in the spatial representation of large objects and large spaces such as buildings and city neighborhoods. In these cases, both perception and language resort to qualitative descriptions such as maps and guides (Gallistel, 1990).

Similarly, there is evidence that we use visual routines to perform visual tasks (Ulmann, 1997). The idea of routines can now be extended to language as well. I have argued that language represents the Topological Structure and Coordinate Frame levels of **E**. It follows that language should represent Topological Structure and Coordinate Frame routines as well. We can test this hypothesis on prepositions. As before, let us assume that each preposition has a default meaning given by the presence or absence of a geometric feature. If language uses the Topological Structure and Coordinate Frame routines and also obeys the minimality criterion, we should predict the following hypothesis:

Linguistic Routine Hypothesis: The meaning of a spatial preposition is the minimal sequence of Topological/Coordinate Frames states and Topological/Coordinate Frame routines ending in affirming or denying the presence of the default meaning of the preposition.

TABLE 5.1. *Table of prepositions*

Preposition	about	above	across	after	against	along	alongside	amid	among	around	at
Central Meaning	N/A	GF	GI	N/A	NGI	MA	MA	GI	GI	GI	BL
Preposition	atop	behind	below	beneath	beside	between	betwixt	beyond	by	down	from
Central Meaning	BL	MA	GF	GF	MA	GI	GI	GI	N/A	GF	BL
Preposition	in	inside	into	near	nearby	off	on	onto	opposite	out	outside
Central Meaning	GI	GI	GI	GI	GI	GI	NGI	NGI	MA	GI	GI
Preposition	over	past	through	throughout	to	toward	under	underneath	up	upon	via
Central Meaning	GF	N/A	GI	GI	BL	BL	MA	MA	GF	BL	BL
Preposition	with	within	without	afterward	apart	away	back	backward	downstairs	downward	east
Central Meaning	N/A	GI	GI	N/A	GI	GI	N/A	MA	GF	GF	MA
Preposition	forward	here	inward	left	north	outward	right	sideways	south	there	together
Central Meaning	MA	BL	GI	MA	MA	GI	MA	MA	MA	BL	NGI
Preposition	upstairs	upward	west								
Central Meaning	GF	GF	MA								

Note: Gravitational Frame (GF) is the universal vertical frame defined by gravitation. Blob-location (BL) represents a Blob at a particular location. Principal Axis-Location (PA) represents a principal axis of an object at a given location while Minor Axis-Location (MA) represents a Minor Axis at a given location. Blobs (B) are undifferentiated spatial representations, with no internal structure. Generic spatial invariants (GI) are those spatial invariants that do not change when the stimulus is perturbed slightly. Non-generic invariants (NGI) are those spatial invariants that change when perturbed along certain direction.

TABLE 5.2. *Prepositions by spatial type*

Lattice Type	GF	GI	BL	PA	Other
Frequency	10	28	9	16	6

For example, assuming that the default meaning of *on* is 'support', we can define *on* as follows:

Definition: on(X, Y) if and only if there is a (minimal) sequence of states and routines $S_1, S_2 \ldots S_n$ such that $S_1 = X$ and SUPPORT(S_{n-1}, S_n) and $S_n = Y$.

So, for example, in Fig. 5.1a, there are only two states, Black-Book and Table satisfying SUPPORT(Black-Book, Table). In Fig. 5.1b, we have four states, Black-Book, Middle-Book, Lower-Book, and Table corresponding to the four objects in the figure such that SUPPORT(Black-Book, Middle-Book), SUPPORT(Middle-Book, Lower-Book), SUPPORT(Lower-Book, Table). Similarly,

Definition: in(X, Y) if and only if there is a (minimal) sequence of states and routines $S_1, S_2 \ldots S_n$ such that $S_1 = X$ and CONTAINED(S_{n-1}, S_n) and $S_n = Y$.

More speculatively, ecological analysis may also be useful in other aspects of the semantics of natural language. For example, let us look at the notion of conceptual structure (Jackendoff, 1990). Conceptual Structure is based on the existence of a basic set of semantic features. Some of these features are: THING, PLACE, PATH, EVENT, DIRECTION, MANNER, AMOUNT, STATE. The relationship between the above semantic features and the three level representations discussed earlier in this chapter is quite direct. PLACE and DIRECTION are linked to a Coordinate frame and THING, PATH, EVENT are linked to topological structures. The following sentence provides an example of a coordinate frame:

(1)   The ship is going east.

Now consider:

(2)   John walked into the room.

Sentence (2) is topological for it does not specify where in the room John walked, only that he was in the room at the end. The shape and size of John are not specified. The metric–topological–coordinate frame distinction can possibly provide an explanation of why these semantic features are more important than others.

5.5   Conclusions

The goal of this chapter was to show that the language–perception interface may have more regularities than previously thought. The acceptance of the canonical model has led to mistaken hypotheses about the language–perception interface. Instead, by looking at common ecological constraints, I constructed a structure lattice for spatial representation. The top levels of the structure lattice also capture many properties of spatial language. I focused only on navigation and spatial reasoning. A complete theory of spatial representation should also include spatial representations for object recognition and categorization. Another important problem is to understand the representation of temporal and functional aspects of perceptual and linguistic representations. Temporal relations, causality being an important example, intertwine with spatial relations in the representation of action. Similarly, functional considerations interface with spatial relations in support and containment relations. More work needs to be done in fleshing out the relationship between spatial representation, temporal, and functional relations. The invariance-based model outlined in this chapter can possibly be expanded to include functional features by using a variant of functional geometry (Coventry and Garrod, this volume, Ch. 10; Cohn, Bennett, Gooday, and Gotts, 1997). At this point it is not clear if these three terms are psychologically distinct. To conclude, the ecological approach will not make the problems of perception and language less complex. However, by situating the problems in an ecological context, the ecological approach facilitates the understanding of the regularities of spatial representation.

6

Contextual, Functional, and Geometric Components in the Semantics of Projective Terms

CAROLA ESCHENBACH

Abstract

The projective terms of a natural language can differ regarding their syntactic properties, their dependence on reference systems, and their contextual dependency regarding objects or regions of comparison. While the dependence of projective prepositions on reference systems has been considered in linguistics and psycholinguistics in detail, the other aspects are less well studied. This article concerns a collection of German projective terms including prepositions, post-positions, adverbs, and adjectives. Its goal is to identify similarities between different items and map them to common semantic components or syntactic regularities. The semantics of the lexemes combine geometric components representing spatial aspects and functional components representing the principal directions on the basis of a reference system. The influence of the context on the interpretation of projective terms is mapped to the distinction between variables belonging to the argument structure of the lexemes and free variables occurring in the semantic form. The description of the semantics of the German terms in this framework shows that the similarities and variations between the lexemes can be modeled by combining a small set of semantic components in different ways.

Functional components

Components in the semantic forms of spatial terms that cannot completely be described in a geometric framework. Functional components considered in this

The research reported in this chapter was supported by the Center for Advanced Study in Berlin and carried out in the context of the project 'Axiomatics of Spatial Concepts' (Ha 1237/7) supported by the Deutsche Forschungsgemeinschaft (DFG) in the priority program on 'Spatial Cognition'. I want to thank Laura Carlson, Christopher Habel, Susan Olsen, Hedda Schmidtke, Ladina Tschander, and Emile van der Zee for commenting on an earlier version of this text.

chapter relate to perceptual and behavioral features that select principal directions based on a given reference system.

6.1   Introduction

Spatial situations or configurations can be described with natural language expressions. This simple observation is the backbone of the wide field of research on spatial language that is assumed to lead to insights into the system of spatial concepts that derive from different ways of perceiving and acting in space (Herskovits, 1986; Lang, Carstensen, and Simmons, 1991; Landau and Jackendoff, 1993; Bloom, Peterson, Nadel, and Garrett, 1996; van der Zee and Slack, 2000).

Both language and space are inherently structured. The structure of natural languages derives from the linguistic abilities of humans. A grammar and a corresponding lexicon can describe the linguistic structure. The mental lexicon interrelates different levels of linguistic structure such as the phonological form, syntactic features, the argument structure, and the semantic form of a lexeme (cf. Bierwisch, 1989). Syntactic features and the argument structure guide the derivation of the semantic form of a composite expression from the meaning of the components. The objective of lexical semantics is to describe the argument structures and the semantic forms of lexemes such that common aspects of different uses are made explicit and meaning relations between complex expressions involving the terms can be formally derived.

Characteristics of spatial structure are described by geometry (Habel and Eschenbach, 1997). However, mental representations of space include aspects that are not purely geometric. An example is the force of gravity, which causes and constrains movement and asymmetries in natural kinds (as asymmetries between roots and crowns of trees or feet and heads of humans). The semantic forms of spatial terms interrelate different levels of spatial knowledge. My proposals include semantic components that stand for geometric, functional, and contextual aspects of the meaning of the expressions. Geometric components can be characterized in a purely geometric framework. The appendix gives an axiomatic specification of the geometric relations used in the proposals below. Functional components relate to perceptual and behavioral features that select principal directions based on a given reference system. My notion of 'functional component' is rather broad and contrasts with 'geometric component'. Semantic components that cannot completely be described in a geometric framework are called 'functional'. Contextual components are represented as free variables in the semantic form. Non-compositional aspects of interpreting natural language expressions derive from interpreting such variables relative to the context (cf. Bierwisch, 1988). Thus, the contextual components stand for the lexemes' requirements on the context.

TABLE 6.1. *German projective terms*[2]

	Syntax	UP	DOWN	FRONT	BACK	RIGHT	LEFT
Loc	Prep [+dat]	*über*	*unter*	*vor*	*hinter*		
Dir	Prep [+acc]	*über*	*unter*	*vor*	*hinter*		
Loc	Prep [+poss]	*oberhalb*	*unterhalb*			*rechts*	*links*
Loc	Adjective	*ober*	*unter*	*vorder*	*hinter*	*recht*	*link*
Loc	Adverb	*oben*	*unten*	*vorne*	*hinten, zurück*	*rechts*	*links*
Dir	Adverb	*nach oben*	*nach unten*	*nach vorne*	*nach hinten*	*nach rechts*	*nach links*
Dir	Adverb	*von oben*	*von unten*	*von vorne*	*von hinten*	*von rechts*	*von links*
Dir	Adverb	*rauf*	*runter*	*vor*	*zurück*		
Dir	Postp [+acc]	*rauf*	*runter*		*zurück*		
Dir	Adverb	*herauf*	*herunter, herab*	*hervor*			
Dir	Postp [+acc]	*herauf*	*herunter, herab*				
Dir	Adverb	*hinauf*	*hinunter, hinab*				
Dir	Postp [+acc]	*hinauf*	*hinunter, hinab*				
Dir	Adverb	*aufwärts*	*abwärts*	*vorwärts*	*rückwärts*		
Dir	Postp [+acc]	*aufwärts*	*abwärts*				
Dir	Adverb			*voraus, voran*	*hinterher*		
Dir	Postp [+dat]			*voraus, voran*	*hinterher*		

The study of the semantics of projective terms in natural languages focuses on a small set of expressions, like the English prepositions *above, below, in front of, in back of, right of,* and *left of* or the corresponding German prepositions *über, unter, vor, hinter, rechts,* and *links.* In this chapter, I will look at a larger range of projective terms in German that relate to the six principal directions, which will be designated by the symbols UP, DOWN, FRONT, BACK, RIGHT, LEFT.

Table 6.1 lists the German projective terms to be discussed in this article.[1,2] The first two columns indicate syntactic and related semantic properties of the

[1] Please notice that the discussion in this chapter concerns only the German expressions listed in Table 6.1. The direct transfer to the field of English lexemes is not intended, even though I give English glosses for the German examples.

[2] *Über* has horizontal uses comparable to 'over'/'across'. *Unter* is also used in the sense of 'among'. These uses will be completely ignored in the following. The preposition *auf* (used similarly to 'on' describing (vertical) support) has been excluded to avoid the detailed discussion of the spatial and functional aspects of support.

Rechts, links, oberhalb, and *unterhalb* have to be combined with genitive noun phrases (*oberhalb der Tür,* 'above the door') or *von*-PPs (*rechts von der Tür,* 'to the right of the door'). The syntactic feature [+poss(essive)] stands for both options.

TABLE 6.2. *A possible lexical entry for the projective locative preposition* vor *('in front of')*

Lexeme	Argument structure	Semantic form
vor	$\lambda G_{[+\text{dat}]}\ \lambda \underline{F}$	$F \subset \textbf{ext-reg}(\textbf{front-axis}(RSYS),\ G)$

lexemes. For example, the first row presents prepositions that are combined with dative noun phrases to form a locative prepositional phrase. As the second row shows, the same prepositions can be combined with accusative noun phrases yielding directional prepositional phrases. (Other German prepositions such as *in* ('in', 'into'), *auf*, and *an* ('on', 'onto') exhibit the same case alternation scheme.) Some terms (e.g. *aufwärts*, 'upward') can occur both as adverb and as postposition. The syntactic and semantic details and the consequences for the analysis will be discussed in Section 6.4. At present I just want to convey that there is a larger group of German lexemes relating to the principal directions. The principal directions UP and DOWN show the largest range of lexemes, and RIGHT and LEFT the smallest range.

6.2   A Common Model of Reference Systems and Projective Prepositions

Projective prepositions relate two objects in space (*Die Fliege ist über dem Tisch*, 'the fly is above the table'), which are traditionally called 'figure' (the fly) and 'ground' (the table), relative to a spatial reference system. According to Levinson (1996a), the various uses of projective prepositions can be classified as 'intrinsic', 'absolute', and 'relative'. This classification reflects how the respective reference systems are related to figure and ground (Eschenbach, 1999). The ground object serves as the reference system in intrinsic uses, the environment of figure and ground is the reference system in absolute uses, and a viewer, external to both figure and ground, is the reference system of relative uses.

Table 6.2 gives a possible lexical entry for the German projective preposition *vor*. It reformulates proposals from the literature on the semantics of locative prepositions and elaborates them regarding the projective aspects of the selected set of lexemes (cf. Jackendoff, 1983; Wunderlich and Herweg, 1991; Kaufmann, 1995).

The argument structure determines how the syntactic embedding of the lexeme can lead to the specification of the bound variables (cf. Higginbotham, 1985; Eschenbach, 1995). Internal arguments of lexemes ($\lambda G_{[+\text{dat}]}$) are annotated with the case imposed on the selected noun phrase. For example, the ground object (G) of the locative preposition *vor* has to be given by a noun phrase with dative case. The figure is the external argument ($\lambda_{\underline{F}}$), which is indicated by underlining the variable.

In the semantic form, the symbols ⊂, **ext-reg, front-axis**, etc. stand for semantic components. All bold symbols stand for geometric relations or entities; italicized symbols are contextual components. For example, the symbol **front-axis** represents the mapping that extracts the geometric representative of the principal direction FRONT from a reference system. F ⊂ **ext-reg**(**front-axis**(*RSYS*), G) symbolizes that the figure is spatially included in a region that is derived from G and the principal direction FRONT as given by a reference system *RSYS*. The symbol *RSYS* is a contextual component. It can be identified with the intrinsic reference system of the ground object or with some other reference system such as the speaker's or the listener's relative reference system. Contextual components are not tied to syntactic features that guide their interpretation. Nevertheless, certain expressions can be added for the purpose of specifying such variables (e.g. *from my view point*).

The lexical entries for the projective prepositions *hinter, über, unter, rechts,* and *links* can be derived from the specification in Table 6.2 by replacing the mapping **front-axis** with other mappings corresponding to the respective principal direction. The six mappings have to be anchored in representations of object categories, for example, in the form of systems of labeled axes tied to the mental representation of the shape of the objects (Landau and Jackendoff, 1993).

This model of the lexical entries and the role and representation of reference systems generalizes several observations about the use of projective prepositions. However, it has to be refined. First, it does not explain the assignment of the labels and the selection of the axes across different object categories. Therefore, I will replace the labels by semantic components that relate to functional asymmetries. The specification of the lexemes can account for the spatial opposition of UP/DOWN, FRONT/BACK, and RIGHT/LEFT, respectively. Second, the model suggests a uniform geometric representation for all six principal directions. Depending on the different functional sources, I will employ different geometric representations below. Third, the proposal in Table 6.2 does not suggest analyses of further prepositions (*oberhalb, unterhalb*) or other lexemes that both fit into the general scheme and represent the observable differences in comparison to the other prepositions. The proposal presented below covers the complete range of expressions listed in Table 6.1.

6.3 Functional Asymmetries and Principal Directions

Objects or environmental features that can serve as reference systems show functional asymmetries, which are exploited to determine the principal directions.

Two principal directions can make use of the same functional asymmetry such that they yield a pair of opposite directions.

6.3.1   UP/DOWN

The principal directions UP and DOWN relate to the asymmetric influence of gravity in the environment. In the following discussion, all proposals for semantic forms of lexemes relating to the principal directions UP and DOWN include the symbolic form BEARING(RSYS) (cf. Levinson, 1996a; Eschenbach, 1999). The asymmetric structure of humans, animals, and artifacts originating from the influence of gravity can also be a source for determining such a bearing (cf. H. H. Clark, 1973; Carlson, 1999). That a body is in standard orientation regarding the environment can then be expressed as alignment of the bearing provided by the body and the bearing of the environment (B-ALIGN(BEARING (BODY), BEARING(ENV))). Also, the organization of visual perception in humans leads to a uniform mapping of the gravitational axis on retinal coordinates, given that the head is canonically oriented (B-ALIGN(BEARING(EYE), BEARING(ENV))) (Friederici and Levelt, 1990). Moreover, the retinal orientation can be transferred to pages, diagrams, or texts for which a standard orientation of viewing is important (B-ALIGN(BEARING(PAGE), BEARING(EYE(VIEWER(PAGE)))))).

On the geometric level, I will distinguish two types of geometric bearings corresponding to two types of motion caused by the force of gravity. First, if an object like a stone is released from one's hand, it moves in a straight path to the ground. I will use the symbolic form **strict**(BEARING(RSYS)) to refer to the geometric representation of this linear direction (see Fig. 6.1a). Second, a fluid or a ball on a non-horizontal plane moves toward the lower level. A horizontal plane is a plane of equal level with regard to the force of gravity. Thus, gravity also distinguishes deviations from the horizontal. I will use the symbolic form **lax**(BEARING(RSYS)) for this more general or relaxed form of

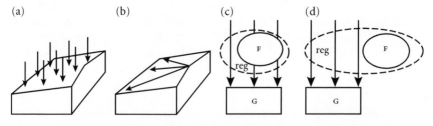

FIG. 6.1. The arrows indicate a strict geometric bearing (a) and a lax geometric bearing (b) on a tilted plane. Relative to the strict bearing, F is to a higher degree *über* ('over', 'above') G in (c) than in (d).

gravitational influence (see Fig. 6.1b). The alignment conditions for bearings are given in the appendix.

Both types of geometric bearings are directions. Every direction can be reversed. Correspondingly, I will use two (ternary) symbols $\lesssim$ and $\gtrsim$ to relate two objects relative to a bearing. The symbol $\lesssim$ will be read 'precedes', and it will be used to describe the semantic form of the terms relating to UP. The symbol $\gtrsim$ is read 'succeeds', and it occurs in the semantic form of the terms relating to DOWN. In this sense, the bearing of gravity stands for both the force driving objects to the ground and the counteracting force raising objects from the ground. In the next section, the specification of a lexeme from the DOWN-group is skipped if it can be derived from an UP-lexeme by substituting $\gtrsim$ for $\lesssim$.

Logan and Sadler (1996) and Carlson-Radvansky and Logan (1997) showed that the degree of acceptability of some projective prepositions (especially *over, above, under, below*) depends on the vertical alignment of figure and ground. Descriptions involving *above* and *below* are rated less acceptable for misaligned configuration (Fig. 6.1d) than for aligned configurations (Fig. 6.1c). Gapp (1995) reports corresponding experiments regarding some German projective prepositions. His results show, for example, that the vertical alignment of the objects affects the ratings of descriptions based on *über* and *unter*. The experiments do not cover the prepositions *oberhalb* ('above', 'higher up') or *unterhalb* ('below', 'at a lower level'). However, judgments of native speakers give evidence that *oberhalb* and *unterhalb* are neutral in regard to alignment in the vertical dimension. The difference in dependence on vertical alignment can be reflected by referring to the strict bearing in the semantic form of the lexemes that are affected by vertical alignment (e.g. *über* and *unter*) and by referring to the lax bearing in the description of lexemes that do not express vertical alignment (*oberhalb* and *unterhalb*).

Logan and Sadler (1996) call the geometric structure of the acceptability pattern a 'spatial template'. Such spatial template effects can result from the assumption that the region related to the ground object is not the exact region of the figure but some (larger) region (**reg**) including the figure. The degree of acceptability is inversely proportional to the extent of the difference in space occupied between **reg** and F as illustrated in Figure 6.1c–d. F is to a higher degree *über* ('above') G in (a) than in (b) because in (a) the region (**reg**) that is firmly above the ground is smaller than in (b).

At this stage of the discussion, we have introduced all components that are involved in the semantics of the German prepositions *über, unter, oberhalb,* and *unterhalb*. To offer a (nearly) English gloss, the locative preposition *über* is analyzed here as follows: the figure is spatially included in a region that precedes the ground relative to the strict geometric bearing of a reference system to be provided by the context. Regarding the interaction of syntax and semantics, I assume that the region **reg** plays the role of a referential argument (marked by an underlined abstractor symbol) for the locative preposition (cf. Rauh, 1997).

The prepositions *oberhalb* and *unterhalb* are analyzed with reference to the lax geometric bearing of the reference system.

über	$\lambda G_{[+dat]}\ \lambda\underline{F}\ \lambda\mathbf{reg}$	$F \subset \mathbf{reg} \wedge \lesssim(\mathbf{strict}(\text{BEARING}(RSYS))),\ \mathbf{reg},\ G)$
unter	$\lambda G_{[+dat]}\ \lambda\underline{F}\ \lambda\mathbf{reg}$	$F \subset \mathbf{reg} \wedge \gtrsim(\mathbf{strict}(\text{BEARING}(RSYS))),\ \mathbf{reg},\ G)$
oberhalb	$\lambda G_{[+poss]}\ \lambda\underline{F}\ \lambda\mathbf{reg}$	$F \subset \mathbf{reg} \wedge \lesssim(\mathbf{lax}(\text{BEARING}(RSYS))),\ \mathbf{reg},\ G)$
unterhalb	$\lambda G_{[+poss]}\ \lambda\underline{F}\ \lambda\mathbf{reg}$	$F \subset \mathbf{reg} \wedge \gtrsim(\mathbf{lax}(\text{BEARING}(RSYS))),\ \mathbf{reg},\ G)$

6.3.2   FRONT/BACK

The principal directions FRONT and BACK are related to orders of accessibility and time (Clark, 1973; Franklin and Tversky, 1990). Accessibility in space is influenced both by the functional asymmetries of bodies and by distance and occlusion. For example, the region (intrinsically) in front of a person (V) is the region of his or her best access by vision, manipulation, and motion. The region behind the person is the opposite region, which can be accessed less well. Figure 6.2a illustrates the corresponding division of space. Relative uses of *vor* and *hinter*, in contrast, deal with distance and occlusion. The figure is in front of the ground object relative to a person (V) if the figure (partially) occludes the ground or is closer to the person than the ground (Fig. 6.2b).

Both the intrinsic and the relative use can employ V's perspective or view. However, the intrinsic and the relative judgments of accessibility do not concur spatially. The spatial opposition of *vor* and *hinter* is based on a cluster of local functional asymmetries that cannot be integrated into a single global ordering. A pragmatic motivation for such complex 'perspectives' derives from the regular spatial configuration of interaction and communication between two people (Fig. 6.3a). In situations of confrontation ('canonical encounter', Clark, 1973), both participants have their own (complex) perspective. In spite of that, when they relate an object to either participant using *vor* or *hinter*, they refer to the same region in space independently of the chosen perspective (Fig. 6.3a). Thus, they agree about which region is *hinter* X ('behind X'), *vor* X ('in front of X'), *vor* Y ('in front of Y'), or *hinter* Y ('behind Y'). Nevertheless, when they relate a figure to some other ground object (for example to an object G located between them), the different perspectives will lead to different descriptions (Fig. 6.3b).

(a)   (b)

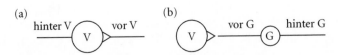

FIG. 6.2.   (a) Intrinsic use of *vor* V ('in front of V') and *hinter* V ('behind V'). (b) *Vor* G ('in front of G') and *hinter* G ('behind G') relative to V.

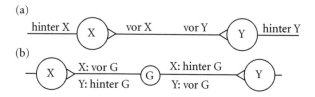

FIG. 6.3. Partitioning of space in situations of confrontation, relative to the perspectives of both participants.

Different access orders can depend on different reference systems and different types of access. I will use the symbolic form **access-ord**($RSYS$, $TYPE$) to refer to a geometric representation of an access order derived from a reference system $RSYS$ based on a type of access (such as INTR for intrinsic or REL relative).[3] Access orders need not be linear and different modes of access can favor different areas. This corresponds to the fact that the areas of good or bad access do not reduce to a single line (cf. Franklin, Henkel, and Zangas, 1995). The intrinsic access orders ascribed to artifacts depend on the standard spatial configuration between the artifact and its user. The intrinsic access order of encounter artifacts (desks, wardrobes, houses) is the same as the relative access order of the user (**access-ord**(ARTIF, INTR) = **access-ord**(USER(ARTIF), REL)) while the intrinsic access order of artifacts that serve as body extensions (such as chairs, cars, pens) is the intrinsic access order of the user (**access-ord**(ARTIF, INTR) = **access-ord** (USER(ARTIF), INTR)).

The German preposition *vor* is also a temporal preposition comparable to the English term 'before'. Its temporal opposite is *nach* ('after'). The temporal order addressed by *vor* and *nach* is linked to the order of access induced by motion. However, the assignment of *vor* and *hinter* on the basis of a path of motion depends on whether immobile locations or moving objects are related.

Relative to a path of motion, an immobile location is spatially *vor* ('in front of') another one if it is encountered temporally *vor* ('before') the other one. This spatial ordering of locations on a path will be symbolized as **access-ord**(PATH, LOC). If a mobile object moves along a path in standard orientation, then the access order relative to the object is the location order of the path (**access-ord**(MOBILE, REL) = **access-ord**(PATH(MOBILE), LOC)). Similarly, the intrinsic access order ascribed to a text is the location order of the path of scanning the text (**access-ord**(TEXT, INTR) = **access-ord**(SCAN-PATH(TEXT), LOC)).

---

[3] Language communities or individual speakers differ regarding the applicability of intrinsic access orders. If the ground object is taken to be the reference system then the intrinsic order is systematically used. Speakers of Hausa use the direction of intrinsic access orders even in a large range of cases where the ground object and the reference system differ (Hill, 1982). Native speakers of German mostly prefer the relative access order when the ground object and the reference system are distinct.

If both figure and ground move along the same path, then the figure is *vor* ('ahead of') the ground if it is leading (Eschenbach, 1999). The order of moving objects on a path is the same as the intrinsic access order of the moving entities (**access-ord**(PATH(MOBILE), M-OBJ) = **access-ord**(MOBILE, INTR)).[4] Thus, the temporal order of encounter is the unifying aspect between the different path-based uses of *vor* and *hinter*. Depending on the mobility of figure and ground, the spatial order of the locations on the path or of the objects moving along the path determine the order of encounter.

The specifications of *vor* and *hinter* display the same structure as the entry of *über*. They say that the figure is spatially included in a region that relates to the ground object. In this case, the region is related to the ground regarding an access order. As before, the two symbols $\lesssim$ and $\gtrsim$ stand for precedence (FRONT) and succession (BACK).

vor $\lambda G_{[+\text{dat}]} \, \lambda \underline{E} \, \underline{\lambda}\textbf{reg}$ $F \subset \textbf{reg} \wedge \lesssim(\textbf{access-ord}(RSYS, TYPE), \textbf{reg}, G)$

hinter $\lambda G_{[+\text{dat}]} \, \lambda \underline{E} \, \underline{\lambda}\textbf{reg}$ $F \subset \textbf{reg} \wedge \gtrsim(\textbf{access-ord}(RSYS, TYPE), \textbf{reg}, G)$

6.3.3   RIGHT/LEFT

The principal directions RIGHT and LEFT are grounded in a spatially symmetric subdivision of human bodies (Farrell, 1979; Franklin and Tversky, 1990). Regarding both geometric and functional aspects, bodies are largely symmetric with a vertical plane of symmetry. Slight functional asymmetries such as hand preference form the basis for naming the two sides of this division. Nevertheless, the geometric and functional symmetry of human bodies is a source of systematic difficulties in identifying and naming the principal directions RIGHT and LEFT (Corballis and Beale, 1976).

A body-based reference system for RIGHT and LEFT has to supply one or two markers (RIGHT-MARKER(RSYS), LEFT-MARKER(RSYS)) distinguishing the sides relative to a largely symmetric division of space (**sym-plane**(RSYS)) (Eschenbach and Kulik, 1997). I will use half-spaces as the geometric representatives of the principal directions RIGHT and LEFT, since a half-space codes both the dividing plane and the marked side. The primary right space of the reference system (**p-right-space**(RSYS)) is a half-space that is bordered by the plane of symmetry and includes the right marker but does not intersect the left marker of the reference system (see Fig. 6.4a).

Although hand preference seems to be the main functional asymmetry that forms the basis of RIGHT and LEFT, the term *right hand* does not invariably refer to a

---

[4] Paths are conceptual entities that provide two access orderings. Therefore, paths themselves are not geometric entities. To derive a uniform labeling of the types of access orders, the location order of a path can be considered as the relative and the mobile-object order as the intrinsic access order of the path (LOC = REL and M-OBJ = INTR).

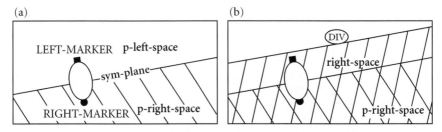

Fig. 6.4. (a) Primary and (b) secondary division of space for the assignment of RIGHT and LEFT.

person's preferred hand. Rather, there exists a regular geometric scheme for assigning RIGHT and LEFT to human bodies in which the term *right hand* refers to the hand most people prefer. Thus, a geometric scheme overwrites the functional background regarding the assignment of the labels. The identification of another person's left or right is based on geometric transformations of a known reference system, rather than on the observation of bodily asymmetries. In this sense, RIGHT and LEFT are 'more geometric and less functional' than the other principal directions.

The geometric transfer scheme asserts that if the intrinsic access orders and bearings are aligned, then the primary right spaces of two bodies are compatible (**p-right-space**(BODY1) ≳ **p-right-space**(BODY2)). Similarly, paths of motion (and rivers) are commonly ascribed primary right and left spaces compatible with a moving object (**p-right-space**(PATH(MOBILE)) ≳ **p-right-space**(MOBILE)) whenever the object moves forward (i.e. into the standard direction of motion) and is upright relative to the environment. This is the basis for interpreting expressions such as *in Fahrtrichtung rechts* ('right relative to the direction of traveling') or *rechts der Donau* ('to the right of the Danube'). The assignment of primary right and left spaces to artifacts (cars, wardrobes, texts, depictions) is based on compatibility between the primary right space of the artifact and the user (**p-right-space**(ARTIF) ≳ **p-right-space**(USER(ARTIF))).

German uses of *rechts* ('right') and *links* ('left') allow both figure and ground to be located in the same half-space resulting from the division induced by the reference system. For example, I can say that a red dot is *rechts* ('right') of a blue dot even if both dots are to my right or to my left. The language Tenejapa does not allow corresponding uses (Brown and Levinson, 1992). This suggests that Tenejapa considers only the primary division while the use of the German terms allows a secondary division. The secondary division is based on an additional divider (DIV) that is independent of the reference system (see Fig. 6.4b). DIV borders the relative right space (**right-space**(RSYS, DIV)), which additionally is compatible with the primary right space of the reference system. The left half-space can be characterized analogously.

The proposals for *rechts* and *links* differ only regarding the specification of the half-space. The German prepositions *rechts* says that the figure is spatially included in a region that is included in the right space identified by the reference system and the ground object, which plays the role of the secondary divider (Eschenbach, 1999). The findings of Brown and Levinson (1992) suggest that for the semantic form of the corresponding lexeme of Tenejapa, **p-right-space** is more the appropriate semantic component.

rechts	$\lambda G_{[+poss]} \, \lambda F \, \underline{\lambda} reg$	F ⊂ **reg** ∧ **reg** ⊂ **right-space**(RSYS, G)
links	$\lambda G_{[+poss]} \, \lambda F \, \underline{\lambda} reg$	F ⊂ **reg** ∧ **reg** ⊂ **left-space**(RSYS, G)

6.4   German Projective Terms beyond Prepositions

The functional and geometric components introduced above are essential components in the description of the semantics of the other projective terms, as presented in this section. In the glosses of the semantic forms, I will refer mainly to the lexeme of the principal direction UP. The other lexemes are addressed explicitly only if their analyses strongly deviate from this example.

6.4.1   Locative uses of projective adverbs and adjectives

In contrast to prepositions, adverbs do not have internal arguments. Thus, projective adverbs (*oben*) do not relate the figure to a linguistically specified ground object. Nevertheless, the locative adverbs specify regions similar to prepositions. They relate the figure to a contrasting location (*cl*), which the context provides. The contrasting location can be some focused object in the context. For example, Zimmer, Speiser, Baus, Blocher, and Stopp (1998) report experiments in which the participants used adverbs and combinations of adverbs to relate a target to a focused reference object. The reference system and the contrasting location can have independent sources. For example, the interpretation of the sentence *Das Messer liegt rechts* ('the knife is on the right') can use the speaker's reference system for RSYS and a contextually provided plate as the contrasting location (*cl*).

The projective adjectives (*ober*) deviate from other German adjectives in several respects. For the current discussion, it is relevant that their semantics is inherently relational. Projective adjectives cannot be used in predicative position (**Das Buch ist ober/vorder*, 'the book is upper/front'.) They can be used only as restrictive modifiers to select an object (the figure) in contrast to another object (called here 'ground') of the same category. Thus, *das obere Buch* ('the upper book') refers to a book that is in a higher position than another book present. Nevertheless, in the context of a projective adjective the ground object cannot be specified by linguistic means but has to be provided by the situation of utterance. Following Higginbotham's (1985) proposal, the argument structure of projective adjectives includes a position that binds the head noun ($\lambda P_{[+\text{head}]}$) and an external argument (λ_F). In the semantic form, the predicate supplied by the noun is applied to both the figure and the ground.

The use of the adverbs *oben* and *unten* and the adjectives *ober* and *unter* does not require alignment of the figure and the contrasting location or ground. Thus, these lexemes are specified with reference to the lax geometric bearing of the reference system. The main contrast between the adverbs and the adjectives derives from the differences in the argument structure. While the adverbs refer to regions that are related to contextually given places, the adjectives relate the figure to a contextually given ground object of the same category.

oben	$\lambda_F\,\boldsymbol{\lambda}\text{reg}$	$\text{F} \subset \textbf{reg} \wedge \lesssim (\textbf{lax}(\text{BEARING}(\textit{RSYS})),\, \textbf{reg},\, \textbf{\textit{cl}}\,)$
vorne	$\lambda_F\,\boldsymbol{\lambda}\text{reg}$	$\text{F} \subset \textbf{reg} \wedge \lesssim (\textbf{access-ord}(\textit{RSYS},\, \textit{TYPE}),\, \textbf{reg},\, \textbf{\textit{cl}}\,)$
rechts	$\lambda_F\,\boldsymbol{\lambda}\text{reg}$	$\text{F} \subset \textbf{reg} \wedge \textbf{reg} \subset \textbf{right-space}(\textit{RSYS},\, \textbf{\textit{cl}}\,)$
ober	$\lambda P_{[+\text{head}]}\,\lambda_F$	$\text{P}(\text{F}) \wedge \text{P}(G) \wedge \lesssim (\textbf{lax}(\text{BEARING}(\textit{RSYS})),\, \text{F},\, G)$
vorder	$\lambda P_{[+\text{head}]}\,\lambda_F$	$\text{P}(\text{F}) \wedge \text{P}(G) \wedge \lesssim (\textbf{access-ord}(\textit{RSYS},\, \textit{TYPE}),\, \text{F},\, G)$
recht	$\lambda P_{[+\text{head}]}\,\lambda_F$	$\text{P}(\text{F}) \wedge \text{P}(G) \wedge \text{F} \subset \textbf{right-space}(\textit{RSYS},\, G)$

6.4.2 Directional uses of projective prepositions and adverbs

The directional use of the prepositions *über, unter, vor,* and *hinter* is signaled by the accusative case of the noun phrase specifying the internal argument. The directional use of a preposition refers to a path that leads into a region as characterized by the locative use of the same preposition. Combinations of *nach* ('to') or *von* ('from') with one of the locative adverbs form directional adverbial expressions. *Nach oben* ('upward') specifies a path that leads to a region which precedes a contextually specified location relative to the bearing of the reference system. *Von oben* ('from above') specifies a path that leaves such a region. More generally, the spatial condition expressed by the adverb (e.g. *oben*) specifies the goal region (*nach oben*) or the origin (*von oben*) of the path the composite expression refers to.

The difference between locative and directional uses of the prepositions and adverbs is reflected in the argument structure and the semantic form. The referential argument of a directional preposition or adverb is a path, and an existential quantifier binds the region variable. Directional prepositions describe a path of the figure ($D(\text{F}, \text{PATH})$) that ends (but does not start) in a region ($\text{TO}(\text{PATH}, \textbf{reg})$) to which the locative use of the preposition applies (Eschenbach, Tschander, Habel, and Kulik, 2000). In combination with a verb of motion (*unter den Tisch rollen*, 'roll underneath the table'), the contextual component D is interpreted such that the path is the path of motion of the figure. In the context of a verb of orientation (*unter den Tisch zeigen*, 'point underneath the table') the verb can specify other types of paths (cf. Kaufmann, 1995; Eschenbach *et al.*, 2000; Schmidtke, Tschander, Eschenbach, and Habel, 2003). The entries for the directional forms of the projective adverbs can be constructed based on the same scheme. The contrasting location (*cl*) can be interpreted as the origin (in the case of *nach*) or as the goal (in the case of *von*) of the path.

über	$\lambda G_{[+acc]} \, \lambda \underline{F} \, \underline{\lambda} PATH$	$\exists \mathbf{reg} \, [D(F, PATH) \land TO(PATH, \mathbf{reg}) \land \lesssim (\mathbf{strict}(BEARING(RSYS)), \mathbf{reg}, G)]$
nach oben	$\lambda \underline{F} \, \underline{\lambda} PATH$	$\exists \mathbf{reg} \, [D(F, PATH) \land TO(PATH, \mathbf{reg}) \land \lesssim (\mathbf{lax}(BEARING(RSYS)), \mathbf{reg}, \mathbf{cl})]$
von oben	$\lambda \underline{F} \, \underline{\lambda} PATH$	$\exists \mathbf{reg} \, [D(F, PATH) \land FROM(PATH, \mathbf{reg}) \land \lesssim (\mathbf{lax}(BEARING(RSYS)), \mathbf{reg}, \mathbf{cl})]$
vor	$\lambda G_{[+acc]} \, \lambda \underline{F} \, \underline{\lambda} PATH$	$\exists \mathbf{reg} \, [D(F, PATH) \land TO(PATH, \mathbf{reg}) \land \lesssim (\mathbf{access\text{-}ord}(RSYS, TYPE)), \mathbf{reg}, G)]$
nach rechts	$\lambda \underline{F} \, \underline{\lambda} PATH$	$\exists \mathbf{reg} \, [D(F, PATH) \land TO(PATH, \mathbf{reg}) \lesssim \mathbf{reg} \subset \mathbf{right\text{-}space}(RSYS, \mathbf{cl})]$

6.4.3 Directional adverbs and postpositions

The expressions discussed up to now display strong morphological regularities in their word stems. But there are directional adverbs that deviate in this respect. The stem *rück* is employed in the BACK-group (the noun *Rücken* denotes the body-part back). *Auf* appears in the group of UP (the preposition *auf* is used similarly to 'on' to describe situations of (vertical) support). *Ab* ('off') belongs to the stems of the DOWN group.

Table 6.1 shows that a large range of directional adverbs can be used as postpositions that are combined with accusative noun phrases. Examples are *den Berg rauf* ('up the mountain'), *den Berg herauf* ('hither, up the mountain'), *den Fluß abwärts* ('down the river'), and *den Weg zurück* ('back along the path'). For the sake of simplicity, I will call the referent of the embedded noun phrases 'ground object'. The postpositions impose strong restrictions on the ground object and express that the path is included in the surface of the ground object. Apart from this, the directional adverbs and the postposition specify the same condition.

$Postp_{[+acc]} \quad \lambda G_{[+acc]} \, \lambda \underline{F} \, \underline{\lambda} PATH \quad PATH \subset \mathbf{surface}(G) \land \dots$

The adverbs *rauf* ('up', 'upward') and *runter* ('down') are shortened forms of *herauf* and *herunter*. *Her* is a directional deictic particle. Corresponding to the directional use of the English adverb 'here' (*Komm her!*, 'Come here!'), *her* expresses that the path leads to a proximal region. The kindred lexemes *hinauf* and *hinunter* include the directional deictic particle *hin* that expresses a direction to a distant goal region. Whether a region is considered proximal or distant is generally a matter of the context. The shortened forms (*rauf, runter*) are less pronounced with regard to the deictic properties than the original.

The conditions mentioned are reflected in the analysis as follows. The adverb *rauf* states that the path ends in a region (**reg**) that precedes the origin of the path (**or**(PATH)) in regard to the lax geometric bearing. The condition that the goal region is proximal (*PROX*(**reg**)) or distant (*DIST*(**reg**)) expresses the stronger deictic character of *herauf* and *hinauf*. Using $\gtrsim$ instead of $\lesssim$ leads to corresponding proposals for the adverbs *runter, herunter, herab* and *hinunter, hinab*. A further directional adverb derived from the addition of a directional deictic particle is *hervor* ('to the front'). The directional adverb *hervor* specifies a path to a region that is more accessible than a (contextually given) ground object in a relative access order. Example uses are *hinter der Abdeckung hervor kommen* ('come (from) behind the cover to the front') and *hervor treten* ('step/stick (out of the line) to the front').

rauf	$\lambda_F \lambda$PATH	$\exists$**reg** $[D(F, \text{PATH}) \land \text{TO}(\text{PATH}, \textbf{reg}) \land$ $\lesssim(\textbf{lax}(\text{BEARING}(\textit{RSYS})), \textbf{reg}, \textbf{or}(\text{PATH}))]$
herauf	$\lambda_F \lambda$PATH	$\exists$**reg** $[D(F, \text{PATH}) \land \text{TO}(\text{PATH}, \textbf{reg}) \land$ $\lesssim(\textbf{lax}(\text{BEARING}(\textit{RSYS})), \textbf{reg}, \textbf{or}(\text{PATH})) \land \textit{PROX}(\textbf{reg})]$
hinauf	$\lambda_F \lambda$PATH	$\exists$**reg** $[D(F, \text{PATH}) \land \text{TO}(\text{PATH}, \textbf{reg}) \land$ $\lesssim(\textbf{lax}(\text{BEARING}(\textit{RSYS})), \textbf{reg}, \textbf{or}(\text{PATH})) \land \textit{DIST}(\textbf{reg})]$
hervor	$\lambda_F \lambda$PATH	$\exists$**reg** $[D(F, \text{PATH}) \land \text{TO}(\text{PATH}, \textbf{reg}) \land$ $\lesssim(\textbf{access-ord}(\textit{RSYS}, \text{REL}), \textbf{reg}, G)]$

The adverbs *aufwärts* ('upward') and *abwärts* ('downward') specify the alignment of a path with a bearing. For example, *aufwärts* describes a path that is monotonously leading upwards. This condition is stronger than the condition formulated for the adverbs *rauf* or *nach oben* where only the origin and the goal of the path are related.

Aufwärts and *abwärts* specify motion against or with the force of gravity, but do not express vertical alignment. Therefore, the lax geometric bearing suffices to specify the spatial condition for these adverbs. One way to express the semantics of these adverbs is to say that *aufwärts* employs the object order of the path while *abwärts* employs the location order of the path with the lax geometric bearing. Thus, a path leads *aufwärts* ('upward') if the leading object is above the following one. A path leads *abwärts* ('downward') if the location reached earlier is above the location reached later.

aufwärts	$\lambda_F \lambda$PATH	$D(F, \text{PATH}) \land$ **align**(**access-ord**(PATH, M-OBJ), **lax**(BEARING(*RSYS*)))
abwärts	$\lambda_F \lambda$PATH	$D(F, \text{PATH}) \land$ **align**(**access-ord**(PATH, LOC), **lax**(BEARING(*RSYS*)))

The adverbs *vorwärts, rückwärts,* and *seitwärts* ('forward', 'backward', 'sideways') specify the alignment of a path relative to the intrinsic reference system of the figure. *Vorwärts* ('forward') expresses that the direction of motion is in accordance with the intrinsic orientation of the body. Thus, the reference system is bound to be intrinsic to the figure and cannot be specified differently by contextual influences. The geometric condition can be described as the alignment of the object order of the path with the intrinsic access order of the figure. The lexeme *rückwärts* is morphologically related to the noun *Rücken* (the body-part 'back') and *seitwärts* to the noun *Seite* ('side'). *Rückwärts* ('backward') expresses that the backside of the moving figure (BACK-BP(F)) is leading, that is, it precedes the center. Correspondingly, *seitwärts* ('sideways') can be used to say that a lateral side of the moving figure is leading.

vorwärts	$\lambda_F \lambda$PATH	$D($F, PATH$) \wedge$
		align(access-ord(PATH, M-OBJ),
		access-ord(F, INTR))
rückwärts	$\lambda_F \lambda$PATH	$D($F, PATH$) \wedge$
		$\lesssim($**access-ord**(PATH, M-OBJ),
		BACK-BP(F), CENTER(F))
seitwärts	$\lambda_F \lambda$PATH	$D($F, PATH$) \wedge \exists$S [SIDE-BP(S, F) $\wedge$
		$\lesssim($**access-ord**(PATH, M-OBJ), S, CENTER(F))]

The directional adverbs *zurück* ('back') and *vor* ('to the front') also specify paths relative to intrinsic reference systems. There are three uses of *zurück* that I want to distinguish. An example of the first use is *Treten Sie bitte zurück* ('Please, step back.'). The adverb indicates that the goal region of the path is in the intrinsic back region of the figure. Thus, the figure plays a role similar to the ground object in other constructions. *Vor* can be used in the corresponding manner. In a second use (as in *Er kommt zurück,* 'he is coming back' or *Er sieht zurück,* 'he is looking back'), *zurück* refers to a path whose goal region (**reg**) is such that another path of the figure (PATH′) started there. The goal region (**reg**) can be contextually given. Finally, *zurück* can be used to specify a region, thus, as a locative adverb (*Er bleibt zurück,* 'he stays back'). Such uses imply that there is another moving (ground) object in the context, such that the region that includes the figure succeeds the ground object relative to the object order of its path.

vor	$\lambda_F \lambda$PATH	$\exists$**reg** [$D($F, PATH$) \wedge$ TO(PATH, **reg**) $\wedge$
		$\lesssim($**access-ord**(F, INTR), **reg**, F)]
zurück	$\lambda_F \lambda$PATH	$\exists$**reg** [$D($F, PATH$) \wedge$ TO(PATH, **reg**) $\wedge$
		$\gtrsim($**access-ord**(F, INTR), **reg**, F)]
zurück	$\lambda_F \lambda$PATH	$D($F, PATH$) \wedge$ TO(PATH, **reg**) $\wedge \exists$PATH′ [$D($F, PATH′$) \wedge$
		FROM(PATH′, **reg**)]
zurück	$\lambda_F \lambda$**reg**	F $\subset$ **reg** $\wedge \exists$PATH [$D($g, PATH$) \wedge$
		$\gtrsim($**access-ord**(PATH, M-OBJ), **reg**, G)]

The lexemes *voraus, voran,* and *hinterher* can be used as directional adverbs or as directional postpositions. In contrast to the other postpositions listed in Table 6.1, *voraus, voran,* and *hinterher* select noun phrases with dative case. Correspondingly, the semantic embedding of the ground object deviates from the pattern of postpositions selecting accusative case. In this case, the ground object supplies a path ($D(G, PATH)$) and serves as the object of comparison. *Voraus* and *voran* can be used to say that the figure is moving ahead of the ground object. *Hinterher* specifies in a corresponding manner that the figure is following. If these terms are used as directional adverbs, then the only difference is that the ground object has to be supplied by the context.

voraus, voran	$\lambda G_{[+dat]}\ \lambda \underline{F}\ \underline{\lambda}PATH$	$D(F, PATH) \wedge D'(G, PATH) \wedge$ $\lesssim(\textbf{access-ord}(PATH, \text{M-OBJ}), F, G)$
hinterher	$\lambda G_{[+dat]}\ \lambda \underline{F}\ \underline{\lambda}PATH$	$D(F, PATH) \wedge D'(G, PATH) \wedge$ $\gtrsim(\textbf{access-ord}(PATH, \text{M-OBJ}), F, G)$
voraus, voran	$\lambda \underline{F}\ \lambda PATH$	$D(F, PATH) \wedge D'(g, PATH) \wedge$ $\lesssim(\textbf{access-ord}(PATH, \text{M-OBJ}), F, G)$
hinterher	$\lambda \underline{F}\ \underline{\lambda}PATH$	$D(F, PATH) \wedge D'(g, PATH) \wedge$ $\gtrsim(\textbf{access-ord}(PATH, \text{M-OBJ}), F, G)$

6.5 Conclusion

The German language includes a variety of projective terms that relate to the six principal directions UP, DOWN, FRONT, BACK, RIGHT, and LEFT. This chapter has presented analyses of several lexemes. The analyses reflect syntactic and semantic similarities and differences among terms of the same principal direction. The grouping according to the principal direction is reflected in the embedding of semantic components referring to their functional source. Syntactic similarities are reflected by the uniformity of the argument structure. Semantic components that have to be anchored to the context of an expression indicate the requirements on the context for the interpretation of an expression.

The inspection of the larger inventory of German projective terms reveals that lexemes that belong to the same principal direction differ regarding the influence of the reference system. For example, the groups named UP and DOWN are not homogeneous in terms of vertical alignment. The semantic description calls for two different geometrical models representing the functional asymmetries deriving from gravity. While a large group of the lexemes discussed rely on the context in regard to the specification of the reference system, some lexemes in the groups named FRONT and BACK specify the reference system and the type of access-order (intrinsic or relative) in their semantic forms. Furthermore, the set of German terms of the principal directions RIGHT and LEFT is notably smaller than the other groups. This corresponds, on the one hand, to the weak functional basis of this distinction, and, on the other hand, to the geometric character that is based on the symmetric division of space rather than a geometric direction.

Appendix

Areas

Straight lines (**l**), planes (**pl**), half-spaces (**hs**), and regions (**reg**) are areas. The Greek letter ε is used in the following as a variable for areas. $\mathbf{p} \iota \varepsilon$ expresses that point **p** lies in or on ε. (D1) defines inclusion ($\subset$) and (D2) intersection ($\circ$) for areas. Two areas are congruent ($\gtreqless$) iff one of them is part of the other (D3).

(D1)	$\varepsilon \subset \varepsilon'$	$\Leftrightarrow_{\mathrm{def}} \forall \mathbf{p}\ [\mathbf{p} \iota \varepsilon \Rightarrow \mathbf{p} \iota \varepsilon']$
(D2)	$\varepsilon \circ \varepsilon'$	$\Leftrightarrow_{\mathrm{def}} \exists \mathbf{p}\ [\mathbf{p} \iota \varepsilon \wedge \mathbf{p} \iota \varepsilon']$
(D3)	$\varepsilon \gtreqless \varepsilon'$	$\Leftrightarrow_{\mathrm{def}} \varepsilon \subset \varepsilon' \vee \varepsilon' \subset \varepsilon$

Straight lines have at least two points on them (A1), any two points lie on a common line (A2), and different lines share at most one point (A3). Three different points that lie on the same line are called collinear (D4).

(A1)	$\forall \mathbf{l}\ \exists \mathbf{p}\ \mathbf{q}$	$[\mathbf{p} \neq \mathbf{q} \wedge \mathbf{p} \iota \mathbf{l} \wedge \mathbf{q} \iota \mathbf{l}]$
(A2)	$\forall \mathbf{p}\ \mathbf{q}\ \exists \mathbf{l}$	$[\mathbf{p} \iota \mathbf{l} \wedge \mathbf{q} \iota \mathbf{l}]$
(A3)	$\forall \mathbf{p}\ \mathbf{q}\ \mathbf{l}\ \mathbf{l}'$	$[\mathbf{p} \neq \mathbf{q} \wedge \mathbf{p} \iota \mathbf{l} \wedge \mathbf{q} \iota \mathbf{l} \wedge \mathbf{p} \iota \mathbf{l}' \wedge \mathbf{q} \iota \mathbf{l}' \Rightarrow \mathbf{l} = \mathbf{l}']$
(D4)	$\mathbf{col(p, q, r)}$	$\Leftrightarrow_{\mathrm{def}} \mathbf{p} \neq \mathbf{q} \wedge \mathbf{p} \neq \mathbf{r} \wedge \mathbf{q} \neq \mathbf{r} \wedge \exists \mathbf{l}\ [\mathbf{p} \iota \mathbf{l} \wedge \mathbf{q} \iota \mathbf{l} \wedge \mathbf{r} \iota \mathbf{l}]$

Planes have at least three non-collinear points on them (A4) and any three points lie on a common plane (A5). If a straight line and a plane share two points, then the line is included in the plane (A6). Different planes share at most one line (A7).

(A4)	$\forall \mathbf{pl}\ \exists \mathbf{p}\ \mathbf{q}\ \mathbf{r}$	$[\mathbf{p} \neq \mathbf{q} \wedge \mathbf{p} \neq \mathbf{r} \wedge \mathbf{q} \neq \mathbf{r} \wedge \neg\, \mathbf{col(p, q, r)} \wedge$
		$\mathbf{p} \iota \mathbf{pl} \wedge \mathbf{q} \iota \mathbf{pl} \wedge \mathbf{r} \iota \mathbf{pl}]$
(A5)	$\forall \mathbf{p}\ \mathbf{q}\ \mathbf{r}\ \exists \mathbf{pl}$	$[\mathbf{p} \iota \mathbf{pl} \wedge \mathbf{q} \iota \mathbf{pl} \wedge \mathbf{r} \iota \mathbf{pl}]$
(A6)	$\forall \mathbf{p}\ \mathbf{q}\ \mathbf{l}\ \mathbf{pl}$	$[\mathbf{p} \neq \mathbf{q} \wedge \mathbf{p} \iota \mathbf{l} \wedge \mathbf{q} \iota \mathbf{l} \wedge \mathbf{p} \iota \mathbf{pl} \wedge \mathbf{q} \iota \mathbf{pl} \Rightarrow \mathbf{l} \subset \mathbf{pl}]$
(A7)	$\forall \mathbf{pl}\ \mathbf{pl}'\ \mathbf{l}\ \mathbf{l}'$	$[\mathbf{l} \neq \mathbf{l}' \wedge \mathbf{l} \subset \mathbf{pl} \wedge \mathbf{l}' \subset \mathbf{pl} \wedge \mathbf{l} \subset \mathbf{pl}' \wedge \mathbf{l}' \subset \mathbf{pl}' \Rightarrow \mathbf{pl} = \mathbf{pl}']$

The ternary relation β glossed here as 'between' relates collinear points (β1), (β4). It is symmetric wrt. the first and third argument position (β2) and asymmetric wrt. the first and second one (β3). If **q** is between **p** and **r** and **q**' is collinear with **q** and **p**, then **q** lies between **p** and **q**' or between **r** and **q**' (β5). For any two points

p and **q** there is a point **r** such that **q** is between **p** and **r** (β6). And if three points and a line lie in the same plane such that the points do not lie on the line and the line intersects the segment between two of the points, then the line intersects one of the other segments as well (β7).

(β1)	$\forall$**p q r**	$[\beta(\mathbf{p}, \mathbf{q}, \mathbf{r}) \Rightarrow \mathrm{col}(\mathbf{p}, \mathbf{q}, \mathbf{r})]$
(β2)	$\forall$**p q r**	$[\beta(\mathbf{p}, \mathbf{q}, \mathbf{r}) \Rightarrow \beta(\mathbf{r}, \mathbf{q}, \mathbf{p})]$
(β3)	$\forall$**p q r**	$[\beta(\mathbf{p}, \mathbf{q}, \mathbf{r}) \Rightarrow \neg\,\beta(\mathbf{q}, \mathbf{p}, \mathbf{r})]$
(β4)	$\forall$**p q r**	$[\mathrm{col}(\mathbf{p}, \mathbf{q}, \mathbf{r}) \Rightarrow (\beta(\mathbf{p}, \mathbf{q}, \mathbf{r}) \vee \beta(\mathbf{q}, \mathbf{p}, \mathbf{r}) \vee \beta(\mathbf{p}, \mathbf{r}, \mathbf{q}))]$
(β5)	$\forall$**p q r q$'$**	$[\beta(\mathbf{p}, \mathbf{q}, \mathbf{r}) \wedge \mathrm{col}(\mathbf{q}, \mathbf{q}', \mathbf{p}) \Rightarrow (\beta(\mathbf{p}, \mathbf{q}, \mathbf{q}') \vee \beta(\mathbf{q}', \mathbf{q}, \mathbf{r}))]$
(β6)	$\forall$**p q**	$[\mathbf{p} \neq \mathbf{q} \Rightarrow \exists\mathbf{r}\,[\beta(\mathbf{p}, \mathbf{q}, \mathbf{r})]\,]$
(β7)	$\forall$**p$_1$ p$_2$ p$_3$ l**	$[\exists\mathbf{pl}\,[\mathbf{p}_1 \iota \mathbf{pl} \wedge \mathbf{p}_2 \iota \mathbf{pl} \wedge \mathbf{p}_3 \iota \mathbf{pl} \wedge \mathbf{l} \subset \mathbf{pl}] \wedge \neg\,(\mathbf{p}_1 \iota \mathbf{l}) \wedge$
		$\neg\,(\mathbf{p}_2 \iota \mathbf{l}) \wedge \neg\,(\mathbf{p}_3 \iota \mathbf{l}) \wedge \exists\mathbf{q}\,[\mathbf{q}\iota\mathbf{l} \wedge \beta(\mathbf{p}_1, \mathbf{q}, \mathbf{p}_3)]] \Rightarrow$
		$\exists\mathbf{r}\,[\mathbf{r}\iota\mathbf{l} \wedge (\beta(\mathbf{p}_1, \mathbf{r}, \mathbf{p}_2) \vee \beta(\mathbf{p}_2, \mathbf{r}, \mathbf{p}_3))]\,]$

A boundary point for an area is a point **p** such that all points between **p** and some point in the area are in the area, and all points between **p** and some other point not in the area are not in the area (D5). Area ε borders area ε$'$ iff a boundary point of ε$'$ is also a boundary point of ε, and ε and ε$'$ share nothing but boundary points of ε$'$ (D6). The surface of an area ε is the area on which the boundary points of ε lie.

(D5)	**bdpt**(ε, **p**)	$\Leftrightarrow_{\mathrm{def}} \exists\mathbf{r}\,[\mathbf{r}\iota\varepsilon \wedge \forall\mathbf{q}\,[\beta(\mathbf{p}, \mathbf{q}, \mathbf{r}) \Rightarrow \mathbf{q}\iota\varepsilon]\,] \wedge$
		$\exists\mathbf{r}\,[\neg\mathbf{r}\iota\varepsilon \wedge \forall\mathbf{q}\,[\beta(\mathbf{p}, \mathbf{q}, \mathbf{r}) \Rightarrow \neg\mathbf{q}\iota\varepsilon]\,]$
(D6)	**borders**(ε, ε$'$)	$\Leftrightarrow_{\mathrm{def}} \exists\mathbf{p}\,[\mathbf{bdpt}(\varepsilon', \mathbf{p}) \wedge \mathbf{bdpt}(\varepsilon, \mathbf{p})] \wedge$
		$\forall\mathbf{p}\,[\mathbf{p}\iota\varepsilon \wedge \mathbf{p}\iota\varepsilon' \Rightarrow \mathbf{bdpt}(\varepsilon', \mathbf{p})]$
(A8)	$\forall$ε **p**	$[\mathbf{p}\iota\,\mathbf{surface}(\varepsilon) \Leftrightarrow \mathbf{bdpt}(\varepsilon, \mathbf{p})]$

A half-space is convex (it includes any point that lies between two of its points) (A9) and has a continuous boundary (between any point inside and any point outside there is a boundary point) (A10). The surface of a half-space is a plane (A11).

(A9)	$\forall$**hs p q r**	$[\beta(\mathbf{p}, \mathbf{q}, \mathbf{r}) \wedge \mathbf{p}\iota\mathbf{hs} \wedge \mathbf{r}\iota\mathbf{hs} \Rightarrow \mathbf{q}\iota\mathbf{hs}]$
(A10)	$\forall$**hs p r** $\exists$**q**	$[\mathbf{p}\iota\mathbf{hs} \wedge \neg\,\mathbf{bdpt}(\mathbf{hs}, \mathbf{p}) \wedge \neg\mathbf{r}\iota\mathbf{hs} \wedge \neg\,\mathbf{bdpt}(\mathbf{hs}, \mathbf{r}) \Rightarrow$
		$\beta(\mathbf{p}, \mathbf{q}, \mathbf{r}) \wedge \mathbf{bdpt}(\mathbf{hs}, \mathbf{q})]$
(A11)	$\forall$**hs** $\exists$**pl**	$[\mathbf{pl} = \mathbf{surface}(\mathbf{hs})]$

The primary right space of the reference system is a half-space that is bordered by the plane of symmetry and includes the right marker but does not intersect the left marker of the reference system. The right space relative to a divider DI (**right-space**(RSYS, DI)) is bordered by DI and compatible with the primary right space (A13).

(A12) ∀RSYS **rhs**   [**rhs** = **p-right-space**(RSYS) ⟺
                          borders(**sym-plane**(RSYS), **rhs**) ∧
                          RIGHT-MARKER(RSYS) ⊂ **rhs** ∧
                          ¬ LEFT-MARKER(RSYS) ∘ **rhs**]

(A13) ∀RSYS DI **hs**   [**hs** = **right-space**(RSYS, DI) ⟺ **borders**(DI, **hs**) ∧
                          hs ⪎ **p-right-space**(RSYS)]

Directions

Access orders and geometric bearings are grouped under the term of geometric direction (δ). $\lesssim(\delta, \mathbf{p}, \mathbf{q})$ symbolizes that point $\mathbf{p}$ precedes point $\mathbf{q}$ with respect to direction δ. For all directions, precedence is a transitive (A14) and asymmetric relation (A15). (D7) defines precedence for areas based on precedence for points. Given any direction, precedence ($\lesssim$) and succession ($\gtrsim$) are converse (D8). Direction δ is aligned with direction δ' iff every point $\mathbf{p}$ that precedes a point $\mathbf{q}$ regarding δ, also precedes $\mathbf{q}$ regarding δ' (D9). Alignment in this sense is not symmetrical.

(A14) ∀δ **p q r**   [$\lesssim(\delta, \mathbf{p}, \mathbf{q}) \wedge \lesssim(\delta, \mathbf{q}, \mathbf{r}) \Rightarrow \lesssim(\delta, \mathbf{p}, \mathbf{r})$]

(A15) ∀δ **p q**   [$\lesssim(\delta, \mathbf{p}, \mathbf{q}) \Rightarrow \neg \lesssim(\delta, \mathbf{q}, \mathbf{p})$]

(D7) $\lesssim(\delta, \varepsilon, \varepsilon')$ $\Leftrightarrow_{def}$ ∃**p q** [**p** ι ε' ∧ **q** ι ε ∧ $\lesssim(\delta, \mathbf{p}, \mathbf{q})$] ∧
                          ∀**p q** [**p** ι ε' ∧ **q** ι ε ⇒ ¬ $\lesssim(\delta, \mathbf{q}, \mathbf{p})$]]

(D8) $\gtrsim(\delta, \varepsilon, \varepsilon')$ $\Leftrightarrow_{def} \lesssim(\delta, \varepsilon', \varepsilon)$

(D9)   **align**(δ, δ') $\Leftrightarrow_{def}$ ∀**p q** [$\lesssim(\delta, \mathbf{p}, \mathbf{q}) \Rightarrow \lesssim(\delta', \mathbf{p}, \mathbf{q})$]

Geometric bearings are straight directions. That means, if $\mathbf{p}$ precedes $\mathbf{r}$ relative to bearing $\mathbf{b}$ and $\mathbf{q}$ is between $\mathbf{p}$ and $\mathbf{r}$, then $\mathbf{p}$ precedes $\mathbf{q}$ and $\mathbf{q}$ precedes $\mathbf{r}$ relative to bearing $\mathbf{b}$ (A16). The lax geometric bearing of a reference system is such that for every point there is a plane that includes exactly those points that do not precede or succeed $\mathbf{p}$ (A17). The strict geometric bearing of a reference system is such that for every point $\mathbf{p}$ there is a straight line $\mathbf{l}$ such that the points of $\mathbf{l}$ are $\mathbf{p}$ and the predecessors and successors of $\mathbf{p}$ regarding the geometric bearing (A18). (The geometric bearings introduced by Eschenbach (1999) are strict geometric bearings.)

(A16) ∀**b p q r**   [$\lesssim(\mathbf{b}, \mathbf{p}, \mathbf{r}) \wedge \beta(\mathbf{p}, \mathbf{q}, \mathbf{r}) \Rightarrow \lesssim(\mathbf{b}, \mathbf{p}, \mathbf{q}) \wedge \lesssim(\mathbf{b}, \mathbf{q}, \mathbf{r})$]

(A17) ∀BEARING **p**   ∃**pl** ∀**q** [**q** ι **pl** ⟺ ¬ $\lesssim(\textbf{lax}(\text{BEARING}), \mathbf{p}, \mathbf{q})$ ∧
                          ¬ $\lesssim(\textbf{lax}(\text{BEARING}), \mathbf{q}, \mathbf{p})$]

(A18) ∀BEARING **p**   ∃**l** ∀**q** [**q** ι **l** ⟺ (**q** = **p** ∨ $\lesssim(\textbf{strict}(\text{BEARING}), \mathbf{p}, \mathbf{q})$ ∨
                          $\lesssim(\textbf{strict}(\text{BEARING}), \mathbf{q}, \mathbf{p})$)]

For every reference system, the strict geometric bearing is aligned with the lax geometric bearing (A19). The alignment of bearings (B-ALIGN) is defined (D10) as alignment of the strict and the lax geometric bearings.

(A19) $\forall$BEARING $[\mathbf{align}(\mathbf{strict}(\text{BEARING}), \mathbf{lax}(\text{BEARING}))]$

(D10)   B-ALIGN(B_1, B_2) $\Leftrightarrow_{\text{def}} \mathbf{align}(\mathbf{strict}(B_1), \mathbf{strict}(B_2)) \wedge$
$\mathbf{align}(\mathbf{lax}(B_1), \mathbf{lax}(B_2))$

For every access order intrinsic to x, the front of x precedes and the back of x succeeds the center of x.

(A20) $\forall$x $[\lesssim(\mathbf{access\text{-}ord}(\text{x}, \text{INTR}), \text{FRONT-BP}(\text{x}), \text{CENTER}(\text{x}))]$

(A21) $\forall$x $[\gtrsim(\mathbf{access\text{-}ord}(\text{x}, \text{INTR}), \text{BACK-BP}(\text{x}), \text{CENTER}(\text{x}))]$

A point lies on a path iff it precedes or succeeds another point wrt. the location order of the path (D11).

(D11)   **p** ι PATH $\Leftrightarrow_{\text{def}} \exists\mathbf{q} \ [\lesssim(\mathbf{access\text{-}ord}(\text{PATH}, \text{LOC}), \mathbf{p}, \mathbf{q}) \vee$
$\lesssim(\mathbf{access\text{-}ord}(\text{PATH}, \text{LOC}), \mathbf{q}, \mathbf{p})]$

The origin of a path is a point that lies on the path but does not succeed any other point of the path wrt. the location order (D12). The final point of a path is a point of the path that does not precede any other point wrt. the location order (D13). A path leads to a region iff its final point is included in the region but its origin is not (D14). And a path comes from a region iff its origin is included in the region but the final point is not (D15).

(D12) $\mathbf{or}(\text{PATH}) = \mathbf{p}$ $\Leftrightarrow_{\text{def}} \mathbf{p} \ \iota \ \text{PATH} \wedge$
$\neg \exists\mathbf{q} \ [\lesssim(\mathbf{access\text{-}ord}(\text{PATH}, \text{LOC}), \mathbf{q}, \mathbf{p})]$

(D13) $\mathbf{fin}(\text{PATH}) = \mathbf{p}$ $\Leftrightarrow_{\text{def}} \mathbf{p} \ \iota \ \text{PATH} \wedge$
$\neg \exists\mathbf{q} \ [\lesssim(\mathbf{access\text{-}ord}(\text{PATH}, \text{LOC}), \mathbf{p}, \mathbf{q})]$

(D14)   TO(PATH, **reg**) $\Leftrightarrow_{\text{def}} \mathbf{fin}(\text{PATH}) \ \iota \ \mathbf{reg} \wedge \neg \mathbf{or}(\text{PATH}) \ \iota \ \mathbf{reg}$

(D15)   FROM(PATH, **reg**) $\Leftrightarrow_{\text{def}} \mathbf{or}(\text{PATH}) \ \iota \ \mathbf{reg} \wedge \neg \mathbf{fin}(\text{PATH}) \ \iota \ \mathbf{reg}$

7

Verbs and Directions: The Interaction of Geometry and Function in Determining Orientation

CHRISTOPHER HABEL

Abstract

Describing verbally changes in space is based on the ability to focus on spatial properties and relations. Change of orientation is a specific type of spatial change, which has to be expressed by special verbs, for example the German *drehen* ('turn'). Furthermore, there are adverbials peculiar to modifying a change of orientation VPs, for example, *rechtsherum* ('clockwise'). In the present chapter situations of turning, verbally encoded by *drehen*-descriptions, are used to exemplify the linguistic principles of encoding ORIENTATION and CHANGE OF ORIENTATION: the BEARER OF TURNING, that is the object that performs a change of orientation, provides a FRONT-AXIS, whose direction changes during the temporal phase focused in the utterance. In selecting the FRONT-AXIS and choosing relations to describe specific properties, as final orientation or direction of turning, speakers' assumptions about functional properties and relations are the frame for establishing the spatial concept fundamental for verbalization, namely ORIENTATION.

Functional concepts

Components in the conceptual representation of spatial terms that cannot completely be described in a geometric framework; especially, concepts that

The research reported in this chapter was partially supported by a grant (project 'Axiomatics of Spatial Concepts', Ha 1237/7) of the Deutsche Forschungsgemeinschaft (DFG) in the priority program on 'Spatial Cognition'. I want to thank Carola Eschenbach, Hedda Schmidtke, and Ladina Tschander for important comments and fruitful discussions on the topic 'Orientation and change of orientation'. Parts of our co-operation have been materialized as Schmidtke *et al.* (2003).

concern actions for which an artifact is designed, or specific activities a person usually performs in order to act and interact successfully, such as seeing, grasping, or moving.

7.1 Introduction

Natural language descriptions of dynamic spatial situations frequently involve the interaction of two types of expressions connected to spatial structure: a verb of 'change in space' (such as *go, turn, rotate*) and an adverbial, which gives further information about the change in question, for example, about direction or the goal of motion. Directional phrases play a major role in the process of semantic composition. The most obvious—and widely discussed—examples are verbs of motion that systematically combine with directional prepositional phrases (*Paul walks into the house*). The verb expresses that a BEARER OF MOTION (referred to by *Paul*) traverses a PATH, and the directional prepositional phrase specifies the direction of this path of motion. The systematic characteristics of such combinations suggest that the semantics of verbs of motion contain a uniform component that specifies the interrelation between the BEARER OF MOTION, that is the entity that performs a change in space, and the PATH OF MOTION (Eschenbach, Tschander, Habel, and Kulik, 2000).

There is only a small class of verbs that can be combined with directional prepositional phrases. In contrast, non-directional local prepositional phrases, which specify the location of entities or situations, can be added to most verbal phrases (*Paul opened the present in the garden*) as a modifier. This suggests that verbs have to specify explicitly semantic conditions with respect to directional information in order to be combined with directional prepositional phrases.[1] In addition to verbs of motion, some other groups of verbs can be modified by directional prepositional phrases (Schmidtke, Tschander, Eschenbach, and Habel, 2003). Among them are verbs of change of orientation (e.g. *drehen, turn,* Habel, 1999) and verbs such as *point, aim, direct, shout, yell, call, look, stare, gaze,* that do not focus on paths of motion.[2] Beyond directional prepositional phrases, some other classes of adverbials—namely rotational adverbs *rechtsherum, linksherum* ('clockwise', 'counterclockwise') and orientational adverbs *vorwärts, rückwärts, seitwärts* ('forward', 'backward', 'sideways')—can be used to specify some changes of orientation. This chapter will use German to illustrate the phenomena,

---

[1] These semantic conditions, which are exemplified in Section 7.3, correspond to well-formedness conditions with respect to DIRECTIONAL-features and DIR-functions in Nikanne's approach (1990, 2000).

[2] The common characteristic between these 'verbs of orientation' is their reference to static object orientations, for example induced by a line of perception in the case of verbs of visual perception. In general, the static object orientation either holds during the situation described or is established by it.

on the one hand, because the differences between German and English give interesting insight in the phenomena, on the other hand, because the author and most of his informants are native speakers of German.

The objectives of this chapter are twofold: first, I specify the general structures that underlie and sanction the combinations between verbs of change of orientation and orientation-sensitive prepositions. By subtly analyzing these special cases the relation between the conceptions of orientation and direction are clarified in a way that can be applied in a wider range of phenomena. These analyses concern the interplay of the levels of conceptual representations and spatial representations (Jackendoff, 1997). Second, there are two—often interacting—types of factors, which determine whether a combination of a verb of change of orientation and a modifying directional prepositional phrase or a rotational adverb is acceptable, and how this combined expression is interpreted. On the one hand, purely geometrical properties and relations of the entities involved in a change of orientation have to be considered, for example, regions, axes, etc. On the other hand, additional functional aspects come into play, as REGULAR_DIRECTION_OF_ MOTION (e.g. people, animals, vehicles), REGULAR_DIRECTION_OF_PERCEPTION (e.g. people, animals, cameras, microphones), REGULAR_DIRECTION_OF_ INTERACTION (e.g. tip of a pen, tip of finger,...).[3] The interplay between geometrical and functional aspects is bi-directional. Some entities in the world can be conceptualized with respect to more than one functional aspect, for example a person's REGULAR_DIRECTION_OF_MOTION can be different from the ACTUAL_DIRECTION_OF_PERCEPTION, if she has turned her head to a side. In such cases, the geometric aspects of a situation can be used to select the functional aspect the speaker intended to mention.

In Section 7.2 the verbal means German speakers use to describe turning situations are exemplified and two perspectives on turning are presented, namely a result-perspective and a process-perspective. In Section 7.3, I give a formal, geometrical specification of the concepts and spatial entities involved in verbal descriptions of turning situations. Furthermore, it is shown how functional information about the participants of a turning situation stipulates the primary geometric entities of the spatial representation level.

7.2   Describing Turning Situations Using the German Verb *drehen*

CHANGE OF LOCATION and CHANGE OF ORIENTATION are two separate aspects of conceptualizing dynamics in space (Schmidtke *et al.*, 2003). Some verbal expressions can be used to describe the combination of a CHANGE OF LOCATION and a CHANGE OF ORIENTATION, for example *John turns off into Main Street.*

---

[3] The notion of 'functional aspect' is used here in a broad sense, not restricted to artifacts, but also applicable to some 'functions of living beings'.

Other expressions are committed to refer to only one of these changes: whereas *Mary turns the key* refers to a pure CHANGE OF ORIENTATION, *The stone fell down* describes a pure CHANGE OF LOCATION. Furthermore, expressions can be neutral with respect to one of the changes, for example, *Mary walks into the garden* describes a CHANGE OF LOCATION but leaves it open, whether Mary changes her orientation. In contrast to this, there are some verbs that always refer to a combination of different types of spatial change, e.g. *tumble* and *roll*, as in the sentences *The rock tumbled down* or *The car rolled down the hill.*[4]

Although the German verb *drehen* is primarily a CHANGE OF ORIENTATION verb, *drehen* as well as some prefix verbs derived from *drehen* can transport information about both CHANGE OF ORIENTATION and CHANGE OF LOCATION.[5] I start with a short overview of *drehen*-constructions in German, and contrast these with their English counterparts.[6] If the BEARER OF TURNING, that is the entity that performs a change of orientation, is also the agent of the turning, *drehen* requires the use of a reflexive pronoun, see (1.a)–(1.a″), a grammatical phenomenon I will not discuss in this chapter.

(1) a. *Maria dreht sich.*   *Maria turns REFL.*
     a′. *Maria dreht sich zum Fenster.*   *Maria turns REFL towards the window.*
     a″. *Maria dreht sich um.*   *Maria turns around.*
     b. *Maria dreht den Schlüssel.*   *Maria turns the key.*
     c. *Maria dreht den Türknopf.*   *Maria turns the doorknob.*
     c′. *Der Türknopf dreht sich.*   *The doorknob turns REFL.*
     d. *Maria dreht den Ball.*   *Maria turns the ball.*
                                               [Maria spins the ball.]
     e. *Die Erde dreht sich um die Sonne.*   *The earth turns around the sun.*
                                               [The earth revolves around the sun.]

Whereas (1.a)–(1.b) describe situations in which orientation changes, (1.e) describes only a process of changing location. (1.c) and (1.d) do not fit well in this schema: first, the location of the turned object—the doorknob or the ball—is

---

[4] The core concept in the semantics of *roll*—see *The ball rolled down the hill*—is ROTATION, which has some relevant aspects in common with CHANGE OF ORIENTATION, as I argue in Section 7.3.3. Additionally, the case of *rolling cars* is special: CHANGE OF LOCATION and ROTATION concern different entities, namely the car, as BEARER OF MOTION, and the wheels, that is parts of the car, as BEARER OF ROTATION. In contrast, in the case of a rolling ball, both BEARER roles are filled by the same entity.

[5] German *abdrehen*, as in *Das Schiff dreht nach Norden ab* ('The ship changes course to the north'), as well as prefix verbs, such as *abbiegen*, and corresponding English expressions, such as *turn off*, will not be discussed in this chapter.

[6] Note that in this chapter the German examples are translated literally, although such English translations do not always replicate the acceptability rating of the German expression. The literal translations are augmented by further information if this is useful for non-native speakers of German, for example I use REFL to translate the reflexive pronoun in *sich drehen*.

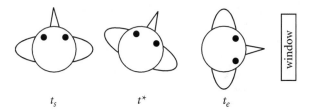

$$t_s \qquad\qquad t^* \qquad\qquad t_e$$

FIG. 7.1. The turning of a person.

constant during the situation in question. Second, neither (1.c) nor (1.d) seem to be a cases of change of orientation, since balls—as long as they do not change their location—do not have an orientation,[7] and doorknobs do not have an orientation of that type that is inherent in the concept of turning. Nevertheless, in this chapter, I will present a unifying analysis, which is based on the idea of a change of orientation, for all cases exemplified in (1).

What happens when we see that Maria turns as depicted in Fig. 7.1 and describe this verbally? In other words, what do we conceptualize, when we perceive such a situation of TURNING, and why do we verbalize this by means of a verb as *turn* (in English) or *drehen* (in German) combined with a spatial adverbial as exemplified with (2.a)–(2.c)?

(2) a. *Maria dreht sich.*   *Maria turns REFL.*
     b. *Maria dreht sich rechtsherum.* *Maria turns REFL clockwise.*
     c. *Maria dreht sich zum Fenster.* *Maria turns REFL towards the window.*

Although all three of these sentences can be used to describe the situation in question, they do this in a different manner. Uttering (2.a) is neutral with respect to the 'Drehsinn' ('sense of turning'),[8] a concept that I call in the following DIRECTION OF TURNING, that is the sentence can be used for veridical descriptions of a clockwise as well as of a counterclockwise turning. Furthermore, (2.a) gives no information about the orientation of the protagonist after the turning. In contrast to this, (2.b) is sensitive to the way the turning is performed, namely, that it is done clockwise. This means, that a turning, which starts at time t_s and ends at time t_e, has to respect some requirements for the course of turning, to be describable by a *rechtsherum drehen* phrase: If t^* is a time between t_s and t_e, then the ORIENTATION of the BEARER OF TURNING, that is the entity that performs a change of orientation, has to be at time t^* between the START-ORIENTATION

---

[7] Balls that change location, that is rolling balls inducing a trajectory, can inherit an orientation by their movement (Eschenbach, 1999).

[8] The compound noun *Drehsinn* is used in technical German in the areas of mathematics, physics, and engineering. There is also an English counterpart, namely the mathematical usage of *sense*: 'one of the two directions of ROTATION, that is, either CLOCKWISE or ANTICLOCKWISE' (E. J. Borowsky and J. M. Borwein, *Collins Dictionary of Mathematics*, 1989, p. 530).

TABLE 7.1. *Linguistic ways of expressing aspects of turning*

	Basic sentence	Rotational adverb	Directional PP
	Maria dreht sich	*rechtsherum*	*zum Fenster*
Direction of turning	neutral	+	−
Final orientation of the protagonist	neutral	−	+
Focused event type	neutral	process	resulting state

(at t_s) and the END-ORIENTATION (at t_e).[9] Furthermore, this betweenness-condition on the course of turning also holds for the sub-courses between t_s and t^* and that between t^* and t_e. Thus, this description of turning, which distinguishes *rechtsherum drehen* and *linksherum drehen*, takes the process aspect in the foreground. On the other hand, (2.b) does not hold information about the resulting state of the turning, that is about the orientation after the turning. The conditions for using (2.c) are different: here the resulting state is focused on, namely the orientation of the protagonist at time t_e. The sense of turning is not expressed by the sentence, that is both clockwise and counterclockwise turnings are compatible with (2.c).

To summarize (see Table 7.1): the core sentence (2.a) is neutral with respect to the direction of turning, the final orientation of the protagonist and the event type.[10] The combination of the core sentence with the rotational adverbial *rechtsherum* or with the directional prepositional phrase *zum Fenster* provides further information, and by this, these augmented sentences can focus on specific aspects of the turning.

The scheme—depicted in Table 7.1—for combining basic sentences with rotational adverbials and directional prepositional phrases does not lead to acceptable sentences for every kind of turning situation. The basic sentences in (3.a) are used as a starting point. Whereas the combination with a rotational

[9] This idea of an orientation between two other orientations can formally be described by the geometric concept of *betweenness* of *directions*, which we discussed in detail in Schmidtke *et al.* (2003). I exemplify this idea informally with the case of the directions of a compass. NE is a direction between N and E, and furthermore, NNE is a direction between N and NE. But, S is not a direction between N and E. The *directions*, which are *between* N and S, can be categorized via *betweenness* into two distinguished classes, namely, the W-directions and the E-directions.

[10] The analysis of *drehen*, in particular, and verbs of change of orientation, in general, presented in this chapter—and also in Eschenbach *et al.* (2000) and Schmidtke *et al.* (2003)—as well as my usage of 'process' and 'state', which follows the Vendler (1957) tradition of analyzing verbs, corresponds to Pustejovsky's (1991) approach of event types and type shifting.

adverbial leads to well-accepted sentences (3.b), the combination with a directional prepositional phrase is not acceptable (3.c). The second column of this example shows that the acceptability rating is independent of the syntactic position of *Ball*, namely whether it is subject or direct object. Additionally, the contrast between (3.c) and (3.d) gives evidence that being an artifact or having the lexical feature [−ANIMATE] cannot be the cause for the unacceptability of (3.c).

(3) a. *Maria dreht den Ball.*   *Der Ball dreht sich.*
        Maria turns the ball.   The ball turns REFL.
     b. *Maria dreht den Ball rechtsherum.*   *Der Ball dreht sich rechtsherum.*
        Maria turns the ball clockwise.   The ball turns REFL clockwise.
     c. **Maria dreht den Ball zum*   **Der Ball dreht sich zum*
        Fenster.   *Fenster.*
        Maria turns the ball towards the   The ball turns REFL towards
        window.   the window.
     d. *Maria dreht den Sessel zum Fenster.*
        Maria turns the armchair towards
        the window.

Before I summarize the first analyses, I come back to a further type of using *drehen* in German, the case of the revolving earth (1.e), that is the case of a rotation around an external axis.[11] Starting from the acceptable sentence (4.a), not only the modification by a directional PP (4.c), but also modification by a rotational adverb leads to a less acceptable sentence (4.b).[12]

(4) a. *Die Erde dreht sich um die Sonne.*   The earth revolves around the sun.
     b. *?Die Erde dreht sich rechtsherum*   The earth revolves clockwise
        (um die Sonne).   (around the sun).
     c. **Die Erde dreht sich zum Jupiter*   The earth revolves towards
        (um die Sonne).   Jupiter (around the sun).

These analyses of examples (2)–(4) lead to the following questions:

Q1 What are the common aspects of the turning of a human, for example Maria, and the rotation of a ball and the revolution of the earth around the sun leading to usage of the same German verb *drehen*? In other words, what is the common core in conceptualizing turning situations?[13]

---

[11] In contrast to this case, the axes of rotation of turning balls, spinning tops or rolling wheels are called 'internal'.

[12] In these examples, (4.b) and (4.c), I use the clumsy sentence with PP *um die Sonne*, since *Die Erde dreht sich* sentences are preferentially interpreted as referring to rotation with internal axis.

[13] By 'common core' I refer to abstract representational schemata on the conceptual level, which have to be extended with specific information from the linguistic—or extra-linguistic—context, not to a prototype (see Jackendoff (1996*b*) on polysemy).

Q2   What distinguishes the turning of Maria from the turning of a ball or the revolution of the earth, and which aspects of turning are responsible for the differences in the semantic judgments of using directional PPs or modification by rotational adverbs?

I will conclude this section by giving a preliminary answer to parts of question 2: since people possess intrinsic orientations, their turning actions can be characterized by changes of the intrinsic orientation, which are caused by this turning. Specifically, the resulting orientation can be specified by the linguistic means of a directional PP. On the other hand, balls or the earth do not possess an intrinsic orientation. Thus, it is not possible to refer to changes of their orientation, and as a consequence, the rotation of a ball or the revolution of the earth cannot be characterized by a resulting orientation.

7.3   Conceptual Semantics for the German Verb *drehen*

7.3.1   Orientation and change of orientation[14]

Objects can only be oriented if they have a distinguished AXIS. For example, in describing a ship as oriented *to the north*, we refer implicitly to the maximal axis of its hull. On the other hand, the orientation of the masts—strictly speaking, the difference in alignment between verticality and the ship's secondary axis induced by them—is perceptual evidence for a vessel's lift during a strong storm. Both types of axes—primary as well as secondary—are mainly based on the spatial properties of the objects and can be ascribed to them by use of visually perceivable spatial information. This idea can be based on Biederman's (1987) recognition-by-component approach in two ways: (1) For one-geon objects the specifying axis is the primary one. Other, orthogonal axes—for example in the case of a brick; see Lang (1990) for a kindred approach—can function as secondary or even ternary axes; (2) for two-geon or more-than-two-geon objects often—as in the case of a vessel—there exist perceptually or functionally distinguished geons, that provide a primary axis. As the example of a vessel demonstrates, axes based on visual, geometrical properties of an object are mostly connected with its functional properties: the geometrically prominent, maximal axis of a ship hull, is also the functional prominent axis of the 'direction of intended regular motion'—in contrast to a (mostly unintended) drift off of a ship.

The axis system of humans exemplifies the intricate relationship between spatially determined axes and their functional properties. In particular, functionality influences the determining of relevance or salience of an axis, for

---

[14] The conception of ORIENTATION used in this chapter is described in more detail in Schmidtke *et al.* (2003). In the present chapter I give only an overview on the geometrical framework to the analysis of direction and orientation, and apply this framework in the analysis of turning-situations in general and the German verb *drehen* in particular.

example the spatially prominent HEAD-TO-FEET AXIS of the human body seems not to be its functionally primary axis. In most situations, the FRONT–BACK AXIS—connected to important functions of interaction with the environment, as visual perception, locomotion, and manipulation—is functionally more important (H. H. Clark, 1973; Franklin and Tversky, 1990; Tversky, 1996).

The idea of AXES provides one important way to characterize SPATIAL REFERENCE SYSTEMS (SRS), which are the fundamental structures for the usage of spatial concepts in language and cognition (Carlson, 1999; Eschenbach, 1999). Axes are the basis of most geometrical models of SRS, which I call 'frames of reference' (Eschenbach, 1999). I characterize the SRs providing orientations by systems of axes that are characterized by *half-lines* (cf. Schmidtke *et al.*, 2003). This conception of SRSs is sometimes described as a system of so called 'half-axes', for example, in the case of humans these are: FRONT-, BACK-, HEAD-, FEET-, LEFT-, and RIGHT-AXIS. These six axes constitute a system of three pairs of axes, namely (FRONT-AXIS, BACK-AXIS), (HEAD-AXIS, FEET-AXIS), and (LEFT-AXIS, RIGHT-AXIS), each pair consisting of two axes opposite to each other.[15]

By use of the geometric concept *equidirection*—cf. Schmidtke *et al.* (2003)—it is possible to distinguish between the following relations between two objects, (1) having the same orientation, (2) having opposite orientations, and (3) being differently oriented, but having opposite orientations. ORIENTATION and CHANGE OF ORIENTATION are the core concepts for the description of turning situations. I will now exemplify this with sentence (2.c) now renumbered as (5), which describes a situation as depicted in Fig. 7.2.

(5) *Maria dreht sich zum Fenster.   Maria turns REFL towards the window.*

This situation can be specified as follows: (i) Maria performs a movement of her body, which changes her orientation. (ii) The movement results in an orientation towards the window. (iii) When she started this movement, she had an orientation different from her final orientation, that is she was not oriented to the window. The beginning and the end of the action described by (5) are depicted in Fig. 7.2 with Maria's orientation given by her FRONT-AXIS. To sum up, this analysis of *drehen* is based on ORIENTATION and CHANGE OF ORIENTATION specified as follows: ORIENTATION is characterized by a *half-line* directed towards a *region* (in space), for example the region of the window mentioned in (5). CHANGE OF ORIENTATION depends on regarding two or more orientations as being different, specified by *equidirection*, for example the orientations specified by Maria's FRONT-AXIS at time t_s and at time t_e.

In Fig. 7.2, Maria's orientation is depicted via a FRONT-AXIS that is induced by her head. Although the head-induced axis is of primary importance, there are

---

[15] The reader should be aware that a pair (FRONT-AXIS, BACK-AXIS), that is geometrically characterized by two *half-lines*, differs from a FRONT-BACK-AXIS, that would geometrically be characterized by one *line*.

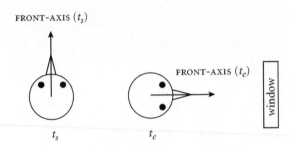

FIG. 7.2. Turning towards a window.

other body-induced axes, especially the trunk-induced, that can be used as a basis of a person's orientation, too. Furthermore, since the head-induced axis and the trunk-induced axis have most of the time—completely or nearly—the same orientation, this common orientation, that I call BODY ORIENTATION, is seen as the standard orientation of a person. Since sentence (5) does not give information about a specific axis, (5) is interpreted as a turning with respect to one of the two primary axes, head-induced axis or trunk-induced axis. Dependency and independency between the orientations of an object as a whole, for example the human body, and some parts, for example the head, the trunk, or the back, has to be considered in production and comprehension of *drehen* expressions such as (6).

(6) a. *Maria dreht den Kopf zum Fenster.*   *Maria turns her head towards the window.*

   b. *Maria dreht ihren Rücken zum Fenster.*   *Maria turns her back towards the window.*

   b′. *Maria dreht sich mit dem Rücken zum Fenster.*   *Maria turns REFL with the back towards the window.*

   c. *Maria dreht sich mit dem Kopf zum Fenster.*   *Maria turns REFL with the head towards the window.*

Sentence (6.a) gives—through the object NP *den Kopf* (*the head*)—specific information about the body part, which Maria turns. Therefore, the resulting state of the CHANGE OF ORIENTATION is specified by FRONT-AXIS (HEAD_OF (Maria)), see Fig. 7.3a. Comprehension of (6.a) leads to the assumption that head orientation and body orientation of Maria are uncoupled. (6.b) has syntactically the same structure as (6.a): having the same agent, Maria, while the entities which are the BEARERS OF TURNING, head or back, are different. Thus for (6.b), the reference axis of the CHANGE OF ORIENTATION has to be provided by another part of Maria's body, namely the back, formally, BACK_OF (Maria). Therefore, a body-part specific FRONT-AXIS is chosen specified by the *half-line* beginning at the center of the body and crossing the surface of the body part in question,

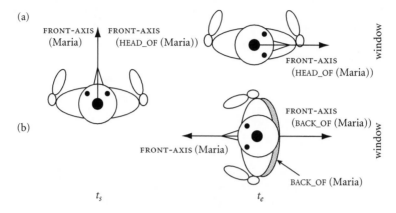

FIG. 7.3. Changing the orientation of the head or of the back.

for example the back, in its center, as depicted in Fig. 7.3b.[16] That FRONT-AXIS (BACK_OF(Maria)) and BACK-AXIS (Maria) have the same orientation, is due to the anatomy of human beings, namely that the trunk and the back (as part of the trunk) cannot be uncoupled, and more specifically, that the front and the back of human beings are oppositely oriented—in contrast to horses, for example. In sentence (6.b′) Maria is agent as well as—via the reflexive *sich*—BEARER OF TURNING. The PP *mit dem Rücken* gives information to allow a choice of an appropriate axis and by this to select a distinguished orientation. The resulting axis and orientation are identical to that induced by (6.b), but the perspectives are different: whereas in sentence (6.b′) Maria's back plays the role of an orientation device and Maria's body is the object to be reoriented, in (6.b) Maria's back is the primary object of turning and, due to human anatomy, her body performs a turning, too. In contrast to the human back, our head can take another orientation to our trunk (cf. Fig. 7.3a). Therefore, the situations described by (6.a) and by (6.c) are different: analogously to (6.b′) the PP *mit dem Kopf* provides an orientation, which is specified by an axis from the center of the body through the head, and which has the function of orientation device for the turning of the whole body. (Note, that this axis is different from the head's front axis.) Thus, a typical situation described by (6.c) is—for example—a reorientation of a person lying on the floor or changing sleeping position in a hotel bed.

To summarize, in specific situations—as depicted in Fig. 7.3a, in which the head orientation and body orientation are uncoupled—it is necessary to make explicit which of the canonical orientations, induced by a major function of

---

[16] This characterization, that obviously neglects some aspects of three-dimensional space, is sufficient for the purpose of the present chapter. To consider three-dimensional geometry and three-dimensional space, the conception of FRONT-AXIS has to be extended to a family of *equidirected* FRONT-AXES. Geometric characterizations of this type are presented in Schmidtke *et al.*, 2003.

interacting with the environment, is used. Whether focusing on the orientation of a body part—instead of mentioning the orientation of a person—leads to an orientation different to the orientation of the person, is a matter of human anatomy, not of language.

7.3.2   *drehen*—Linguistic characterization and geometric specification

The analysis of sentence (5) can be characterized as a 'precondition–postcondition' analysis. Conceptualizing the turning situation as an event leading to a result takes two orientations of the BEARER OF TURNING into consideration: (a) its final orientation has to be considered, and (b) the distinctness of the initial and the final orientation has to be guaranteed. These orientations are given by the FRONT-AXIS with respect to the selected spatial reference system of the bearer of turning, SRS(BOC)—in the following I use the more general term BEARER OF CHANGE OF ORIENTATION, abbreviated by BOC. Since orientations are time dependent, time parameters have to be considered. The distinctness condition (b) for initial and final orientation can be specified in a formal manner by (7.a). '*front-axis*(SRS(x, t))' refers to the *half-line* that represents the FRONT-AXIS of a SPATIAL REFERENCE SYSTEM provided by an object x at time t. In other words, it is not the case that the FRONT-AXIS of the bearer's selected system of reference at time t_s, that is when the turning starts, has the SAME ORIENTATION AS the FRONT-AXIS at t_e, that is when the turning ends.

(7.a) $\neg$ [*front-axis*(SRS(BoC, t_s)) $\upuparrows$ *front-axis*(SRS(BoC, t_e))]

($\upuparrows$ standing for '*equidirected*' is the geometric means of specifying 'having the same orientation'; for details, see Schmidtke *et al.* (2003).)

Furthermore, the geometrical specification of being oriented towards a region has to be part of the analysis of sentence (5). This can be done using the relation $\otimes$, which holds for *lines* or *half-lines* and *regions* having common *points*, that is points which overlap. (7.b) exemplifies this for the specific entities involved in the situation described by (5).

(7.b)   *front-axis*(SRS(*Maria*, t_e)) $\otimes$ *region*(*window*)

Thus, the geometric characterization (7.c) of a *drehen dir.PP* construction, that is a construction of the type *X turns towards Y* which specifies the FINAL ORIENTATION (fin.or), contains two parts, the specification of the resulting orientation and the distinctness condition.

(7.c)   drehen_fin.or $(X, Y, t_s, t_e) \Rightarrow$ *front-axis*(SRS(X, t_e)) $\otimes$ *region*(Y)
   $\neg$[*front-axis*(SRS(X, t_s)) $\upuparrows$ *front-axis*(SRS(X, t_e))]

If only *Maria dreht sich* is uttered—that is if no directional PP, for example *zum Fenster*, is mentioned explicitly—then there is no verbally specified postcondition of Maria's change of orientation. As a consequence, the distinctness condition

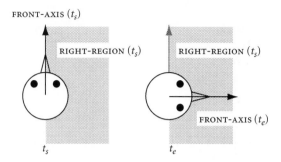

FIG. 7.4. Reorientation with respect to two temporal instances of one spatial reference system.

(7.a) concerns the difference between the orientation when the turning starts, and some subsequent orientation (at time $t > t_s$). This leads to condition (8) constituting the core meaning of *drehen* for those objects X that possess a distinguished orientation.

(8)   drehen $(X, t_s, t_e) \Leftrightarrow \exists t : [t_s < t \leq t_e] \wedge \neg [front\text{-}axis(\text{Srs}(X, t_s))$
        $\Uparrow front\text{-}axis(\text{Srs}(X, t))]$[17]

Up to now, we have discussed anchoring in an external system: the window as reference object specifying the final orientation is independent from Maria's reference system which is basic for the change of orientation. In sentence (9) the expression *nach rechts* specifies the final orientation of the turning with respect to a reference region dependent on Maria. Two instances of the reference system induced by Maria are involved (see Fig. 7.4). The first instance provided by the beginning of the turning at time t_s, establishes a *front-axis*(Srs(*Maria*, t_s)) and a specific region, *right-region*(Srs(*Maria*, t_s)).[18] The second instance—considering the resulting state of the turning at time t_e—supplies the *front-axis*(Srs(*Maria*, t_e)), which has to be anchored with respect to the *right-region* of the t_s-instance, to determine the final orientation (10). What is to the right of Maria at the end of the turning, that is at time t_e, is not relevant for specifying the turning; only what is to her right when starting the turning (time t_s) determines a possible final orientation. Both types of directional adverbials, that is *zum Fenster* and *nach rechts*, constrain the final orientation by an overlap condition, that is they provide

---

[17] Van der Zee (2000) proposes GOING_AROUND(x, AXIS_OF(y)) for the lexical structure of *draaien*, which is the Dutch counterpart of *drehen* (I use here an adaptation of van der Zee's notation). Whereas van der Zee starts with the MOTION aspect of *draaien*, and thus discusses PATHS induced by the verb, I focus on the CHANGE OF ORIENTATION aspect of *drehen*, and thus ORIENTATION of an object in motion. Both aspects are systematically interrelated, in language and cognition as well as in physical reality of solid objects, Habel (1999).

[18] The concept RIGHT REGION and its geometric counterpart *right region* are based on Eschenbach and Kulik (1997) and Eschenbach *et al.* (2002). In Eschenbach (Ch. 6) the kindred geometric concept *p-right-space* is used in the analysis of German *rechts* ('right of').

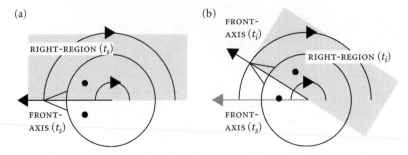

FIG. 7.5. Turning clockwise.

a region, which has to overlap with the *front-axis* determining the final orientation (compare (7.b) and (10)).

(9) *Maria dreht sich nach rechts.*   *Maria turns to the right.*
(10) *front-axis*(SRS(*Maria, t_e*)) ⊗ *right-region*(SRS(*Maria, t_s*))

Now I come back to the case of rotational adverbials such as sentence (2.b), now renumbered as (11), which takes a process perspective on the turning depicted in Fig. 7.1. In other words, not the result of the turning but the course of the turning is foregrounded by the verbal description.

(11) *Maria dreht sich rechtsherum.*   *Maria turns REFL clockwise.*

The adverbial *rechtsherum* specifies the conditions of this process with respect to the concept DIRECTION OF TURNING (see fn. 9). Starting with an initial front axis, that is with *front-axis*(t_s), there are two possible options to changing orientation, namely to orient towards RIGHT-REGION(t_s) or towards LEFT-REGION(t_s). But the condition for *rechtsherum drehen*, that is for a clockwise turning, is stricter than the condition (10) for *nach rechts drehen*: at any time t_i during such a turning the same condition, namely to orient immediately after t_i towards RIGHT-REGION(t_i), holds (see Fig. 7.5).

This has two relevant consequences, which I want to mention here: (a) the DIRECTION OF TURNING, that is the rotational direction, of a clockwise turning is persistent, and (b) the final orientation of a clockwise turning does not have to be in *right-region*(t_s), that is turning clockwise and turning to the right are different changes of orientation. The idea of persistence of rotational direction can be formally specified using different methods. In the following I present a characterization of *turning clockwise* continuously, (12), which focuses on the most important properties of rotational direction and thus of rotational adverbials.[19]

---

[19] Cases of discrete or interrupted turning, for example the movement of a minute hand taking discrete one-minute steps, require some modifications of condition (iii) and of the sequences of time entities to be considered. Since during the phases of standstill of the bearer of turning the betweenness condition (iii) would not be fulfilled, it has to be weakened.

(12) drehen_rot.dir $(X, \textbf{right}, t_s, t_e) \Rightarrow$
There is a sequence $t_0, t_1, \ldots t_{n-1}, t_n$ of time entities, with $t_0 = t_s$ and
$t_n = t_e$, such that for all $i = 0, \ldots n - 1$ holds:
(i) $t_i < t_{i+1}$
(ii) $front\text{-}axis(\textsc{Srs}(X, t_{i+1})) \otimes right\text{-}region(\textsc{Srs}(X, t_i))$
(iii) for all t^*, with $t_i < t^* < t_{i+1}$:
$[front\text{-}axis(\textsc{Srs}(X, t^*)) \otimes right\text{-}region(\textsc{Srs}(X, t_i))] \wedge$
$[front\text{-}axis(\textsc{Srs}(X, t^*)) \otimes left\text{-}region(\textsc{Srs}(X, t_{i+1}))]$

Condition (i) says that the temporal entities, which are used in this specification, are ordered: t_s is the first and t_e the last element of the sequence. Condition (ii) specifies that for every time t_i the next element of the sequence is in the respective *right-region*(t_i), thus, (ii) guarantees the persistency property. And (iii) states that between the time t_i and the time t_{i+1} the front axis of the bearer is oriented between the orientation *front-axis*(t_i) and *front-axis*(t_{i+1}).[20] The parameter RIGHT in (12) is an abbreviation for the contribution of the rotational adverb *rechtsherum*. Thus, for the independent characterization of the meaning of *rechtsherum* the condition schema for the sequence $t_0, \ldots, t_n$ has to be abstracted from characterization (12).[21]

Applying characterization (12) in the conceptual analysis of sentence (9) leads to intended consequences. First, the condition schema for the sequence of temporal entities corresponds to the process interpretation of (9), and second, since characterization (12) does not contain any constraint that relates the final orientation to the initial orientation, no information about this final orientation has to be coded in natural language.

On the other hand, the combination of a directional PP and a rotational adverbial as in (13.a) is possible. Combining the two characterizations the following happens: The directional PP contributes the condition on the final orientation (13.b) and the rotational adverb specifies the direction of turning (13.c), via the characterization schema (12). The condition about distinctness of initial and final orientation (13.d, corresponding to 7.c), which is contributed by the directional PP, does not conflict with the conditions (13.c) given by *linksherum*.

(13) a. *Maria dreht sich*   Maria turns REFL anticlockwise
linksherum zur Tür.   towards the door.

---

[20] From a mathematical point of view, characterization (12), especially condition (iii), is based on assuming the density of orientations. Thus the formalization given here is suitable both for dense and for continuous models of space and time. 'Betweenness of directions' is described in detail in Schmidtke *et al.* (2003).
[21] I skip this step in presenting the formal characterizations, since it would produce a detour from the main argument. The term 'abstract' gives a hint of the type of formal language I propose for the complete characterization, namely λ-expressions.

   b. *front-axis*(Srs(*Maria*, t_e)) $\otimes$ *region*(door)
   c. (ii) *front-axis*(Srs(*Maria*, t_{i+1})) $\otimes$ *left-region*(Srs(*Maria*, t_i))
      (iii) for all t^*, with $t_i < t^* < t_{i+1}$:
        [*front-axis*(Srs(*Maria*, t^*)) $\otimes$ *left-region*(Srs(*Maria*, t_i))] $\wedge$
        [*front-axis*(Srs(*Maria*, t^*)) $\otimes$ *right-region*(Srs(*Maria*, t_{i+1}))]
   d. $\neg$ [*front-axis*(Srs(*Maria*, t_s)) $\upuparrows$ *front-axis*(Srs(*Maria*, t_e))]

I conclude this section focusing on an important aspect that all types of change of orientation have in common: in describing a change of orientation, it is necessary to consider more than one spatial reference system at a time, namely at least two Srs, that are—temporally determined—instances of the frame of reference of the BEARER OF CHANGE OF ORIENTATION. To conceptualize a movement as a CHANGE OF ORIENTATION presupposes that two different ORIENTATIONS are involved in the movement, and this difference is the manifestation of two Srs provided by the object performing the movement.

7.3.3 Turning balls, knobs, and screws

The analyses presented in Sections 7.3.1 and 7.3.2 are based on canonical orientations of an object. In other words, they are based on the existence of a spatial reference system induced by the BEARER OF TURNING, which provides a time-variant *front-axis*(Srs(BOC, t)). In this section I will discuss how the prior analyses of turning objects with canonical orientations have to be extended for analyzing sentences such as (3), which describe situations containing turning balls, that is objects, which do not possess a spatial reference system providing FRONT-AXES.

    The absence of a canonical FRONT-AXIS(Srs(BOC, t)) explains why both instances from (3.c)—renumbered as (14.a)—are not acceptable. The use of the directional PP *zum Fenster* requires that the FRONT-AXIS of the BEARER OF TURNING is taken into consideration. On the other hand, the question is open why both variants of (14.b) = (3.b) are fully acceptable.

(14) a. **Maria dreht den Ball zum Fenster.*   **Der Ball dreht sich zum Fenster.*

      Maria turns the ball towards the window.   *The ball turns REFL towards the window.*

   b. *Maria dreht den Ball rechtsherum.*   *Der Ball dreht sich rechtsherum.*

      Maria turns the ball clockwise.   *The ball turns REFL clockwise.*

Even if an object, as a ball, does not possess an appropriate spatial reference system of its own, it is possible that the object inherits the relevant information about rotation otherwise. I start with a gedanken-experiment: we choose any point on the surface of a rotating ball we like, which is not on the axis of rotation, for example point₁ of Fig. 7.6a. During rotation of the ball this point changes its place. Now we look on that axis that begins at the axis of rotation and that meets

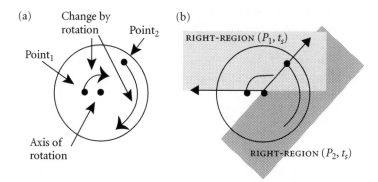

FIG. 7.6. Rotation of a ball.

point$_1$, compare Fig. 7.6b. This axis, *front-axis*(Srs(*ball*, P_1, t_s)), which is induced by point$_1$, also specifies a *right-region*(Srs(*ball*, P_1, t_s)). The same gedanken-experiment is possible with respect to other points on the surface, for example point$_2$. Since the ball is a solid object, a rotation of the ball leads to a regular behavior in changes of orientation for the *front-axis*(Srs(*ball*, P^*, t_s)) of all points P^* not on the axis of rotation: the characterization of turning clockwise (12) holds either for all points of the ball not lying on the rotational axis or for none of these points.

In other words, any point of the ball not lying on the axis of rotation is a good representative for characterizing rotational direction. This property is central for perceiving a rotation visually or haptically. But note that assigning a rotational direction, that is conceptualizing it as clockwise or counterclockwise, can depend on the position of the observer.

In contrast to rotational adverbs, using the choosing-any-point-you-like method is not successful with respect to combinations of *drehen* with a directional PP, as in (14.a). The directional PP requires the fulfillment of a final orientation condition of type (7.b). Using the corresponding condition (14.c), different points P^*—with different directed *front-axes*(Srs(*ball*, P^*, t_e))—could lead to different conditions on final orientation. Thus, this method cannot provide a final orientation of the ball.

(14.c)   **front-axis**(Srs(*ball*, P^*, t_e)) ⊗ **region**(*window*)

To summarize, by the choosing-any-point-you-like method it is only possible to choose P_1-specific *front-axes*, but it is not possible to determine a unique *front-axis* of the ball, and thus to conceptualize a FRONT-AXIS of the ball. As a consequence, this method is sufficient to specify whether there is any rotation at all, or what the rotational direction is, but it is—due to the absence of a unique FRONT-AXIS—too weak to specify other relevant conditions, as the final orientation condition. For extreme cases, as a ball with one perceptually salient, distinguished dot on the surface, the analysis given above predicts that some people will accept (14.a), since they conceptualize *front-axis*(Srs(*ball, dot, t*)) as *front-axis*(Srs(*ball, t*)), whereas other people will see (14.a) as not acceptable, since they do not allow a FRONT-AXIS to be attributed to balls.

These analyses given for turning balls are transferable to other rotating objects without inherent spatial reference systems. This is independent of the type of rotation, namely whether the rotational axis is internal, as in the case of the ball or of a carousel, or whether the rotational axis is external, as in the case of the earth revolving around the sun, cf. (4). (15.a), internal axis of rotation, as well as (15.b), external axis of rotation, seem to be not fully acceptable, which is due to the fact that there is no regular position of an observer that would justify a distinction between clockwise and counterclockwise.[22]

(15) a. ?*Die Erde dreht sich rechtsherum.*   *The earth revolves clockwise.*
     b. ?*Die Erde dreht sich rechtsherum*   *The earth revolves clockwise*
       um die Sonne.   *around the sun.*

I will now come back to the influence of functional properties on verbal description of *drehen*-situations. I focus in the following mainly on the use of directional PPs in turning descriptions with respect to objects that can possess functionally determined Srs, for example chairs, plants, doorknobs, keys, and screws.

(16) a. *Maria dreht den Stuhl zum Fenster.*   *Maria turns the chair towards the window.*
     b. *Maria dreht die Palme zum Fenster.*   *Maria turns the palm (tree) towards the window.*
     c. *Maria dreht die Stehlampe zum Schreibtisch.*   *Maria turns the floor lamp towards the desk.*
     c'. *Dreh die Stehlampe bitte zum Schreibtisch.*   *Please, turn the floor lamp towards the desk.*

Following the analyses I have proposed above the object that performs a turning, that is the BEARER OF TURNING, has to provide a *front-axis* connected with an Srs to specify the final-orientation of *drehen*. In (16.a), the FRONT-AXIS of the chair is induced via the primary function of chairs, namely the function to sit on them, that is the *front-axis* of a (regular) chair is *equidirected* with the axis of perception of a person sitting on the chair; see Fillmore (1997) and Miller and Johnson-Laird (1976) for this type of argumentation. But, if the chair in question does not stand up but is lying, its functional front is not primary any more. Thus the hearer of (16.a) could also assume a geometrically salient axis, for example given by the back of the chair, as specifying the final orientation towards the window. In contrast to artifacts such as chairs, plants possess other functional properties and

---

[22] This acceptability rating changes to 'fully acceptable', if a globe, that is a concrete small-scale model of earth, is referred to. I thank the editors for this example.

relations to provide SRs and *front-axes*. In the case of (16.b), there is a functional interaction between the plant and its environment, which makes available an SRs, namely the relationship between a plant needing light for photosynthesis and a window as a source of light. Since regular sources of light often have an effect on the shape and structure of indoor plants, the TOWARD_THE_LIGHT_SIDE of a plant, that is the side which in the past was regularly oriented to light, as well as its OPPOSITE_TO_THE_LIGHT_SIDE, that is the side which in the past was not regularly oriented to light, are visually perceivable in most cases. Thus, due to different functional consequences, two standard interpretations of (16.b) exist, that can be paraphrased as follows: 'Maria turns the palm such that {*the 'light'-side/the 'shadow'-side*} of the palm will be directed to the window after finishing the act of turning, since she wants {*not to change/to change*} the conditions of regular lighting'. Case (16.c–c′) combines both types of functional aspects discussed above: the functionally determined *front-axis* of the lamp is *equidirected* with the *line* of light given by the lamp. Furthermore, the function of a desk, namely to perform acts of writing or reading on specific subareas of the top of the desk, can influence how the SRs is imposed on an individual desk. If, for example, Maria uses the left half of her desk for doing computer work, and the right half for paperwork and reading, than comprehending (16.c)—in visual awareness of the situation—or following the request (16.c′) should make use of a FINAL ORIENTATION of the lamp towards the right half of the desk.[23]

I conclude this section with a short discussion of objects whose functional prominent axes are identical with the axes of rotation, for example doorknobs, keys, and screws. Since there is no other salient axis of a doorknob or a key in those situations in which these artifacts are used to fulfill their intended function, in German, verbal descriptions of their turning show linguistically and conceptually similar behavior to that of rotating balls (17). The usage of *drehen* + rotational adverbs is prominent whereas *drehen* + directional PPs is less, or not acceptable. In the specific construction using the directional adverbial *nach rechts*, there is a widespread tendency in German to accept this for some types of these objects (without prominent axes), and to reject it for other types: doorknobs and keys belong to different classes (17.a, b).[24] On the other hand, a key lying on a table can be turned in direction toward another object. In this case, the

---

[23] Carlson (2000) argues convincingly for the influence of function on imposing reference frames. Her studies consider primarily the case of projective spatial relations, for example ABOVE, in situations in which the spatial reference system provided by the reference object has primary influence on processing spatial relations. In contrast, for CHANGE OF ORIENTATION situations the reference system of the BEARER OF TURNING has the primary influence. Nevertheless, I assume that Carlson's view on functional influence holds for the case of CHANGE OF ORIENTATION situations in a corresponding manner. The example (16.c–c′) shows how stimuli for experimental investigations could be designed.

[24] Currently, it is unclear which properties of objects with rotational axes but without a visually or geometrically prominent secondary axis determine that combinations of *drehen* with *nach rechts* are used more or less frequently.

shape of the key induced by the main axis, which is the axis of rotation with respect to the intended function, provides a perceptually induced axis determining the FRONT of the key.

(17) a. *Maria dreht den   Türknopf rechtsherum. *nach rechts. *zur Wand.*
     *Maria turns the   doorknob clockwise.   *to the right. *towards the wall.*
  b. *Maria dreht den   Schlüssel rechtsherum. nach rechts. *zur Wand.*
     *Maria turns the   key   clockwise.   to the right.   *towards the wall.*

Furthermore, other artifacts, such as screws, can lead to other types of *drehen* + directional PPs, as in (18). Knowledge about the functional properties of screws is necessary to interpret the spatial change described by (18). Since we know, that in the turning of a screw two changes in space interact, namely a rotation and— caused by this—a movement in the direction of axis of rotation, it is possible to use the conceptual contribution of the directional PP as specification of the second, inferred movement.

(18)   *Maria dreht die Schraube in den   Maria turns the screw into the*
      Tisch.   table.

7.4 Conclusion

The German verb *drehen*, which corresponds to members of the English group of verbs containing *turn*, *rotate*, and *revolve*, possesses a complex behavior pattern in combination with adverbials specifying direction of rotation. The conceptual analyses of these linguistic ways of describing turning situations give evidence about the inventory on the conceptual level: spatial reference systems, SRSs, which induce a system of axes, are the core basis for conceptualizing and describing turning situations. The SRS provides further concepts, as FRONT-AXIS and RIGHT-REGION, which are the conceptual basis for characterizing the meaning of *drehen* as well as for the specification of the contribution of rotational adverbs and directional PPs to the meaning of the whole sentence. Furthermore, functional properties of the bearer of motion, that is the object, which performs the turning or rotation, determine the specific SRS, which is selected in production or comprehension of the sentence in question.

8

Between Space and Function: How Spatial and Functional Features Determine the Comprehension of *between*

EMILE VAN DER ZEE and MATT WATSON

Abstract

It is often assumed that the spatial meaning of *between* is only based on *spatial features* (geometrically definable cognitive representations; see, e.g. Johnston and Slobin, 1979). This chapter first considers how spatial features represent the meaning of *between*. It then considers a possible impact of *visual functional features* (visually perceived spatial features, like cartoon-like eyes, that invite a particular object categorization, such as 'this is an animal'), *linguistic functional features* (lexical concepts inviting a particular categorization, as derived from 'this is a thumb'), *general functional features* (features contributed by cognitive processes found across cognitive systems, like cognitive effort), and *dynamic–kinematic features* (features specifying actual or potential interactions between physical entities). After considering why *between* can correspond to more than one *spatial prototype* it is discussed which of the above features are *lexical features*, which features are *contextual features*, and how features of different types may interact to specify the meaning of *between* in context.

Feature

A feature is a cognitive representation of some aspect of the internal or external world.

8.1   Introduction

Let us start by considering some linguistic facts about the English preposition *between*. What does *between* refer to? The following sentence provides an example in which *between* is used:

(1)   Our car is between those trees.

It appears that *those trees* in (1) must be interpreted so that the car is standing between two trees, or two groups of trees. If one were to assign a reading to *those trees* in which there are, for example, three trees, an English native speaker would no longer find the example acceptable. This means that English *between* is different from, for example, Dutch *tussen*, French *entre*, and German *zwischen* (see Habel, 1989). In these languages an example like (1) can be used to describe a situation in which a car is among more than two trees, while these trees are not grouped together as two separate entities. In English *between* thus refers to a situation in which a *Figure* (e.g. the car in (1)) is located in relation to two *Referents* (e.g. two trees or two groups of trees).

Between belongs to a small family of prepositions that is sensitive to the number of Referents involved, as well as to the distribution of those Referents. For example, *among(st)* refers to the location of a Figure relative to a small set of Referents, and *amid(st)* refers to the location of a Figure in relation to as many Referents as are necessary to be conceptualized as a continuous mass (Talmy, 2000, pp. 191–2). In both cases, however, the Referents must surround the Figure. *In the middle of* seems to have a similar meaning as *amid(st)*, with the extra requirement that the Figure must be located close to the perceived midpoint of the entities forming the Referent structure. *Betwixt* and *in between* behave like *between*. These prepositions describe the location of a Figure in relation to two Referents. As in the case of *between* the Referents cannot be just anywhere in relation to the Figure. If two Referents are on one side of the Figure, *between* cannot be used. So, what Referent distributions are allowed? The next section considers what Referent distributions are permitted, and which spatial features define such distributions.

8.2   Spatial Features Representing Referent Distributions

8.2.1   Ordered space

Johnston and Slobin (1979, pp. 530–1) argue that '*between*...requires a coordination of two proximity relations' and O'Keefe (1996, p. 300) writes that 'A...definition of *between* is that the sum of the distances from each of the reference entities to the target entity is not greater than the distance between

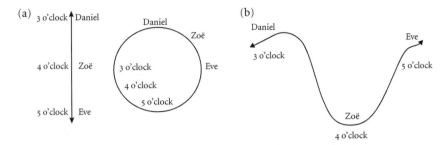

FIG. 8.1. The one-dimensional version of ordered space can be formalized as a path, connecting different points in time or space, thus defining a point in space or time between two other points.

the two reference entities'. Both statements thus indicate that *between* assumes an ordering of space. How could such an ordering be defined?

In discussing the meaning of German *zwischen* ('between') Habel (1989) describes ordered space in terms of an ordering of points along a path. Informally, if a path can be constructed from A to B, and from B to C, then B is between A and C. This idea covers all one-dimensional and higher dimensional orderings in time and space. For example it can explain why 4 o'clock is between 3 o'clock and 5 o'clock, and why Zoë is between Eve and Daniel, no matter what the shape of the path through time or space is, or what inherent direction the path has (Fig. 8.1).

Ordering space in terms of a path assumes that the Figure and the two Referents can be idealized as points: a starting point, an endpoint, and a point on the same path not equal to the starting point or endpoint. Such an idealization is not always desirable, however, as we will see in the next section.

8.2.2   Idealized geometric structures and spatial prototypes

Talmy (2000, p. 191) observes that *between* locates one entity in relation to two other entities, the latter of which can be schematized as point-like structures. Figure 8.2, however, shows that idealizing two Referents as two point-like structures leads to a loss of information about the internal structure of the between-region. In Figs 8.2a and 8.2b the Referents are elongated shapes. Differences in Figure positions with respect to Referents give rise to differences in the acceptability of *x* being *between y and z*.

Hayward and Tarr (1995), Logan and Sadler (1996), and Regier and Carlson (2001) show that locative expressions like *above x* do not refer to an isotropic region in space. Locative prepositional phrases like *above x* correspond to a *spatial prototype*, giving rise to a region of graded acceptability for such a phrase. Figure 8.2 points out that a theory on the meaning of *between* should not only

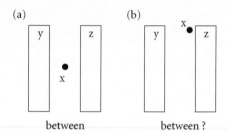

FIG. 8.2. If two Referents are not idealized as point-like structures the between-region behaves like a spatial prototype, that is by having different levels of acceptability at which *between* applies.

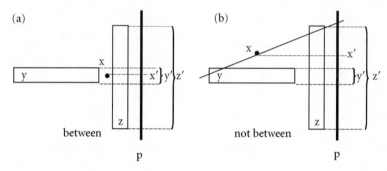

FIG. 8.3. The projections x′, y′, and z′ of x, y, and z on projection plane p must be such that x′ is included in y′ and z′ (compare a and b).

account for the number of Referents involved, and their distribution, but also for the non-isotropic nature of a between-region. The spatial features discussed below focus on all these aspects.

8.2.3   Projection

In Fig. 8.3b a line first intersects y, then x, and finally z. But, even though space is ordered, English native speakers could not say that *x is between y and z*. Van der Zee, Watson, and Fletcher (submitted) argue that it follows from Fig. 8.3a that for x to be *between y and z* space must not only be ordered, but that there must also be a projection plane p containing the projections x′, y′, and z′ of x, y, and z respectively, on which x′ must be included as a part of both y′ and z′.

8.2.4   Representing the projection plane in a reference frame

There is a widespread misunderstanding that the meaning of *between* is not based on direction or the use of a reference frame. (e.g. Landau and Jackendoff, 1993;

O'Keefe, 1996). Van der Zee, Watson, and Fletcher (submitted) show as well, that *between* is a preposition that—like *above* and *to the left of*—assumes the use of a reference frame. If one would turn the page such that the line intersecting x, y, and z in Fig. 8.3b is parallel to your line of sight (which thus forms the projection plane), it may be possible to say that *x is between y and z.* This shows that also the reference frame in which the projection plane is represented has an influence on the comprehension of *between*.

8.2.5   Boundaries for the spatial prototype *between y and z*

The region representing *between y and z* on the basis of ordered space and projection is called the *BOP region* here (Between based on Ordered space and Projection). Van der Zee, Watson, and Fletcher (submitted) show that subjects put more dots in the BOP region when asked to put a dot between two objects (their experiment 3), and subjects overall assign greater acceptability to dots in this region compared to dots outside this region (experiment 4).

The BOP region, however, is not a reliable representation of the region *between y and z.* As shown in Fig. 8.4, and as argued before, a between-region is not isotropic, and the way in which a BOP region is defined assumes isotropy for such a region. Still, a BOP region can be said to represent the possible outer boundaries of a spatial prototype *between y and z* if no other features but spatial features play a role in a reference situation. The generation of a spatial prototype *between y and z* can be considered as a transformation of the BOP region, internally structuring this region, enlarging it, or changing its shape. High acceptability for *between* along the axis around which the Referents are mirror symmetric in Fig. 8.4b—and low acceptability close to the Referents' contours—can be explained by such a transformation. The remainder of this section considers spatial features transforming the BOP region into a graded structure.

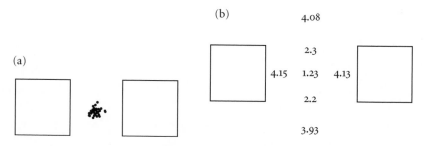

FIG. 8.4. A selection of some results from van der Zee, Watson, and Fletcher (submitted) showing that subjects connect the BOP region with a region between two objects (both in dot placements (a) and acceptability ratings of dots (b)). Ratings are represented at locations of dots rated and range from 1 (highly acceptable) to 7 (not acceptable).

8.2.6   Symmetry

Because using *between* involves access to two Referents, the issue of spatial symmetry automatically presents itself. Wagemans (1995) shows that symmetry detection is an important property of our visual system, and argues that mirror symmetry is perceptually more salient than rotational symmetry. Van der Zee, Watson, and Fletcher (submitted) therefore investigated the use of *between* in relation to both kinds of symmetry.

Figure 8.5 shows that subjects tend to place dots *between two Referents* along an axis around which the Referents are mirror symmetric or rotationally symmetric (experiment 1). If the Referents are close a dot placement task reveals two distinct spatial prototypes in the rotationally symmetric condition (Fig. 8.5b). In the mirror symmetric condition it is less clear whether two distinct prototypes exist (see Fig. 8.5a). The reverse obtains if the inter-Referent distance is larger. This points not only to different effects of rotational symmetry and mirror symmetry, but also to an inter-Referent distance effect. Inter-Referent distance is discussed in Section 8.2.8.

In another experiment (experiment 2) subjects carried out acceptability ratings for *between* in relation to the points shown in Fig. 8.6. Acceptability ratings of the points are higher if the two Referents are mirror symmetric instead of rotationally symmetric around an axis. These results suggest that perceptual saliency—via symmetry type—impacts on the acceptability of *between*.

8.2.7   Inter-referent distance

If we consider the effect of inter-Referent distance on acceptability ratings for *between* a mixed picture presents itself. If square-shaped Referents are involved (as in Fig. 8.4, but rotated to form diamond shapes) acceptability judgments are higher for Referents that are close compared to Referents that are far. However, if elongated Referents are used (as in Fig. 8.5) ratings are better for the far com-

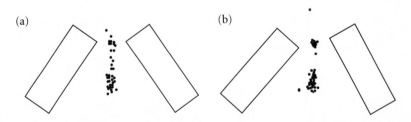

FIG. 8.5. A selection of some results from van der Zee, Watson, and Fletcher (submitted) showing that dot placements tend to cluster along an axis around which Referents are mirror (a) or rotationally symmetric (b).

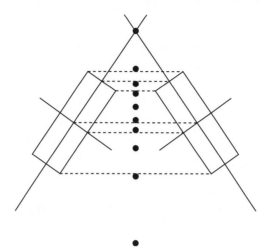

Fig. 8.6. Points for which acceptability ratings for *between* were carried out in van der Zee, Watson, and Fletcher's (submitted) experiments 2 and 7, abstracting over Referent structure orientation, symmetry type, and inter-Referent distance.

pared to the close condition. The latter effect is mainly due to a condition in which the Referents are rotated 180° in relation to the depicted situation in Figs 8.5 and 8.6. This brings us to the issue of possible effects of Referent structure orientation.

8.2.8   Referent structure orientation and shape

If one abstracts from inter-Referent distance there is no overall difference in acceptability of *between* for rectangular-shaped Referents that differ 180° in orientation. However, there is such a difference for square-shaped Referent structures that differ 90° in orientation. In the latter case dots around horizontally aligned Referents give more acceptable *between* judgments than dots around vertically aligned Referents.

8.2.9   Referent contours and centers of gravity

Regier and Carlson (2001) show that acceptability judgments for *above* are influenced by a Referent's contour and center of gravity (see also below). The dot placements in Fig. 8.5 show that one spatial prototype is close to where the Referents' contours meet, and that another prototype is at one center of gravity of the region bounded by a line connecting the close contours and the bottom grazing line. It thus seems that notions playing a role in explaining the graded structure of *above* also play a role in explaining the graded structure of *between*.

8.2.10   Intrinsic referent axes

Van der Zee (1996) and van der Zee and Eshuis (2003) show that the meaning of Dutch directional prepositions like *voor* ('in front of') is specified in relation to the internal axial structure of a Referent. The internal axial structure of a Referent does not influence acceptability judgments for *between* of the points illustrated in Fig. 8.6. This indicates that *between* is not sensitive to just any spatial features considered in isolation.

8.2.11   Spatial feature combinations

Although it was observed that certain spatial features do not have an effect on either dot placements or on acceptability ratings for *between*, it could be argued that a combined influence of such features exists. As shown in Fig. 8.4a many dot placements can be found in the middle of the BOP region. Acceptability judgments for the exact midpoint are also much higher than acceptability judgments for *between* in relation to other points in the same reference situation (see Fig. 8.4b). These results could be due to the intrinsic axes of the BOP region and its center of gravity, and/or to the intrinsic axes of the Referents and the line connecting their centers of gravity—in combination with the axis around which the Referents are mirror symmetric. Whichever alternative is valid as an interpretation of the results in Fig. 8.4, the results are based on a combination of spatial features that in isolation do not have such an impact.

  This section has revealed that certain spatial features impact on the use of *between*, that others don't, but that even if spatial features do not have an impact in isolation they may do so in combination. This leaves us with the question, which spatial features—or combinations—are part of the lexical structure of *between*, and which features are contextual? This question is answered in Section 8.8. Let us first, however, consider some other types of features.

8.3   Visual Functional Features

Landau (1996) showed that cartoon-like eyes and a tail-like feature lead to more object placements and higher acceptability ratings for *in front of* at that side of a circle where the eyes are located. Apparently such visual features enable subjects to determine the function of an object side, namely as having a 'front'. Van der Zee, Watson, and Fletcher (submitted) used cartoon-like eyes to determine whether such features influence the construction of a spatial prototype corresponding to *between y and z*.

  Cartoon-like eyes have a very limited influence on dot placement. Out of thirteen different stimuli with cartoon-like eyes an effect was only found in one case: when two Referents—and their eyes—are oriented such that the eyes are

(a)   (b)   (c)

FIG. 8.7. A selection of some results from van der Zee, Watson, and Fletcher (submitted) showing a slight influence of cartoon-like eyes when they are directed at a shared region (a), compared to a situation in which the eyes look in different directions (b), or where no eyes are present (c).

directed at a shared region (Fig. 8.7). Cartoon-like eyes do not have an influence on acceptability judgments for *between*. In a control experiment van der Zee, Watson, and Fletcher (submitted) determined that there is an influence of the cartoon-like eyes used on acceptability ratings for *in front of*, thereby replicating Landau, and establishing that the absence of an effect for *between* is not due to problems with the stimuli.

The results thus indicate that although visual functional features influence the acceptability of *in front of*, these features only have a limited influence on the use of *between*. But, how is such an influence on *between*—limited though it may be—possible at all, if only spatial features are part of the lexical structure of *between*? The answer to this question is presented in Section 8.8. Let us consider linguistic functional features next.

8.4 Linguistic Functional Features

Using the same stimuli as in Figs 8.5 and 8.6, van der Zee, Watson, and Fletcher (submitted) told subjects that one rectangle represented a thumb and the other rectangle an index finger (experiments 6 and 7). It was assumed that this would invite a categorization of the stimuli on the basis of the lexical concepts THUMB and INDEX FINGER, and in doing so would possibly assign a grasping function to the Referents involved (i.e. a grasping of the dot to be placed, or the point to be rated).

In contrast to the results from the experiments testing spatial features, extra dot clusters are found close to the outer boundaries of the BOP region when the above linguistic functional features are present (Fig. 8.8). Also, in contrast to what was found in the spatial feature experiments, a Referent structure orientation effect is observed when linguistic functional features are present (compare Figs 8.8a and 8.8b). In addition, there are clear spatial prototypes in the close condition compared to the far condition, an effect that is reversed if no linguistic functional features are present.

Acceptability ratings for *between* are also slightly different when linguistic functional features are present, compared to when these features are not present.

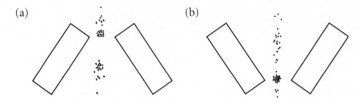

Fig. 8.8. A selection of some results from van der Zee, Watson, and Fletcher (submitted) showing that dot placements tend to cluster in the same areas as in Fig. 8.5, but in addition cluster close to the outer BOP region boundaries (a and b). Comparing (a) with (b) shows that there is an effect of Referent structure orientation.

When linguistic functional features are present acceptability ratings do not show a distance effect, do show a Referent structure orientation effect, and the spatial prototype in the lower BOP region is relatively large. When linguistic functional features are absent the reverse is the case.

The results indicate that linguistically assigning a function to spatial structures, like THUMB and INDEX FINGER, or possibly even GRASP, influences the use of *between*. How can such contextual influences have an effect? Also the answer to this question must be postponed until Section 8.8, where the relative influence of all feature types is discussed. Consider general functional features next.

8.5   General Functional Features

Between seems cognitively more expensive, compared to other locative prepositions. For example, it seems easier to respond to a question *Where is the hammer?* with *in front of the washing machine*, than with *in between the washing machine and the sink*. The former answer seems easier, because it only involves specifying the position of a Figure in relation to one Referent, compared to specifying its position in relation to two Referents. Quinn (this volume, Ch. 19) holds the same factor responsible for the order in which spatial relations are acquired. He finds that children acquire abstract knowledge of the spatial relation BETWEEN between six–seven and nine–ten months, whereas children acquire abstract knowledge of ABOVE and BELOW before six–seven months.

Cognitive effort may thus have a different impact on the use and development of *above* compared to *between*. Does this mean that a feature representing cognitive effort is part of the lexical structure of words? This is highly unlikely. The measurement of cognitive effort is an on-line process, and not the hallmark of our long-term memory for words (the mental lexicon). But, general cognitive features representing such things as cognitive effort, attention, and focus are part of the context in which words are used. In that sense they contribute 'meaning' to a context. Section 8.8 discusses how such features can be built into the contextual meaning of *between*. Consider one more feature type.

8.6   Dynamic–Kinematic Features

Coventry and Garrod (in press) show that also dynamic–kinematic features play a role in the use of *between*. These authors point out that, according to the *Oxford English Dictionary*, *between* locates an object that physically or mentally separates two Referents. They report an experiment in which subjects are either presented with a ball between two rectangles without any alternative connection (Fig. 8.9a), with a loose alternative connection (Fig. 8.9b), or with a rigid alternative connection (Fig. 8.9c).

Because increasingly less control can be attributed to the ball separating the two rectangles when going from Fig. 8.9a to 8.9b and 8.9c, it is predicted that acceptability ratings for *between* drop from 8.9a, to 8.9b, to 8.9c. The authors interpret an empirical confirmation of this prediction as evidence for a role of dynamic–kinematic features. Are such features part of the lexical structure of *between*? Before we can answer this question, and all other questions posed so far, we must briefly consider the relation between *between* and its possible spatial prototypes. We have so far seen that *between* may refer to one spatial prototype, but—depending on the experimental context—also to more spatial prototypes. It is only after clarifying the relation between *between* and its spatial

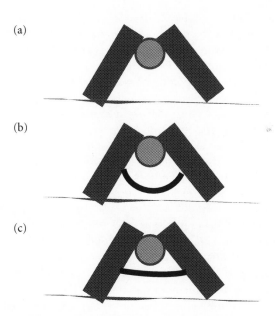

Fig. 8.9. Reference situations in Coventry and Garrod (2004) where a ball separates two rectangles without any alternative connection (a), with a loose alternative connection (b), or with a rigid alternative connection (c).

prototype that we can investigate which features are lexical and which features are contextual.

8.7 One Lexical Concept but more than one Corresponding Spatial Prototype

We have seen that there are circumstances in which the concept BETWEEN maps to at least two spatial prototypes (see, e.g. Fig. 8.5b). Is this due to the lexical structure of *between*, or not? Let us consider similar cases.

There seem to be three types of spatial prepositions that map onto more than one spatial prototype. The first type is exemplified by Dutch *naast* ('beside' or 'to the side of'). *Naast* locates a Figure at two possible sides of a Referent (its left and right side). It is part of the meaning of *naast* that two spatial prototypes must exist—whatever the spatial context in which the Figure occurs. If *naast* can be used, two regions in space are referred to. This means that it is part of the lexical structure of *naast* that this preposition corresponds to two prototypes.

The second type of spatial preposition maps to more than one spatial prototype if its lexical structure and the spatial context both allow it. An example is *along(side)*. *Along(side)* only takes object nouns that refer to idealized one-dimensional entities: *along(side) the wall, along(side) the river, along(side) the line*, but **along(side) the marble, *along(side) the coin*, etc. *Along(side)* refers to one spatial prototype if in some context only one side of a one-dimensional Referent can be accessed (e.g. *Billy walked along the wall* if only the inside or the outside of the house are accessible), or if the context idealizes the surface of the Referent to one side (e.g. *The ant walked along(side) the pencil*). If the context allows access to two sides, then *along(side)* refers to two spatial prototypes. For example, if both sides of a river, wall, or line are equally accessible to Billy then *Billy walked along(side) the river/wall/line* refers to Billy being in two possible locations. *Along* is thus an example of a preposition where the lexical structure in combination with the context determines how many spatial prototypes are generated: the lexical structure of *along* specifies that the object of the preposition must refer to a one-dimensional object, but depending on the number of object sides that are accessible (one or two), one or two spatial prototypes are generated.

The third type of spatial preposition maps to more than one spatial prototype if certain spatial features are present in the context in which that preposition is used. Let us consider what those spatial features might be. *Through x* normally refers to only one spatial prototype. For example, although *A pen through my eye* may refer to a pen being through my eye in many different ways, the fact that the pen is sticking out of my eye from two different places is enough to declare the entire inner region of my eye as a potential region corresponding to *through my eye*. But, the region that *through* preferably maps to is sensitive to the shape properties of the reference object. Take the sentence *The stick is through the box*.

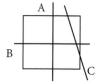

FIG. 8.10. One rather prefers *The stick through the box* to refer to situations A and B, then to C.

Because of the shape properties of the box, one rather prefers the stick in Fig. 8.10 to be through the box in (A) and (B), then in (C). In Fig. 8.10 there are thus two spatial prototypes corresponding to *through the box*. The generation of these prototypes follows from the symmetry properties of the Referent.

Between is not like *naast* or *along*, but is more like *through*. Since there are cases where *between y and z* refers to only one prototype (e.g. Fig. 8.4a), *between* cannot be like *naast*. That is, it cannot be part of the lexical structure of *between* that it must always refer to two prototypes. Could *between* be like *along*? Although such a possibility cannot be dismissed outright, it is unlikely. Which violation of one of its lexical specifications would make it possible for *between* to refer to two possible prototypes in Fig. 8.5b? It seems more likely that the two prototypes in Fig. 8.5b are due to the spatial properties of the Reference structure. For instance, if mirror symmetry is involved (Fig. 8.5a) instead of rotational symmetry (Fig. 8.5b), then the distinctness of the two spatial prototypes fades. It therefore seems more likely that *between* is like *through*.

The nature of the contextual factors that cause *between* to map to at least two spatial prototypes is not entirely clear. As observed, symmetry type may have an influence, and distance may, but further research—for example cognitive modeling—would be needed to quantify the relative impact of such factors. What is important at this point, however, is that nothing in the lexical specification of *between* invites a generation of more than one prototype. Let us now consider how lexical and contextual features together can explain the meaning of *between* in context.

8.8   The Meaning of *between* in Context

The simplest possible explanation for the meaning of *between* in context assumes a lexical specification of *between* as corresponding to a BOP region, and the demand that a spatial prototype must be generated. The latter can be performed by highlighting sub-regions in the BOP region on the basis of *perceptual saliency* (based on such spatial features as symmetry) and—if applicable—on the basis of extra-geometrical features pointing out regions of *potential interaction* (in the sense of Carlson and Covell, this volume, Ch. 12; Barsalou *et al.*, this volume,

Ch. 9; Glenberg and Kaschak, this volume, Ch. 2). Perceptual saliency and potential interaction are primarily represented in relation to the two Referents involved. Let us consider how this explanation connects to the phenomena discussed.

Based on the evidence reviewed above the BOP-region seems to describe the outer boundaries of possible spatial prototypes corresponding to the meaning of *between*. The spatial features that transform the BOP region into one or more spatial prototypes are symmetry and a combination of such spatial features as intrinsic axes, a center of gravity, and symmetry. An effect of inter-Referent distance and Referent structure orientation seems dependent on the shape of the Referents used.

As argued by Wagemans (1995) symmetry differences relate to differences in perceptual saliency. And, the fact that some other spatial features only have an influence in combination makes it plausible that their influence derives from a cumulative saliency effect in visual processing. Although a quantitative model studying feature interactions would provide stronger evidence for perceptual saliency, the information presented here points out some circumstantial evidence for an influence of perceptual saliency.

Three different feature types suggest that 'potential interaction' is a possible factor highlighting parts of the BOP region. Visual functional features only seemed to have an impact on the comprehension of *between* if the eyes of the Referents were directed at a shared region. But, even though the impact of visual functional features was limited, the observed effect does suggest an influence of potential interaction: in a normal context a region at which two pairs of eyes are directed is a likely region of interaction between two agents. It is also quite likely that the linguistic functional features studied here give rise to a transformation of the BOP region because of a potential interaction between the Referents involved: lexical concepts categorizing two rectangles as a THUMB and an INDEX FINGER in combination with an available dot may suggest a grasping action. The third type of feature encoding potential interaction is the dynamic–kinematic feature. Work by Coventry and Garrod (in press) studying this type of feature showed that the more likely a possible interaction between two Referents was prevented, the better the between-ratings became. It thus seems that the impact of three feature types can be accounted for—post-hoc—by the idea that potential interaction—or the prevention of it—may transform a BOP region into a spatial prototype.

General functional features may either play a role in spatial prototype selection or in prototype formation. Features representing cognitive effort appeared to select certain types of spatial relations with a greater likelihood for further processing (e.g. those corresponding to *in front of the washing machine*), compared to other relations (e.g. those corresponding to *between the washing machine and the sink*). Insofar as the contextual meaning of *between* is determined by the selection of the term itself, features representing cognitive effort

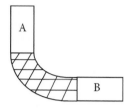

FIG. 8.11. The striped region is predicted to have a higher acceptability for *between* if this region is assigned a potential zone of interaction.

thus play a role. But, there are also general functional features that are candidates for prototype formation. As indicated by Regier and Carlson (2001) attention plays a role in the formation of a spatial prototype corresponding to *above x*. This role can be interpreted as highlighting the influence of certain spatial features (e.g. inter-Referent distance and the center of gravity of the Referent structure). General functional features can thus—in principle—play different possible roles in the contextual meaning of spatial prepositions, and possibly in relation to *between*.

Even though the explanation offered here for the contextual meaning of *between* is clearly post-hoc, it is by no means ad-hoc. For example, it is possible to assign potential interactions to otherwise meaningless stimuli, and thereby study the possible impact of such potential interactions. One prediction that follows from interpreting rectangles A and B in Fig. 8.11 as cars, while suggesting that cars A and B may run into each other, is that the entire path of potential interaction would generate a higher acceptability for *between* than any other points in space.

Summarizing, we can say that the explanation for the meaning of *between* offered here assigns a dominant role to spatial features, as also suggested in the literature, albeit a more elaborate version of it. As shown by the prediction in Fig. 8.11, however, it is also necessary to assign a role to contextual features. We assume that the meaning of *between* in context derives from its lexical specification—generating a BOP region—and an extra-lexical instruction to amend this ideal based on contextual factors.

Part Two

Function: Definitions and Influence

9

The HIPE Theory of Function

LAWRENCE BARSALOU, STEVEN SLOMAN,
and SERGIO CHAIGNEAU

Abstract

We propose that function is a complex relational concept that draws on many conceptual domains for its content. According to the HIPE theory, these domains include **H**istory, **I**ntentional perspective, the **P**hysical environment, and **E**vent sequences. The function of a particular entity does not have a single sense. Instead many different senses can be constructed that depend on the conceptualizer's current goal, setting, and personal history. On a given occasion, relevant knowledge is assembled across conceptual domains to construct a relevant sense, represented as a mental simulation and structured by a causal chain.

Function

The role that an entity plays in serving the goal of an agent, or its role in the operation of a larger system such as a geology, ecology, or religion.

9.1 Introduction

Although function is a central construct across the cognitive sciences and neurosciences, its detailed structure has received little attention (but see Wimsatt, 1972; Wright, 1973).[1] Often an entity's function is viewed as a single unanalyzed

This work was supported by National Science Foundation Grant SBR-9905024 and BCS-0212134 to Lawrence W. Barsalou, and by a NASA grant NCC2-1217 to Steven A. Sloman. We are grateful to Laura Carlson and Emile van der Zee for the opportunity to write this chapter, and for superb editorial advice on revising it. We are also grateful to Mojdeh Zamani, Philippe Rochat, Robert McCauley, and Laura Namy for helpful discussion of this work.

[1] These articles were brought to our attention after developing the HIPE theory and writing this chapter. Although these authors had different aims than ours, they made similar points and reached similar conclusions.

property. In many theories, a function is just another amodal symbol abstracted from perception and action. When functional properties are viewed modally, they are often assigned to a single modality, namely, the motor system.

We propose that function is a much more elaborate construct. First, a function is a complex relational structure, not a single unanalyzed property. Second, the complex relational structure that represents a function is distributed across many modalities, not just one. Third, there is not just one sense of an entity's function, there are many.

The HIPE theory is an account of people's knowledge about function. It describes the content of this knowledge and how it is used, both for artifacts and natural kinds. The HIPE theory is not an account of the physical world. Although functional knowledge may often correspond to the world, significant departures arise (e.g. the roles and essences described later for history). Also we do not view functional knowledge as an independent module in the brain. Rather functional knowledge emerges as people integrate information across diverse conceptual domains. In general, HIPE provides an analysis of how functional knowledge is represented and processed.

We will assume that mental simulations represent the complex relational knowledge in functions. By *mental simulation* we mean reenactments of experience in sensory-motor systems, similar to mental imagery. See Barsalou (1999) for further discussion of theory, and Barsalou (2003) for empirical evidence. As will become clear, we further assume that causal chains underlie function (e.g. Glymour, 2001; Pearl, 2000; also see Sloman, Love, and Ahn, 1998), with causal relations producing transitions between states of functional simulations. For a review of HIPE's relation to the literatures on function, see Chaigneau and Barsalou (in press). For empirical tests of HIPE, see Chaigneau (2002) and Chaigneau, Barsalou, and Zamani (2004).

9.2   The HIPE Theory

HIPE specifies that representations of function integrate four types of conceptual knowledge: History, Intentional perspective, Physical environment, and Event sequences. Table 9.1 summarizes the relevant knowledge and presents a notation for representing it. In this section, we focus on HIPE's conceptual content; in the next, we address the causal chains that represent function.

9.2.1   Intentional perspective (I)

When representing an entity's function, many different senses can be conceived. Just as there is tremendous diversity in how people represent a category (Barsalou, 1987, 1989, 1993), so are there many different ways to represent an entity's function. An agent's intentional perspective, **I**, is the gateway into

TABLE 9.1. *Summary of the HIPE components for artifacts and natural kinds*

Notation		Description
Artifacts	Natural kinds	
I:	I:	International Perspective
MP	MP	Meta-Cognitive Purpose
POV	POV	Point of View
H:	H:	History
R	R	Role
IV	EGR	InVention or Evolution/Geology/Religion
M	C	Manufacture or Creation
UH	LH	Use History or Life History
P:	P:	Physical Environment
FO(PS, G*)	FO(PS, G*)	Focal Object (Physical Structure, Goal*)
S	S	Setting
EA (PS, G, IACT)		External Agent (Physical Structure, Goal, Initiating ACTion)
E:	E:	Events
B	B	Behaviors
O	O	Outcome

* optional component.

functional knowledge, with **I** determining the information retrieved about function on a given occasion.[2]

As Table 9.1 illustrates, **I** includes a meta-cognitive purpose, **MP**, and a point-of-view, **POV**. When representing an entity's function, an agent typically has a meta-cognitive purpose in doing so, namely, the reason why the agent—at the meta-cognitive level—is accessing knowledge about the entity's function (as opposed to the concrete purpose of actually using the object). For example, an agent may have the goal of establishing the origin of an entity's function. Under this **MP**, the agent retrieves a subset of functional knowledge that establishes this origin. On another occasion, the agent may have the goal of identifying physical properties that produce optimal functional outcomes. Under this **MP**, the agent recalls successful uses of the entity and attempts to identify correlated physical properties. On another occasion, an agent may have the goal of using an entity to achieve its standard function (e.g. using a hammer to pound in a nail). Under this **MP**, the agent retrieves a procedure for using the entity. Many other **MP**s are

[2] The notational symbols in the text and Table 9.1 are variables that become bound to values. These symbols do *not* refer to specific propositions. Thus **I** does not refer to a particular proposition about an agent's intention, but is a variable that takes a specific intention as a value.

possible, each retrieving different subsets of functional knowledge. Thus an entity's function has many senses—not just one—with the current **MP** determining the relevant sense. In principle, a wide variety of **MP**s are possible; in practice, a few probably dominate, such as those just described.

In simulating a function, the agent's **MP** always leads to a particular point of view, **POV**. If the agent's **MP** is to pound in a nail herself with a hammer, the agent adopts her own **POV** to guide action. In contrast, imagine that the agent is asked whether her roommate could use a hammer to hang a picture. The **MP** is still to use a hammer for its standard function. However the simulation of this functional sense now takes the **POV** of the roommate. Similarly imagine that the agent speculates on why hammers have the function they do. Under this **MP**, the agent might adopt the **POV** of an inventor, or perhaps some prehistoric figure making a hammer. Finally imagine that the agent is asked to think about the optimal physical properties to achieve a hammer's function. Under this **MP**, the agent may adopt the **POV** of an omniscient observer looking across the distribution of functional simulations currently accessible. As these examples illustrate, the current **MP** causally initiates the **POV**:

$$MP \rightarrow POV \tag{1}$$

Once an **MP** and a **POV** are in place, they determine the remaining content of a functional simulation.

9.2.2   History (H)

Researchers have argued recently that history is central to an object's function (e.g. Bloom, 1996, 1998; Gelman and Bloom, 2000; Matan and Carey, 2001; Prasada, 1999*a*). According to these views, people believe that an object's physical structure depends on the original purpose it was intended to serve at the time of its creation—the design stance. As Table 9.1 illustrates, history, **H**, has a parallel structure for artifacts and natural kinds that differs in their respective realizations. For artifacts, **H** includes a role, **R**, an invention process, **IV**, a manufacturing process, **M**, and a use history, **UH**. The role, **R**, is the purpose that the artifact was originally intended to serve at the time of its invention, **IV**. Thus cars were created for transportation, and telephones for communication. Specific instances of the artifact are created during a manufacturing process, **M**, and then acquire a particular use history, **UH**, once agents acquire them. For example, a particular hammer might only be used as a paper weight. As a result, this non-standard function may dominate the hammer's use history, thereby obscuring its standard role, **R**. Use history is important later when we address non-intended uses of entities, such as ad hoc categories (Barsalou, 1983, 1985, 1991).

Whereas **R** and **IV** together constitute the long-term history of an artifact category, **M** and **UH** together constitute the immediate history of an instance.

An agent may not know all of the long-term and immediate history for an artifact, and what they know may be incorrect. Even when knowledge is non-optimal, however, agents are likely to know that **R, IV, M**, and **UH** are relevant at a meta-level (i.e. they know that such knowledge probably exists and is relevant). Most importantly, agents believe that an artifact's long- and short-term histories are central to its function.

For natural kinds, **H** has a parallel structure. A given natural kind category plays a role, **R**, in an ecology. Thus plants provide food for animals, and fertilizer for other plants. Animals control other populations of animals, clean the environment through scavenging, fertilize plants, and so forth. Geological kinds such as water provide sustenance for plants and animals. A natural kind comes to achieve its role, **R**, through some sort of evolutionary, geological, or religious process, **EGR**. Individuals who subscribe to scientific thinking may typically believe that the roles of natural kinds arise through evolution and geology, whereas individuals who subscribe to religious thinking may view creationism as important. Specific instances of a natural kind are created in some manner, **C**, and then acquire a particular life history, **LH**. For example, plants and animals are created via reproduction and birth, whereas water is created via condensation. Analogous to an artifact having a use history, **UH**, a natural kind may have a life history, **LH**, that may depart from its original role, **R** (e.g. a porcupine that becomes a pet).

Whereas **R** and **EGR** together constitute the long-term history of a natural kind, **C** and **LH** constitute the immediate history of an instance. An agent may not know all of the history for a natural kind, and what they know may be incorrect. Even when knowledge is non-optimal, however, people are likely to know that **R**, **EGR, C**, and **LH** are relevant at a meta-level. Most importantly, people believe that a natural kind's long- and short-term histories are central to its function.

We offer several additional proposals about history. First, we assume that simulations represent the content in **H**. For example, people might simulate the invention or manufacture of an artifact, or they might simulate two animals producing offspring.

Second, historical chains arise in various ways. Sometimes a role exists that leads to the creation of an entity. For example, there may be an historical need for a tool, which eventually leads to its invention and manufacture:

$$R \rightarrow IV \rightarrow M \tag{2}$$

Alternatively, an inventor may explore a domain and in the process discover a role that consumers never knew had use, although they appreciate it once the manufacturing process creates the product:

$$IV \rightarrow R \rightarrow M \tag{3}$$

For natural kinds, roles and evolution/geology/religion may be intertwined in such complex ways that it is impossible to determine which came first.

Thus people may often view creation as the outcome of roles coupled with evolution/geology/religion:

$$R \searrow \atop EGR \nearrow \mkern-18mu C \qquad (4)$$

Ultimately how agents represent causal chains to themselves is an empirical question. As these examples illustrate, HIPE can represent a number of possibilities.

Third, we view roles, **R**, as detached historically from the events in which entities actually perform their functions. An artifact's role is the purpose that its inventor was trying to achieve in designing it originally. A natural kind's role is the purpose that a scientist or religious figure defined it as playing in some theoretical framework. Whereas roles reside in past history, goals and outcomes attempt to realize them in specific functional events.

Finally, roles, goals, and outcomes are closely related, as just described. An agent's goal, **G**, to use an artifact often corresponds to its historical role, **R**. Similarly, the outcome of using the artifact, **O**, hopefully realizes the goal. For example, an agent's goal to pound in a nail with a hammer instantiates the hammer's more general role. Similarly the agent's goal is realized when the intended outcome occurs, namely, the nail is pounded in completely. Thus **R**, **G**, and **O** are highly similar, given that they all represent using a hammer to pound something in successfully. Nevertheless **R**, **G**, and **O** differ in important ways. As just noted, **R** is the role of an artifact in the mind of an inventor or manufacturer. For a natural kind, **R** is a role within a scientific or religious framework. In contrast, **G** and **O** are specific realizations of **R** at different points in functional event sequences. A goal is an agent's intention to realize a role on a given occasion, and an outcome is an event that hopefully realizes the goal. Later we will see how alignment between roles, goals, and outcomes in causal chains produces a variety of functional phenomena.

9.2.3   Physical environment (P)

In this section and the next, we turn to the content of a functional event sequence, **E**, that occurs in the physical environment, **P**. In HIPE, **P** revolves around **FO**, the focal object whose function is of interest. Nevertheless other parts of **P** are important as well, including relevant aspects of the setting, **S**, and optionally an external agent, **EA**. We treat each in turn. Again we assume that simulations represent these components in functional reasoning.

As Table 9.1 illustrates, a focal object has physical structure, **PS**, and may optionally have internal goals, **G**. An entity's function obviously depends on its physical structure (e.g. Gibson, 1979*a*, 1979*b*). For example, the handle and head of a hammer allow it to function as a hammer but not as a screwdriver. Although people may not view most artifacts as having internal goals, they may believe that some do (e.g. robots, automatic teller machines, car alarms). Animals clearly have internal goals, and plants can be viewed as having related tendencies to thrive, reproduce, and avoid threats. Like most artifacts, geological kinds do not have goals. Under various circumstances, however, artifacts and geological kinds may be imbued with internal forces that enter into causal explanation. Religious history, **EGR**, may infuse artifacts, geological kinds, and living things with intentionality, and so may people's proclivity to anthropomorphize. Similarly, when people believe that an entity's history implants an essence in its physical structure, the essence may have a goal-like character (e.g. Gelman and Diesendruck, 1999).

Knowledge of background settings, **S**, typically contributes to understanding the functions of focal objects. Knowing the physical structure of a hammer, for example, is not sufficient for knowing its function. Knowledge about nails and wood is also essential. Similarly, knowing the setting of a tree is necessary for understanding its functional role in the environment. In general, **S** includes knowledge about objects and locations central to understanding functions. We do not specify the components of **S** here, given that many are possible. For a sense of the variety, see the components of situations in Wu and Barsalou's (2004) coding scheme.

Finally, external agents, **EA**, are central to understanding the functions of artifacts. We define an **EA** as an agent who helps a focal entity achieve a function it cannot achieve on its own. Whereas some entities achieve their functions without external agents, others require them. As just described, animals, plants, and some artifacts have internal goals that drive their behavior towards their historical roles, **R**. Although these entities are clearly agents, they are not external agents. In contrast, a hammer cannot achieve its function without an external agent using it. Interesting cases arise when agents such as plants and animals become artifacts for humans (e.g. food, transportation, pets). Under these conditions, humans become external agents who contribute to plants and animals developing new functions that differ from their evolutionary/religious roles, **R**. Other interesting cases arise when humans help plants and animals achieve their evolutionary functions, as when bringing back endangered species. In these latter cases, both internal and external agency contribute to achieving a species' original role.

As Table 9.1 illustrates, external agents have a physical structure, **PS**, they adopt goals, **G**, and they take initiating actions, **IACT**, that trigger event sequences, **E**. An agent's physical structure, **PS**, is central to the functional affordance of a focal object, **FO**. The functions that the focal object can play depend not only on its physical structure but also on the agent's physical structure (Gibson, 1979*a*, 1979*b*). Thus a ceiling can function as a resting place for a mosquito but not for a cat. An agent's goal, **G**, is also central to what occurs functionally. For example, a hammer's function depends on whether an agent intends to use it for nailing, smashing, etc. Finally we include initiating actions, **IACT**, in the physical environment, **P**, because they belong to the full set of physical conditions required to begin the causal chain that realizes a function. All other resulting events will be included in the subsequent event sequence, **E**. Together, a focal object, **FO**, a setting, **S**, and an optional external agent, **EA**, constitute a physical system that is sufficient to produce a functional outcome.

9.2.4 Event sequences (E)

Once the full physical system, **P**, for achieving a function is present, full causal power is achieved, and an event sequence, **E**, is simulated (i.e. **P → E**). **E** includes two components. First, **E** contains the behaviors, **B**, of the focal object and of all relevant setting objects. Second, **E** concludes with the outcome, **O**. Typically **B** may include many behaviors of the focal and setting objects, with all these behaviors jointly contributing to **O**. If certain critical behaviors do not occur, the desired **O** may not follow.

When all of the causal conditions for achieving an entity's historical role, **R**, reside in **P**, and when no competing causes exist, a sequence of behaviors, **B**, culminates in an outcome, **O**, that realizes **R**. When **P** takes some other form, or when competing causes exist, **B** and ultimately **O** may take other forms. For example, if an entity's physical structure, **PS**, is altered or damaged in some way, **O** may depart from **R** (e.g. an animal unable to forage because of a damaged olfactory system). Similarly, when organisms learn, they may acquire new goals, **G**, from settings, **S**, that cause their behaviors to diverge from evolutionary roles (e.g. when a dog learns to chase cars). Finally, when an agent, **A**, has a goal, **G**, that differs from an artifact's historical role, **R**, the outcome, **O** may diverge from **R**. For example, if an agent wants to hold some paper down with a hammer, a non-standard function of the hammer may be realized. Thus **R** is only realized when all its conditions are realized in **P**, and no competing causes exist.

9.3 Causal Chains in HIPE

The HIPE theory assumes that people typically have knowledge about history, intentional perspective, the physical environment, and events for a given entity. By no means, however, does HIPE assume that people have complete knowledge in any of these domains. Indeed people may often lack knowledge of some components in Table 9.1, and those they do know may be represented partially or incorrectly. We merely propose that people's knowledge about function typically follows the structure in Table 9.1, and that when they lack knowledge about specific components, their meta-knowledge specifies that such knowledge probably exists and may be relevant.

As discussed earlier, we make several other assumptions about how people represent functions. On a given occasion, people only access a subset of the relevant HIPE knowledge. To represent the subset retrieved, they reenact it in a multi-modal simulation. A causal chain underlies the simulated event sequence, producing transitions between states of the simulation.

Finally we make two assumptions about the properties of causal chains. First, an individual relation, $X \rightarrow Y$, is causal when X and Y are correlated, when the expected temporal relation holds (Y does not precede X), and when the expected kind of intervention is supported (manipulating the value of X changes the value of Y). Second, when multiple causes produce an effect, the effect is some as yet unspecified function of the joint causes. In (4), for example, we assume that C is some function of R and EGR. Each cause plays a role, but its size and relation to the other cause may be unknown.

9.3.1 Flexibility and falsifiability

As will be seen shortly, many causal chains can be constructed from the HIPE knowledge for an entity. Rather than only thinking about the entity's function in a single way, people can think about it in many different ways, depending on the circumstances. The HIPE theory is designed to capture this flexibility. On different occasions, different subsets of HIPE knowledge are accessed and configured into different causal chains, each representing one particular belief about the entity's function.

One concern might be that this theory is so powerful as to be unfalsifiable. Perhaps it can represent any proposed hypothesis about function. We believe that HIPE is falsifiable in at least three ways. First, it predicts that function is a complex relational structure distributed across modalities. If the representation of function turns out to be atomistic, unimodal, or amodal, HIPE would be falsified. Second, HIPE predicts that knowledge about function is flexible, not rigid. If knowledge of function turns out to be rigid, HIPE would be rejected. Because previous theories have not proposed that function is flexible (to our knowledge), this strikes us as non-obvious. Finally, HIPE predicts that representations of function are drawn from four types of conceptual knowledge (H, I, P, and E), and that the componential structure in Table 9.1 captures the central content of this knowledge. HIPE is falsified if general types of knowledge must be added or deleted, or if the componential structure for a type of knowledge must be modified significantly.[3]

9.3.2 Causal initiation

As discussed earlier, we believe that intentional perspective, I, plays a central role in accessing specific subsets of HIPE knowledge. In general, I determines the specific functional sense, Fn, simulated on a given occasion for an entity. Thus:

$$I \rightarrow Fn \tag{5}$$

---

[3] A related issue is whether principled constraints govern the functional representations possible within HIPE. Clearly not every possible combination of HIPE's components constitutes a meaningful representation. At this time, specific constraints on this process remain to be developed.

where **Fn** is some configuration of components from the **H**, **P**, and **E** domains. As Table 9.1 illustrates, **I** in (5) can be decomposed to yield:

$$MP \rightarrow POV \rightarrow Fn \tag{6}$$

Thus an agent's meta-cognitive purpose and point of view produce the functional sense simulated for an entity on a given occasion. In general, **I** can be viewed as an operator that, first, establishes a **MP** and a **POV**, which in turn operate on knowledge to produce a particular **Fn**. When the same **I** is applied to knowledge of different entities, a different **Fn** results for each entity. Conversely, when different **I**s are applied to knowledge of the same entity, a different **Fn** results for each **I**.

In many situations, an agent's intentional perspective may arise internally as goals are generated in a top-down manner. For example, an agent who likes music may create the goal of attending a concert, which is then realized in a functional event, **Fn**. In other situations, however, an agent's intentional perspective may be triggered by a state of the physical environment, **P**, or by an event sequence, **E**, occurring in it—the agent may not have the goal beforehand. Under these conditions, the causal sequence takes one of the following forms:

$$P \rightarrow I \rightarrow Fn$$
$$E \rightarrow I \rightarrow Fn \tag{7}$$

Analogous to the decomposition of (5) into (6), **P**, **E**, and **I** in (7) could be expanded using more specific components from Table 9.1. Depending on the situation, different aspects of **P** or **E** might trigger the resultant intentional perspective, **I**, to represent a particular functional sense, **Fn**.

For the remainder of this section, we delete intentional perspective from most causal chains. By simplifying them in this manner, the relevant components become more salient. Of course, an intentional perspective is always present, and it always plays a central role in shaping causal chains.

9.3.3   Causal level

As the decomposition of (5) into (6) illustrates, causal chains can be represented at different levels of specificity. It is an open question whether people represent causal chains at multiple levels or just one. Regardless, representing these chains at different levels is useful notationally for theoretical purposes.

For example, we can distinguish different theories of function most directly at the general level. Consider affordance theories, which propose that function depends on both the physical structure of an entity and the physical structure of the organism using the entity (Gibson, 1979*a*, 1979*b*). We can represent this general view as:

$$P \rightarrow E \tag{8}$$

P includes the physical structures of the focal object and the agent, which determine the functional events, **E**, that follow. In contrast, historical views propose that the physical structure of an entity depends on its history (e.g. Bloom, 1996, 1998; Gelman and Bloom, 2000; Matan and Carey, 2001; Prasada, 1999*a*). We can represent the design stance as:

$$H \rightarrow P \qquad (9)$$

Here an entity's history, **H**, produces a physical structure, **P**, that achieves the entity's historically intended role.[4] At this general level, it is easy to see the difference between these theories. Whereas the affordance view predicts that people ignore history when assessing function, the historical view predicts that people take history into account. Similarly, (8) and (9) illustrate how physical structure is a cause in affordance theories but an effect in historical theories.

When people actually reason about function, they may reason at a level that is more specific than the level in (8) and (9). For example, someone reasoning about affordances at a more specific level might decompose (8), **P → E**, into the following causal chains:

Geological kinds

$$
\begin{array}{c}
FO(PS) \searrow \\
\quad\quad\; B \longrightarrow O \\
S \nearrow
\end{array}
$$

Living things

$$
\begin{array}{c}
FO(PS, G) \searrow \\
\quad\quad\quad\; B \longrightarrow O \\
S \nearrow
\end{array}
\qquad (10)
$$

Artifacts

$$
\begin{array}{c}
FO(PS) \searrow \\
S \longrightarrow B \longrightarrow O \\
EA(PS, G, IACT) \nearrow
\end{array}
$$

For a geological kind, its physical structure and setting are the cause of its function. For a living thing, its physical structure, internal goals, and setting constitute the critical cause. For an artifact, its physical structure and setting, together with an external agent, produce its function. These specific causal chains capture the prediction that people believe different configurations of physical components cause the functions of artifacts, living things, and geological kinds. As (10) illustrates, constructing causal chains in the HIPE framework brings out the functional differences between different types of concepts.

[4] For the design stance, an object's intended role would presumably be conceptualized in its designer's mind as an affordance, namely, **P → E**. Once the object exists and has the required structure, it can produce the desired event. Nevertheless the focus of the design stance is on designing a physical object that eventually achieves a desired affordance, not on instances of the affordance being realized.

We can similarly decompose the causal chain in (9), $\mathbf{H} \to \mathbf{P}$, for the historical perspective into more specific causal chains:

Geological kinds
$$\begin{array}{c} R \searrow \\ C \longrightarrow FO(PS) \\ EGR \nearrow \end{array}$$

Living things
$$\begin{array}{c} R \searrow \\ C \longrightarrow FO(PS, G) \\ EGR \nearrow \end{array} \qquad (11)$$

Artifacts
$$\begin{array}{c} R \searrow \\ M \longrightarrow FO(PS) \\ IV \nearrow \end{array}$$

As (11) illustrates, people might conclude that the physical structure of a geological kind is the result of its ecological role, a long-term geological process, and a more recent creation process. People might reason similarly about living things, but conclude further that a living thing's internal goals—not just its physical structure—reflect its history. Finally people might reason that an artifact's physical structure reflects its intended role, invention, and manufacturing history.

Although theories differ on whether affordances or history are central to function, HIPE assumes that people reason in both ways. Depending on $\mathbf{I}$, people represent the functional sense most relevant in the current situation.

9.3.4　Causal alignment

By assessing the alignment of components across HIPE domains, non-standard forms of function, including functional failure and ad hoc categories can be represented. Two components—outcomes and goals—appear particularly important for alignment. We address each in turn.

When a standard function is achieved successfully, the outcome, $\mathbf{O}$, corresponds both to the historical role, $\mathbf{R}$, and to any relevant goals, $\mathbf{G}$. Consider the standard function of a hammer to pound in a nail. When a nail has been pounded in successfully, $\mathbf{O}$ corresponds both to the external agent's goal, $\mathbf{G_{EA}}$, and to the hammer's historical role, $\mathbf{R}$.[5] Thus:

$$\begin{array}{c} R \searrow \\ M \longrightarrow FO(PS) \searrow \\ IV \nearrow S \longrightarrow B \longrightarrow O \qquad O \sim G_{EA} \sim R \\ EA(PS, G, IACT) \nearrow \end{array} \qquad (12)$$

---

[5] Because $\mathbf{G}$ occurs twice in the notation, subscripts will distinguish the goals of external agents, $\mathbf{G_{EA}}$, from the goals of focal objects, $\mathbf{G_{FO}}$, as needed. Similarly subscripts will distinguish the physical structure of external agents, $\mathbf{PS_{EA}}$, from the physical structure of focal objects,

Similarly consider one function ascribed to deer, namely, to consume vegetation. When a deer consumes vegetation successfully, **O** corresponds both to the deer's internal goal, $\mathbf{G_{FO}}$, and to its historical role, **R**:

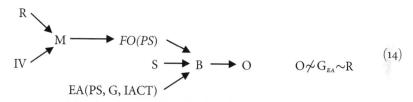

$$O \sim G_{FO} \sim R \qquad (13)$$

As these examples illustrate, HIPE predicts that people assess whether $\mathbf{O} \sim \mathbf{G} \sim \mathbf{R}$ to determine whether an entity's standard function has been achieved successfully.

HIPE can similarly represent when attempts to achieve standard functions fail. Imagine that a hammer's wooden handle has shattered, such that the hammer can no longer pound in nails effectively. This state of affairs can be represented as follows:[6]

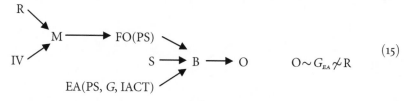

$$O \not\sim G_{EA} \sim R \qquad (14)$$

As (14) states, the outcome, **O**, does not correspond to $\mathbf{G_{EA}}$ or **R**, presumably because the focal object's physical structure, $\mathbf{PS_{FO}}$, is not as expected. Because of this alignment failure, an agent would conclude that the hammer's standard function had not been achieved successfully. As (12), (13), and (14) illustrate, causal chains in HIPE can capture both success and failure in achieving standard functions.

HIPE can also represent non-standard functions through the non-alignment of goals, **G**, with roles, **R**. Of interest here are ad hoc categories (Barsalou, 1983, 1985, 1991). For example, a hammer might be used as a paper weight such that:

$$O \sim G_{EA} \not\sim R \qquad (15)$$

$\mathbf{PS_{FO}}$. Finally, $\sim$ will indicate correspondence between roles, goals, and outcomes, whereas $\not\sim$ will indicate lack of correspondence.

[6] We will use italics to indicate that components in causal chains take unusual values and thereby produce atypical outcomes. Thus, *FO(PS)* is in italics for (14), as is G_{EA} for (15), G_{FO} for (16), and both G_{EA} and *S* for (17).

In (15), the external agent, **EA**, has a goal for using the hammer, $\mathbf{G_{EA}}$, that differs from its standard role, **R**. As a result, the outcome, **O**, corresponds to the non-standard goal but not to the standard role, assuming that all of the conditions for achieving the non-standard outcome are present.

A similar causal chain could be constructed for a living thing that performs a non-standard function:

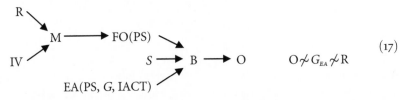

$$ (16) $$

For example, if a dog chases a car, its internal goal, $\mathbf{G_{FO}}$, no longer corresponds to its historical role, **R**. Again the outcome, **O**, corresponds to the non-standard goal when the conditions for achieving it are met.

HIPE can also represent cases where a non-standard goal fails. For example, imagine that a hammer fails as a paperweight due to high winds. This failure can be captured as:

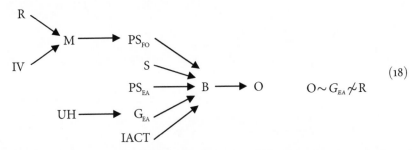

$$ (17) $$

As (17) illustrates, the hammer plays a non-standard role, $\mathbf{G_{EA}} \not\sim \mathbf{R}$, and the outcome fails to achieve it, $\mathbf{O} \not\sim \mathbf{G_{EA}}$, due to an atypical property of the setting, **S**.

Finally, the frequent pursuit of a non-standard goal establishes an unusual use history, **UH**, in an artifact's history, **H**. For example, a hammer only ever used as a paperweight establishes a use history that displaces its standard role, **R**. On encountering this particular hammer, **UH** may trigger its non-standard role through the external agent's goal, $\mathbf{G_{EA}}$:

$$ (18) $$

When **UH** is stronger than **R**, **IV**, and **M**, the non-standard goal occurs in **B** and **O**. As (18) illustrates, complex HIPE components such as **EA(PS, G, IACT)** can be broken out into their more specific sub-components as needed. Breaking out **EA(PS, G, IACT)** allows showing that **UH** affects G_{EA} specifically, not **EA** as a whole. This further illustrates HIPE's ability to represent causal chains at multiple levels of specificity (compare 8, 10, and 18).

In general, **UH** for artifacts and **LH** for natural kinds may establish entrenched senses of function that compete with standard roles, **R**. As a result, **UH** and **LH** bias the intentional perspectives, **I**, that determine the functional senses, **Fn**, simulated for entities:

$$UH \rightarrow I \rightarrow Fn \qquad (19)$$

$$LH \rightarrow I \rightarrow Fn$$

As described in the section on causal initiation, other factors determine **I** as well, such as the agent's goal and the current setting (see (7)). Nevertheless the personal histories in **UH** and **LH** may often play a central role, thereby producing variability in how people conceptualize function (analogous to the role of personal history in Barsalou, 1987, 1989, 1993).

9.4   Applications

We have offered a theory of function and a notation for representing it. A key question is what can this theory do? Is it just an armchair theory, or is it useful in generating predictions and explaining findings? To address this question, we offer examples of how we have found HIPE useful in our own work.

First, HIPE offers a novel account of function. Rather than being a simple unanalyzed property, an entity's function is a complex relational construct, drawing on many modalities for its content, structured by causal chains. Furthermore, an entity's function has many senses, not just one, depending on an agent's current goal, setting, and personal history. HIPE also provides hypotheses about the different causal chains underlying the functions of artifacts, living things, and geological kinds (see (10)).

Second, HIPE generates useful predictions. Consider again the affordance account of artifact function from (10):

$$\begin{array}{c} FO(PS) \searrow \\ S \longrightarrow B \longrightarrow O \qquad (20) \\ EA(PS, G, IACT) \nearrow \end{array}$$

As (20) states, the functional outcome, **O**, cannot occur until all of the conditions in the physical environment, **P**, are present, namely, **FO(PS)**, **S**, and **EA(PS, G, IACT)**. Once these conditions exist, they produce the relevant behaviors, **B**, followed by **O**. Chaigneau *et al.* (2004) tested this prediction by manipulating the information about the physical environment, **P**, that participants received while trying to understand the function of a novel object. When participants received only the physical structure of the focal object, PS_{FO}, they were poor at specifying the object's function. When participants further received the relevant setting, **S**, along with PS_{FO}, their ability to specify the focal object's function improved but was far from perfect. Only when the agent's action, **IACT**, was presented along with **S** and PS_{FO} were participants able to fully specify the object's function. These results support HIPE's central assumption that a complex configuration of entities and events underlies people's understanding of a functional event. Only when this entire configuration exists does understanding become complete.

As described earlier, another of HIPE's predictions is that the function of an entity has many senses, not just one. Juxtaposing Chaigneau *et al.*'s results with others in the literature demonstrates this multiplicity. As just described, Chaigneau *et al.* found that participants could fully understand an object's function based solely on the physical environment, **P**. Participants did not need to know the object's history, **H**, to have an adequate understanding (they learned nothing about history in these experiments). In contrast, a number of researchers have found that an object's function *does* depend on its history (e.g. Bloom, 1996, 1998; Gelman and Bloom, 2000; Matan and Carey, 2001; Prasada, 1999a). This apparently conflicting pattern of results is consistent with HIPE's prediction that function takes different senses. On some occasions, participants' intentional perspective, **I**, orients them towards an object's physical affordances; on other occasions, a different **I**, orients participants towards the object's history.

Chaigneau *et al.*'s finding that **H** was irrelevant when **P** was fully specified illustrates the distance principle of causal chains (cf. Pearl, 1988). In the causal chain, $A \rightarrow B \rightarrow C$, cause **A** is irrelevant to effect **C** because **B**'s closeness to **C** is sufficient for causing **C**. Consider how the distance principle applies to the causal chain that results from combining (8) and (9):

$$H \rightarrow P \rightarrow E \qquad (21)$$

Once **P** is fixed in (21), **H** becomes distant and should matter little, which is what Chaigneau *et al.* observed.

Besides producing novel predictions, HIPE explains and integrates findings. Consider Gelman and Bloom's (2000) finding that history is central to function. In their work, children were told that a makeshift object was created either intentionally or accidentally to serve a function. For example, a newspaper was formed into a hat intentionally by an agent, or was formed accidentally by a car running over the newspaper. Under these conditions, children thought that 'hat' better named the intentional object than the accidental one. Note, however, that the children never received other information that HIPE specifies as central to function, such as the setting, actions, and events involved in actually wearing the hat. In recent work, Chaigneau (2002) added these additional factors into situations like these and found that intentional vs. accidental history became a relatively minor factor (see also Chaigneau, Barsalou and Sloman, 2004).

HIPE explains these divergent results. In Gelman and Bloom's study, children only received history, **H**, and physical structure, **P**. As a result, they had the requisite conceptual material to develop historical causal chains like those in (9) and (11). In contrast, Chaigneau's participants received much more knowledge about **P** and **E**, thereby providing them with the critical elements for constructing affordance chains like those in (8) and (10). Under these latter conditions, history became distant from the functional outcome, thereby decreasing in importance (Pearl, 1988).

HIPE similarly explains the importance of history in Matan and Carey (2001). In these experiments, participants were told that a makeshift object was constructed to serve a particular function (e.g. a teapot), but were told little about the object's physical structure. Later, participants were told that the object actually performed some other function (e.g. a watering can). Under these conditions, participants believed that 'teapot' was a better name for the object than 'watering can'. HIPE explains the importance of history here in terms of alignment, namely, 'teapot' maximizes the correspondence between **R**, G_{EA}, and **O**, whereas 'watering can' does not (compare (12) vs. (16)). When history is salient, participants like to maximize alignment. HIPE further predicts, however, that if the object's history of use, **UH**, became biased over time towards the watering can, participants might come to prefer naming it with 'watering can' (see (18)). Finally HIPE further predicts that if participants receive more information about the object's physical structure that affords using it as a watering can, then history might become distant and play less of a role. When Chaigneau's (2002) participants received more complete knowledge about PS_{FO} in situations like these, history's role diminished considerably, supporting this prediction.

In summary, HIPE offers a detailed conceptual account of function and the various senses it takes. It also illustrates the power of expressing knowledge as causal graphs. As just illustrated, HIPE provides a useful framework for explaining current findings, and for resolving apparent discrepancies between them. HIPE may require significant revision in the face of future data and further theoretical considerations. Hopefully, however, HIPE will provide useful insights into the construct of function, and into the literature addressing it. We would find ourselves chagrined to discover that this theory of function was all hype.

10

Towards a Classification of Extra-geometric Influences on the Comprehension of Spatial Prepositions

KENNY COVENTRY and SIMON GARROD

Abstract

There is much empirical evidence showing that factors other than the relative positions of objects in Euclidean space are important in the comprehension of a wide range of spatial prepositions in English and other languages. Yet thus far attempts at classifying what we will call *extra-geometric* constraints have not been forthcoming. In this chapter we survey the range of experimental evidence for extra-geometric constraints, and we provide the first attempt at a classification of these influences. We argue that extra-geometric influences are basically of two types: what we term *dynamic–kinematic* aspects of scenes, and knowledge of the functions of objects and how they usually interact with each other in particular situations. We review the evidence for each of these parameters across a range of types of preposition, and report some new data showing the influence of extra-geometric variables on the comprehension of *between*. We conclude with a discussion of the implications the empirical data and resultant classification have for models of spatial language comprehension.

Extra-geometric influences

Influences that do not have to do with the geometry (usually construed) of the spatial relations being depicted in visual scenes or situations.

10.1 Introduction

All languages have a means of expressing where objects are located in the world, which is unsurprising given that locating objects is essential to survival. Across

We would like to thank Jaqueline Dalimore for collecting the *between* data reported in this chapter.

a range of languages, expressions involving spatial prepositions convey to the hearer where one object (located object) is located in relation to another object (reference object). For example, *The fly is above Steve's head* indicates that the fly is positioned higher than Steve's head, not in contact with his head. Until relatively recently it has been assumed that spatial terms refer to regions of space in the visual scene being described (e.g. Bennett, 1975; Brugman, 1988; Logan and Sadler, 1996). Spatial terms have been mapped onto intuitive concepts such as *interior* and *superior* in some accounts (e.g. Bennett, 1975), while others have tried to map terms more precisely onto the geometric relations in scenes (e.g. Herskovits, 1986; Logan and Sadler, 1996). In this respect, the objects involved in the visual scene do not matter; it is the relative positions of located and reference objects in (Euclidean) space which determine spatial location of one object with reference to the other object. More recently it has been argued on both theoretical and empirical grounds by a range of authors that *what* objects are influences the descriptions of *where* those objects are (e.g. the various works of Carlson and colleagues, Coventry and colleagues, Garrod and colleagues and Vandeloise). In the first part of this chapter we review the empirical evidence for the importance of what we will term *extra-geometric* variables. Along the way we report some new data showing the influence of extra-geometric variables on the comprehension of *between*. In the final section we consider how geometric and extra-geometric variables may come together, and we outline what we term the *functional geometric framework* (cf. Coventry and Garrod, 2004) to the comprehension and production of spatial prepositions.

10.1.1 Evidence for the importance of extra-geometric factors on the comprehension of spatial prepositions—observations and classifications

Although there is now a considerable body of evidence that factors other than geometry influence spatial language comprehension, the studies concerned involve a range of manipulations which have been variously labeled functional relations, location or functional control relations, object association, animacy effects, context effects, etc. We can term these effects *extra-geometric* because they do not have to do with the geometry (usually construed) of the spatial relations being depicted in the scenes. Given the myriad types of effects in the literature, we need to address the issue of whether there is a single type of effect present, manifest in many different ways, or indeed whether the effects found to date involve a set of different factors at play. Here we briefly review these effects, with a view to extracting a set of types of extra-geometric constraints which need to be taken on board in models of spatial language comprehension.

To anticipate the subsequent discussion, we believe that the relevant extra-geometric factors are mainly of two basic kinds: either they relate to specific knowledge of how objects are likely to interact in standard situations or they relate to inferences (or even direct perceptions) about the dynamic aspects of the scenes being described. We briefly consider the evidence for each of these factors across a range of types of preposition.

10.2 *In* and *On*

10.2.1 Effects due to the perceived dynamics of the interaction

There are various studies that show extra-geometric influences on judgments of spatial relations that reflect how viewers see the dynamics of the interactions in scenes. Vandeloise (1991, 1994), Garrod and Sanford (1989), and Talmy (1988)[1] have all argued that what they variously call functional control, location control, or force dynamics are important factors in spatial language use. Containers have the function of controlling the location of their contents, and therefore evidence that relates to control should influence the appropriateness of *in* (and other prepositions as well). Several studies have shown that alternative control in static scenes (Garrod, Ferrier, and Campbell, 1999), or relative movement of located and reference objects (Coventry, 1998; Richards, Coventry, and Clibbens, 2004; see also Richards and Coventry, this volume, Ch. 11) both influence the comprehension and production of *in* and *on*. For example, Garrod *et al.* (1999) showed participants pictures of objects located in various positions in containers or on supporting surfaces (see Fig. 10.1). One group of participants was given a range of sentences involving prepositions to rate, and another group was asked to judge what would happen to the relative positions of located and reference objects if the bowl were to be moved. Garrod *et al.* (1999) found that the appropriateness ratings of *in* and *on* were indeed affected by whether or not there was an alternative source of location control. Furthermore, there was

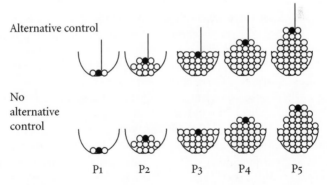

Fig. 10.1. Schematic representation of the scenes used by Garrod *et al.* (1999).

[1] Talmy originally applied force dynamics to verbs of motion, but others have extented the work to spatial language, and spatial prepositions in particular (see Coventry and Garrod, 2004 for a discussion).

a correspondence between confidence in the prepositional description and independent judgments of the perception of location control between the located and reference objects.

Coventry (1998) and Richards, Coventry, and Clibbens (2003; see also L. Richards and Coventry, this volume, Ch. 11) have tested directly whether manipulations of location control do exert any influence on the comprehension and production of *in*. Participants were presented with scenes where a located object was shown at various heights on top of a pile of objects in a container. When the located object was shown to move from side to side together (at the same rate) with the rest of the contents and container (thus demonstrating location control), *in* was rated as being more acceptable than when the whole scene was stationary. Conversely, when the located object was shown moving on its own (wobbling from side to side, but still in contact with the rest of the stationary contents), acceptability ratings for *in* were reduced compared to stationary scenes.

Another way of manipulating location control is by manipulating the animacy of the located object, as has been done by Feist and Gentner (1998). When a coin is resting on a container or supporting surface, it is only the movement of the reference object which can potentially dislodge the coin. However, an animate object, such as a firefly may well fly away of its only volition. Therefore it may be expected that ratings for *in* and *on* would be lower to describe the position of the firefly as compared to the position of the coin when they are in the same position. Indeed, Feist and Gentner found that ratings were lower for animate objects than for inanimate objects when located in the same positions on or in a hand. A greater degree of enclosure was required for the firefly than for the coin for participants to switch from *on* to *in*.

10.2.2   Object knowledge effects and *in* and *on*

A range of object knowledge effects have been documented in the literature for *in* and *on*. These include effects of object-association and object-specific function, and labeling effects. Some studies have examined whether the specific functions of objects influence the appropriateness of prepositions to describe relations between objects. Coventry, Carmichael, and Garrod (1994) found that *in* was used more and was rated to be more appropriate to describe the location of the apple in Fig. 10.2b (solid x in a bowl) as compared with Fig. 10.2c (solid x in a jug). Furthermore, adding liquid to the jug was found to further decrease the production (and rating) of *in*, but made no difference in the case of the bowl (e.g. in Fig. 10.2d *in* was used least and rated to be least appropriate). Thus the addition of water appears to make the object-specific function of the jug more salient, further reducing the appropriateness of the container as a container of solids. Coventry and Prat-Sala (2001) have found the same effect across a greater variety of materials. There is therefore evidence to suggest that *in* is influenced by the object-specific function of the reference object.

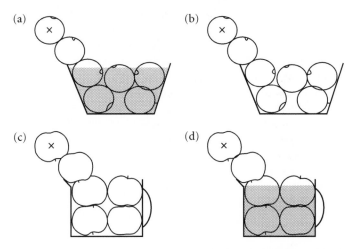

FIG. 10.2. Example scenes used by Coventry, Carmichael, and Garrod (1994), and Coventry and Prat-Sala (2001).

The influence of object specific knowledge is also highlighted in studies of how the labels given to objects in a scene can affect spatial descriptions of the scene. Coventry, Carmichael, and Garrod (1994) found that whether the same object in the visual scene depicted was labeled a *dish* or a *plate* influenced the ratings of *in* and *on* to describe the position of a located object in direct contact with a plate/dish. Feist and Gentner (1998) also found that the same reference object labeled a bowl vs. a plate influenced ratings in a similar way.

10.3 Projective Prepositions: *over, under, above, below, in front of,* and *behind*

10.3.1 Effects due to the perceived dynamics of the interaction

Just as we have seen with the comprehension and production of *in* and *on*, there is a range of types of evidence that actual or potential dynamics present in scenes are also important for the comprehension and production of projective prepositions, such as *over* and *in front of*.

Carlson-Radvansky and Radvansky (1996) found that the presence of a functional relation between objects to be described influences the choice of reference frame used to describe the locations of those objects. Imagine a picture of a mail carrier holding a letter standing near and to the left of a mailbox. When the mail carrier was standing facing the mailbox with hand outstretched as if to be posting the letter, then participants had a preference for using intrinsic descriptions (e.g. *The mail carrier is in front of the mailbox*). In contrast, when the mail carrier was standing with his back to the mailbox, then extrinsic-relative descriptions were preferred (e.g. *The mail carrier is to the left of the mailbox*). Therefore, the use of the intrinsic reference frame is preferred when the located object and reference object are in a position to interact with each other. Following on from this, it might be expected that blocking the mail carrier's access to the mailbox would diminish the appropriateness of *in front of* to describe the mail carrier. Richards (2001) and Richards and Coventry (in submission) tested this by placing a screen between located and reference objects using similar manipulations to those just described. Indeed, as expected, they found that the production of *in front of* (intrinsic reference frame) decreased when access to the reference object was obstructed by the screen in a free production task.

In another study, Carlson-Radvansky, Covey, and Lattanzi (1999) asked participants to rate the appropriateness of *The coin is above the piggy bank* to describe the location of a coin positioned in relation to a piggy bank which had a coin slot in various positions on its back. The position of the slot varied so that it either coincided with a position directly above the centre of mass of the piggy bank or did not. They found that acceptability ratings shifted as a function of slot position. The highest ratings were in cases in which the coin was aligned with the slot, rather than directly higher than the centre of mass of the piggy bank. These results are consistent with the idea that participants use what we term a *dynamic–kinematic routine* (of which *location control* for *in* and *on* is another example) to determine what would happen to the coin should it be dropped towards the piggy bank. If the coin is predicted to fall into a slot, then it is judged to be optimally *above* the piggy bank.

Coventry and Mather (2002) tested more directly whether there is a relationship between comprehension and production of the preposition *over*, and judgments of object interaction over time. Participants were shown a diagram partitioned into segments of a building which lies on the flight-path of an aeroplane, and were asked to indicate in which segment they considered the plane to be *over* the building. There were three conditions: a control condition with no additional context and two experimental conditions in which participants were told that the diagram was of a fighter-bomber on a mission to bomb a building (condition two) or target (condition three). Coventry and Mather found that in the context conditions, there was a significant association between where *over* was appropriate and judgments by the same participants as to where they thought the bomb should be dropped in order to successfully hit the building.

There is also some evidence that there is a greater influence of dynamic–kinematic routines for some prepositions compared to others. Coventry and Mather (2002) found weaker effects of context in their study for *above* as compared to *over*. Furthermore, Coventry, Prat-Sala, and Richards (2001) similarly found a much greater influence of extra-geometric relations for *over* and *under* than for *above* and *below*. In a series of studies investigating the interplay between geometry and function on the comprehension of *over*, *under*, *above*, and *below*,

Coventry *et al.* (2001) manipulated the extent to which an object was fulfilling its protection function. Participants had the task of rating the appropriateness of sentences of the form *the located object is preposition the reference object* in order to describe positions of objects in each scene (see Figs 10.3 and 10.4).

FIG. 10.3. Example scenes manipulating function and geometry from Coventry, Prat-Sala, and Richards (2001).

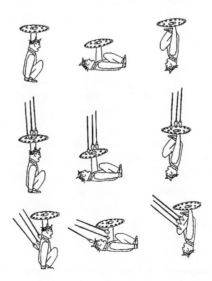

FIG. 10.4. Example scenes manipulating reference frames and function from Coventry, Prat-Sala, and Richards (2001).

Coventry *et al.* found that ratings for functional scenes overall (Fig. 10.3, middle row; mean rating = 3.81) were higher than ratings for control scenes (Fig. 10.3, top row; mean rating = 3.53) which in turn were higher than ratings for non-functional scenes (Fig. 10.3, bottom row; mean rating = 2.87). Furthermore, the functional manipulation was found to influence the ratings of prepositions even in cases where the prototypical higher than relation was present. Even when the located object was positioned directly above the reference object,[2] (in the good region identified in spatial templates; Logan and Sadler, 1996), non-functional scenes were given significantly lower ratings than functional and control scenes. In addition, Coventry *et al.* found that *over* and *under* were more affected by the manipulation of rotation of the located object away from the vertical plane than *above* and *below*, while conversely *above* and *below* were found to be more affected by this geometric manipulation than *over* and *under*. Even more striking differences between these terms were found when frames of reference were found to conflict (see also Carlson-Radvansky and Tang, 2000). Consider the scenes depicted in Fig. 10.4. With scenes on the left, the absolute (gravitational) and intrinsic (object-centred) frames of reference coincide. With scenes in the middle and on the right the absolute and intrinsic frames do not coincide, but conflict. For scenes on the left, one can say that *the shield is above the Viking* for both frames of reference, but for scenes in the middle and on the right *the shield is above the Viking* is appropriate for the absolute frame of reference but inappropriate for the intrinsic frame of reference. Indeed, for *above* and *below* acceptability ratings were found to drop as a function of the degree of frame of reference conflict present in the scene being rated. However, no effect of function was present for *above* and *below*. In contrast, function effects were very much present for *over* and *under*, but the standard frame of reference conflict effects were not observed for these terms.

In a further series of studies, Coventry, Richards, Joyce, and Cargelosi (in preparation) manipulated the degree to which an object can fulfil its function (e.g. through changing its size, or by damaging the object). They then determined effects on the appropriateness of *over*, *under*, *above*, and *below* (using the same types of materials displayed in Fig. 10.3). For example, increasing the size of an umbrella increases the protection function that the object affords, while an umbrella full of holes does not afford much protection from the elements. Indeed, they found that increasing the size of the protecting objects magnified the functional effect for all spatial terms, such that the effects of the functional manipulation occur as strongly for *above/below* as they do for *over/under*. In contrast the addition of holes to the (same-sized) umbrella was found to weaken the influence of function as expected.

---

[2] Or vice versa for inferior relations (i.e. for below and under).

10.3.2   Object knowledge effects and projective terms

There is much evidence that object knowledge influences both the selection of a reference frame, and the comprehension and production of a range of projective terms once that reference frame has been selected.

Carlson-Radvansky and Radvansky (1996), as part of the mail carrier experiment described above, also manipulated the functional relations between the objects. They compared functionally related pairs of objects (e.g. mail carrier and mailbox) to pairs of unrelated objects (e.g. mail carrier and birdhouse) and found that the intrinsic reference frame was produced significantly more for related objects (e.g. *The mail carrier is in front of the mail box*) than for the unrelated objects. In contrast, the relative/absolute frames were produced significantly more for the unrelated objects (e.g. *The mail carrier is to the left of the birdhouse*) than for related objects. This indicates that knowledge of the relations between objects and how they normally interact plays an important role in the selection of reference frames.

Carlson-Radvansky and Tang (2000) also found the intrinsic reference frame is preferred over relative/absolute reference frames for *above*, using a similar task to the one used by Carlson-Radvansky and Radvansky (1996). Located objects positioned in line with the intrinsic frame were rated more acceptable for pictures denoting related objects interacting than in pictures where unrelated objects interact or where the related objects were not shown to interact. This study shows interplay between object knowledge and dynamic–kinematic routines.

Carlson-Radvansky, Covey, and Lattanzi (1999) also report a second study in which they found effects of both located object and the relationship between the located and reference object of placements of one object *above* another object. They presented a range of reference objects in which the functional part was either aligned or misaligned with the object's centre of mass (e.g. the bristles on a toothbrush). They then presented pictures of different located objects which were either functionally related to the reference object (e.g. a toothpaste tube) or unrelated to the reference object (e.g. a tube of paint). The task for participants was to stick the picture of the located object above the reference object. They found that participants positioned the related located objects between the centre of mass and the functional part, and that the deviations toward the functional part were greater for the related objects than for the unrelated objects (see Regier, Carlson, and Corrigan, this volume, Ch. 13 for more discussion of this study).

Coventry, Prat-Sala, and Richards (2001) also investigated the influence of object knowledge in the umbrella-type studies reviewed above. They compared objects which do not have a known protecting function with those that do. For example, a *suitcase* was substituted for the umbrella in the scenes in Fig. 10.3. Clearly a suitcase is not known as something that offers protection against the rain. So the question is whether it will still be judged as *over* the person to the same degree as something like an umbrella which is known to have this function. While they found that the ratings for the inappropriate functional objects were lower overall than for the appropriate protecting objects, no interactions were found between this variable and any of the other variables examined. In other words, the effects of functionality and geometry were present for the non-stereotypically functioning objects just as they were with the stereotypically functioning objects. This is clear evidence that how objects are functioning in context is important, irrespective of our stereotypic knowledge about those objects.

10.4   Other Prepositions: The Case of *between*

There is also evidence for the importance of a range of extra-geometric constraints on the comprehension and production of a variety of other spatial prepositions, such as proximity terms like *near* and *far*. Coventry and Garrod (2004) review this evidence more comprehensively than space permits here. We confine ourselves to the consideration of one further preposition: *between*.

Following the Garrod *et al.* experiments on *in* and *on*, we were interested in whether similar effects of alternative control might be present with *between*. According to the *Oxford English Dictionary* (*OED*), *between* may mean at or to a point in the area or interval bounded by two or more other points in space or time. According to this definition, an object placed in the space separating two objects should be appropriate. In accordance with data on other terms (e.g. Logan and Sadler, 1996; Regier and Carlson, 2001), one might expect that placement of the located object lower or higher than the space bounded by the two reference objects would reduce the appropriateness of *between* (see van der Zee and Watson, this volume, Ch. 8). However, there is another sense of *between*, which involves separation either physically or mentally (again recognized by the *OED*). If this is the case, then part of the meaning of *between* is to functionally restrict contact between the two reference objects. Therefore, just as alternative control of a located object reduces the appropriateness of *in* and *on* in the study of Garrod *et al.* (1999), we can predict that alternative control of reference objects may similarly reduce the appropriateness of *between* to describe the position of a located object.

The experiment presented participants with different arrangements of wooden blocks and wooden spheres and elicited judgments of the appropriateness of descriptions such as *The ball is between the blocks* to describe the position of the ball. Sentences involving a range of prepositions were included.

There were 37 scenes in all and among other things they included the following manipulation: alternative source of connection between the objects—three levels (1) no alternative source, (2) loose alternative—non-rigid like a chain, and (3) rigid and substantial alternative—for example a bolt between the two blocks.

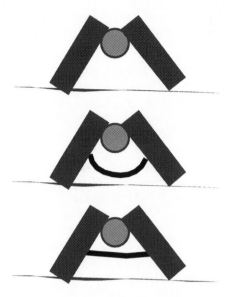

FIG. 10.5. Schematic representation of the *between* scenes.

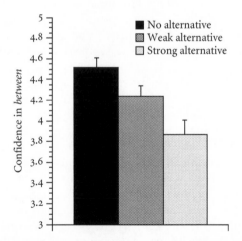

FIG. 10.6. Mean confidence (on a scale from 1 to 5) in *between* judgments for scenes containing increasingly strong alternative connectors for the reference objects.

An example set of materials is shown in Fig. 10.5. Just as expected the confidence in *between* judgments varied systematically with the degree of alternative connection between the blocks, as is illustrated in Fig. 10.6. Like *in* and *on*, alternative control also seems to be important in the comprehension of *between* (see also van der Zee and Watson, this volume, Ch. 8).

10.5   Putting Geometric and Extra-geometric Constraints Together: The Functional Geometric Framework

We have argued that the extra-geometric effects reported in the literature fall into two categories. The first are effects due to knowledge of the specific objects in the scene and the standard situations in which those objects occur. Under this banner come a variety of types of knowledge about objects and situations, including effects of labeling objects in the scene, stored associations between objects, and object-specific functional information. The second type of effect has to do with interaction, which importantly relates to actual or potential dynamics in a scene. In all the studies reviewed, what will happen over time provides the key judgment about the appropriateness of a range of terms. For example, in the case of the piggy bank study (Carlson-Radvansky *et al.*, 1999), the judgment is that the coin will be able to find its way into the piggy bank should the coin be dropped. In the *in* and *on* and *between* location control studies, the judgments have to do with objects successfully fulfilling their functions over time. Thus these results point to action as a key variable in formulating representations of objects in a scene.

The challenge, now that evidence for the existence of these multiple constraints has been established, is to work out how these constraints are put together. As a start, we have developed a functional geometric framework in which to understand the situation specific meaning of spatial expressions (Coventry and Garrod, 2004). In this framework the two types of extra-geometric constraints, dynamic–kinematic routines, and knowledge of objects/situations, come together with what we term *geometric routines* in order to determine the situation-specific meaning of a spatial expression. Geometric and dynamic–kinematic routines ground spatial language in perception, and following Ullman's original notion of routine (1984, 1996), are optional and subject to attentional control. The Attention Vector Sum model (Regier and Carlson, 2001; see also Regier, Carlson, and Corrigan, this volume, Ch. 13) may well turn out to be an adequate characterization of geometric routines for *above* and *below*, but other terms like *in* are likely to require very different routines, possibly involving the application of a region connection calculus (Cohn *et al.*, 1997). Dynamic–kinematic routines can be regarded as another type of routine, distinct from the processing of geometry. Certainly there is good evidence that visual information is not processed in a unitary fashion. At least two different visual pathways exist (Ungerleider and Mishkin, 1982), which Milner and Goodale (1995) have labeled the 'where' and 'how' systems. More recently there is some suggestion that the visual route to action involves an association between structural descriptions for objects and stored semantic descriptions for objects (Rumiati and Humphreys, 1998). Creem and Profitt (2001) provide some preliminary evidence supporting this view. They found that the natural tendency people have to pick up a hand tool in relation to its appropriate use, even though it was the furthest part from the observer, was disrupted using a dual task paradigm. The idea that objects potentiate actions, and that the representation of objects involves an action component, is consonant with the recent claims of Glenberg and colleagues who have argued that language understanding involves the meshing together of affordances derived from indexed objects or perceptual symbols (Glenberg, 1997; Glenberg and Robertson, 2000; Kaschak and Glenberg, 2000).

Whether or not particular routines are applied to a visual scene and how such routines are weighted is affected by knowledge of the objects in the scene, the particular preposition used to describe a scene and the context in which that scene occurs (see Coventry, 1999; see also Tversky, this volume, Ch. 21). In order to deal with context effects, and the integration of multiple sources of information from a variety of routines, the functional geometric framework places situation specific models as necessary elements in the explanation of situation specific meaning (Coventry and Garrod, 2004; see also Carlson, 2000). Situation-specific models are surrogate representations which are built on-line as a function of multiple information sources in a context. Such models are interfaces between language and the world, and do not represent the direct mental representation of a scene or text, but rather represent the important features of a spatial scene or text in the context in which it occurs. Building a situation model for a spatial scene therefore allows the conceptualization of the objects in that scene to be mediated by context. Consider again the toothbrush study of Carlson-Radvansky, Covey, and Lattanzi (1999). Now imagine a context where someone is about to brush his or her teeth and is holding the toothbrush with one hand and the toothpaste with the other. In such a context our intuition is that *the toothpaste is over the toothbrush* would be most appropriate when the toothpaste tube is directly above the head of the toothbrush. Even in a case where the toothpaste tube is replaced by a tube of paint, in the context of an expressionist painter preparing to paint a picture the tube of paint is over the toothbrush when it is in a suitable position for the paint to successfully arrive on the bristles. In this account, what objects are, and how they are labeled, drives the application of routines and weights their appropriateness in context.

A final point to note is that viewers of scenes attempt to construct the most informative spatial model they can of a scene in order that the strongest inferences possible can be made consistent with the visual scene being described. For example, we have reviewed the evidence that suggests that *over* and *under* appear to involve greater weighting for the extra-geometric components in the framework than *above* and *below*, which in turn are weighted more towards geometric routines. Consider now *John is under the ball* vs. *John is below the ball*. In the first expression the inference follows that John is in a position to catch the ball, but this is not necessarily the case in the second expression. Furthermore, the same framework affords extension to the use of prepositions in metaphorical domains (see Garrod and Sanford, 1989 for a discussion). *John works under Steve* suggests that Steve is John's boss, but *John works below Steve* is less likely to lead to this inference.

Exactly how models are built as a function of the multiple constraints we have delineated remains to be established. However, we believe the functional geometric framework provides a starting point within which to construct more specific process models of spatial language comprehension and production.

11

Is it *in* or is it *on*? The Influence of Geometry and Location Control on Children's Descriptions of Containment and Support Events

LYNN RICHARDS and KENNY COVENTRY

Abstract

Spatial language comprehension and production is affected not just by where objects are positioned in space, but also by what those objects are and how they are interacting with each other over time. In this chapter we examine children's production of spatial expressions to describe scenes involving containment and support events which manipulate both the relative positions of objects in those scenes, and the dynamics in the scenes. The latter manipulation was a test of whether children's production of spatial expressions is influenced by what has been termed *location control* (e.g. Garrod, Ferrier, and Campbell, 1999). The study we report finds that even the youngest age group of children (from 3;4) modified the spatial expressions they produced in response to the presence or absence of location control in the scenes being described.

Feature of location control

Location control is a (force dynamic) relationship whereby the position of the located object over time is determined by the position of the reference object.

11.1 Introduction

Prepositions in English are the main lexical items used to identify the location of objects and people in the environment. They also constitute part of the closed

We would like to thank all the children of St Nicholas & St Faith Nursery School and Burraton Primary School, Saltash, Cornwall, for their enthusiasm when participating in the experiment reported here and for the teachers who went out of their way to help. We would also like to thank Sherria Hoskins for her technical help in producing the video scenes.

class set of syntactic forms (but see Gentner and Boroditsky, 2001 for discussion), and play an important role in structuring other (non-spatial) domains (Talmy, 1983). For example, when asked to describe the location of a teapot one might say *the teapot is over the cup, in front of the kettle,* or *in the sink.* In such expressions we will refer to *the teapot* as the located object, and *the cup, the kettle,* and *the sink* as the reference objects. The aim of this chapter is to examine the spatial prepositions *in* and *on* from a developmental perspective, focusing on the relative influences of geometry and the specific extra-geometric factor of *location control* (e.g. Garrod, Ferrier, and Campbell, 1999) on children's production of these terms (see Coventry and Garrod (2004 and this volume, Ch. 10) for a classification of extra-geometric variables more generally). We will begin with an overview of how location control affects the comprehension and production of *in* and *on* in adults. We then consider whether children utilize functional information when naming novel *objects* (i.e. nouns), before looking at infants' *pre-linguistic* knowledge of containment and support and the age of acquisition of *in* and *on.* We then conclude by outlining some findings from a study that investigated the influence of location control on children's descriptions of object locations (i.e. prepositions).

11.2   *In* and *on*: The Importance of the Extra-geometric Factor of Location Control in Adult Comprehension and Production

It has often been assumed that spatial prepositions define *where* objects are in the world. As such, some approaches to the semantics of the preposition *in* have focused on geometry without much consideration of the contextual factors, objects, and speakers involved (e.g. Bennett, 1975; Cooper, 1968; Leech, 1969). For example, in the expression *the x is in the y,* the preposition *in* denotes the relationship of enclosure; the inclusion of an X *in* a Y (Bennett, 1975; Cooper, 1968). Alternatively *in* might refer to dimensional properties of the location whereby 'X is *in* Y' locates X within either a two-dimensional place Y (e.g. a surface or plane) or a three-dimensional place Y (e.g. within a space. e.g. Leech, 1969). Geometric approaches to the preposition *on* primarily highlight *contiguity* with a *surface,* although the notion of support has been recognized (Cooper, 1968; Miller and Johnson-Laird, 1976).

More recently, research has begun to focus on a range of extra-geometric factors, so-called as they have to do with *what* objects are and *how* they are interacting rather than *where* they are located in space with reference to one another. These factors have been shown to influence the comprehension of words such as *in* and *on* (see Coventry and Garrod, this volume, Ch. 10; Coventry, 1998; Coventry, Carmichael, and Garrod, 1994; Garrod and Sanford, 1989; Vandeloise, 1991, 1994, and this volume, Ch. 15). For example, Vandeloise (1991, 1994, and this volume, Ch. 15) has proposed that the container/contained and bearer/burden relationships underlie the representations of the prepositions *dans* (*in*) and *sur* (*on*) in French. Indeed, Vandeloise has also proposed that the container/contained relationship (rather than the purely geometric relationship of enclosure) is one of the complex concepts that underlie children's early meaning for the preposition *dans*. For an object to be a successful container, and likewise for a surface to be successful as a supporting surface, it must be able to constrain the location of objects over time. Similarly, Garrod and Sanford (1989) proposed that the meaning of prepositions such as *in* and *on* is related to the physical/functional relationship between the located and in particular the construct of *location control*. Location control is defined as the constraint of the located object over time by the reference object. According to this account, for example, for a pear to be *in a bowl* means that when the bowl is moved, the pear should move with it. Similarly for a person to be *in a queue*, the queue, and its movement, predicts the location of the person. In the case of *on*, if a picture is *on the wall*, the wall prevents the picture from falling and if a kite is *on a string* the string *functionally supports* the kite against the force of the wind.

Therefore, this type of account contains two elements: extra-geometric information (in particular *location control*) and geometric information (enclosure for *in* and contiguity with a surface for *on*) and these elements *together* determine the meaning of *in* and *on*. Furthermore, location control relates to inherently dynamic mental representations (Freyd, 1987). When viewing a static arrangement, the claim is that how objects will potentially interact with each other, and how their relative positions may change reflects *inferred* dynamic forces between the objects in the scene (see also Talmy, 1988).

A number of studies undertaken with adults have shown that extra-geometric factors such as *location control* do indeed influence adults' production and comprehension of *in* and *on* (e.g. Coventry, 1992, 1998; Ferrier, 1996; Garrod, Ferrier and Campbell, 1999; see Coventry and Garrod, this volume, Ch. 10). For example, imagine a bowl of fruit such that the fruit is piled high above the rim of the container. When the container is so full, the only place that the other pieces of fruit can go is to be piled up higher and higher above the rim of the container. Imagine further that someone is moving the container from one place to another (e.g. from one side of the table to the other). In a scenario such as this, all the fruit remains in the same relative position to the container over time. This illustration demonstrates how a container can afford *location control* of its contents, and has been used in video studies to test the functional element of *in*. In an experimental situation, for scenes such as these not only would one expect an effect for the height of the pile where degrees of enclosure are changing (and therefore there is more likelihood that the located object will fall off the pile of fruit), but one might also expect effects of location control. When the bowl is shown to be constraining the location of the contents over time, one might expect *in* to be highly appropriate. Conversely imagine that the object on the very top of the pile is moving from side to side of its own accord as if it has a life of its own, thereby strongly suggesting that there is no location control being exerted by the bowl. Here, one would expect *in* to be much less appropriate as a description. The comparison scenes for both the location and the non-location control scenes are scenes with the same geometric manipulation but where there is no movement involved. Using manipulations of this type, Coventry (1992, 1998) and Ferrier (1996) found that *in* was used more (in a sentence completion task), and was rated as being more appropriate to describe the location of the highest object in the pile when the video scene involved location control than when the same scene was depicted statically. Conversely, *in* was rated less appropriate and was used less when non-location control was present compared to static scenes. Furthermore, it has also been shown that if a container is tilted, suggesting that its contents will fall out, adults' production and comprehension of *in* is reduced (Coventry, 1992, 1998). Garrod, Ferrier, and Campbell (1999) demonstrate similar effects with static scenes for both *in* and *on* where alternative control of the located object is manipulated with the use of a string connected to the located object.

Thus, location control affects comprehension and production of *in* and *on* in adults in constrained sentence completion tasks. In regard to the development of spatial language, one can also ask whether location control influences *children's* comprehension and production of spatial prepositions, and if so, *when* and *how* it appears within the production of spatial expressions. According to Vandeloise (1987; and this volume, Ch. 15), the container/contained relationship influences children's early understanding of the preposition *dans* (*in*). In contrast, the primacy that geometric relations are accorded in the cognitive linguistic literature (e.g. Lakoff, 1987) may suggest that geometric relations may have a privileged developmental status. For example, Landau and Munnich (1998) suggested that extra-geometric variables might only come into play when geometric constraints do not clearly hold. Following from this, one might expect that understanding of geometry precedes understanding of location control. Indeed, as reviewed next, this is consistent with children's demonstrated attention to form before function in object naming, and consistent with the existing literature on children's understanding of spatial language and their pre-linguistic knowledge.

11.3   Influences of Form and Function: The Development of Object Naming

The question of whether children's lexical learning is influenced by form or function was debated quite fiercely in the 1970s and 1980s with regard to children's acquisition of *nouns* (E. Clark, 1973*b*; Nelson *et al.*, 1978). It had been argued that children are more likely to label two objects with the same name if they share *perceptual similarities*, for example shape (E. Clark, 1973*b*). However, an equally strong assertion was made claiming that the initial categorization and naming of objects is based on some *shared function*, for example, actions that an object is capable of making or actions that children can perform on an object (Nelson, 1974, 1982). As Smith (this volume, Ch. 16) clearly demonstrates, an object's form and its function (as defined by Nelson) are often inextricably linked (see also Tversky, this volume, Ch. 21; Madole and Oakes, this volume, Ch. 18). Indeed, Nelson maintains that the child's semantic development (i.e. organization of word meaning) cannot be considered separate from the acquisition of real world knowledge.

A novel-object, novel-noun paradigm has usually been employed in an attempt to assess the relative influence of form and function (e.g. Landau, Smith, and Jones, 1998; Merriman, Scott, and Marazita, 1993; Smith, Jones, and Landau, 1996). Children are shown a novel object with a novel count noun (e.g. 'stad') and they are encouraged to learn the name of the object. Next, the children are either given some functional information about the novel object (e.g. it can be used to mop up water), or are given no functional information at all. They are then shown additional novel objects. Some of these resemble the original in their form but not their function whereas others resemble the original in their function but not their form. The children are subsequently asked a question such as *is this a stad?*

Many studies using such a paradigm have demonstrated that young children, under five years of age, respond according to the perceptual characteristics of these novel objects rather than their functional abilities (e.g. Gathercole, Cramer, Somerville, and op de Haar, 1995; Gentner, 1978*b*; Landau, Smith, and Jones, 1998; Merriman, Scott, and Marazita, 1993; Smith, Jones, and Landau, 1996; Tomikawa and Dodd, 1980). Moreover, much of this research has suggested that function is more salient for older children (over 5;0) and adults (e.g. Gathercole *et al.*, 1995; Landau *et al.*, 1998; Merriman *et al.*, 1993). Although many of these studies used completely novel artifacts, in one experiment, Landau *et al.* (1998) showed familiar objects (e.g. containers) to younger participants (mean ages 2;6, 3;7, and 5;5) and adults. First they showed them the *standard* object which was both functionally and perceptually ideal. For example, the standard container was four-sided and made of hard clay with a function to carry water. They then showed them other objects that either had the same shape but were functionally useless (e.g. had holes) or could perform the same function but were differently shaped (e.g. oval). Landau *et al.* found that when asked to generalize on the basis of name, only the adults labeled the test objects according to whether or not the object could perform the same function. However, when they were explicitly asked whether or not each test object could perform the same function as the original, the three and five year olds (and adults) responded positively to same-function test objects. In contrast, the two year olds showed no evidence of being able to correctly judge whether or not objects could carry out particular functions.

However, recent research has discovered that children as young as two years old can generalize novel nouns on the basis of function, if that function is salient and relevant to them (Kelmer Nelson, 1999). Consistent with Nelson's (1974) definition of function that highlighted the importance of an objects' actions or actions that children can perform on that object, Kelmer Nelson (1999) found that children's naming of novel objects could be influenced exclusively by functionally relevant properties (including containment) if they had prior experience of interacting with the test objects. Without this direct experience, children largely generalized by global appearance.

It appears, therefore, that children need to have some kind of direct experience if they are to utilize functional information when assigning nouns to new objects. But what of spatial language? Does functional information affect the way children describe the location of objects in a scene? Before we report a study which aimed to establish how the factors of location control and geometry influence the production of spatial expressions developmentally, we briefly examine children's early spatial language development and their pre-linguistic understanding of containment and support relations.

11.4   The Development of *in* and *on* in a Child's Lexicon, and the Pre-linguistic Understanding of Containment and Support

In and *on* are the first spatial prepositions that are typically acquired by children. Indeed, children begin to produce *in* and *on* from around the age of 1;7–2;6 (Durkin, 1980; Halpern, Corrigan, and Aviezer, 1983; Johnston, 1984; Johnston and Slobin, 1979; Sinha, Thorseng, Hayashi, and Plunkett, 1994; Tomasello, 1987; Weist, 1991). Nevertheless, experimental studies looking at the *comprehension* of *in* and *on* suggest that although children as young as 1;6 have demonstrated some ability to associate the preposition *on* with both typical and atypical types of spatial relations, the prepositions *in* and *on* are not fully comprehended until children are in their third year (around 2;3–3;0, E. Clark, 1973a; Meints, Plunkett, Harris, and Dimmock, 2002; Sinha, 1982; Weist, 1991; Wilcox and Palermo, 1975). Similarly *production* studies have shown that *in* and *on* do not become stable members of a child's spatial lexicon until well into their third year or beyond (Johnston, 1984; Sinha *et al.*, 1994).

Well before children begin to comprehend and produce their first prepositions, their general understanding of the spatial relations involved is already quite sophisticated (see Quinn, this volume, Ch. 19, for a review). In order for a child to become familiar with functional information about objects, the child will invariably need to experience that function in some way (see also Madole and Oakes, this volume, Ch. 18). Take for example the concepts of containment and support that have been posited to underlie the meanings of the prepositions *in* and *on* (e.g. Vandeloise, 1987, 1991, 1994). It is only by interacting with containers and surfaces that one might fully understand these concepts. It has been noted that even very young children enjoy putting things into and taking things out of containers, and certainly by the end of their first year many children will have experienced drinking from cups and numerous situations where containment or support fails (Bowerman, 1996*b*). It has been shown that even before children typically demonstrate an adult-like understanding of the preposition *in* (between 2;3–3;0), they have some appreciation of the concept of containment and know the canonical use of containers. For example, by the time infants reach around 10 months of age, they seem to have some expectations about the constraints on the width and height of an object that can be inserted into a container, and the understanding that the position of the container determines the position of its contents, although this only holds for instances where objects that usually fulfill the containment function (cups) are used (Freeman, Lloyd, and Sinha, 1980; Hespos and Baillargeron, 2001*a*). However, it has also been demonstrated that infants as young as 2.5–3.5 months look longer when they see the following unlikely event: an object is lowered into a container, the container is then moved away, revealing the object behind it (Hespos and Baillargeron, 2001*b*). It appears, therefore, that even very young infants might have a rudimentary appreciation that the movement of one object relative to another is a fundamental part of the concept of containment (which in turn is a core element in the factor of location control). It is likely, however, that children do not fully comprehend the basis of containment until very much later. Indeed, although they appear to understand that openings on the surface of an object afford the insertion of something into the opening, it is not until they reach around 1;5–1;8 of age that they understand that these openings need to have supporting bottoms in order for them to contain (Caron, Caron, and Antell, 1998). Thus, children demonstrate a broad understanding of the functional notion of containment by the middle of their second year.

A similar, gradual understanding of the concept of support has been demonstrated (e.g. Baillargeon, Needham, and DeVos, 1992; Needham and Baillargeon, 1993). Infants begin by demonstrating an initial concept of support; at the age of about four-and-a-half months they look longer if an object remains suspended when the visible form of support is removed (Needham and Baillargeon, 1993). By the age of around five-and-a-half months, infants appear to believe that an object can be fully supported when only its corner is in contact with a platform. However, by the age of around six-and-a-half months, infants appear to recognize that a box can fall even when partially supported (Baillargeon *et al.*, 1992).

It appears, therefore, that well before the age at which children demonstrate adult-like comprehension and production of the prepositions *in* and *on*, they have first experienced the purely geometric, visual form of objects in a spatial array and have exhibited behavior that suggests they know something of the concepts of containment and support. However, while function may feature prominently in the child's pre-linguistic conceptual repertoire, it does not necessary follow that function is important in the acquisition of spatial prepositions. For example, as Choi and Bowerman (1991) have shown, early language input can shape how the child learns and extends the meaning of spatial terms. Furthermore, as reviewed earlier, there is some evidence from the domain of object naming that form may precede function in extending the names of novel objects to new objects.

The following section describes an experiment that was designed to investigate for the first time whether the presence or absence of functional information (location control) in scenes depicting containment events affects the spatial language children produce when they describe the relative positions of objects in those scenes (Richards, Coventry, and Clibbens, 2004). The specific prepositions that were focused upon were the 'simple' topological terms of *in* and *on* (cf. Piaget and Inhelder, 1956.)

11.5   Where's the Orange? Geometric and Functional Factors in Children's Production of *in* and *on*

The purpose of the study was to determine whether children's descriptions of containment events would also reflect the functional nature of the scenes as defined by location control. In an attempt to elicit natural language production, a series of video scenes depicting two puppets hiding real objects were shown to the children. The manipulations were similar to those in the Coventry studies conducted with adults (See Fig. 11.1 where the located object is indicated by a star).

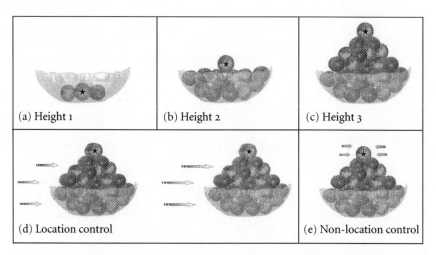

(a) Height 1

(b) Height 2

(c) Height 3

(d) Location control

(e) Non-location control

Fig. 11.1. The main bowl manipulations used by Richards, Coventry, and Clibbens, 2004.

Three levels of geometry of the scene were manipulated by systematically altering the height of the pile of the objects in a bowl. Either the located object was positioned below the rim of the bowl (Fig. 11.1*a*), level with the rim (Fig. 11.1*b*) or it was situated high above the rim of the bowl (Fig. 11.1*c*). Functional information was manipulated by way of depicting location control of the target object by the bowl where the target object and bowl are shown to move together at the same rate (Fig. 11.1d, where double headed arrows denote a sideways movement), non-location control where the target object moved independently of the bowl (Fig. 11.1e) and static scenes).

Scenes depicting the above manipulations were interleaved with a number of other manipulations/distractor scenes of a variety of spatial arrangements (e.g. in/on/over) and were subsequently edited into four separate videos. Each video involved 32 spatial scenes presented as a 'game' for the children to play with puppets (that were also present for the duration of the experiment). The child's role was to tell a puppet wearing a blindfold where another puppet had 'hidden' the target object (a free response paradigm). We were interested to see which factors (geometric and/or location control) children considered to be important in the scenes. Indeed, if children did consider such factors to be important, we wanted to know *how* they communicated this (if at all) when describing locations. For example, in Fig. 11.1e, where is the orange? Is it *in the bowl* or is it *on the apples*? For this task, the children needed to be able to produce both *in* and *on* in reasonably large quantities in order for their utterances to be usefully categorized and analyzed. Therefore 80 children across four age groups between the ages of 3;4 and 7;8 participated in this experiment (the youngest group had a mean age of 4;1).[1]

Due to the complexity of the data and large number of manipulations involved, we will concentrate on the scenes involving the bowls and other objects in contact with canonically positioned bowls as described in detail (and shown in Fig. 11.1).

When we looked at the range and complexity of the types of completions produced by the children to describe the spatial scenes, we found that their responses fell into one of two broad categories. The first category comprised single phrase utterances, minimally containing a preposition and a noun phrase (e.g. *in the bowl*, and *on top of the oranges*). The second category of responses comprised utterances containing two single prepositional phrases combined together in a single utterance (e.g. *on the blue blocks in a plastic bowl; in a bowl with some balls*). The production of two prepositional phrases increased significantly with age. A similar developmental difference in the length of utterances

---

[1] The younger children we piloted had difficulties in that they usually stuck to one preposition (typically *in*) even though they saw plates and bowls with other objects in/on/over them. We did, however, still expect to find differences across the age groups given that children's production of *in* and *on* is not fully established until around 3;0 (Johnston, 1984; Sinha *et al.*, 1994) and that many studies have shown that children do not typically utilize functional information in their naming of objects until around the age of 5;0.

has also been found in other studies using a free response paradigm (e.g. Plumert, Ewert, and Spear, 1995). Indeed, Plumert *et al.* (1995) found that the word order children produced was important for disambiguating the location of an object. Their results indicated that the first place mentioned in these children's utterances was the main locational focus of attention, with the secondary land-mark being mentioned as merely additional information (see also Flores d'Arcais, 1987; MacWhinney, 1977). To investigate how the focus of the children's descriptions changed as a function of the manipulated factors in our study, we analyzed the data in terms of whether *in the bowl* was produced as the first (or only) prepositional phrase. For example, *the orange is on top of other oranges in the bowl* would be considered a use of *on top of oranges* as first mention, while *the orange is in the bowl on top of other oranges* would be considered as a use of *in the bowl* as first mention.

The data are summarized in Table 11.1. Children in all age groups illustrated knowledge of geometric relations in that higher piles were associated with lower production of *in the bowl* as the first (or only) prepositional phrase. Interestingly, there was an age trend, with older children displaying reliably greater changes in their production of *in the bowl* as the first (or only) description of the scenes in response to changes in the height of the pile than younger children. If geometry were the primary construct in the development of spatial prepositions, one would not expect this distinction to show an age trend. However, with con-tainment events, geometry and location control are highly correlated. When the target object is enclosed in the container, location control is also present; the higher the pile, the more likely it is that the target object will fall out should the reference object be moved (as has been reported by Garrod *et al.*, 1999). Therefore, in order to assess whether children were responding according to the

TABLE 11.1. *Mean percentage of in-bowl first (or only) utterances across age groups, N = 77*

Age group	Height 1 (Low)			Height 2 (Medium)			Height 3 (High)		
	ST	NLC	LC	ST	NLC	LC	ST	NLC	LC
1 (mean 4;1)	81	81	78	62	62	67	43	41	54
2 (mean 5;5)	88	86	91	74	72	75	58	55	60
3 (mean 6;1)	94	94	94	67	68	72	40	38	48
4 (mean 7;1)	95	94	95	71	67	71	44	39	46
All Ages	90	89	90	69	67	71	46	43	52

Note: Locational control abbreviations: ST = Static, NLC = Non-Locational Control, LC = Locational Control.

functional information in the scene we needed to examine the manipulation of location control.

When we examined the descriptions of location control we discovered that even children in the very youngest age group (range 3;4 to 4;5) not only produced *in the bowl* as their first (or only) prepositional phrase according to the geometric relationship depicted in the scene, but also depending upon whether or not the bowl was successfully fulfilling its containment function. They produced *in the bowl* as the first or only prepositional phrase significantly more when the bowl demonstrated location control than for static and non-location control scenes. Moreover, the effects of location control were present only when the target was located outside the space that the bowl occupies (i.e. heights 2 and 3). However, when the target object is contained inside the bowl, not only is the geometric constraint at its optimum, but so too is location control (see Vandeloise, this volume, Ch. 15, for a discussion of this point). These findings mirror the effects found for adults and strongly suggest that both geometry and location control are important in learning how to produce prepositions appropriately.

11.6   Summary and Conclusions

Overall, the results reported above (and more detailed analyses of all the scenes described in Richards *et al.*, 2004) show that young children are aware of and use both geometric and extra-geometric constraints when describing the relative positions of objects to containers (and supporting surfaces). Furthermore, as they become more sophisticated in their descriptions they express this information by altering the syntactic construction of their sentences. These results have also been extended for other prepositions (Richards, 2001; Richards and Coventry, submitted). Indeed, we have found evidence that the extra-geometric information in a scene is a central influencing factor for children. Even the youngest children we tested made verbal distinctions in their description of locations of objects and people in line with extra-geometric distinctions between scenes, whereas distinctions according to geometric aspects of a scene displayed a developmental trend, possibly not fully developed until much later (Richards and Coventry, submitted). However, although we have evidence that children are influenced by extra-geometric factors, it is somewhat premature to argue that these relations precede the influence of geometry in the earliest understanding of *in* and *on*. This specific question might only be answered by looking at spatial language *comprehension* rather than production. Comprehension allows the possibility of testing children as young as 1;3 for the prepositions *in* and *on* using appropriate methodologies (e.g. Choi, McDonough, Bowerman, and Mandler, 1999). Additionally, such comprehension methodologies will have the advantage of reaching any fine-grained differences between the various factors manipulated and individual prepositions examined in a way that these production studies could not.

12

Defining Functional Features for Spatial Language

LAURA CARLSON and EDWIN COVELL

Abstract

Spatial terms such as *above* are typically used to specify the location of a desired object by indicating its spatial relationship to a reference object whose location is presumed known. Use of such terms requires that the space around the reference object be parsed into particular regions (e.g. **above, below**). Previous research has demonstrated that the construction of these regions are influenced not only by geometric properties of the reference object (such as its center-of-mass) but also by its functional parts. For example, in a placement task in which participants were asked to put one object above another object, objects were more likely to be placed away from the center of the object, toward its functional part (Carlson-Radvansky, Covey, and Lattanzi, 1999). Moreover, this bias was stronger for objects that were functionally related (e.g. a coin vs. a ring placed above a piggy bank). The goal of the current chapter is to begin to define 'functionally related' by focusing on the contributions of various characteristics (e.g. surface, use, or functional features) of the reference object. To do this, we systematically analyzed the reference objects used by Carlson-Radvansky *et al.*, classifying them in various ways, and asking whether such classifications mediated the bias toward the functional part. We conclude with a discussion of the contribution of the located object, and a reflection on how to define functional features for spatial language more generally.

Functional feature

A functional feature is a part of an object that is central to its use. This feature can be flexibly determined, based on the context and manner in which the object is used.

12.1 Introduction

As H. Clark (1996) notes, language is a communicative act that is undertaken to accomplish a shared goal. In the case of spatial language, one typical goal is for a speaker to inform a listener about the location of a sought-for object (hence-forth, located object). The most efficient means of accomplishing this goal is to describe the located object's position by spatially relating it to an object whose location is already known (henceforth, reference object). An example is:

(1)   The sheet of paper is behind the printer.

Given that the world is cluttered with many objects, one might wonder what defines the printer in (1) as an appropriate reference object for the located object, the sheet of paper. For example, my desk is cluttered with not only paper and a printer but also books, a computer, a telephone, journals, a coffee mug, manuscripts to review and so on. Talmy (1983) has argued that reference objects tend to be larger and more permanent, whereas located objects tend to be smaller and more moveable (see also de Vega, Rodrigo, Dehn, Barquero, and Ato, 2002). This makes sense in terms of the goal of the utterance, because larger and less movable objects can act as more stable landmarks. This leads to an asymmetry, in that utterance (2) is much less acceptable than utterance (1).

(2)   The printer is in front of the sheet of paper.

Another factor that could influence selection of a reference object is the func-tional relationship between the objects being spatially related. For example, Ullmer-Ehrich (1982) noted that people who were describing the spatial layouts of their apartments tended to describe clusters of objects that were functionally related. Moreover, Carlson-Radvansky and Radvansky (1996; see also Carlson-Radvansky and Tang, 2000) showed that participants rated sentences describing the spatial relationship between two objects as more acceptable when the objects were functionally related and positioned in a typical interactive manner (see mail carrier and mailbox in Fig. 12.1a) than either (a) when they were functionally related but not positioned in a typical interactive manger (see Fig. 12.1b) or (b) were not functionally related (see mail carrier and birdhouse in Fig. 12.1c). Pairwise comparison of these three conditions highlights two distinct aspects of this effect. First, there is the contribution provided by the reference object itself, as indicated by the greater acceptability associated with the picture for mail-box vs. the picture with the birdhouse. Note that the sentence referring to the birdhouse is not nonsensical—the mail carrier may be trying to coax a bird to land on his hand. Nevertheless, participants seemed to prefer reference objects that depict a more typical functional interaction, and in that sense, that are more functionally related. Second, there is the contribution provided by the portrayed interaction between the located and reference objects, as indicated by the pref-erence for the mail carrier facing toward the mailbox rather than facing away. This suggests a preference for positioning objects in a manner that allows or affords their typical interaction (in the sense of Barsalou, 1999 and Glenberg, 1997; see also Barsalou, Sloman, and Chaigneau, this volume, Ch. 9; Glenberg and Kaschak, Ch. 2). Note that there also may be a contribution of the located object

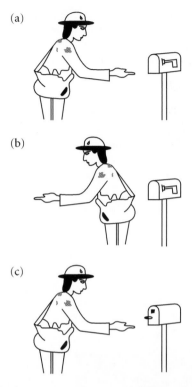

FIG. 12.1. Panels (a)–(c) show various degrees of functional relatedness. Specifically, Panel (a) depicts a mail carrier and mailbox in a typical functional interaction. Panel (b) depicts the mail carrier and mailbox in a non-functional interaction. Panel (c) depicts the mail carrier and a birdhouse in a functional interaction.

Source: Adapted from Carlson-Radvansky and Radvansky (1996).

itself, although this was not tested in Carlson-Radvansky and Radvansky (1996). In combination, these results may suggest that the most appropriate reference object would be one that is functionally related to and potentially interactive with the located object.

In the current chapter, we begin an analysis of what 'functionally related' means by focusing on the contributions of the reference object. To do this, we provide an extensive analysis of the items from Carlson-Radvansky, Covey, and Lattanzi (1999) in which we compare different classifications of reference objects to determine the features (surface, use, and functional as defined in Section 12.3) to which subjects seemed especially sensitive. We adopted two approaches: first we hypothesized dimensions that may be used to classify the objects, and then explored whether these dimensions altered the functional effect. Second, we adopted an atheoretical approach in which we performed a principal components analysis of the data to create clusters of objects from which we then tried to infer relevant dimensions. We end with a discussion of the contribution of the located object, and the implications of these analyses for defining functional relatedness for spatial language more generally.

12.2   The Functional Bias

Carlson-Radvansky, Covey, and Lattanzi (1999) presented subjects with pairs of pictures of located and reference objects, and asked subjects to place the located object above or below the reference object. Critical reference objects had a functionally important part that was offset from the center of the object, and interaction with this functional part was from above or below. Figure 12.2 shows three examples that vary in the size of the offset between the functional part and the object's center (the head of a hammer, the lens holder for a contact case, and the nozzle for a ketchup pump). A complete list of reference objects and their functional parts appears in Table 12.1. Using objects with a functional part that was offset from the center of the reference object enabled an assessment of whether participants were defining *above* with respect to geometric features of the reference object (i.e. its center-of-mass, Gapp, 1995; Regier, 1996; Regier and Carlson, 2001) or with respect to its functional parts. The identity of the located

Hammer
(head)

Contact case
(Lens holder)

Ketchup pump
(nozzle)

Fɪɢ. 12.2. Sample reference objects (hammer, contact case, ketchup pump). The functional part indicated in parentheses.

Source: Carlson-Radvansky, Covey, and Lattanzi (1999).

TABLE 12.1. *Item information from Carlson-Radvansky, Covey, and Lattanzi (1999).*

Reference object	Functional part	Deviation (mm)	Offset (mm)	Deviation (%)
Basketball hoop	Basket	14.06	24	59
Blender	Pitcher	4.50	7	64
Can opener	Blade	11.19	23	49
Cassette player	Door	10.19	26	39
CD player	Drawer	19.44	32	61
Contact case	Container	6.69	8	84
Crane	Hoist	25.13	52	48
Dishwasher	Tray	17.44	42	42
File cabinet	Drawer	11.81	29	41
Fire extinguisher	Nozzle	20.00	39	51
Fishing pole	Line	8.13	38	21
Gas pump	Nozzle	29.44	30	98
Hammer	Head	35.88	52	69
Hand dryer	Nozzle	15.75	18	88
Hand mixer	Blades	8.13	15	54
ID scanner	Scanner	15.13	15	101
Ketchup pump	Nozzle	22.63	40	57
Light	Shade	18.38	20	92
Newspaper dispenser	Door	16.63	29	57
Pencil sharpener	Hole	12.19	11	111
Piggy bank	Slot	7.00	11	64
Recycle bin	Hole	9.88	23	44
Soda fountain	Nozzle	8.50	13	65
Tea kettle	Spout	17.75	40	44
Toilet bowl	Opening	14.63	20	73
Toothbrush	Bristles	17.56	41	43
Typewriter	Paper cylinder	5.38	16	34
Video game system	Game slot	4.19	11	38
Watering can	Spout	30.75	50	62

object was also manipulated, such that some located objects were functionally related to the reference object (e.g. a hamburger for the ketchup pump or a nail for the hammer) and some located objects were not functionally related (a hockey puck for the ketchup pump or a toothpick for the hammer). Note that these latter objects are nonfunctional in the sense that they are not typically used in conjunction with the reference object, although it is plausible that a function relating the two may be imagined. These nonfunctional located objects were matched in size and shape to the functionally related located objects. The critical dependent measure was the deviation (in mm) of the placement of the located object from a line running through the center of mass of the reference object. Deviations in the direction of the functional part were coded as positive; deviations away from the functional part were coded as negative.

The critical finding was that placements of the located object were significantly biased toward the functional part of the reference object, as indicated by the positive direction of the effect. While this functional bias was stronger for functionally related located objects, it was also present for functionally unrelated located objects. Accordingly, henceforth we will collapse across this distinction, enabling us to focus exclusively on the contribution of the reference object to the functional bias effect. Note that this is appropriate, because both the functionally related and unrelated located objects were selected to interact with the reference object in the same manner. Thus, the same function of the reference object was portrayed across the two located objects (e.g. a coin and a ring dropping into a piggy bank; a tube of toothpaste or tube of oil paint squeezed onto a toothbrush). Table 12.1 provides the mean deviation of the placement (averaged across subjects) for each of the reference objects. In addition, Table 12.1 provides a measure (in mm) of the offset of the functional part, defined as the distance between a line running through center of the reference object and a line running through the functional part. The deviations coded as percentages of this distance are also provided. Note that 0 percent deviation would be perfectly aligned with the center-of-mass of the object, and 100 percent deviation would be aligned with the functional part. Intermediate deviations reflect biases toward the functional part but not coincident with it. For example, a deviation of 59 percent (i.e. the basketball hoop) indicates that the average placement of the located object was at a location that was 59 percent of the distance away from the center towards the functional part. Comparisons across objects on the basis of percent deviation are thus standardized with respect to the offset. This is important because the size of the offset (obviously) sets the range of absolute placements, as evidenced by the significant correlation between distance and deviations ($r = .72$). Accordingly, percent deviation will be used as the critical measure in the subsequent analyses.

As is evident from Table 12.1, while all deviations were greater than 0 (indicating a functional bias) the magnitude of this bias varied across the set of reference objects. We were interested in identifying the features of the reference object that were responsible for modulating the size of the functional bias. Accordingly, we classified the objects along a number of different dimensions, and asked whether the functional bias significantly differed across the classifications within a particular dimension. Due to the relatively small data set, we dichotomized each dimension, usually in terms of the presence or absence of a feature. The logic underlying our approach was that if subjects were selectively attending to a particular feature of the reference object, and if that feature had a significant impact on their placements, then a group of objects that all had that feature should show a larger functional bias than a group of objects that did not have that feature. Classification of the objects into groups was based on the first impressions of the authors, consistent with the manner in which we suspected subjects approached the original task. We only report dimensions for which each of the two groups of objects contained at least five items. Finally, our analyses are based on the 29 items described in Table 12.1; we excluded an additional item (the dolly) due to its extreme deviation (295 percent, corresponding to a placement in the direction of the functional part, but well on the other side of it).

12.3 Classificatory Features of the Reference Objects

Table 12.2 reports the features that we used as the basis of our classifications, including the number of objects falling into each group, the mean percent deviation, and an indication of the significance of an independent items one-tailed *t*-test comparing the two groups. The dimensions are grouped into surface-based features, use features, and functional features. As these different feature groups indicate, we did not restrict ourselves to strictly functional features. Indeed, for many of the surface-based and use features, it is difficult to come up with an account by which the features would modulate the functional bias. This was intentional, because this offered an opportunity to falsify our contention that the functional bias reflects a sensitivity to functional features. As such, we expected that most of the surface-based and use features would *not* modulate the functional bias. With respect to the functional features, we tried to generate dimensions that were related to the function of the object that could plausibly influence the bias.

12.3.1 Surface features

Significant factors

Breakable contrasted objects with parts that were breakable (i.e. blender, typewriter, cassette player; $N = 7$) with objects without obviously breakable parts (i.e. recycle bin, hammer; $N = 22$). The functional bias was greater for breakable objects than nonbreakable objects.

Marginally significant factors

Size contrasted whether the conceptual size of the reference object (that is, as occurs in the real world and not the actual size portrayed in the pictures) was small or large, with small objects operationally defined as those that could fit within a breadbox. The functional bias was greater for small objects (i.e. hammer, toothbrush, contact case; $N = 14$) than for large objects (i.e. newspaper dispenser, crane, basketball hoop; $N = 15$).

Nonsignificant factors

Shape contrasted the overall shape of the reference object, comparing objects that were box-like (i.e. recycle bin, hand dryer, typewriter; $N = 16$) with objects that were more elongated (i.e. hammer, can opener, toothbrush; $N = 13$).

TABLE 12.2. *Classifications of reference objects from Carlson-Radvansky, Covey, and Lattanzi (1999)*

Dimension	Categories		
Surface Features			
Breakable	Yes	No	*
	65%	46%	
Size	Small	Large	†
	67%	54%	
Shape	Elongated	Squat	ns
	59%	61%	
Material	Metal	Other	ns
	62%	57%	
Sound	Noisy	Quiet	ns
	61%	60%	
Electric	Yes	No	ns
	66%	57%	
Writing on object	Yes	No	ns
	61%	60%	
Design	Aesthetic appeal	Strictly Functional	ns
	60%	61%	
Use Features			
Location of use	Strictly indoor	Outdoor/either	†
	65%	54%	
Ownership	Private	Public	†
	56%	70%	
Type of use	Home	Business	ns
	57%	66%	
Handheld	Yes	No	ns
	60%	60%	
Functional Features			
Size of offset	Small	Large	*
	68	52	
Interaction changes located object	Yes	No	*
	66%	53%	
Is functional part vital?	Yes	No	*
	67%	54%	
Direction of functional interaction	Above	Below	ns
	57%	63%	
Contains located object	Yes	No	ns
	60%	61%	
Dispenser	Yes	No	ns
	58%	64%	

Note: * = significant difference between groups at $p \leq .05$; † = marginally significant difference between groups at $p \leq .08$; ns = not significantly different.

Material contrasted objects that contained metal (i.e. can opener, crane, file cabinet; $N = 22$) and objects that were made from non-metallic materials (i.e. piggy bank, contact case, recycle bin; $N = 7$).

Sound contrasted objects that made noise when being used in conjunction with the located object (i.e. blender, pencil sharpener, cassette player; $N = 16$) and objects whose use was quiet (i.e. light, recycle bin, tea kettle; $N = 13$).

Electric contrasted objects whose use required electricity (i.e. dishwasher, blender; $N = 12$) with objects that did not require electricity (i.e. piggy bank, recycle bin, contact case; $N = 17$).

Writing contrasted objects with writing on them (for the pictures that we used) (i.e. soda fountain, recycle bin, hand dryer; $N = 9$) with items without writing on them (i.e. light, can opener; $N = 20$).

Design contrasted objects whose design had an aesthetic character (i.e. designed to look good; aesthetic appeal of the item was important—i.e. tea kettle, watering can, piggy bank; $N = 12$) and those objects that were strictly functional (aesthetic appeal was irrelevant—i.e. hammer, file cabinet, ketchup pump; $N = 17$).

Summary

From a functional perspective, it is not surprising that many of these surface features did not modulate the functional bias. Theoretically, it is somewhat unclear why the material, general shape, sound, and other such 'perceptual' features would potentially alter the manner in which the located object would interact with the functional part. Certainly many of these features are correlated with an object's function (an object that exerts force may typically be metallic, make noise, etc.). However, these contrasts suggest that these dimensions in and of themselves are not sufficient to characterize the functional bias, and lend credence to the idea that the bias reflects a sensitivity to the function of the reference object.

The two surface features that seemed to modulate the functional bias were breakability and size. It is possible that these two dimensions are correlated, in that agents may be more likely to break small objects than large objects. As such, these features may be related to the fact that for large objects, the size of the offset between their centers and the functional parts may be larger than the size of the offset for smaller objects, and as noted below, the size of the offset significantly impacts the functional bias. As such, these surface features may only modulate the functional effect by virtue of another more functional feature.

12.3.2   Use features

Marginally significant factors

Location of use. This dimension contrasted objects that were strictly used indoors (i.e. can opener, contact case, dishwasher, pencil sharpener; $N = 15$) and objects that were used strictly outdoors or either indoors or outdoors (i.e. watering can, hammer, gas pump; $N=15$), with the functional bias greater for indoor than indoor/outdoor items.

Ownership. This dimension contrasted objects that are privately owned (i.e. toothbrush, can opener, hammer, light; $N=20$) with objects that are available for public use (i.e. recycle bin, newspaper dispenser, ketchup pump; $N=9$), with the functional bias smaller for privately owned objects than for publicly used objects.

Nonsignificant factors

Type of use. This dimension contrasted objects used within the home (i.e. can opener, contact case, basketball hoop; $N=17$) with objects used in a business (i.e. typewriter, soda fountain, recycle bin; $N=13$).

Handheld. This dimension contrasted objects that are held in the hand during use (i.e. hammer, gas pump, can opener; $N=9$) and objects that are not handheld (i.e. newspaper dispenser, crane, CD player; $N=20$).

Summary

Again, from a functional perspective, it is not necessarily surprising that these features did not play a strong role in modulating the functional effect. With respect to the two dimensions that had a marginal influence, one might think that these dimensions are somewhat redundant (e.g. indoor objects are more privately used). However, the modulation of the functional bias was not consistent for these dimensions (e.g. it was larger for indoor items than indoor/outdoor items; and larger for public items than privately used).

12.3.3   Functional features

Significant factors

Size of offset. This dimension contrasts objects with a small vs. large offset between the center-of-mass of the object and a line running through its functional part, with the functional bias smaller for objects with a small offset (i.e. basketball hoop, can opener, hand dryer; $N=15$) than for objects with a large offset (i.e. toothbrush, file cabinet, hammer; $N=14$).

Interaction changes the located object. This dimension contrasted objects that changed the functionally related located object (i.e. blender, ketchup pump, light, can opener; $N=13$) with items that did not change the located object but rather served a storage function (i.e. recycle bin, newspaper dispenser, file cabinet; $N=16$). The functional bias was larger for those that changed the located object than for objects that did not change the located object.

Functional part is most vital. The functional parts of the items were selected to satisfy the criteria that they were interacted with from above or below and that they were offset from the object's center. Accordingly, there is no guarantee that the functional part that we selected was actually the functional part that was considered most vital to the object's function. To determine whether the importance of the functional part mediated the functional bias, we took each of the reference objects, and drew bounding boxes around definable parts. For each object, we had 31 naive observers select the part that was most vital to the object's function. We then contrasted the functional bias for objects whose most vital part corresponded to our functional part (i.e. basketball hoop, contact case, can opener; $N = 14$) with objects that had different functional part selected as most vital (i.e. fishing pole, cassette player, dishwasher; $N = 15$). Objects whose most vital part coincided with our functional part had a significantly larger functional bias than objects whose most vital part did not coincide with our functional parts.

Nonsignificant factors

Direction of functional interaction. This dimension contrasted objects for which interaction with the functional part was from above (i.e. toothbrush, dishwasher, blender; $N = 14$) with objects for which interaction with the functional part is from below (i.e. can opener, fishing pole, hand dryer).

Contains located object. This dimension contrasted objects that contained at least part of the located object (i.e. newspaper dispenser, contact case, piggy bank; $N = 12$) and items that did not contain any part of the located object (i.e. ketchup pump, tea kettle, crane; $N = 19$).

Dispenser. This dimension contrasted objects that dispensed something (i.e. light, ketchup pump, typewriter; $N = 13$) with items that did not dispense anything (i.e. crane, CD player, basketball hoop; $N = 18$).

Summary

Three functional dimensions were important: the size of the offset, whether the reference object changed the located object, and whether the functional part was selected as most vital. The size of the offset is presumably correlated with the size of the object (as portrayed). Note, however, that the direction of the effect is opposite to that expected strictly on the basis of error variation according to which smaller offsets would show a larger error (because the same mm deviation converts to a larger percentage of the distance for small offsets than for large offsets). Rather, smaller offsets showed a smaller functional bias. It has been suggested that both geometric and functional features may influence spatial language use (Carlson, 2000; Carlson-Radvansky *et al.*, 1999; Coventry, Prat-Sala, and Richards, 2001). This dimension may reflect the fact that the weights assigned to the functional and geometric components vary as a function of their separability. This is an interesting question for future work. In addition, the finding that the functional bias is mediated by one type of function (change the located object) but not another (dispensing) suggests another source of variance in the functional bias that is worthy of investigation. Finally, the function bias was larger for objects whose most vital part coincided with our functional part than objects whose most vital part did not coincide with our functional parts. This suggests that the perceived importance of the functional part played a role in modulating the functional bias—that is, the observed bias to our functional part was larger when participants agreed with us that our functional part was most salient vs. when they believed another part to be most salient. Nevertheless, it should be noted that a significant functional bias occurred toward our functional part, even when participants believed another part to be most salient. This suggests that the functional bias may be defined with respect to multiple parts of an object, with its weight influenced by the relative salience of the part. This is an issue we are currently exploring. For example, one way in which to change the relative salience of a part is to change the identity of the located object. For example, for a watering can as a reference object, a plant as a located object emphasizes the spout whereas a faucet as the located object emphasizes the hole into which water is first poured (see Kenny and Carlson, in preparation).

12.4   Principal Components Analysis of the Reference Objects

The dimensions that were examined in the preceding analyses were ones that were generated by looking at the pictures of the objects and hypothesizing possible factors, both ones that we expected could modulate the functional bias (i.e. functional features), and ones that we did not expect to modulate the bias (i.e. surface and use features). In contrast, a complementary atheoretical approach would be to make no assumptions as to the relevant dimensions, but instead use the data to generate components that formed clusters of objects. Then, given the clusters of objects, one could try to infer the relevant dimensions. The advantage of this approach is that it might generate dimensions that are not tied to particular theoretical commitments.

As an example of this approach, we submitted a matrix of items and their deviations to a principal components analysis followed by varimax rotation. Sixteen subjects contributed data to each item (collapsing across the identity of the located object), with different subjects contributing to different items. We discuss only components that accounted for more than 10 percent of the variance in the correlation matrix. Items were considered to load onto a component if they had a factor loading greater than .4.

Table 12.3 presents the five components that emerged from this analysis, the variance accounted for by each component, our best guess as to the underlying dimension, and a list of the items that loaded on each component, along with their factor loadings. Note that this analysis assumes that the components are orthogonal; thus, items primarily loaded onto a single component. In the few cases in which an item loaded on multiple components, it is

TABLE 12.3. *Factor loadings from a principle components analysis of the item data from Carlson-Radvansky, Covey, and Lattanzi (1999); only loadings greater than .40 are listed*

Component Description	Component 1: Dispenses object or substance; Take or get something out of it	Component 2: Located object interacts with object through its opening	Components 3: Requires precision for use	Component 4: Functional part has flat surface that object is placed on VS a hole object is placed into	Components 5: Use is specific to certain object VS general use
Variance accounted for	15%	14%	14%	11%	10%
Objects					
Cassette Player	.925				
Ketchup Pump	.807				
Fire Extinguisher	.643				
Newspaper Box	.670				
Video Game	.487				
Contact Case		.921			
Piggy Bank		.756			
Kettle		.595			
Hand Dryer		.427			
Hand Mixer		−.891			
Pencil Sharpener			.926		
Soda Fountain			.922		
Watering Can			.714	.511	
Toothbrush			.649		
Toilet			−.562		−.662
CD Player				.818	
Hammer				.486	
Blender				−.889	
VideoGame Unit				−.513	
Lighter					.942
Can Opener					.666
ID Scanner					.547
Dishwasher					.484

assumed that independent features of the item are differentially loading onto the components. Also, in some cases the items loaded negatively onto a component, as indicated by the negative factor loading. Finally, note that each of the rotated components captured approximately the same amount of variance (range 14–10 percent).

12.4.1   The components

The first component

This component seems to include reference objects that either dispense an object or a substance. These are reference objects that one takes or gets something out of. Examples include the ketchup pump that dispenses ketchup; the newspaper box that dispenses newspapers, or the cassette player that dispenses a tape—note that this functional component of the cassette player was particularly emphasized by the sideways view of the object with its door (where you put the tape) open. According to this component, one identifiable functional feature across the set of reference objects may be the ability to dispense. Note, however, that this definition is a bit broader than the dispensing function defined in the classificatory analysis (that was not a significant factor), in that it includes the ability to 'eject'—those items that best instantiated that feature (cassette player and video game) were not classified as dispensing objects in the earlier classification analysis.

The second component

This component can best be described as discriminating reference objects whose located objects interact with the reference object through an opening: contacts are placed inside the contact case; coins are dropped into piggy banks; hands are placed around the opening of a hand dryer to receive warm air. The negatively loaded item for this component (hand mixer) does not have a single opening into which the located object is placed. According to this component, one identifiable functional feature across the set of reference objects may be containment.

The third component

This component refers to the amount of precision that is required for using the reference object in conjunction with the located object: a pencil must be placed within a very constrained hole in the pencil sharpener; the cup must be placed rather exactly under the nozzle at the soda fountain, toothpaste on a toothbrush, the small spout of the watering can. In contrast, the negatively loaded item (toilet) allows more general, less precise interaction with the located object (toilet brush—imagine moving the brush at all angles while cleaning). According to this component, an identifiable functional feature may be precision of use.

The fourth component

This component seems to differentiate between a flat surface on the functional part that provides support vs. a hole in the functional part into which an object is inserted. Examples of the supporting class of objects include the tray in the CD player, the bristles on the toothbrush, the claw of the hammer. In contrast, examples of the inserting class of objects include the blender into which ice is placed and the video recorder into which the video is inserted. According to this component, two somewhat opposing functional features can be identified: supporting and inserting.

The fifth component

This component refers to the fact that the reference object is typically used with a very constrained set of located objects: can with can opener, dishes with dishwasher. The negatively loaded item (toilet) can be used more generally—indeed, it may be the case that this item instantiates the opposite end of this component because a brush is not the most typically interactive located object for this reference object. According to this component, an identifiable functional feature may be specificity of use.

12.5   Implications and Conclusions

Based on the principal components analysis, one can derive a list of features that influenced the functional bias, and one can infer which functional features of the reference object participants were attending to. Across the five components the following functional features were identified: ability to dispense, containment, precision of use, supporting, inserting, and specificity of use. These functional features augment the functional features that were observed in the object classification phase: that the degree of functional bias varied as a function of the size of the offset, suggesting a tradeoff between geometry and function; that the bias varied as a function of the salience of the functional part; and that the bias varied with the degree to which the reference object in some way altered the located object. In some sense, these two different approaches reveal different levels of functional features, with the principal components analysis corresponding to features defined on the basis of the particular functional part as characterized by the interaction between a (typical) located object and the reference object. In contrast, the classification phase corresponds to features defined on the basis of the object as a whole, be they surface, use, or function. How these different emergent functional features interact is an obvious area for future research.

Viewing these approaches as mapping onto different levels of functional features also serves to highlight a point we began with: functional relatedness has to do with not only the function of the reference object but also the interaction between it and the located object. Following a Glenbergian approach (e.g. Glenberg, 1997; Glenberg and Kaschak, Ch. 2), another way to put this distinction is as follows: based on its particular physical characteristics a given reference object may subserve a given number of functions. That is, a shoe may serve to protect the foot or to squash a bug; however, it could not be used to comb your hair or to tighten a screw. However, given the class of functions that it could subserve, the role of the located object (foot or bug) would be to select a particular function by helping to establish the context in which the reference object will be used. In this sense, the contribution of investigating the reference object in isolation is to identify the range of possible functions. The contribution of investigating the reference object in conjunction with a located object is to identify the conditions under which each of these functions may operate.

Thus, defining functional features for spatial language in many ways is isomorphic to defining functional relatedness, in that the situational context and purpose for which the reference object and located object are used are critically important in serving to highlight particular aspects of the reference object (see Barsalou, Sloman, and Chaigneau, this volume, Ch. 9). This then has a corresponding influence on the manner in which space around the reference object is parsed and consequently described.

13

Attention in Spatial Language: Bridging Geometry and Function

TERRY REGIER, LAURA CARLSON, and
BRYCE CORRIGAN

Abstract

In this chapter, we argue that spatial language is determined in part by attentional deployment over objects. We argue further that this attentional deployment may be driven by both geometry and habitual object function. Thus, geometric and functional influences on spatial language, while separate in origin, may act through the same psychological mechanism: attention. We make this argument concrete through a computational model of projective spatial terms, the Attentional Vector Sum (AVS) model. We first review the success of this model in accounting for some purely geometric aspects of spatial language, in terms of attention. We then present a natural extension to the model, one that allows an influence of object function on attentional deployment, and thus on predicted spatial language use. We demonstrate that this extended version of the model is capable of accounting for data that indicate an influence of object function on spatial language. These results suggest that attention may serve as a unifying level of description in spatial language, bridging geometry and function.

Object function

The purpose for which a particular object is conventionally used.

13.1. Introduction

Spatial language expresses a blend of geometric and functional information. Consider, for example, the sentence 'The smoker lit the match and held it *above* his pipe.' In part, this sentence describes a purely geometric relation between the match and the pipe: we know that the match is held somewhere in a region that projects upwards from the pipe. But the sentence also suggests something more specific. We are led to imagine that the match is poised near the bowl of the pipe, that is, near the part of the pipe that is most functionally significant for the purpose of smoking—rather than over the pipe's center of mass, for instance. Such an influence of object function on spatial term meaning has been empirically demonstrated (Carlson-Radvansky and Radvansky, 1996; Carlson-Radvansky, Covey, and Lattanzi, 1999; Coventry, Prat-Sala, and Richards, 2001). Thus, the interpretation of even very simple spatial descriptions appears to be colored by object function, in addition to geometry.

How does this occur? What is the mechanism by which geometric and functional considerations are brought together in spatial meaning? We propose that this occurs in part through *attention*. Specifically, we argue that attentional deployment may be driven by both geometric and functional considerations—but that once attention is determined, spatial term use may flow from it. On this view, then, attention serves as a crucial mediating force in spatial language.

We pursue this idea as follows. We first present an attentionally based computational model of spatial language, the Attentional Vector Sum (AVS) model (Regier and Carlson, 2001). We briefly review this model's success in accounting for spatial term use relative to objects that do *not* have any intended function. This demonstrates the model's ability to account for purely geometric aspects of spatial language. We then demonstrate that a natural extension of this model (Carlson and Regier, in preparation) can also account for functional effects on spatial term use. In both cases, the attentional component of the model is critical to its success. We conclude with a discussion of the ramifications of such a demonstration.

13.2   An Attentional Account of Spatial Terms

Simple English projective spatial terms such as *above* display a graded category structure, as shown in Fig. 13.1. Here, all three circles are *above* the rectangular reference object to some degree. But of the three, A appears to be the best example of *above*, B a somewhat weaker example, and C the weakest example. What underlies such graded judgments? We argue that the structure of such *linguistic* spatial categories can be explained in the light of two observations, concerning *nonlinguistic* spatial perception and representation.

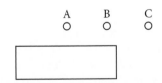

Fig. 13.1. Graded category structure for *above*.

The first observation is that the apprehension of spatial relations involves attention. Logan (1994) has shown that a visual search for a target in a field of distractors is slow and increases linearly with the number of distractors when the only difference between targets and distractors is the spatial relation (above, below, left, or right) between their elements. This finding suggests that spatial relations do not pre-attentively *pop out* of the visual field, as some visual features do (Treisman and Gormican, 1988). Rather, the perception of spatial relations appears to require the focus of attention.

The second observation is that in some neural subsystems, overall direction is represented as the vector sum of a set of constituent directions. For example, Georgopoulos, Schwartz, and Kettner (1986) examined the area of monkey motor cortex representing the animal's arm, in order to determine the cortical representation of intended arm movement direction. They found a population of broadly directionally tuned cells, such that each cell responded maximally when the monkey's arm movement was in the cell's preferred direction. The direction of arm motion was accurately predicted by a vector sum over the population of cells as a whole:

$$\sum_{i \in population} a_i \vec{v}_i$$

Here, a_i is a measure of the activity of cell i, and $\vec{v}_i$ is the preferred direction of cell i. This vector sum formulation of direction also accounts well for some aspects of motion perception (Wilson and Kim, 1994), suggesting that the representation is a widely used one.

We bring together these two observations, concerning attention and vector sum representation, in the Attentional Vector Sum (AVS) model. The model predicts spatial term acceptability judgments, such as those discussed above, based on these non-linguistic considerations. The operation of the model, and its grounding in attention and vector sum coding, are illustrated in Fig. 13.2.

In (a), we see an attentional beam focused on the reference object, or landmark. The beam is centered on that part of the landmark top that is vertically aligned with the located object, or nearest to being so aligned. Attentional strength is maximal at the focus of the beam, and then drops off with distance (Downing and Pinker, 1985; LaBerge and Brown, 1989)—indicated by the concentric circles in the figure. Thus, some parts of the landmark receive considerable amounts of attention, while others receive much less. The width of the attentional beam, and therefore the amount of the landmark that is well-attended, varies with the distance between the two objects: the farther apart the two objects are, the wider the beam, and the greater the extent of the landmark that is well-attended. It is natural to broaden the attentional beam with distance in this fashion, as the perceiver must include both objects in the attentional beam. This then is the attentional component of the AVS model.

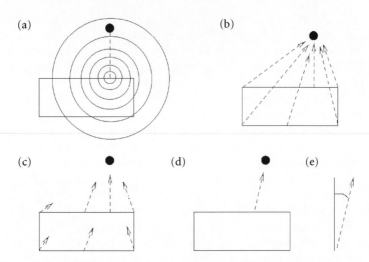

FIG. 13.2. The Attentional Vector Sum (AVS) model.

The vectorial component is shown in the next frame, (b). We define a vector projecting from each point of the landmark object toward the located object—yielding a population of such vectors.

The attentional and vectorial components of the model are joined in an *attentionally weighted vector sum*. Specifically, we use the same vector sum formula as before, namely $\sum_i a_i \vec{v}_i$ but now a_i is the amount of attention paid to landmark point i, and $\vec{v}_i$ is the vector rooted at point i. Thus, each vector is multiplied by the attentional strength at its root. This yields a population of attentionally weighted vectors, as shown in (c). These are then summed, and the result indicates the overall spatial orientation between the two objects, as shown in (d). We then measure the alignment of this vector sum with a reference axis, such as upright vertical for *above*. This is shown in (e). Perfect alignment corresponds to a perfect example of the spatial term in question—and deviations from perfect alignment correspond linearly to poorer examples. There is also a cutoff, perpendicular to the reference axis: for instance, points that are strictly lower than the highest point on the landmark are considered poor examples of *above*, regardless of the vector sum. The model has four free parameters: the (1) slope and (2) y-intercept of the linear alignment function, measuring how well the vector sum aligns with the reference axis, (3) the default width of the attentional field (attentional field width is modulated both by this parameter and by inter-object distance), and (4) the sharpness of the perpendicular cutoff. Regier and Carlson (2001) provide a more detailed formal presentation of the AVS model.

This then is a proposed account of projective spatial terms, an account that relies critically on attention. As we shall see, this model accounts well for spatial term judgments relative to a variety of simple objects.

13.3   Testing the AVS Model

There is an instructive prediction made by the AVS model, which highlights the interaction of attention and vector summation. Imagine a marble located a half-inch above a large book lying on a table. Now imagine moving the marble around over the surface of the book, but maintaining the half-inch height—and noting how good an example of *above* each positioning produces. The AVS model predicts that at low elevations of this sort, *above* ratings will not vary much as we move the marble around over the book. At higher elevations, however, ratings will vary more, peaking directly above the center of the book. Why should this be? Because at low heights, the attentional beam will be quite narrow, as beam width varies with inter-object distance. This means that attention will be restricted to the region of the book directly beneath the marble, and nearby. Critically, the edges of the book will not receive much attention—meaning that for all intents and purposes, the marble is located above a limitless plane. Thus, the vector sum will be nearly upright for a wide range of positionings. At higher elevations, however, the attentional beam will span a larger area, such that the edges of the book receive more attention—and this will affect the vector sum, resulting in greater deviations from upright vertical. Under these circumstances, a strong *above* rating is predicted only if the marble is well-centered over the book.

This prediction is not made by an intuitively reasonable-seeming competing model, the Bounding Box (BB) model. The BB model holds that a point is *above* a landmark to the extent that it falls within the rectangular region bounded by the vertical line on the right edge of the landmark object, the vertical line on the left edge, and the horizontal line at the top of the object. This region is highlighted in Fig. 13.3. The BB model predicts that the only quantities that will affect *above* ratings are the horizontal and vertical distances of the located point from the three bounding lines. When we apply the example of the marble being moved around over the book at two different heights to this model, we find that the two elevations are distinguished only by the distance from the horizontal line. And that distance will be the same across points at a given elevation. Thus, there is no prediction of greater sensitivity to centeredness at higher elevations, in contrast with the AVS model.

Regier and Carlson (2001) tested this contrasting prediction. We showed participants scenes in which a small object was located relative to a large rectangular landmark object. The array of placements of the located object, relative to the landmark, is shown in Fig. 13.4. At each point in time, the located object appeared in one of the indicated locations, and the participant indicated how good an example of *above* the resulting spatial relation was, on a 10-point (0–9) scale. We obtained a mean rating for each position by averaging the responses of all participants to that position. We then determined how well the

FIG. 13.3. The Bounding Box (BB) model.

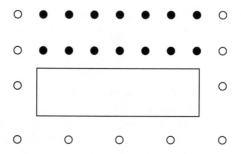

FIG. 13.4. Spatial stimuli for investigating the centeredness prediction.

AVS model, and a set of competing models, including the BB model, fit these empirically obtained data. Free parameters in the models were adjusted to fit these data as closely as possible.

The highlighted positions, shown in black in Fig. 13.4, are the critical ones that allow us to test the prediction. The AVS model predicts that ratings from the higher row will be more sensitive to centeredness than those from the lower row. The BB model and other competitors do not make this prediction.

Figure 13.5a displays the experimentally obtained *above* ratings for these critical points—with the top and bottom rows shown separately. As predicted by the AVS model, the top row is more sensitive to centeredness than the bottom row, which is comparatively flat. This difference between rows with respect to centeredness is statistically significant (Regier and Carlson, 2001: Experiment 7). Figure 13.5b shows the fit of the AVS model to these data—it is qualitatively

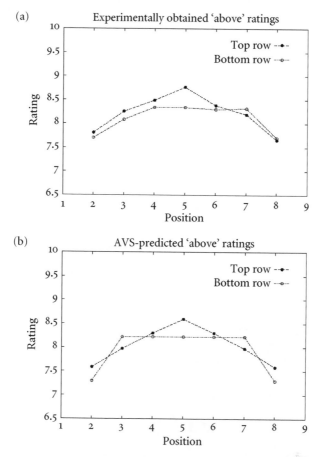

FIG. 13.5. Empirical and model responses, in testing the centeredness prediction.

similar, and quantitatively quite close ($r^2 = .888$ over these critical points; $r^2 = .985$ over all positions shown in Fig. 13.5). The AVS model also exhibited the same qualitative behavior under different parameter values, obtained by fitting the AVS model to a different set of *above* ratings. No competing model, including the BB model, was able to produce the qualitative effect shown here, even when fit directly to these data, and none had a tighter quantitative fit.

In a series of experiments, we similarly tested other predictions of AVS and the competing models, relative to a variety of landmark objects. These are shown in Fig. 13.6, with sample placements of the located object.

The AVS model provided the tightest overall quantitative fit to our data. The AVS model's fit to all our data, pooled over seven experiments, is shown in Fig. 13.7. The fit is good ($r^2 = .970$, over 337 data points), and better than those

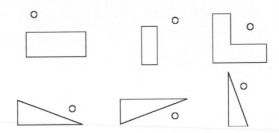

FIG. 13.6. Further spatial stimuli used in testing the AVS model.

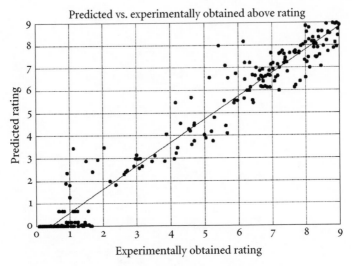

FIG. 13.7. Overall fit of the AVS model ($r^2 = .970$).

of competing models (e.g. BB $r^2 = .953$). Critically, only the AVS model also passed all of our qualitative tests.

In all of these cases, however, the objects were abstract geometric figures, and had no particular intended function. Thus, the model's success on such figures is limited in scope; it accounts for merely geometric aspects of spatial language. Could the same model also account for instances in which there *was* an intended function for the objects, as in the smoker's-pipe example with which we opened this chapter? This was the question we turned to next.

13.4 Bridging Geometry and Function

A number of researchers have demonstrated that the intended function of objects affects spatial term use and acceptability judgments (Carlson-Radvansky *et al.*,

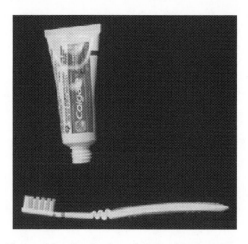

FIG. 13.8. The toothbrush stimulus of Carlson-Radvansky *et al.* (1999).

1999; Coventry *et al.*, 2001). We focus in particular on the results of Carlson-Radvansky *et al.* (1999), who found effects of object function on simple projective spatial terms such as *above*.

In one experiment, Carlson-Radvansky *et al.* (1999) showed participants pictures of objects that were functionally related (e.g. a toothbrush with its bristles pointed upwards, and a toothpaste tube). The participants were asked to place one object 'above' the other (e.g. 'Place the toothpaste tube above the toothbrush'). A possible example of such a placement is shown in Fig. 13.8.

The question of interest was just where above the toothbrush participants would place the tube: directly above the center of mass of the toothbrush, above the functional part of the toothbrush (the bristles), or elsewhere. (Although multiple reference and located objects were used in this experiment, we refer to the toothbrush and toothpaste tube, for ease of exposition.) Carlson-Radvansky *et al.* (1999) found that participants tended to place the tube above the toothbrush somewhere *between* the toothbrush's center of mass and the functionally relevant part: the bristles. Figure 13.8 captures this intermediate placement. When the two objects to be located were clearly functionally related, as in the toothbrush/toothpaste tube example, the mean horizontal displacement from the center of mass toward the functional part was 72 percent. In contrast, when the located object was not directly functionally related to the reference object (e.g. a tube of oil paint placed relative to a toothbrush), the effect was weaker: the mean horizontal displacement was 45 percent of the way from the center of mass toward the functional part of the object.

There are two points of significance in these results. First, even for simple projective spatial terms such as *above*, there appears to be an effect of object function, such that optimal *above* placements are biased toward the functional part of the reference object. Second, the amount of bias varies with the functional relatedness of the two objects. This strengthens the conclusion that the effect is one of object function.

13.5   Object Function, Attention, and the AVS Model

What might account for these functional effects? A clue lies in an observation made by Lin and Murphy (1997). They found evidence suggesting that people pay more *attention* to functional than non-functional parts of objects. Specifically, they found that people are quicker and more accurate in detecting that an object part is missing from an object when that part is a functional, rather than non-functional, part of the object. This is the pattern one would expect if people paid more attention to the functional parts of objects.

This idea of preferential attention to functional parts helps to make sense of Carlson-Radvansky *et al.*'s (1999) findings, when considered in light of the AVS model. Imagine the toothbrush and toothpaste tube of Fig. 13.8. If the bristles on the toothbrush were non-functional, and were therefore attended just as any other part of the object would be, the AVS model would yield *above* ratings that peaked somewhere near the center of mass of the toothbrush. This holds since the vector sum would be nearest upright vertical for such placements (see Regier and Carlson, 2001). However, if the bristles were to receive more attention than other parts of the object, by virtue of being functionally relevant, the vectors rooted in the bristles would come to contribute more strongly to the overall vector sum. This would cause the vector sum to deviate from upright vertical, and therefore to yield sub-maximal responses, for a located object above the center of mass. An upright vector sum, and therefore a maximal response, would be obtained when the located object was placed somewhere between the center of mass and the bristles—as in Carlson-Radvansky *et al.*'s (1999) 'toothbrush' findings.

13.6   Can the AVS Model Account for Functional Effects?

In order to test these intuitions, Carlson and Regier (in preparation) extended the AVS model to allow greater attention to functionally relevant parts of objects. Let a_i be the amount of attention paid to landmark point i under the original model, determined solely by distance as specified earlier. We now let A_i denote the total amount of attention at point i, with the understanding that this attention has both distance-based and function-based components. Specifically, we let:

$$A_i = a_i(1 + f_i)$$

Here, f_i denotes the functional status of point i. That is, $f_i = 0$ if point i is not included in some functional part of the object, and $f_i > 0$ if point i is included in a functional part. Note that if there is no functional part of the object, $f_i = 0$ for all i, and therefore $A_i = a_i$ for all i, and the model is equivalent to the original purely geometric version. However, if $f_i > 0$ for some point(s) in the object, both geometry and function will affect attentional deployment—and will thus affect the vector sum, and spatial term acceptability.

In our simulations, we set all f_i in the functional part of the object to the same single value F. The specific values of F used in our simulations are discussed below. High values of F correspond to large amounts of functionally modulated attention being paid to the functional part of the object—this is what one would expect for a toothpaste tube located relative to a toothbrush, for instance, since the two objects are functionally related to each other. Lower values of F (but still greater than 0) indicate that less functionally modulated attention is being paid to the functional part of the object. This is what one would expect for a tube of oil paint located above a toothbrush: the two objects are not functionally related, but the bristles are still a functional part of the toothbrush.

We tested this model on a version of the toothbrush experiment of Carlson-Radvansky *et al.* (1999). We created a toothbrush-like object, shown in Fig. 13.9, and set the 'bristles' to be functional—that is, we set $f_i = F > 0$ for points in the bristles, and $f_i = 0$ elsewhere.

We also specified two rows of potential locations for a located object relative to the toothbrush. These rows are also shown in the figure. We then determined whether the newly modified AVS model could account for Carlson-Radvansky *et al.*'s (1999) findings. We were interested in two specific questions. First, are the highest *above* ratings found somewhere between the middle of the toothbrush

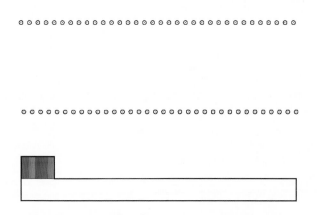

Fig. 13.9. A simplified toothbrush stimulus, investigated in simulations.

and the bristles? Second, does stronger functionally modulated attention to the bristles result in the highest ratings moving closer to the bristles?

To address these questions, we obtained an AVS-predicted *above* rating for each placement of the located object relative to the toothbrush, shown in Fig. 13.9. The model has five free parameters: the four geometric parameters described earlier, plus one functional parameter. The four geometric parameters were set by fitting the model to the spatial term data of Logan and Sadler (1996). The objects in their data are simply an 'X' located relative to an 'O'. Since these objects have no clear functional parts, the data may reasonably be considered to reflect purely geometric factors. The remaining free parameter was the functional value F, just described, controlling the strength of functionally modulated attention to the functional part of the reference object. We varied this parameter in an attempt to account for Carlson-Radvansky *et al.*'s (1999) findings.

Figure 13.10 displays the AVS-predicted *above* ratings across the top row of points (from Fig. 13.9), under three conditions. In these three conditions, the strength of functionally modulated attention, controlled by F, is either none ($F=0$), weak ($F=.3$), or strong ($F=.8$). We focus on these parameter values since they provide a good fit to the empirical data. The toothbrush at the bottom of the figure is drawn to indicate where above the toothbrush each rating was obtained.

As the figure demonstrates, functionally modulated attention to the bristles does affect *above* ratings, in the manner observed by Carlson-Radvansky *et al.* (1999). With no functional attention to the bristles ($F=0$), the ratings peak

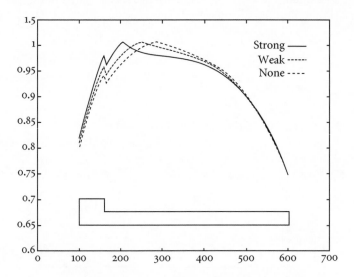

FIG. 13.10. AVS responses, exhibiting effects of object function.

approximately 25 percent of the way between the center of mass of the tooth-brush, and the nearest point of the bristles. Thus, even a purely geometric version of the AVS model exhibits a maximal response biased somewhat toward the bristles. However, the effect of function becomes clear when examining the other two cases. With weak attention to the bristles ($F = .3$), the best example of *above* is located 46 percent of the way from the center of mass of the toothbrush to the nearest edge of the bristles. This closely matches one of Carlson-Radvansky *et al.*'s (1999) empirical findings: participants placed the tube of oil paint an average of 45 percent of the way from the center of mass toward the bristles. When stronger attention is paid to the bristles ($F = .8$), AVS's best example of *above* is located 73 percent of the way toward the bristles. This in turn closely matches another of Carlson-Radvansky *et al.*'s (1999) findings, with objects that were directly functionally related: participants placed the toothpaste tube an average of 72 percent of the way toward the bristles. In general, stronger values of F cause the peak in *above* ratings to move closer toward the functional part of the object.

The AVS model thus suggests an interpretation of the empirical findings. On this model, participants tended to place located objects near the functional part of the reference object because they preferentially paid *attention* to that func-tional part (Lin and Murphy, 1997). And they tended to place directly func-tionally related objects (e.g. toothpaste tube) nearer the functional part than they did non-related objects (e.g. oil paint tube) because the function was clearer in the former case, which caused more attention to be paid to the functional part of the reference object.

13.7   Discussion

Geometric and functional features are both central to the linguistic description of space. There may sometimes be a temptation to view these two contributing forces as different in kind. After all, geometric features concern aspects of spatial reality that are quite independent of human use and convention, while functional features concern precisely those aspects of space that *are* governed by the ways in which humans interact with the world.

Nonetheless, we have argued for a commonality between geometry and func-tion. Both geometry and function may cause *attention* to be allocated to particular parts of objects, and in some instances, spatial term use may then flow from that. We have demonstrated the viability of this idea through an attentionally-based computational model, the AVS model. This model, which originally accounted for spatial term acceptability ratings relative to functionless objects, now also accounts for some effects of object function. In both cases, the deployment of attention is central to the model's success.

The significance of this work lies not so much in the specific equations that define the AVS model, but rather in the more general notion of attention as a unifying level of description, bridging geometry and function. Although these two contributors to spatial meaning are of course different in nature, it may not always be necessary, or even useful, to view them that way. It is possible that geometric and functional features have common psychological effects, and that it is those effects in turn that influence the way we speak about space.

14

Being Near the Ceramic, but not Near the Mug: On the Role of Construal in Spatial Language

SANDEEP PRASADA

Abstract

The way we construe an entity has systematic consequences for the ways in which we think and speak about it. Construals or conceptions are particular ways of understanding what something is, and, as such, they embody explanatory structures. This chapter presents a theory of the formal explanatory structures embodied in our different construals of entities as objects and as stuff, and illustrates how this difference accounts for a number of differences in the ways in which we use spatial language to talk about objects and stuff. It is argued that functional properties are central to our conceptions of many kinds of objects. They are understood to be capacities to act or be acted upon that are understood to follow in virtue of the object being the kind of thing it is (and thus properties that follow in virtue of the object's structure). Furthermore, they provide an explanation for the existence of the object and/or its structure. It is argued that construals and the formal explanatory structures they embody affect spatial language when a given construal specifies a particular way of thinking about the geometric properties of an entity. Specific situations in which this is the case are discussed.

Function

The function of artifacts and parts of living things are represented as functional capacities that can also characterize a living thing as a whole. Functional

This research was supported in part by National Science Foundation grant SBR-9618712. I would like to thank Krag Ferenz for helpful discussions and the editors for their helpful comments on an earlier draft of the chapter. This chapter was written in part while I was a visitor at the Rutgers University Center for Cognitive Science. I am grateful to the Center, Rochel Gelman, and Alan Leslie for their hospitality.

capacities are capacities of an object to act or be acted upon in a specific manner that (i) are understood to follow in virtue of the object being the kind of thing it is (and thus properties that follow in virtue of the object's structure), and (ii) provide an explanation for the existence of the object and/or its structure.

14.1 Introduction

We naturally think of the world as consisting of various kinds of things and stuff. Qualities, actions, locations, quantities, relations, and events are all naturally understood to be *of*, or involving, things and stuff. The fundamental role that things and stuff play in our conceptual systems is reflected in the fact that we usually inquire about what something is, before inquiring about other properties of the thing. Furthermore, different ways of conceiving of what an entity is can have important implications for how we think and talk about the entity. For example, if we conceive of an entity as a mug, then it makes sense to ask whether it is upside down or not, whereas, if we conceive of that *same* entity as some ceramic, then it does not make sense to determine its orientation. Similarly, conceiving of the entity as a mug allows us to ask how many parts it has, but this question makes no sense if we think of it as simply some ceramic. Finally, we can describe something that is near the interior surface of the mug as being near the ceramic, but cannot describe it as being near the mug. These differences, and others like them, do not just happen to be true of mugs and ceramic, but instead seem to follow from our understanding of what mugs and ceramic are. As such, they should be derivable from our conceptual representation of mugs and ceramic.

In what follows, I describe some recent work on the conceptual representation of things and stuff that accounts for many of these phenomena. As will be evident, this approach accords a central role to functional information in our conceptions of things and stuff. Conceptions or construals are particular ways of understanding what something is.[1] As such, they require that the entity being thought about be represented from a particular perspective or point of view. This chapter focuses on two modes of construal that are central to our thought—those that allow us to think of entities as objects and those that allow us to think of entities as stuff. The first part of the chapter presents a theory of object and substance construals, the role of functional information in this theory, and the theory's relation to other theories of conceptual representation. The second part of the chapter illustrates how this approach to construals and functional information can account for some of the phenomena mentioned above.

---

[1] I will use the terms *construal* and *conception* interchangeably.

14.2 Object and Substance Construals and Functional Information

14.2.1 Approaches to conceptual representation

Theories of conceptual representation have traditionally viewed concepts as centrally involved in categorization. Consequently, they have been concerned with specifying what has to be true of an entity in order for it to be categorized in a given manner. In particular, feature theories of conceptual representation have sought to represent concepts in terms of combinations of features that form the basis for categorization. The classical theory of concepts differs from prototype theory and its derivatives in that the former represents combinations in logical terms, whereas the latter represents combinations in statistical terms. By focusing on what has to be true of entities (logically or statistically), these approaches are able to account for a range of phenomena related to categorization, but are unable to account for the manner in which concepts mediate understanding and explanation (Murphy and Medin, 1985).

Understanding and explanation require knowing not simply what is true (how things are), but also what is responsible for things being as they are. The concepts-as-theories approach recognizes the central role that concepts play in understanding and explanation, and thus views concepts as theory-like explanatory structures (Carey, 1985; Murphy and Medin, 1985; Keil, 1989; Gelman, 1996). According to this approach, concepts in different domains are structured in terms of knowledge of domain-specific constructs and causal mechanisms.

The approach to conceptual representation that I describe below shares with the concepts-as-theories view the idea that concepts provide specific ways of understanding things. It differs from the concepts-as-theories approach, however, in that it seeks to specify the *formal* explanatory structures (FES) that are embodied in our common sense conceptions. For the sake of convenience, we may call this the FES approach to conceptual representation. This approach shares similarities with Gelman's (1990) notion of skeletal mental structures, and Keil's (1994) notion of modes of construal, in that it seeks to determine the relatively content-free structures that guide common sense conception.

14.2.2 The formal aspect of explanation and understanding in common sense conception

Unlike the theory view of concepts, which draws upon modern scientific practice in emphasizing the role of causal mechanisms in explanation, the FES approach draws upon an Aristotelian approach to explanation and understanding which makes use of a number of non-mechanistic modes of explanation and understanding.[2] Explanation of a fact (e.g. why A is B) is achieved by identifying (C)—that which is responsible for the fact. That is, that in virtue of which A is B. Importantly, there is no need to have any knowledge of *how* it is that C is responsible for A being B, only that it is.[3] In particular, we need not know anything about any causal mechanisms that may be necessary for production of the fact.[4]

This mode of understanding is illustrated in (1)–(2). These examples display the fact that the four-leggedness of dogs is understood to derive from their being dogs and not from their being animals, brown, or any other property. It is important to note that this is not a linguistic fact, but a fact about what we understand to be responsible for the four-leggedness of dogs.

(1)   Why does Fido have four legs?
(1a)   Because he is a dog.
(1b)   #Because he is an animal.[5]
(1c)   #Because he is brown.
(2)   Dogs are four-legged.
(2a)   Dogs, in virtue of being dogs, are four-legged.

Because this mode of understanding does not make reference to causal mechanisms, it is applicable to facts whose explanation does not depend on any type of causal mechanism (3)–(4). For example, there is no causal mechanism that links being an animal and the capacity to move by itself. The capacity is simply part of being an animal (3). Similarly, there is no causal mechanism that connects the property of being a triangle and a figure having internal angles that add up to 180°. We nevertheless identify the property of being a triangle as being the property of the figure that is responsible for the internal angles of the figure adding up to 180°.

(3)   Why is Fido capable of moving on his own?
(3a)   Because he is an animal.
(4)   Why do the internal angles of that figure add up to 180°?
(4a)   Because it is a triangle.
(4b)   #Because it is an isoceles triangle.
(4c)   #Because it is a plane figure.

---

[2] In this the approach builds on similar work by Moravcsik (1975, 1981, 1990) and Pustejovsky (1995).

[3] The nature of explanation is a complex and large topic (see, for example, papers in Keil and Wilson, 2000). My purpose here is only to elucidate the nature of the explanatory structures that I see as being operative in our common sense conceptions of things and stuff. The account of explanation assumed here is similar in many respects to that proposed by Wilson and Keil (2000).

[4] In this respect this mode of understanding is similar to that provided by the 'design stance' (Dennett, 1987, 1996).

[5] I will use the symbol # to denote that the sentence is in some way inappropriate or unacceptable in the given context.

It is important to note that this mode of explanation and understanding applies equally well to cases in which causal mechanisms are at work (5). So, for example, we can identify the hitting of the window by a rock as that which is responsible for the window's breaking. In doing so we explain the event without making reference to the causal mechanisms that are at work. The next section illustrates how this formal mode of explanation and understanding enters into our conceptions of things and stuff.

(5) Why did the window break?

(5a) Because it was hit by a rock.

14.2.3 Formal explanatory structures in our conception of things and stuff

We get insight into our conceptions of things and stuff by considering what descriptions (6)–(8) reveal about our understanding of a given entity.

(6) I have no idea what that is, but it is smooth, hard, brown, weighs 10 lbs...

(7) That is a chair.

(8) That is a hunk of wood.

The first sentence, (6), merely describes the entity and does not provide any understanding of what the entity is. In contrast, (7) and (8) provide different ways of understanding what the entity is. They do so by identifying the entity as an instance of a particular kind of thing or stuff. In doing so, they state that the entity can be thought of as being essentially the same as indefinitely many other entities of the same kind (Prasada, 2003). This is the classificatory aspect of conception. This is not, however, all that there is to conceiving of the entity in a particular way. Each of these ways of conceiving of the entity (as an instance of some kind of thing or some kind of stuff) renders different aspects of the entity intelligible.

Conceiving of an entity as an object of some kind, as in (7), renders its structure intelligible.[6] On the other hand, conceiving of the entity as an amount of stuff, as in (8), does not render its structure intelligible. Evidence that this is the case comes from a number of sources including the fact that we find (10), but not (11), to be an acceptable answer to (9).

(9) Why does that have the structure it does?

(10) Because it is a chair.

(11) Because it is (a hunk of) wood.

Prasada, Ferenz, and Haskell (2002) propose that when we conceive of an entity as an object of some kind, we understand it to have the structure it does, and not

---

[6] For present purposes, structure can be thought to be simply the three-dimensional organization of the entity at a nonmicroscopic level.

some other structure, because it is the kind of thing it is. That is, we understand the structure to be *nonarbitrary*. It could not be just any other way and still be that kind of object. Having that structure is partially constitutive of being that kind of thing.[7] In contrast, Prasada *et al.* propose that when we conceive of an entity as an amount of stuff, we do not understand it to have the structure it does because it is the kind of thing it is. One must look to something other than what kind of thing the entity is to understand why it has the structure it does. Thought of as stuff, we understand the entity's structure to be *arbitrary*. Having that structure is not even partially constitutive of being that kind of stuff.[8]

Given this proposal as to what it means to make an object or substance construal, the question arises as to how we determine whether to think of the structure of an entity to be arbitrary or nonarbitrary. If our construals are not simply capricious, there must exist reasons for thinking of the structure of an entity as being arbitrary or nonarbitrary, and thus to think of it as an amount of stuff or as an object. Prasada *et al.* identify various types of reasons for thinking of the structure of an entity as being nonarbitrary. Two of these reasons are of particular interest here. They are: (i) knowledge of the existence of a generative process that is directed at producing the structure, and (ii) knowledge of the existence of structure-dependent functions/functional capacities. Knowledge to the contrary provides reasons to think of the structure as arbitrary and the entity as an amount of stuff.

Knowledge that the structure of an entity is the result of a process directed at producing that structure provides a reason to think that the structure couldn't be just any other way—why else would the process be directed at producing *this* structure? Furthermore, it provides an account of why the structure of the entity is what it is—it is what it is because there is a process directed at producing that structure. Similarly, knowledge that an entity functions in a manner that requires it to have the structure it does provides a reason for thinking that the structure of

---

[7] This may seem to preclude the possibility of non-prototypical instances of a category such as beanbag chairs, but it does not in fact do so. Very briefly, if we want to explain the structure of a beanbag chair, we cannot do so by pointing to the fact that it is a chair but must do so by pointing to the fact that it is a beanbag chair. Having that structure is understood to be a consequence of being a beanbag chair, not of being a chair. Beanbag chairs are understood to be chairs on grounds other than their having the specific structure they do (Malt and Johnson, 1992; Bloom, 1996). Clearly, much more needs to be said, however, my purpose here is to show that the theory allows for non-prototypical instances and give an indication of how this is so (see also Prasada, 1999*b*).

[8] This does not mean that the nature of stuff does not place constraints on the form of instances of stuff. Clearly, solid stuff can have shapes that nonsolids cannot and stuffs of different granularity may have different constraints on the forms that instances of the stuff can assume. The point is that the form of any instance of stuff cannot be explained by its being the kind of stuff it is. Furthermore, having a particular shape is not what (even partially) makes an instance of stuff the kind of stuff it is. In contrast, having a particular structure/shape is what (partially) makes an instance of an object kind the kind of object it is.

the entity couldn't be just any other way—otherwise the entity would be unable to do what it does. Furthermore, it also provides an account of why the structure of the entity is what it is—it is what it is because that structure is needed in order for the entity to function in the way it does. Prasada, Ferenz, and Haskell (2002) showed that participants were more likely to construe an entity as an object if they were presented with reasons to think that its structure was the result of a structure-generating process, or were given evidence for the existence of structure-dependent functions. Thus, the existence of structure-generating processes and structure-dependent functional capacities both provide reasons for thinking of the structure of an entity as being nonarbitrary. Importantly, the existence of a structure-generating process and structure-dependent functions can also provide explanations for why the entity exists and/or has the structure it does.

We are now in a position to summarize the formal explanatory structures embodied in our conception of things and stuff.[9] The structure of an object is understood to be a consequence of its being the kind of object it is. The structure of the object is not accounted for by its being constituted of what (the stuff) it is constituted of. The existence of an object (and its structure) can be accounted for by identifying that which is responsible for the structure-generating process, and thus the production of the object itself. This must be something other than the object itself and cannot be an aspect of the object. The production of an object can be accounted for by identifying the sake for which that object is produced. This could be the production of the object itself (for the sake of *re*production), or an aspect of the object, though it must be a structure-dependent aspect (e.g. a structure-dependent functional capacity). These formal explanatory relations may, at first glance, seem to be vacuous, but this is an illusion created by their obviousness. Furthermore, their obviousness is their primary virtue. These are ways in which we can't help but make sense of things.

14.2.4 The nature of function in the FES theory of conceptual representation

According to the FES theory there is a teleological or functional component to our conception of many kinds of things. This component has two key properties. First, it represents capacities to act or be acted upon that are understood to follow in virtue of the object being the kind of thing it is (and thus properties that follow in virtue of the object's structure). Second, the capacity to function in this manner provides an explanation for the existence of the thing and/or its structure.

The fact that functions are understood to be capacities to act or be acted upon that follow from the structure of the entity makes them similar in some respects

---

[9] For a more detailed and formal presentation see Prasada (2000).

to affordances (Gibson, 1979a). There are some important differences, however. Gibson's notion of affordance involves the perception of functional properties of things directly from their perceptual appearances. The notion of function that is relevant to the FES theory of conceptual representation, on the other hand, does not require the functional capacities of entities to be directly perceivable from their perceptual structure. What distinguishes conception of an entity as an object from conception of an entity as an amount of stuff is the attribution of a nonarbitrary structure in the former case, but not in the latter. This structure is understood to allow the object to function in certain ways that depend on its structure. We do not, however, have any general expectations as to how much of this structure is perceptible, and whether the link between the perceptible structure and functioning of an object is clear and direct or not. In this respect, the theory may be said to rely on a notion of *conceptual affordance* rather than one of perceptual affordance (see also Glenberg and Kaschak, this volume, Ch. 2; Barsalou, Sloman, and Chaigneau, this volume, Ch. 9). A conceptual affordance would be what we know about how an entity functions based on our understanding of *what* it is, rather than on the basis of how it looks/feels/sounds/smells/tastes. Functional properties of objects are understood to depend on their structures; however, objects can differ in how transparently their functional properties are related to their perceptual properties.

A second way in which functions in the FES approach differ from affordances is that they are understood not only to follow from the structure of an object, but also to provide an explanation for the existence of the object and its structure. Consequently, FES theory makes a distinction between capacities to act and be acted upon that (i) both follow from the structure of the object and explain why objects of that sort exist and/or have the structure they do, and (ii) other activities that the object is capable of performing because of its structure but that do not explain the existence and structure of the object. This distinction is reflected linguistically between what something is for (12) and what something can do (13). The difference is also reflected in the difference in the asymmetries in (14) and (15). Furthermore, while (17) is understood to be an appropriate response to (16), it is not an appropriate response to other functions that a chair may perform (18).

(12)   Chairs are for sitting on.

(13)   Chairs can be used for sitting on, hanging shirts on, resting one's feet,...

(14)   Chairs are for sitting on, but you can hang shirts on them too.

(15)   #Chairs are for hanging shirts on, but you can sit on them too.

(16)   Why can you sit on that?

(17)   Because it is a chair.

(18)   Why can you hang your shirt on it?

Finally, it is worth noting that the teleological component is realized in different ways depending on what object is being understood. It represents the activity that is called the *function* of artifacts (e.g. chairs) and parts of living things (e.g. heart), whereas it corresponds to various *functional capacities* (e.g. to fly, to reproduce) in the case of living things as a whole (e.g. birds). In all of these cases, the teleological component refers to an activity that is a consequence of the structure of the object under consideration, and that provides an explanation for the existence and structure of that object.

14.3   Construal, Functional Properties, and Spatial Language

Given the understanding of object and substance construals and functional capacities outlined above, I turn to a consideration of some of the ways in which construals and functional information enter into the use of spatial language.

14.3.1   Being near the ceramic but not the mug

Consider why it is that we can describe something near the interior surface of a container-like entity as being near the stuff of which the entity is made (e.g. ceramic), but not as being near the object (e.g. mug)? It is plausible that the answer involves the idea that we think of the interior region in different ways when we think of the entity as an object than when we think of the entity as an amount of stuff. Specifically, it seems natural to think of the space as a part of the object, but not to think of it as a part of the stuff (Chomsky, 1992). If the space is considered to be part of the object, then the pattern of use would be readily explained. In this case, an object in the interior region would actually be in contact with the object, and thus could not be considered near it, given that things that are near one another cannot be in contact with one another. In contrast, if the space is not considered to be part of the stuff, an object in that region would not be in contact with the stuff, and thus could not be near it. Thus the crucial question becomes: What is responsible for thinking of the interior region as a part of the object?

Two possibilities suggest themselves. The first follows from the account of object and substance construals presented above and in Prasada, Ferenz, and Haskell (2002). This is the *arbitrariness of structure* hypothesis. It hypothesizes that the space is considered to be a part of the object because construal of an entity as an object involves thinking of its structure as being nonarbitrary, and a consequence of being that kind of object. Given this, the entity is understood to have the structure it does, and the enclosed space created by the structure, in virtue of its being the kind of thing it is. Thus the space is considered to be part of the object because it has to be there in order for the object to have the structure it does and thus be the kind of thing it is. This would not be the case if the entity is thought of as an amount of stuff. In that case the structure is understood to be arbitrary, and thus neither the structure of the entity nor the space it creates is a consequence of its being the kind of stuff it is. The *functionality of space* hypothesis is that the space is considered part of the object, only if there is a function that renders the space and thus structure of the entity necessary.

Both hypotheses predict that it should be possible to describe objects as being near the interior surface of container-like entities if the entity is referred to as stuff. They differ, however, in that the functionality of space hypothesis predicts that it should also be acceptable to do so when the entity is referred to as an object, if the enclosed region is nonfunctional. Ferenz (2000) conducted an experiment that investigates these possibilities.[10] In the object construal condition, subjects were shown container-like novel entities and told what their functions were. There were two types of functions that depended on the enclosed region (containment, and covering). The third type of object had a function that didn't depend on the enclosed region (e.g. podium). Participants were shown a ball near the interior and exterior surfaces of each of the objects, and asked to rate how natural it was to describe the ball as being *near* the object. The substance condition was identical, except that participants were asked to rate how natural it was to describe the object as being near the substance. The results lend support to the arbitrariness of structure hypothesis. Specifically, when the ball was in the enclosed region, participants found the description of the ball as being near the substance more natural than the description of the ball as being near the object. However, when the ball was near the exterior surface they found the descriptions equally natural. Furthermore, there were no effects of the functionality of space.

These findings suggest that the restrictions on the use of *near* are sensitive to whether we think of the entity as an object or as stuff, but not to what kind of object it is, and, in particular, how its structure is related to its functional properties.[11] This result makes sense if we consider our understanding of natural objects like caves, which are not thought to have any specific function, but nevertheless must have the structures they do in order to be the kinds of things they are. Based on the results of the experiment described above, one might expect that things that can be described as being in caves cannot also be described as being near caves, though they may be described as being near the dirt or whatever stuff constitutes the interior surface of the cave. What matters is whether or not the structure of an entity (and thus the enclosure) exists in virtue of the entity being what it is.

---

[10] For details see Ferenz (2000). My presentation and interpretation of the experiment differs from his in detail, but not spirit.

[11] There may be some concern that participants were not thinking of the entity simply as stuff in the substance condition and were rating whether it is acceptable to say that the ball is near the stuff of which the object is constituted. Either way, the structure of the entity, and thus the enclosure is not understood to be the consequence of the stuff and so (as found) it should be possible to refer to the ball as being near the stuff.

These findings also highlight the conclusion that restrictions on the use of spatial prepositions cannot be stated by reference only to the geometric properties of the entities in question. How we construe the entities also matters. A difference in construal (as an object or as stuff) that depended upon whether the entity's structure was considered to be arbitrary or nonarbitrary influenced spatial language use. However, a difference in conception that depended upon a difference in the way in which functional properties of the object were, or were not, related to its structure (i.e. in type of object) did not affect spatial language use. This shows that not all differences in the way we think about an entity are relevant to how we speak about its location. Furthermore, it suggests that it may be that only changes in construal that depend on different ways of thinking about the geometric structure of an entity may influence spatial language use. This possibility receives further support if we consider the ways in which we conceive of geometric notions such as a line, point, and surface, and the manner in which nongeometric entities are conceived of in relation to these notions.

14.3.2   Drawing lines and making grooves

Imagine that I take a stick and drag it in a straight line through some sand. What have I done? Have I drawn a line in the sand or made a groove? Clearly, the answer depends on my intention. However, the question I want to focus on is what constitutes the difference between drawing a line and making a groove, given that the entity produced can be thought of in either way (no matter what my intention in producing it might have been).

An accurate description of the entity produced would reflect (at least) the entity's extension in all three dimensions and the material in which it exists. Conceiving of the entity as a line or as a groove renders different aspects of the entity intelligible. In conceiving of it as a line, we understand its extension in one dimension to be a consequence of its being a line, whereas, we think of its extension in the other two dimensions as not being a consequence of its being a line. In fact, they are understood to be imperfections. It is part of our conception of lines that lines, in virtue of being lines, *cannot* be extended in more than one dimension. Furthermore, the fact that it exists in matter is understood not to follow in virtue of its being a line. In fact, it is this realization of the line in matter that we hold responsible for the imperfections. In contrast, in conceiving of the entity as a groove, we understand its extension in all three dimensions to be a consequence of its being a groove, as is its existence in matter (Bierwisch, 1996). Given this difference in the manner in which we conceive of lines and grooves we can readily explain why it would be natural to say something like (19), but not (20).

(19)   The stick is in the groove.
(20)   #The stick is in the line.

Similar considerations can account for why we prefer to describe things as being in an entity described to be a (shallow) dish, but prefer describing things as being on it if it is described to be a plate (Coventry, Carmichael, and Garrod, 1994). Our understanding of what dishes and plates are leads us to think and speak about the entity in different ways. Specifically, whether its extension in the vertical dimension should be thought to be a consequence of being what it is (dish/plate) or not. Dishes are thought to be essentially three-dimensional, whereas plates are thought to be essentially two-dimensional entities. Furthermore, this difference in the way we think of the structure of dishes and plates is accounted for by what we take to be the functions of dishes and plates. The function of dishes is understood to involve containment, and thus the vertical dimension of the entity is understood to exist in virtue of its being a dish. In contrast, the function of plates is to serve as a clean surface upon which food may be served. It is the difference in function that accounts for the fact that plates are generally shallower than dishes.

In this case, unlike that of the use of *near* discussed in the previous section, the identity of the kind of object and its functional properties affect spatial preposition use. How might we account for this discrepancy? A crucial difference between the two studies involved the type of stimuli used. The Coventry *et al.* (1994) experiment used entities that were plausibly ambiguous with respect to whether they should be conceived of as being three-dimensional or two-dimensional entities. In contrast, the entities used by Ferenz (2000) were unambiguously three-dimensional and all object descriptions required them to be three-dimensional. The crucial difference seems to be that functional information could play an explanatory role in how to think about the structure of entities in the Coventry *et al.* experiment, but could not do so in the Ferenz (2000) experiment. This suggests that functional properties of entities will influence the manner in which spatial language is used insofar as it is unclear how one should think about the spatial structure of entities or spatial relations between entities and functional properties can provide a reason to think of the spatial structure in a specific manner (e.g. as two- or three-dimensional) (Landau and Munnich, 1998).

This explanatory role of functional information is also evident in its role in determining the intrinsic orientation of objects. While it is possible to assign an object an axial structure on the basis of its geometric properties (Jackendoff, 1996a; Narsimhan, 1993), and we can sometimes label these axes on the basis of geometric information (van der Zee and Eshuis, 2003), functional information also plays a role in determining the intrinsic orientation of objects (Ferenz, 2000). Functional information, unlike geometric information, can play an explanatory role by specifying *why* an object *should* be oriented in a particular manner. Similarly, normative statements about distance, for example, whether the TV is too near the couch, can only be made with respect to a standard that is determined by the functional properties of the things in question (Prasada and Ferenz, 2001). In these cases, making reference to functional properties of the things being spoken about is necessary. It is only by reference to objects' functional properties that one can provide an account of how they should be oriented, or how much distance there should be between objects.

There are, of course, other contexts in which functional information has been shown to influence the use of spatial language (e.g. Carlson-Radvansky and Radvansky, 1996; Carlson-Radvansky, Covey, and Lattanzi, 1999; Carlson-Radvansky and Tang, 2000; Coventry, Carmichael, and Garrod, 1994; Coventry, Prat-Sala, and Richards, 2001; Garrod, Ferrier, and Campbell, 1999). Here, I've been interested only in showing how construal of *what* an entity is and any functional properties it possesses in virtue of being that kind of thing may influence how we speak about where things are.

14.4 A Note on Conventional Objects

Finally, it should be mentioned that the account of things and stuff developed above reflects the FES of 'standard' objects such as tables, trees, and dogs. For objects of this sort, both the form and functional properties of the things are understood to be a consequence of what the thing is *and* the functional properties depend on the object's form. Thus, there is an explanatory relation between what an object is and its form (i.e. it has the form it does because it is the kind of thing it is), and between what it is and its functional properties (i.e. it functions the way it does because it is the kind of thing it is), as well as an explanatory relation between its form and function (i.e. it functions the way it does because it has the form it does). Conventional objects such as pawns, coins, and words, on the other hand, possess a different FES. Conventional objects possess the forms and functions they do because they are what they are, but their functional properties are not a consequence of the object's form. Consequently, there is no explanatory relation between the form and functional properties of the object. The link between the structure and function of conventional objects is understood to be produced either by agreement or stipulation, rather than being intrinsic.

14.5 Conclusion

Our construal of what something is has wide ranging consequences for the ways in which we think and speak about it. This chapter has sought to illustrate some of the formal explanatory relations that are embedded in our conceptions of objects and stuff, and how they enter into how we use spatial language to speak about objects and stuff. These include explanatory relations that make reference to functional properties. Functional properties are understood to be capacities to act or be acted upon that follow in virtue of what kind of thing an object is.

Furthermore, they can explain the existence and/or the structure of standard objects, and the existence but not the structure of conventional objects. In all of these cases, functional properties are explained by or explain some aspect of what something is. As such, functional properties are understood in relational terms and their representation requires appropriate relational representational structures (Gelman and Williams, 1998; Prasada, 2000, 2003). An important task for future research is to discover the types of formal explanatory structures embedded in our common sense conceptions of things, and the relational resources needed in order to represent them, as well as their relation to the types of correlational structures that arise from feature theories of conceptual representation.

Construals and the FESs they embody affect spatial language when a given construal specifies a particular way of thinking about the geometric properties of an entity. Object construals require thinking of an entity's structure, including its geometric structure, as being nonarbitrary, and thus spatial language that makes reference to an entity as an object of some kind can be expected to be sensitive to the object's configurational properties. In contrast, substance construals require thinking of the entity's form as being the consequence of something other than what (stuff) it is and thus spatial language that refers to the entity as some stuff will be generally insensitive to the form of the entity. In other cases, the specific kind of object something is construed to be (e.g. dish/plate; line/groove) can influence the use of spatial language. In these cases, the kind of object the entity is construed to be specifies how we should think about the dimensional structure of the entity. Insofar as the functional capacities of a particular kind of object are intrinsic to our conception of that kind of thing, and the functional capacities depend on the geometric structure of the entity, functional capacities will influence spatial language. A third way in which construals influence spatial language is by specifying information that may not be specified on the basis of geometric information alone, for example, the labeling of axes that is necessary for representing the intrinsic orientation of objects. Further research on the different kinds of FESs embodied in our common sense conception of things should help further specify the ways in which our construal of what something is affects the ways in which we talk about where it is.

15

Force and Function in the Acquisition of the Preposition *in*

CLAUDE VANDELOISE

Abstract

Containment, an essential relation in the activities of human beings, has an important role in the development of the spatial uses of the preposition *in*. Relations between the container and its content are characterized by static, kinetic, and dynamic properties. The preposition *in* is often defined in terms of static properties such as topological inclusion or geometric concavity. This chapter, in contrast, puts the kinetic and dynamic properties to the fore and presents envelopment and concavity as consequences of the function of containment. Whereas all properties of containment are met for many uses of *in*, some extensions are justified by only some properties. These properties, thus, behave as the features of a family resemblance. Because of this representation, containment is a complex concept. It may be called a COMPLEX PRIMITIVE because preverbal children are aware of the static and kinetic characteristics of containment. Complete knowledge of this concept develops later, when children manipulate containers and realize the dynamic aspects of containment and its function.

Features

Spatial relationships are not described by markers or conjointly sufficient conditions but by family resemblance. Prototypical situations conveyed by *in* meet all the features whereas marginal situations satisfy only some of them.

Function

The function of an object or relation is its role in the survival and well-being of infants and adults in the world. All the family resemblance features describing a functional relation are FUNCTIONAL RELATIVE TO THIS RELATION. They may be SPATIAL at the same time. For example, concavity is mainly spatial if one describes the shape of a nose but it is functional relative to containment because concave objects only can control a content in more than one direction.

15.1   Introduction

This chapter evaluates the relative importance of the topological concept of INCLUSION and the functional relationship of CONTAINMENT in the acquisition and use of the preposition *in*. The next section is devoted to terminological clarfications. First, the introduction of the term KINETIC helps to clarify the relationship between STATIC and DYNAMIC. Next, the correlations between DYNAMICS and FUNCTION are investigated. The important role of force in the use of the preposition *in* is often underestimated. This question is addressed in Section 15.3. The role of force establishes that inclusion alone cannot completely account for the distribution of *in*. This leads to an analysis of *in* in terms of containment, proposed in Section 15.4. Containment, an essential relationship in human activities, is required to completely explain the distribution of this preposition. Containment is characterized by a set of properties, including the enclosure of some content in a container and the positional control of the content by the container. During development the preposition *in* is first connected to prototypical containment, for which all the properties are satisfied. Afterwards, the use of this word is extended to situations that meet only some of the properties of containment. Each situation to which *in* is applicable shares at least one property with another situation in the set. These properties constitute the set of family resemblance features, which determines the extension of the preposition *in*. The extensions of the concept IN conveying containment are language dependent. Section 15.5 deals with the acquisition of the English preposition *in*. The pre-linguistic schematic concept of containment proposed by Mandler (1992) is compared with the COMPLEX PRIMITIVE of containment advocated in Vandeloise (1991). In the last section of this chapter, I turn back to the relative importance of envelopment and containment. In discourse, envelopment constitutes a determinant criterion for the use of the preposition *in*. As far as the motivation of the extension of this preposition is concerned, however, force is an important characteristic of containment, essential in the acquisition of this word. As a conclusion, spatial features alone cannot provide an accurate definition of the preposition *in*.

15.2   Force, Movement, and Function

According to its Greek etymology, DYNAMIC suggests the presence of force. However, this term is also used to describe events where movement is involved.[1]

---

[1] Habel (this volume, Ch. 7) clearly identifies kinetics with dynamics when he presents change of location and change of direction as two separate aspects of dynamics.

In this sense, it is opposed to STATIC. As a consequence, STATIC is often understood as an opposite of the former sense of DYNAMIC, meaning the absence of force. This is unfortunate since any interaction between material objects involves force. The only difference between static situations and so-called dynamic situations is that in the former case action and reaction (force and counter-force) are equal whereas in the case of movement, one force is stronger than the other. For example, if a pencil lies on a table, the force exerted by gravity on the pencil is balanced out by the counter-force of the table supporting the pencil. Take the table away and there will be movement because the gravitational force on the pencil is stronger than counter-force of the air. To avoid a connection between 'static' and an 'absence of force', I will oppose STATIC (absence of movement) to KINETIC (presence of movement). All static and kinetic interactions are dynamic, in the sense that some force plays a role. Instead of the binary opposition STATIC/ DYNAMIC, we propose the set of oppositions, shown in Fig. 15.1.

Geometrical properties such as shapes and topological relationships such as inclusion are not dynamic. The relation between force and movement must be clarified. Even though both are often considered as physical notions, force as a physical concept has been questioned by many physicists like Lagrange and Mach (cf. Jammers, 1957). Indeed, whereas forces may be defined as causes of movements, only their consequences, moving objects, may be observed. Therefore, forces have sometimes been considered as mystical notions unworthy of an empirical science. In the case of static dynamic relations, however, movements are only potential: the burden would fall without the bearer and the water would spill without the container. If we give up forces, then, we have to introduce a new distinction between actual movements and potential movements. Therefore, I do adhere to the concept of 'force' in this chapter. Another reason for adhering to the notion of 'force' is that outside the spatial domain, the force concept is instrumental in interpreting linguistic phenomena such as agentivity and transitivity (Talmy, 1985; Langacker, 1986), in which energy flows from the agent to the patient. Finally, humans are psychologically aware of strength. They experience action (force) through effort and reaction (counter-force) through pleasure or pain, when their body reacts to pleasant or disagreeable moving objects.

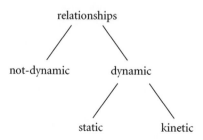

FIG. 15.1. Set of oppositions.

This psychological notion of 'force' supports the idea that this concept is instrumental in the description of language.

Most affordances needed for our survival or our well-being are based on movements or prospective movements. Even our visual perception of the environment is often linked with prospective movements that might be required for the survival or well-being of the observer confronted with the situation. Therefore, there is a strong correlation between function and movement.[2] Nevertheless, the two terms should not be considered identical. First, some movements may be out of place or without purpose. Second, and more importantly, static relationships may be functional. This is certainly the case for the relationship between a bearer and a burden (support). Even though this relation is static, the relation is dynamic at the same time: the weight of the burden may be considered as a cause for potential movement which, because of gravity, would result in falling without the counter-force exerted by the bearer. Shape, a non-dynamic property of objects, may also be functional. Even though concavity in a nose is only aesthetic, concavity in a container is a functional property. Once again, this functionality may be expressed in terms of potential movements. Indeed, concavity is needed in order to prevent the movement of the content in more than one direction. As we will see in Section 15.4, this property is an essential condition for containment.

15.3   The Role of Force in the Use of the Preposition *in*

Topological and dynamic analyses of the preposition *in* should be distinguished. Topological solutions have been proposed notably in Miller and Johnson-Laird (1976), Wunderlich (1985), and Herweg (1989) whereas dynamic descriptions have been advocated by Garrod and Sanford (1988) and Vandeloise (1986, 1994).

According to the topological interpretation, *x is in y* if *x* is included in *y*. Strictly speaking, topological inclusion of a set *x* in a set *y* means that any element of *x* is an element of *y*. In other words, *x* must be a subset of *y*. This is obviously not the case for material objects such as jewels in a box. Therefore, a strict application of topological inclusion requires the substitution of the material entities, the jewels and the box, by the places they occupy. This topological relationship is not dynamic, because force does not play any role in a topological definition. It has been demonstrated (Vandeloise, 1991, 1994) that a strictly topological definition of the preposition *in* for open containers is untenable. Here, we will replace topological inclusion by a deliberately vague notion of spatial envelopment: *x is in y* if *y* envelops *x*.

---

[2] Madole and Oakes (this volume, Ch. 18) claim that functional properties encompass dynamic rather than static information.

FIG. 15.2. A bulb in a socket.

Figure 15.2, which might represent a bottle and a cap as well as a socket and a bulb clearly demonstrates that topology alone cannot explain all the uses of the preposition *in*. Indeed, this figure can be described by sentence (1) but not by sentence (2):

(1)   The bulb is in the socket.

(2)   *The bottle is in the cap.

Since the spatial relationships between the bottle and the cap on the one hand and between the bulb and the socket on the other are similar, neither geometry nor topology can explain this contrast in acceptability. Dynamic factors are clearly involved in this discrepancy. Indeed, the socket determines the position of the bulb whereas the reverse is true with the bottle and the cap. From this example, one may surmise that the object designated by the term that is in the scope of the preposition *in* (its LANDMARK) must determine the position of the object designated by the term on the left of *in* (its TARGET). Sentence (1) fulfills this dynamic condition but sentence (2) does not.

The role of force in the use of the preposition *in* demonstrates that it cannot be exclusively defined by the topological concept of inclusion. In the next section, I will rely on previous analyses of the distribution of the French preposition *dans* (Vandeloise, 1986, 1994). The data, consistent with the behavior of the English preposition *in*, introduce the notion of CONTAINMENT. This functional relationship, primordial in our everyday life, explains the contrast between sentences (1) and (2) because one of the characteristics of the container is to determine the position of its content. The socket in sentence (1) satisfies this condition but the cap does not. Many prototypical configurations for which *in* can be used, such as jewels *in* a box, may be described by *the box contains the jewels*. However, in sentence (1), even though the socket determines the position of the bulb, it does not *contain* it. In order to explain the use of the preposition *in* in this sentence, we have to leave the physical world to enter the intricacies of language and lexical categories. All the situations conveyed by *in* share at least one family resemblance feature with prototypical containment. The list of the combinations of features sanctioning the use of *in* are called the FAMILY RESEMBLANCE CONTAINER/CONTAINED (C/c).

15.4   Containment and the Family Resemblance C/c

The lexical category *in* is considered a NATURAL CATEGORY (Rosch, 1973; Rosch and Mervis, 1975) with prototypical and marginal uses. The former uses, such as *the jewels in the box*, are associated with prototypical containment and are learned first by children. Prototypical relationships of containment in the world are characterized by the following requirements:

(a) The position of the content relative to the container does not change when the container is moving.
(b) The container prevents the content from transgressing its limits in more than one direction.
(c) Before containment, the content moves toward the container rather than the reverse.
(d) The container envelops the content.
(e) The container protects the content.
(f) The container hides the content.

Conditions (a) and (b) describe the POSITIONAL CONTROL of the content by the container. A closed container may control the content in all the directions. For a fluid, the container prevents the content from transgressing its limits in many directions at the same time. Depending on its prospective movements, a material entity that does not fulfill completely the container may be blocked in different directions at different times.[3] Bearers, which control the position of the burden in the vertical direction only, do not meet requirement (b). In prototypical uses of *x is in y*, all of the above requirements are met. However, numerous relationships in the world, such as the bulb in the socket, meet only some of these conditions. Confronted with such situations, languages may either coin a new word or extend the use of *in* to describe the marginal situation. As we know, in order to keep the size of the lexicon under control, the second solution is often chosen and the lexical category *in* looks like an exploded structure, as in Fig. 15.3 in which the circles represent the extension of the configurations meeting requirements (a), (b), and (c) respectively. Configurations in the intersection are prototypical relationships satisfying all the requirements.

Whereas the jewels in the box meet requirements (a) through (f), the bulb in the socket meets properties (a), (b), and (c) but not properties (d), (e), and (f).

---

[3] In my former analyses of the preposition *in*, conditions (a) and (b) were collapsed in one condition mentioning the control of the content by the container. The need for clarification was pointed out to me by the editors of this volume. Instead of CONTROL, Richards and Coventry (this volume, Ch. 11) use LOCATIONAL CONTROL.

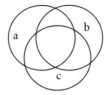

FIG. 15.3. Prototypical and marginal configurations.

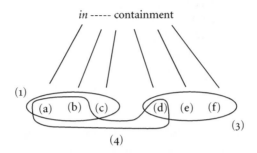

FIG. 15.4. *In* and the family resemblance C/c.

Condition (c) not fulfilled by sentences (3) and (4). Furthermore, as a corollary of requirement (b), the container must be more solid than the content in order to control its position. Such is rarely the case for the wrapping and the gift.

(3) The gift is in the wrapping.

(4) The ladle is in the soup.

These properties, then, are not necessary. Neither is condition (a) sufficient since, in a moving train, the position of a truck on the train does not change relative to the locomotive but it is certainly not contained by the locomotive. However, each circumstance in which *in* is used shares at least one of the above conditions with the other circumstances allowing for the use of this preposition. The conditions describing the situations conveyed by the preposition *in*, then, are FAMILY RESEMBLANCE FEATURES (Rosch and Mervis, 1975). The core of this split family is motivated by the relationship of containment but its extensions are determined by the conventions of each language. The set of combinations of family resemblance features sanctioning the use of *in* is called the FAMILY RESEMBLANCE C/c. Figure 15.4 illustrates the relationship of the preposition *in* with prototypical containment and shows some of the extensions allowed by English in sentences (1), (3), and (4). These sentences are acceptable because the situations they describe meet conditions (a), (b), and (c), conditions (d), (e), and (f) and conditions (a), (b), and (d)[4] respectively.

---

[4] Only the functional part of the ladle is enclosed in the soup.

In the array of properties of containment, each language chooses different features (or combinations of features) by which it extends the use of the word associated with prototypical containment to marginal manifestations of this relation. Among the extralinguistic properties of containment, then, linguists must recognize the PERTINENT FEATURES for the language they are describing. A condition F for containment is PERTINENT if there is at least one pair of combinations of conditions in which the presence or the absence of F makes the use of the word associated to containment acceptable or unacceptable. They constitute the family resemblance features that determine the extensions of the lexical category associated with containment in each language. To the best of my knowledge, French and English do not rely on condition (f) (hiding) to extend the use of the prepositions *dans* or *in*.[5] Cora, in contrast, an Indian language of south-east Mexico, takes advantage of this property to develop the use of the particle *u*, used to describe the prototypical situations represented by the preposition *in* in English (Casad and Langacker, 1985). Indeed, in addition to these uses, the particle *u* can also describe an entity going out of the visual field of the speaker. Pertinent for Cora, condition (f) is not pertinent for English and French and should be discarded from the family resemblances C/c which describe the prepositions *in* and *dans* in these languages. As we will see later, however, hiding has a role in the acquisition of the relationship of containment.

15.5   The Acquisition of the Preposition *in*

The acquisition of the preposition *in* might help linguists to assess the respective importance of topological inclusion and dynamic containment in the representation of this word. Unfortunately, psycho-linguists often blur the distinction between these two concepts. Choi and Bowerman (1991) and Bowerman (1996a, 1996b) mainly associate *in* with INCLUSION. Mandler (1992), on the other hand, relates *in* to a pre-linguistic schema called CONTAINMENT. In an article that Choi and Bowerman wrote with McDonough and Mandler (Choi *et al.*, 1999), they endorse CONTAINMENT as a concept described by *in*. But the same paper (p. 247) associates CONTAINMENT to the description of *in* proposed by Herskovits (1986), an analysis mainly based on inclusion and three-dimensionality. As a matter of fact, CONTAINMENT, as it is used by Mandler, is closer to envelopment than it is to the notion of containment presented in Section 15.4. Indeed, following Lakoff (1987), Mandler assumes that CONTAINMENT is characterized by three structural elements: INTERIOR, BOUNDARY, and EXTERIOR. As far as INTERIOR and EXTERIOR are concerned, I believe that their knowledge stems from the knowledge of containment rather than the reverse and that the explanation of containment by INTERIOR and EXTERIOR puts the cart before the horse. As for the role of

---

[5] Hiding might be a salient property for infants observing the consequences of containment.

BOUNDARY in containment, I suppose that it concerns the concavity of the container. In this way, Mandler's CONTAINMENT reduces to the envelopment of the target by the landmark and is very close to Bowerman's INCLUSION. According to Mandler, the limitations on infants' manual abilities explain why early analyses of her schema CONTAINMENT are more spatial than forceful. However, the fact that infants do not handle objects does not mean that the representation of CONTAINMENT need to reduce to the observation of non-dynamic envelopment. Indeed, experiments by Hespos and Baillargeon (2001*a*) demonstrate that three-and-a-half month old infants already have kinetic expectations and show surprise if a content in a container stays behind when the container is displaced. These infants also know that a content cannot enter a closed container and eight-and-a-half month old infants (Aguiar and Baillargeon, 1998) express surprise if a large content enters a container with a small opening. Even with handling restrictions, then, the early schema of containment might be kinetic rather than exclusively based on non-dynamic envelopment.

Even if their definitions of *in* are very close, Mandler and Bowerman differ on the role of extralinguistic concepts in the acquisition of language. Whereas Mandler believes that the schema CONTAINMENT is a pre-linguistic spatial concept instrumental in the acquisition of *in*, Bowerman claims that universal concepts are not compatible with the many different ways in which languages represent space. As an example, Choi and Bowerman (1991) propose the Korean verb *kkita* expressing TIGHT FITTING, in sharp contrast with the English preposition *in*, related to INCLUSION. This discrepancy, however, might be an artifact of Bowerman's definition. Indeed, if *in* is not defined by topological inclusion but by the dynamic containment, a strong resemblance appears between this preposition and the Korean verb *kkita*. As a matter of fact, tight fitting satisfies all the properties of prototypical containment and differs only by one additional feature (g) to be added to features (a)–(f) of the family resemblance C/c:

(g) The container is in contact everywhere with the content.

This does not mean that the content is in contact everywhere with the container, as exemplified by a ring around a finger, a situation for which, according to Bowerman, *kkita* may be used. If condition (g) is added, it appears that rather than a different concept, TIGHT FITTING is strongly related to CONTAINMENT. It might even be more prototypical for English infants than loose containment. This is consistent with data provided by Choi *et al.* (1999). The authors present English infants between 18 and 23 months of age with pairs of configurations in which one pair represents containment or tight fitting. Attention on the containment relation is increased if it is accompanied by an utterance of the preposition *in*. The interesting fact for our purpose is that the utterance of the preposition *in* in front of a configuration representing tight fitting elicited even more attention than its utterance in front of loose containment. Indeed, 70 percent of the English infants showed preferential attention for tight fitting whereas loose containment attracted more attention from only 55 percent. The concept of tight fitting, then, might be dominant for English children in the early stage of acquisition of *in*.

As Mandler, I believe in the role of pre-linguistic concepts in the acquisition of spatial words. However, her description of *containment* is in sharp contrast with the functional notion of containment introduced in Section 15.4. This might be because Mandler's schemas are non-dynamic or kinetic precursors of the functional relationships that emerge only later when children are able to manipulate objects. Indeed, the conceptualization of containment by infants may be very different from that of 18 month old children, close to the time when they are ready to use the preposition *in*. Mandler (1998) suggests this two-step development when she comments on Nelson's (1985) emphasis on function. Whereas Mandler is talking about processes that begin earlier in infancy, she agrees with Nelson that analysis of motion may underlie the later development of understanding of function. Caron, Caron, and Antell (1988, p. 626) confirm this development when they say: 'at 14 months and possibly older, infants have not yet differentiated the precise combination of properties that affords containment and a genuine understanding of the causal basis of that function does not begin to emerge until 20 months of age'. Thus, whereas the elaboration of Mandler's image schemas needs only geometric information, a complete command of CONTAINMENT clearly requires handling of objects in order to be completely assimilated.[6] For example, children who passively see objects or liquids disappearing into cups and those objects and liquids moving with the cups on a table cannot perceive the part of the cup that is in contact with the table. Consequently, they cannot deduce on the basis of visual evidence that cavities must have a bottom in order to contain. In Caron *et al.* (1988), 17 month old children trust that vertical cylinders without a bottom can contain sand. Interestingly, MacLean and Schuler (1989) establish that children of 14 months given a focused experience of cups and tubes learn to handle them properly months before children who have a normal experience. This progress, thus, is a result of handling and not of the development of intelligence along the steps proposed by Piaget. The role of function in the full understanding of CONTAINMENT should now be clear enough. The schematic stages of elaboration of these concepts proposed by Mandler may play a role in the organization of the early conceptual thought. These concepts are PRE-LINGUISTIC if this term means that they are acquired before the infant begins to speak. However, in a more demanding sense of the word, a PRE-LINGUISTIC concept is instrumental in the acquisition of the word that designates it. At 18 or 20 months of age, when children begin to use the preposition *in*, a more elaborate dynamic and functional concept emerges. The acquisition of the notion of containment, then, has a passive and an active stage. The passive step, as described by Mandler, is certainly pre-linguistic but is mainly kinetic and certainly not functional. The active step, on the other

---

[6] According to Glenberg and Kaschak (this volume, Ch. 2), the meaning of a situation to an individual is the set of actions available to that individual in that situation.

FIG. 15.5. Loose and tight fitting.

hand, is functional but its acquisition coincides with an age at which children are close to understanding the words conveying the concept IN. Further investigation would be necessary to ascertain whether it is completely pre-linguistic. It is also uncertain whether the functional notion of containment develops continuously from the passive stage to the active stage or whether the active stage is a different notion that replaces the passive stage.

In any case, the final functional notion of containment may be called a COMPLEX PRIMITIVE. It is PRIMITIVE relative to language acquisition because it helps to anchor the use of one of the first words in the experience of the child. It is COMPLEX because the family resemblance C/c proposed in Section 15.3 is needed for its representation. It constitutes the basis for the elaboration of *in* in English as well as for the acquisition of the words related to this concept in different languages.

Concerning the role of the late developments of the concept of containment such as the handling of open tubes, an observation on the use of *in* by adults is worth mentioning. An upside-down bowl, one large open tube, and one small open tube on a table with a ball inside may be described by sentences (5)–(7):

(5) *The ball is in the bowl.

(6) ?The ball is in the large tube.

(7) The ball is in the small tube.

In sentence (5), *in* is unacceptable because the bowl can be moved without triggering a movement of the ball (in violation of the feature (a) of the family resemblance C/c). The large tube does not fare much better as far as control is concerned. Nevertheless, sentence (6) might be chosen instead of the more appropriate formulation: *the tube surrounds the ball*. Interestingly, *in* is more appropriate in sentence (7) for the smallest tube that is in contact with the ball everywhere. This may be so because in this case, friction helps the tube to control the ball. In any event, the contrast between sentences (6) and (7) shows that TIGHT FITTING may trigger the use of the preposition *in* when the conditions of containment are not entirely fulfilled.

15.6 Relative Importance of Geometric and Dynamic Factors in the Use of the Preposition *in*

The family resemblance C/c, which determines the use of *x is in y*, combines dynamic properties such as the positional control of the target *x* by the landmark *y* with topological properties such as the envelopment of the target by the land-mark and geometric concavity. What is the relative importance of these factors in the use of the preposition *in*? In the literature on the acquisition of language, the conclusions of Smith *et al.* (1996) and Landau *et al.* (1998) are in sharp contrast to those of Kemler Nelson (1999). Whereas the former authors emphasize the role of perceptual similarity in the categorization of artifacts,[7] Kemler Nelson reports that pre-schoolers between 28 and 33 months rank function over perceived similarity in the classification of a utensil. The latter author explains this dis-crepancy by the fact that her experiment was closer to everyday life than Smith *et al.*'s testing conditions. Concerning adults, Richards and Coventry (this volume, Ch. 11) and Garrod *et al.* (1999) provide interesting data showing that speakers rely on geometrical factors when concavity and envelopment are con-spicuous but rely on dynamic factors such as the positional control of the target by the landmark otherwise. Consequently, they speak of 'functional geometry' and of a hybrid concept of containment: 'situations where there is a clear geo-metry of enclosure indicate containment irrespective of control, but for the situations where the geometry is marginal we require evidence of location control before perceiving containment' (Garrod *et al.*, 1999, p. 186). In this description, one recognizes properties (a) and (d) of the family resemblance C/c, two important characteristics of containment that play a determinant role in the use of the preposition *in*.

In order to evaluate the respective importance of positional control and sur-rounding, two questions must be distinguished. The first concerns how speakers use the existing lexical category *in*. The second asks how such lexical categories occur in a language. Garrod *et al.* (1999) and Richards and Coventry (this volume, Ch. 11) are obviously concerned with the first question. At this level, speakers are looking for criteria allowing them to determine if a word should be used. The experiments of Garrod *et al.* (1999) demonstrate that clear surrounding represents a cue in which speakers are very confident when they use the pre-position *in*. If envelopment is unclear, speakers resort to different criteria such as positional control. At the level of discourse, then, there is collaboration between the geometric and the dynamic factors with a priority assigned to geometry. This fact explains why a majority of the linguistic analyses of the preposition *in* resort to inclusion or to three-dimensionality.

In my own analysis, I am more interested in the second question: how do lexical categories describing space emerge in languages? This question would be immediately discarded by autonomous linguistics like structuralism according to which language is a structure independent from our conceptualization of the world. The multiplicity of the linguistic descriptions of space, rightly put to the forefront by Bowerman (1996a, 1996b) and Levinson (1996a), might appear

---

[7] In this volume, however, Smith notices that the way children act on objects influences how they perceive shape and how they name objects.

to confirm this theory. True, the diversity and relativity of languages constitute an argument against a rigid determination of language by the nature of the world or by its conceptualization. This does not mean though that this conceptualization does not restrict in interesting ways the number of possible alternatives, however numerous they may be. That is the reason why I proposed (Vandeloise, 1991) the notion of *impetus*, referring to the meaning of a polysemous word that better explains word development towards other meanings. From this point of view, I believe that prototypical containment, represented by the family resemblance C/c, accounts better for the extension of the preposition *in* than envelopment or inclusion by themselves. This is a small wonder since this idea of containment brings together all the properties (including envelopment) that prove to be relevant in the use of this preposition. Concepts like prototypical containment certainly ask for early linguistic expression because of their utmost functional importance in everyday life. Once a word is anchored to such a concept, its use must be stretched to cover different situations for which one does not want to coin a new word. In such extensions, the different aspects of prototypical containment such as positional control, envelopment, protection, and occlusion will be relevant. The area of extension is the place for relativity and variability. Under any circumstances, however, I believe that we are interested in plane surfaces and in concave objects because they support and contain and not in bearers and containers because they are two- and three-dimensional. Therefore, in order to explain the development of words conveying containment, positional control is more important than shape. Later on in life, when we have to deal with the words language imposes on us, the role of envelopment in our choice of words becomes important, as demonstrated by Garrod *et al.* as well as Richards and Coventry.[8] However, a direct association of *in* with inclusion cannot explain why puzzled speakers turn to positional control once geometrical and topological criteria are missing. Positional control, on the other hand, explains the importance of envelopment and concavity in the distribution of the preposition *in* as well as its strong connection with the Korean verb *kkita*.

[8] These authors also stress the importance of positional control.

Part Three

Features that are Functional:
Categorization, Learning,
and Language

16

Shape: A Developmental Product

LINDA B. SMITH

Abstract

What defines sameness in shape? A precise definition has proved elusive despite considerable theoretical and empirical efforts across several disciplines. This chapter considers the idea that the perception of object shape—perceptions of the kind that can yield rapid and reliable object recognition—is learned by young children through their actions on objects and as a product of category learning. Action-based categories create shape caricatures, abstractions, that enable the systematic broadening of recognition beyond specific experiences. Thus the processes that yield facile and reliable object recognition may not be pre-specified in the visual system but rather may be experience dependent.

Functional feature

An abstraction, created in development, the consequence of category learning.

16.1   Introduction

Shape is crucial to object recognition and categorization. Objects labeled by the same common noun are typically similar in shape (Rosch, 1976); adults readily recognize objects from simple line drawings of their global shape (Biederman, 1987); and when asked to introspect on object categories, adults say that shape is a defining property (Samuelson and Smith, 1999; Rosch, 1976). Moreover, even two year olds appear biased to form object categories by sameness in shape (E. Clark, 1973b; Smith, 1999). These facts tell us that shape matters to human object recognition. But they do not tell us what shape is.

The theoretical definition of shape and its role in object recognition are heavily studied topics. Still, there is no accepted theory of shape similarity. The central premise of this chapter is that such a theory must be informed by the study of

This research was supported by NIH HD 28675.

development because sameness in shape is a developmental construction, the product of early interactions with objects and early category learning. I pursue this idea in three steps. First, I present circumstantial evidence from the literature on children's early object categories. Second, I present new evidence that directly tests the idea that children learn to perceive abstract shape similarities by learning common object categories and by acting on objects. Finally, I consider the relation of these developmental findings to contemporary theories of object recognition. It is commonplace to think of perception as the bedrock on which categories are built. This idea is being increasingly challenged by studies showing category learning changes and close-up perception (e.g. Goldstone and Steyvers, 2001; Goldstone, Lippa, and Shiffrin, 2001; Schyns, Goldstone, and Thilbaut, 1998), and it is also challenged here by the finding that children's learning of common categories changes their perception of shape.

16.2 Some Circumstantial Evidence

16.2.1 Shape bias in early naming

Children say their first words at around 12 months and in the early stages of object name learning, they make many mistakes. Reports of these errors include labeling twirling lights as 'helicopter', calling all vehicles from bikes to planes 'car', calling oranges, fingernails, and plates 'moon', or calling swans and robins 'duck' (H. Clark, 1973; Macnamara, 1982; Mervis, 1987; Mervis, Mervis, Johnson, and Bertrand, 1992). From these examples, shape does not appear to be the sole nor necessarily the most compelling similarity driving early overgeneralizations.

However, the character of naming errors may change as children approach their second birthday, becoming more shape-based (see H. Clark, 1973; Gelman, Croft, Panfrang, Clauser, and Gottfried, 1998). In a recent study, Samuelson and Smith (2002) documented the potency of shape in two year olds' naming in a task designed to elicit overgeneralizations. They presented children with nonsense objects of various shapes, colors, and textures as shown in Fig. 16.1. The objects were not named for the children nor were the children asked to name the objects. However, as listed in Fig. 16.1, the children often did offer names for these things and for the most part, these names appear to have been guided by global similarities in shape. Samuelson and Smith (1999) confirmed the role of shape by asking adults to match the objects to the names offered by children. Adults could do so accurately when given information about only object shape but not when given information about only object color or texture. In sum, by about two years of age, but perhaps not before, shape similarity drives children's use of English object names.

Children's performances in laboratory tasks also suggest the progressive tuning of attention to object shape. One widely used task is artificial noun

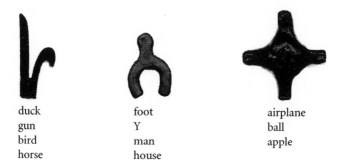

duck	foot	airplane
gun	Y	ball
bird	man	apple
horse	house	

Fig. 16.1. Sample stimulus objects and names spontaneously offered as labels by two year olds in the Samuelson and Smith (2002) study.

learning. In these tasks children are presented with a novel object and it is named with a novel name. Then the experimenter asks what other things have the same name. Findings using this task suggest a developmental progression from linking the name to one particular thing, to generalization of that name to highly similar things, to the broad generalization of the name to a wide variety of things of similar shape. Woodward, Markman, and Fitzsimmons (1994) provide the evidence for an early broadening of generalization between 13 and 18 months. They found that 13 month olds would generalize a name to an object identical to the originally named thing but these young children were much less likely to extend the name to objects that differed even slightly from the original. In contrast, 18 month olds consistently generalized the name to new instances that were non-identical but highly similar overall. Thus, generalization of a just heard name broadens between 13 and 18 months. By the time children are two years old, category extensions expand even further to include objects the same shape as the original exemplar no matter how much they differ in other properties. For example, Landau, Smith, and Jones (1988) found that two and three year old children generalized a novel object name to all new instances with the same shape as the originally named exemplar; they did so even when the test items were 100 times the size of the original and even when they differed radically in textural and material properties from the originally named exemplar (e.g. wood versus sponge or chicken wire). By two years of age, shape dominates children's categorization of novel objects.

   This developmental progression toward shape-based categories occurs at the same time that children's productive vocabularies rapidly expand. Thirteen month olds acquire new object names slowly and use the names they know often only in narrow contexts and with respect to only certain objects (e.g. Mervis, 1987; Woodward, Markman, and Fitzsimmons, 1994). They need repeated experiences with multiple exemplars to determine the full range of category members. By the time children are two years old, however, new object name acquisitions accelerate rapidly to a pace of about three or four new object names *a day* (see, Bloom, 2000 for a review). At this point in development, children often need to hear only a single object named to then use that name correctly across the entire range of the category. Smith (1999; Smith *et al.*, 2002) has suggested that this acceleration is due, at least in part, to children's increased attention to shape and moreover that this increased attention to shape is learned, the product of learning object names during the early slow course of word learning (see Smith *et al.*, 2002).

16.2.2   Symbolic play and the functions of things

During this same developmental period, there are also changes in how children play with objects. As early as 12 months of age, infants show that they recognize object categories by their actions on them—making drinking sounds when playing with an empty cup or using a doll's brush on their own hair (Belsky and Most, 1981). A little later, children direct these actions towards pretend objects— giving a doll a drink from a cup, or brushing a teddy bear's fur. These kinds of activities are called pretend play; children perform characteristic actions on clear instances of well-known categories. Between 18 and 24 months, children add a new and more creative kind of play, called symbolic play, to their repertoire. Here children use objects, often of simple shapes, as stand-ins for the real thing. For example, they might use a banana as a phone, a shoe box as a bed, or a stick as a bottle (see, McCune-Nicolich, 1981*b* for a review). Symbolic play is a signal developmental achievement. It correlates tightly with early vocabulary growth (Corrigan, 1982; Shore, O'Connell, and Bates, 1984; Veneziano, 1981) and is a well-established marker of normal language development. Children who do not engage in symbolic play exhibit significant delays in language acquisition (e.g. McCune-Nicholich, 1981*b*).

No one has previously suggested a link between symbolic play and attention to shape. However, as illustrated in Fig. 16.2, the substitutions reported in the literature suggest that these are shape-based extensions. At the very least, children must be able to perceive the global shape similarity of a banana to a phone and of a box to a bed, if they are to make these kinds of inventive substitutions in play. Importantly, play itself and the actions afforded by object shape may also guide children's perception of shape similarity. Dolls can be placed in beds *and* in boxes and the action of placing may highlight the functionally critical aspect of the shapes of beds and boxes when they serve as beds. Analogously, a phone *and* a banana can be held in similar ways, and holding each so that one end touches an ear and the other the mouth may highlight a particular aspect of shape similarity. Thus, it seems possible that acting on objects, using them in some functional task, may educate children about object shape. Despite an extensive literature on the roles of function and shape in children's categorization, there have been no

FIG. 16.2. Real objects and the simple forms used by children as substitutes for those things in play.

studies of how action may alter the perception of shape. This is because the issue has been cast in terms of a dichotomy between perceptual (e.g. shape-based) versus conceptual (e.g. function-based) categories (e.g. Smith, Jones, and Landau, 1998; Landau, Smith, and Jones, 1996; Kemler Nelson, 1999). Specifically, empirical studies have pitted shape against function and sought to show either that children form categories by shape unaffected by functional information or form categories by function unaffected by shape and perceptual similarity. There are long lists of experiments on both sides of the issue (e.g. Gathercole, Mueller, and Whitfield, 2001; Graham, Williams, and Huber, 1993; Merriman, Scott, and Marazita, 1993; Kemler Nelson, 1999; Smith *et al.*, 1996; Landau *et al.*, 1996). Because these experiments pit how we act on (and use) objects against shape, they provide little insight into the question of whether actions *alter* perceived shape.

However, one series of studies by Kemler Nelson and colleagues (1995; 1999; Kemler Nelson *et al.*, 2000) suggests a possible role for action in defining shape similarities. In one study (Kemler Nelson *et al.*, 2000), two year old children were presented with novel complex objects with multiple parts like those shown in Fig. 16.3. One object, the exemplar, was named with a novel name. In addition, the children were shown a function that depended on one of the parts, for example they were shown how the hinged shape could open, close, and latch. After seeing and manipulating the hinge, the children were more likely to extend the object name to the test objects that also had hinged parts rather than to those that were similar in global shape but lacked the hinge. By Kemler Nelson's interpretation, the children formed conceptually-based functional categories rather

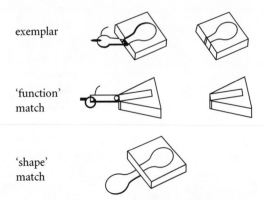

exemplar

'function' match

'shape' match

FIG. 16.3. Illustrations of the objects used by Kemler Nelson *et al.* (2001): the exemplar in its closed and open form and the 'function' matching test object that closes and opens and the 'shape' matching object that does not close.

than shape-based perceptual categories. However, by another interpretation, the actions children performed on the objects may have changed how object shape was perceived. That is, perception itself may be molded by top-down experiences and may not be separable from them (see, Goldstone and Barsalou, 1998).

16.3   New Evidence on Developmental Changes in the Perception of Shape Similarity

The developmental period between 18 months and two years is a momentous one characterized by a rate increase in early object name learning and in the emergence of symbolic play. It may also be a period that is foundational to the definition of shape and shape similarity. The following three hypotheses serve as starting points for pursuing this idea.

Hypothesis 1. Perceived similarities in shape become more abstract as children learn more object categories. As adults, we think of chairs as all having the same shape but all the things we call 'chair' are not exactly the same shape. Kitchen chairs, stuffed chairs, and rocking chairs are similar in shape only under some highly abstract description of shape. When do children have access to these abstract descriptions? One possibility is that children may develop more abstract representations of object shape as they acquire object names. Category learning may blend the specific shapes of specific things to create shape 'caricatures' that preserve the psychologically essential properties of shape.

Hypothesis 2. These shape abstractions broaden the range of objects included in the functional class. Children's object substitutions in symbolic play suggest that they do perceive abstract similarities in shape, ones that encompass the shared shape similarity of shoe boxes and beds, of bananas and phones, and of sticks and bottles. Symbolic play may be a signal developmental achievement precisely because it indicates a perceptual achievement, abstract representations of shape that highlight functionally relevant properties.

Hypothesis 3. Actions on objects directly influence how the shapes of those things are perceived. Just as perceived shape may invite actions, actions may alter perceived shape. If this is so, category learning, action, and perceived shape would form a self-organizing system, each training the other, driving the system toward more abstract, more category relevant, and more functionally appropriate representations of shape.

16.3.1 Experiment 1: recognizing shape caricatures

Figure 16.4 shows pairs of objects: one a simple but recognizable caricature and the other a richly detailed and lifelike form. Can children recognize the category from the minimal shape information provided by the caricature? Does the ability to do so increase as children acquire more extensive knowledge of common object categories? Is recognition of shape caricatures evident in both children's naming and in the actions they perform on objects?

FIG. 16.4. Three-dimensional shape caricatures of common objects and their corresponding lifelike examples.

To answer these questions, Smith (2003) presented Lifelike and Caricature objects were presented to 26 children between 18 and 24 months of age in two tasks: a Play task and a Name comprehension task. The children were divided into two equal groups, those with less than 100 object names in their productive vocabulary and those with more than 100 names in productive vocabulary. The number of object names in productive vocabulary is used as a measure of children's expertise with respect to common object categories. Productive vocabulary was measured by parent report using the MacArthur Communicative Developmental Inventory (Fenson *et al.*, 1994). This is a vocabulary checklist that includes the 300 object names commonly learned first by children learning English.

Lifelike and caricatures versions of 16 common categories were used: cat, chair, pizza, hammer, camera, lollipop, banana, phone, basket, hammer, boat, ice cream, toothbrush, apple, and butterfly. The Life-like instances were all prototypical toy replicas, rich in color, shape, and textural detail. The Shape Caricatures were three-dimensional forms carved from styrofoam and painted a uniform grey. These presented minimal shape detail but were recognizable to adults in a pilot study (see also Biederman, 1987). The three pairs in Fig. 16.4 are photographs of three-dimensional stimuli used in the experiment.

On each trial of the play task, three randomly selected objects were set on the table for one minute and the child was encouraged to play with the objects. None of the objects were named. A child was credited with recognizing an object as a member of the target category if the child performed a category specific action with the object. For example, a child was credited with recognizing an object as a phone if the child pretended to dial a number and/or answer or talk on the object. On each trial of the Name comprehension task, the child was presented with three alternatives and asked to indicate one object by name: For example, 'Where is the phone? Show me the phone'. Each child was tested in both the Play and Name comprehension tasks and the Play task for each object always occurred prior to the Name Comprehension task. Each child was tested with Life-like and Caricature objects in a counterbalanced order. However, no child ever saw both the Lifelike and Caricature version of the same object.

The results suggest that recognition of shape caricatures increases with increasing knowledge of common object categories. The evidence from the Play task is shown in Fig. 16.5. As can be seen, children with fewer than 100 object names and children with more than 100 object names played with the Lifelike objects in category specific ways. For example, they pretended to answer the phone, they made the cat meow and walk, they pretended to lick the ice-cream cone. Thus, both groups of children recognized richly detailed examples of these categories and knew how they are commonly used. However, only children with more extensive category knowledge (as measured by known object names) played with shape caricatures in category specific ways. The children with more extensive object name vocabularies pretended to take pictures with the realistic camera and the

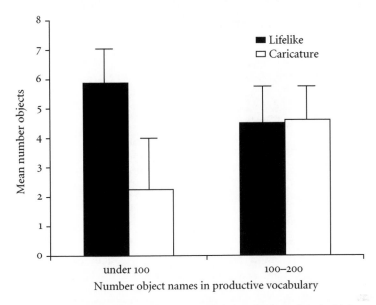

FIG. 16.5. Mean number of objects (maximum eight) that children played with in category specific ways for children with fewer than 100 object names in their productive vocabulary and for children with more than 100 object names in their productive vocabulary.

shape caricature, they pretended to eat the realistic slice of (plastic) pizza and the caricature slice, and so on. For these children, the minimalist shape information in the caricatures was sufficient to elicit actions characteristic of the kind. The children with less extensive vocabularies did play with the caricatures, just not in category specific ways. Figure 16.6 shows children's total actions—of all kinds—on the objects during the Play task. Children in both vocabulary groups manipulated the Lifelike and Caricature objects equally often, for example, by touching them, rolling them, showing them to the experimenter, or using them in play. In sum, the two groups of children differ only in their category specific actions on the Shape Caricatures. This result suggests that during the course of early object name learning, children form abstractions of the shapes of common things, and moreover that these abstracted shapes are linked to functional and category specific actions.

This link between abstract shape recognition and action suggests a new explanation of the emergence of symbolic play. Children's category specific play with the Shape Caricatures is like symbolic play in that the objects are not real instances of the categories; indeed they are very much like the simple forms used in studies of symbolic play (Shore *et al.*, 1984). Consistent with previous research, the present results show a strong link between this kind of play and early vocabulary development. The children who extend category specific actions to objects roughly similar in shape—but perhaps similar along the most category

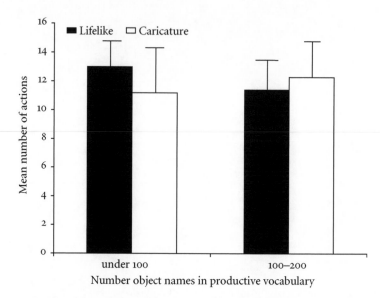

FIG. 16.6. Total number of actions (both nonspecific and category specific) for children with fewer than 100 object names in their productive vocabulary and for children with more than 100 object names in their productive vocabulary.

relevant aspects of shape—are the ones with more developed language. These results suggest further that the link between symbolic play and early vocabulary development may be through the perception of shape, that symbolic play emerges as children begin to form abstract descriptions of object shape and thus can extract the relevant shape similarities across different kinds.

The pattern of results in the Name comprehension task is very much like that in Play task. As shown in Fig. 16.7, children with smaller noun vocabularies recognized the Lifelike objects, selecting the right one 70 percent of the time, but they failed to recognize the Shape Caricatures. In marked contrast, however, the children with larger noun vocabularies recognized both the Lifelike objects and the Caricatures, selecting the named object over 75 percent of the time both for the Lifelike objects and the Shape Caricatures. Thus children with less extensive object name vocabularies appear to need more detail to recognize an object than do children will more extensive object vocabularies who seem to need only a rough caricature of object shape.

These results provide three new insights into the developmental origins of shape. First, young children in the early stages of category learning do not recognize shape caricatures at all, despite their accuracy in recognizing richly detailed instances of the same category. Apparently, the ability to perceive abstract shape similarities is not a given but is instead a developmental product. Second, very young children who are only slightly more advanced in their category knowledge recognize these

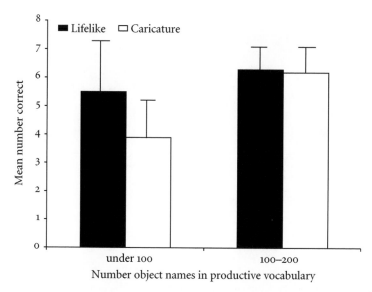

FIG. 16.7. Mean number correct in the Comprehension task for children with fewer than 100 and more than 100 object names in their productive vocabulary.

caricatures of known categories nearly perfectly, that is, as well as they recognize richly detailed instances. Clearly, the processes of object recognition change during this developmental period. Third, there is a link between children's perception of shape and category specific actions. Recognition of shape caricatures may a crucial step in extending actions, in enabling, for example, children to see how a shoe box can stand in for a bed. In this way, developmental changes in the perception of shape may be a key ingredient in the development of symbolic play.

These results also raise new empirical questions. First, the results indicate a strong link between children's knowledge of object names and their recognition of shape caricatures. But they do not tell us the causal direction of that relation— whether the ability to recognize shape caricatures drives category leaning (and object name acquisitions) or whether category learning creates the ability to recognize abstract shapes. The results also do not tell us the nature of the developmental change nor the specific experiences that might drive it. One possibility is that children learn to recognize shape caricatures, category by category. Alternatively, the developmental changes may be more general, changing how children perceive shape similarities for novel as well as known objects. This question was addressed in a second experiment.

16.3.2   Experiment 2: recognizing novel shape caricatures

In a second experiment, 18–24 month old children were introduced to a lifelike but (for young children) novel object, for example, an artichoke. The children

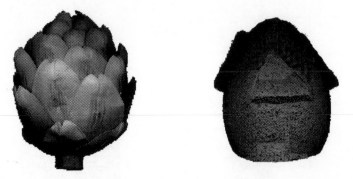

FIG. 16.8. Photographs of a realistic artichoke and a caricature of an artichoke.

were taught the object's name, for example, they were repeatedly told that the object was 'an artichoke' and were trained to select the artichoke from among distractors. On the critical test trial, three shape caricatures were presented to the child, one of which was a shape caricature of the originally named exemplar as shown in Fig. 16.8. The child was asked to indicate the named object, for example, 'Where's the artichoke here?' Children were tested on eight novel objects in this manner. If children must master the relevant shape properties category by category, then this task should be very hard because the caricatured artichoke only preserves some aspects of the original shape. If, however, children are developing general perceptual skills that apply to novel shapes, then children who recognize the caricatures of familiar objects might also recognize the caricatures of novel ones. The results support this second possibility. As shown in Fig. 16.9, children with more than 100 object names in their productive vocabulary (those who readily recognized caricatures of familiar object shapes in Experiment 1) readily recognized the caricature of the newly learned noun. Children with fewer than 100 object names did not. These results strongly suggest that children are learning something general about the shape similarities relevant to object recognition and categorization.

16.3.3   Experiments 3 and 4: Action helps create perceived shape

The third hypothesis states that actions on objects also influence how the shapes of those objects are perceived. A thought experiment illustrates both the idea and the experimental task used to test it. Consider the object in the top of Fig. 16.10. Imagine that you characteristically act on this object by lifting it vertically. Now, consider the objects at the bottom. Which of these belongs to the same category as the original exemplar? The conjecture is that you are more likely to categorize the exemplar with the vertically rather than the horizontally elongated alternative

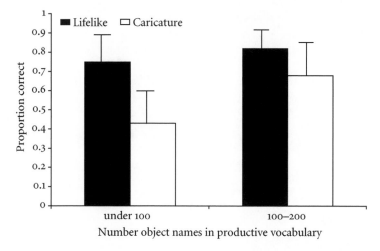

Fɪɢ. 16.9. Mean number of correct choices for children with fewer than 100 and more than 100 object names in their productive vocabulary.

because you moved the object vertically. The conjecture appears to be right, at least for two-and-a-half and three year olds.

In the experiment, 25 children were presented with the exemplar object in the figure and told its name, 'This is a zup.' Thirteen of the children were then shown the object moving vertically and were also given the object so that they could move it vertically along a backdrop. The remaining 12 children were shown the object moving horizontally and then actively moved the object horizontally along the backdrop. The backdrop was a 1 meter square with 'grass' along the bottom edge and a 'tree' along the right side. In the horizontal action condition, children moved the exemplar horizontally along the grass. In the vertical action condition, children moved the exemplar up and down the tree. After acting on the exemplar, it was set down and remained in view as the children were shown individual test objects. The children were asked whether each individual test object was also 'a zup'. There were six unique test objects as shown in Fig. 16.11. Test object H1 was horizontally elongated but differed moderately from the exemplar. Test object H2 was more horizontally elongated and thus differed considerably on this dimension from the exemplar. Test object −H differed from the exemplar only in that it was shortened along the horizontal dimension, thus this object was taller than it was wide. Test objects V1, V2, and −V were similarly constructed, only the changed dimension (relative to the exemplar) was the vertical dimension. The children were queried three times about each test object for a total of 18 trials. After every trial, children were given the exemplar and asked to reperform the action of moving it along the backdrop horizontally or vertically.

Exemplar

Two test objects

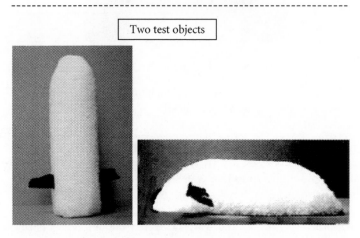

FIG. 16.10. The exemplar and two test objects.

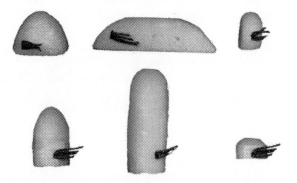

FIG. 16.11. Six test objects. Top row: horizontally extended (H1 and H2) and horizontally decreased (–H) relative to the exemplar (in Fig. 16.10). Bottom row: vertically extended (V1 and V2) and vertically decreased (–V) relative to the exemplar.

If the conjecture about the role of action in perceived shape is correct, then children who moved the exemplar in a horizontal fashion should perceive it as being more horizontally extended than vertically extended and thus should extend the name to test objects H1, H2, and –V more than they should extend the name to test objects V1, V2, and –H. The opposite pattern is expected for children in the vertical action condition.

The expected pattern was strongly present in the children's judgments. As shown in Fig. 16.12, when the children acted by moving the exemplar along a horizontal path, they generalized the name to test objects H1 and H2, the horizontally extended test objects, and also to test object –V, a test object that was also wider than it was tall. When children acted by moving the exemplar along a vertical path, they generalized the name to tests objects V1 and V2, the two vertically extended versions of the exemplar. They did not include test object –H in the category at levels reliably above chance. This evidence suggests that action plays a formative role in the perception of shape. How children use an object influences how they perceive its shape and the shape similarities that organize categories.

This conclusion is also supported by a second study that shows a role for action in the perception of symmetry. In this experiment, children between two-and-a-half and three years of age were shown the exemplar in Fig. 16.13 and told its name, for example, 'This is a zup.' They were also shown and asked to perform

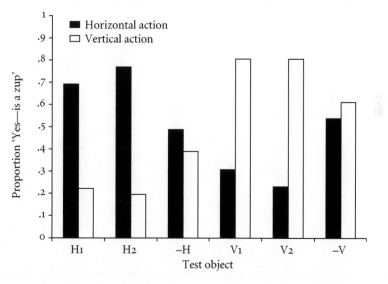

FIG. 16.12. Proportion name extensions to each of the six kinds of test objects for children in the Horizontal and Vertical action conditions.

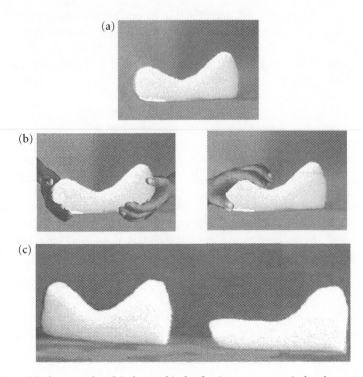

FIG. 16.13. (a): the exemplar. (b): the two kinds of actions—symmetrical and asymmetrical. (c): two of the test objects (S2 and A2).

an action with the object. Half the children were shown and asked to perform and action in which the object was held by its smaller side and waved, as illustrated in Fig. 16.13. Half the children were shown and then were asked to perform an action in which the object is held with two hands, one on each point and then rotated, also as shown in Fig. 16.13. The central question is this: Does asymmetrical action relative to an object's shape increase the likelihood that it is perceived as having an asymmetrical shape? Does symmetrical action increase the likelihood that the object is perceived as being more symmetrical in shape?

A novel noun extension task was again used to answer these questions. After learning the name and acting on the exemplar, the children were presented with individual test objects and asked about each of these 'Is this also a zup?' A series of test objects were constructed that were incrementally more or less symmetrical than the exemplar. Test objects A1, A2, and A3 are progressively more asymmetric and progressively more different than the exemplar. Test objects S1, S2, and S3 are progressively more symmetric and progressively more different from the exemplar. Children were asked about each test object four times (presented in

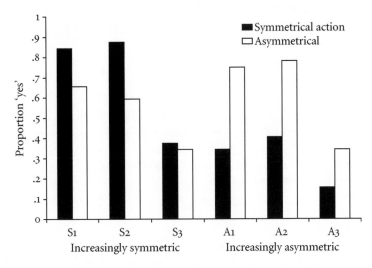

Fɪɢ. 16.14. Proportion names extensions to the six test objects for children in the symmetrical and asymmetrical conditions.

a random order) for a total of 24 trials. After every four trials the child was reshown the action on the exemplar and then given the opportunity to perform that action.

The results are shown in Fig. 16.14. Children who used one part of the exemplar as a handle, extended the name differently than those who had held and moved the object with two hands. Children in the first condition extended the name to new instances that were more asymmetric in their structure than the exemplar but children in the second condition extended the name to new instances that were more symmetric than the exemplar. As is apparent in the figure, magnitude of similarity also mattered, children accepted the smaller deviations toward or away from symmetry depending on condition but not the largest ones (A3 and S3). This similarity effect is consistent with the idea that the effect of action was on perception and not on children's inferences about the kind of object (symmetric or asymmetric) that was suitable for the motion. The action perturbed perceived similarity in the direction of symmetry or asymmetry but did not cause the child to accept shapes well-adapted to the action but dissimilar to the exemplar. In sum, the results suggest that how children act on objects influences how they perceive object shape and the range of allowable shape variation within a category.

The implication of these results is clear: How we use objects influences the aspects of shape children take to be relevant to categorization. These results also provide a means to unify the role of function and shape similarity. Perceived shape and function may not be psychologically separable because the perceived shapes of things determine actions and actions distort in functionally relevant ways perceived object shape.

16.4   Toward a Theory of Shape

These new results strongly indicate that a complete theory of shape will be a developmental theory. The first two experiments show that between the ages of 18 and 24 months, children's perception of shape similarity changes markedly. Children progress from generalizing both actions and names narrowly to a small set of richly similar objects to a broader category encompassing generalizations that seem to depend on an abstract, pared down representation of shape. Experiments 3 and 4 show that actions also influence children's perception of shape, distorting perceived shape in the direction of action.

Because the results are new, there are many empirical gaps, many unanswered questions. But the overall pattern of inter-related developments suggests a potentially powerful story about how and why we perceive object shape the way we do. Children may begin learning about objects by attending to all aspects of shape, those we consider merely decorative may attract attention as much as those that seem (to adults) as essential properties. Thus, to a novice learner the differences in the shape of the chairs in Fig. 16.15 may be just as potent as the similarities. However, as children encounter the full variety of chair shapes and as the child acts on these various chairs in the same way, by sitting, an abstract model of chair shape—one that transcends the specific shapes of specific things—may emerge. These shape models, in turn, will foster further category generalizations and actions, thus refining perceived shape and links to function even further. Thus object shape may be developmentally defined through a child's actions on objects and through category learning. The intriguing implication is that we would perceive the shapes of chairs differently if our culture placed chairs and stools in the same category, or if we used chairs to fight lions rather than to sit on.

FIG. 16.15. Three chairs of different specific shapes but the same general shape.

16.4.1   Theories of object recognition

Contemporary theories of object recognition are not developmentally grounded. They do not take infants and children as their starting point but instead start with the two-dimensional representation on the retina and ask how to build a three-dimensional object from that two-dimensional image. There are two competing classes of theories (e.g. Biederman, 1987; Tarr, 1995). According to Biederman's Recognition-by-Components (RBC) theory, objects are represented in terms of abstract components, generalized cylinders, called geons. These components are abstracted from the two-dimensional image independently of changes in orientation and scale. According to RBC, only a few such components in the proper spatial arrangement are needed to represent a recognizable object. By this account, then, the reason all sorts of chairs are seen as chair shaped is that they all conform to the same componential representation. The shape caricatures used in Experiments 1 and 2 share considerable similarity to the kinds of simplified objects that might be built from Biederman's geons. Although RBC makes no explicit developmental claims, the processes that parse images into componential object representations are typically discussed as unlearned and developmentally stable processes. Contrary to this idea, the present results suggest that the processes that underlie object shape are a developmental product.

Edelman and colleagues (1995, 1999; Edelman and Duvdevani-Bar, 1997) offer a different view of how shape is represented. They propose a theory of recognition and categorization that begins with the premise that perceivers store view-dependent images of objects. Prototypes are formed from multiple images of multiple objects in the same category. These prototypes are interpolated blends of stored images and thus represent simplified and global characteristics of shape. Duvdevani-Bar and Edelman (1999) argue further that once a number of such prototypes have been formed they serve as landmarks, as basis functions, defining the shape space and enabling the recognition of even novel categories. In this view then, early learned object categories *create* the dimensions by which object shape is perceived. The results of Experiments 1 and 2 may be interpreted as providing support for this account.

Neither Biederman nor Edelmann provides a means for connecting perceived shape to action. Both are firmly within Marr's (1982) modular view of vision as a device for deriving general purpose descriptions. This Marrian view contrasts with the Gibsonian (e.g. Gibson, 1987) perspective which sees perception tightly linked to the dynamics of action. Recently, there has been growing interest in the idea that both Marr and Gibson are right, but that each describes a distinct visual system. Goodale and Humphrey (1998) proposed separate but interactive visual systems—one Marrian that evolved to represent objects and one Gibsonian that evolved for the control of action. This idea was based in part on Mishkin, Ungerleider, and Machio's (1983) identitication of two distinct 'streams' of visual processing in the macaque monkey—a ventral stream heavily invested in object

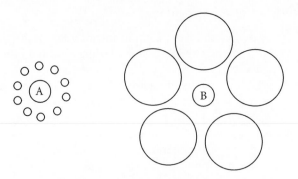

FIG. 16.16. Ebbinghaus Illusion.

recognition and a dorsal stream more heavily invested in spatial vision. Goodale and Humphrey (1998) review a number of results that support this divide between perceiving objects and acting on them.

One compelling result concerns the Ebbinghaus Illusion as illustrated in Fig. 16.16. The standard version of the illusion uses a two-dimensional drawing. The two center circles are the same physical size; however, circle A is surrounded by smaller circles and is perceived as larger and circle B, surrounded by larger circles, is perceived as smaller. Aglioti *et al.* (1995) developed a three-dimensional version of the illusion using poker chips. When viewing these chips in arrays like those in Fig. 16.16, participants still judged circle A to be larger than circle B. Participants were also asked to pick up the disks and their grip aperture was measured. The opening of the fingers during a reach and prior to contact with the object—grip aperture—is a highly sensitive and accurate measure of size. And it was in this case; participants' grip apertures were not affected by the size contrast illusion. These sorts of results suggest that the systems that represents object properties such as size and the action system do not influence each other.

However, this conclusion may be too simplistic. After all, action is driven by the object properties and knowledge of category membership. This appears to be true even when those properties or category membership is irrelevant to the task at hand (see Glenberg and Kaschak, this volume, Ch. 2). For example, Ellis and Tucker (2000) found that in a task in which sounds cue particular hand motions, an irrelevant object in the field perturbs the response in the direction of that appropriate to the object. Similarly, Creem and Proffitt (2001) found that movements toward an object are influenced by the characteristic (but not task relevant) functional use of the object. Finally, frontal lobe patients who are generally over-responsive to the environment also cannot prevent themselves from performing a familiar action with a familiar object (e.g. Lhermitte and Serdaru, 1993; Riddoch, Humphreys, and Edwards, 2000). These results all suggest that our actions are influenced by our representations of objects; and moreover, that our object representations include information about the actions associated with them.

The present results fit this idea in that they suggest that young children form these action-laden representations as they form early categories and as they form more abstract representations of object shape. Experiments 3 and 4 further suggest a direct influence of action on object representation. All the previous studies have shown that object shape (and function) influences action (even when the shape and function are irrelevant to the task). Experiments 3 and 4 show the opposite direction of influence—from action to the perception of shape. I believe this is the first such demonstration that how one uses an object determines its perceived shape. From these two experiments, one cannot make strong conclusions about the mechanisms responsible for this effect. It seems unlikely that movement in a particular way simply increases attention to some dimensions over others. Increased attention to a dimension typically leads to heightened sensitivity to differences on that dimension (e.g. Goldstone and Steyvers, 2001). Thus, if moving an object vertically led to increased attention to the vertical dimension, one would expect increased sensitivity to differences on the vertical dimension. But Experiment 3 indicates the opposite result: the children showed an increased willingness to extend the category to vertically elongated objects.

Rather than increased sensitivity, the results of Experiments 3 and 4 suggest a blurring or blending of the object representation with the action. Memory for the vertical extent of the action, or memory for symmetry of the action, seems to be confused with or combined with the perceived extent or perceived symmetry. Critically, from the current experiments, we cannot tell if it is a combination of perceived action with perceived extent (or symmetry) or whether it is a combination of the felt pattern of body motion with the perceptual properties of the objects. Experiments are underway to address this issue.

16.4.2 Conclusion

Shape similarity develops. It is not a given upon which category formation rests but is, at least partially, a product of category learning—of learning what things are called by the same name and of learning the functional uses of objects. As children's knowledge of common object categories expands, narrow recognition of only richly detailed instances gives way to the recognition of stylized forms for well-known categories and to an increased recognition of abstract shape similarities within novel categories. Shape itself appears to be an abstraction, created in development, the consequence of learning functional categories.

17

Adaptation of Perceptual and Semantic Features

BRIAN ROGOSKY and ROBERT GOLDSTONE

Abstract

This chapter examines the role of features in theories of concepts, perception, and language. The authors define features as psychological representations of properties of the world that can be processed independently of other properties and that are relevant to a task, such as categorization. They discuss the classic view of features as entities that do not change over time. They argue for an alternative view in which features are created and adapted according to the immediate goals and context of tasks, and over longer time periods in terms of perceptual and conceptual learning and development. The authors also discuss the distinction of pairs of dimensions in terms of whether the dimensions can be processed separately (i.e. either dimension can be attended independently of the other) or integrally (i.e. the dimensions cannot be processed independently). They present a study of the classification of linguistic stimuli according to rules based on semantic features (e.g. ferocity and socialness of animals). The results primarily indicate that changes in the integral processing of the dimensions can be induced by tasks that favor the separate processing of one dimension. The findings support the authors' claim that, like perceptual features, semantic features can be adapted during learning.

Feature

(1) A property of a stimulus that can be psychologically processed as a whole, independently from other properties of stimulus. Features are identified by their functional role in cognitive processing, such as the act of including (or excluding) the stimulus as a member of a category.

This research was funded by NIH grant MH56871 and a Gill fellowship to the second author. We would like to thank Robert Goldberg and Mark Orr for helpful comments on earlier drafts. Thanks to Laura Carlson for making us aware of Maslow's quote and for developing, with Emile van der Zee, the theme of the Spatial and Functional Features workshop.

(2) A psychological representation of a property of the world in a form that distinguishes it from other represented properties.

The first meaning emphasizes the role of features in categorizing stimuli; whereas the second meaning relates to the role of features within a representational system.

17.1 Introduction

17.1.1 Features and concepts

A theory of concepts has been and continues to be a fundamental goal of the study of the mind. Concepts are the basic building blocks of thought, and so an understanding of concepts is directly relevant to other cognitive processes and abilities, including memory, language, reasoning, and problem solving. Of these general capacities, concepts are primarily linked with the ability to categorize entities (objects, events, and other concepts). In other words, concepts are the mental constructs that underlie categorization.

Though many different views of concepts continue to be actively pursued, one particularly productive subset of these views holds that concepts consist of a set of features (see Laurence and Margolis, 1999, for a review). Feature-based theories can be the means of addressing the disparate goals of object recognition and language use in similar terms. Our present focus is on features as psychological representations developed from perceptual or conceptual aspects that are relevant to a cognitive task, such as object recognition or categorization (Goldstone, 1994, 2000; Schyns, Goldstone, and Thibaut, 1998; Schyns and Rodet, 1997). The psychological representations may only approximate physical properties of objects (Garner, 1978). For example, the acuity of human perception of sound and light does not correspond exactly to measurable physical dimensions of wavelength and frequency. By defining relevant aspects in a task, it should be possible to establish how different types of features are employed. For example, the structural features (Prasada, this volume, Ch. 14) and the parts (Tversky, this volume, Ch. 21) of an object guide the perception of its functionality. For our purposes we will not focus on the differences between types of features (e.g. spatial versus functional) as described elsewhere in this volume, although we will address such distinctions in regards to language use (Section 17.4.1). Features can also be classified in terms of whether the property is present or absent (a binary feature), has a certain value in an ordered continuum (a dimension), or has a value among some unordered set of values (an attribute). Although binary features, dimensions, and attributes are processed differently (Garner, 1978), we will gloss over these differences in order to discuss featural approaches in general.

Features are psychologically important because they provide a powerful means of processing and representing information about the world. Detection of a single feature in visual search tasks can be done quickly and in parallel, but if a pair of components must be identified that belong to different features, then performance is slow and serial (Treisman and Gelade, 1980). Furthermore, a large array of entities can be efficiently encoded using a small number of constituent features (Goldstone, 2003). The power of features in a compositional structure has been explored in object recognition (e.g. Biederman, 1987) and conceptual semantics (e.g. McNamara and Miller, 1989). Fodor and Pylyshyn (1988) have argued that the lack of compositional representations in connectionist models of language is a critical failure. In the extreme, all our conceptual knowledge may be characterized as a set of related concepts composed of featural concepts that can be further decomposed (Barsalou, 1992). Without a feature-based system, it would be a daunting task to learn and remember perceptual and conceptual information as well as to produce a meaningful description of it.

In this chapter, we will address two aspects of feature-based approaches. First, we will compare the static versus dynamic views of feature sets. The static view treats a concept as a set of features that can be reliably and consistently used to determine the presence or applicability of the concept. The dynamic view proposes instead that the appropriate features can change over time depending on perceptual ability, task constraints, and context. Second, we will consider the relevance of studies of perceptual features to semantic features. Research has examined categorization behavior using perceptual stimuli (often objects or pictures of objects) or linguistic stimuli (single words or descriptions). This perceptual/linguistic division has arisen from the practical goals of the research, that is whether the research was designed to learn about object recognition or about language use. Contrary to this distinction, both perceptual and linguistic processing may share common cognitive systems that can be described by feature-based theories. In support of this view, new data are presented that test the malleability of features of linguistically presented concepts using a classification task commonly employed in perceptual studies.

17.2 Featural Approaches

17.2.1 Static features

Historically, the basic starting point has been to find a common set of distinctive features that, when combined, can account for the diversity of categories and the requirements of categorization tasks. In object recognition, one example of this is Biederman's 'geons': three-dimensional geometric components of objects (Biederman, 1987). Similarly, sets of conceptual (Schank, 1972) and semantic primitives (Wierzbicka, 1992) have been proposed as the basis of all scenarios (e.g. visiting a restaurant) and word meanings, respectively. Such theories of feature primitives imply that the feature set needed to represent any particular object or concept is fixed and only the particular combination of features needs to be learned (cf. Goldstone, Schyns, and Medin, 1997).

The majority of work in categorization, concept learning, and perception has employed experimental tasks in which the features to be learned are determined a priori and remain constant. In concept learning, Bruner, Goodnow, and Austin (1956) studied the strategies used to learn a rule for classifying simple figures. The figures varied on several dimensions (e.g. shape, number, and color) and the category rules were based on logical combinations of certain values of these dimensions (e.g. red and square). In much of their work, they assumed that features, on which the rules are based, are readily available to the perceiver and that they can provide complete definitions for the categorization of instances. This harkens to the classical theory of concepts in which concepts are defined in terms of a limited number of sufficient and necessary features (Laurence and Margolis, 1999). E. Smith, Shoben, and Rips (1974) modeled behavior in sentence verification tasks in which participants decided whether a term was a member of a target category (e.g. *all robins are birds*). They proposed that features are either essential ('defining') or non-essential ('characteristic'). In opposition to definitional features, Rosch and Mervis (1975) argued that all members of a natural category do not necessarily share the same features. Instead, the features of a particular member contribute to the member's degree of relatedness ('family resemblance') and its similarity to a central prototype. Despite their differences, both rule-based and prototype-based views of categories posit features that remain constant.

17.2.2   Separable and integral dimensions

Garner (1974, 1976) and Monahan and Lockhead (1977) examined how combinations of dimensions of a stimulus interact. They designed tasks in which participants classified stimuli as a member of one of two categories. The tasks were meant to gauge how easily one dimension can be processed separately from another dimension. The values on the dimensions were either relevant or irrelevant to the task, or were absent altogether. In a unidimensional task (Fig. 17.1a), the categorization rule that subjects were requested to follow was based on only one dimension but only one value of the other dimension was presented (e.g. red circles versus red squares). In the orthogonal (filter) task (Fig. 17.1b), the rule was based on one dimension and irrelevant variation along the other dimension was present, (e.g. circles versus squares, which could be either red or green). In the correlated categorization task (Fig. 17.1c), there was a perfect correlation between the value on one dimension and the value on the other dimension. Accordingly, either dimension could be used to determine a categorization (e.g. red circles versus green squares).

The performances in these task types were compared for different pairs of dimensions. For some pairs of dimensions (called integral), such as brightness and saturation, response times were faster in the correlated task and slower in the

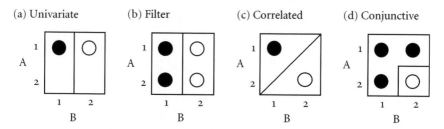

FIG. 17.1. A schematic diagram of several types of classification tasks. A and B represent dimensions, 1 and 2 represent dimension values, and black and white circles represent categories. The solid line shows the classification rule for each task.

filter task compared to the unidimensional task (the control). For other pairs of dimensions (called separable), such as size and shape, there was no facilitation in the correlated task, and no penalty for irrelevant variation in the filter task (Garner, 1976, 1978).

The separable versus integral distinction is further supported by multidimensional scaling solutions of similarity ratings. For integral dimensions, Euclidean distances have been found to fit the similarity space better than city-block distances; whereas the opposite holds for separable dimensions (Garner, 1974). It seems that dimensions of separable stimuli can be attended to separately from each other such that the dissimilarity is additive for each dimension as assumed by the city-block metric (Maddox, 1992). In contrast, integral stimuli are processed more holistically as assumed by the Euclidean metric and attention weighting of the dimensions appears not to be a factor in learning during classification (Nosofsky and Palmeri, 1996). Monahan and Lockhead (1977) proposed that stimuli consisting of integral dimensions are initially processed in terms of overall similarity and then in terms of individual aspects. The reverse may be true for separable dimensions. In general, a multi-dimensional scaling (MDS) solution of similarity ratings can be used to capture the psychological dimensions of the stimuli as well as predict identification and categorization performance based on similarity (e.g. Monahan and Lockhead, 1977; King, Gruenewald, and Lockhead, 1978; Nosofsky, 1987).

17.3 Alternatives to Fixed Features

17.3.1 Overview

In the previous discussion of featural approaches, it has been assumed that the features, whether relevant or irrelevant to the task, and whether separable or integral, remain constant over time. This is part of a larger assumption in which perception is seen as the initial process of gathering information that outputs its results to higher order cognitive modules. These higher order modules are assumed to work with amodal symbolic representations and have little further interaction with perception. Theoretically, this assumption could simply be wrong: cognition could be intertwined with perceptual processing (Barsalou, 1999) and with action (Glenberg and Kaschak, this volume, Ch. 2). Furthermore, even our 'higher' cognitive processes, such as creativity and analogy making, may depend on our ability to perceive patterns (e.g. Hofstadter, 1995).

Perhaps a more conservative hypothesis is that features and dimensions can be adapted over time for specific tasks. As discussed in the Introduction, features within a feature-based system can be combined to encode a large array of entities. This does not mean that a small and fixed set of primitive features can account for all the objects, concepts, and events that we encounter in our world. Instead we need a flexible system that can adaptively re-represent aspects of existing features, and create new features as needed (Goldstone, 2003). Several lines of evidence speak in support of such an alternative notion. One line examines task-related changes due to the interactions between categorization and perception (Goldstone and Barsalou, 1998; Goldstone, Steyvers, Spencer-Smith, and Kersten, 2000). Another line of evidence lies in long-term changes arising from developmental factors (Thelen and Smith, 1994). Both of these changes could be ascribed to the creation of new features and the recombination of existing features that are relevant in determining category membership (Schyns *et al.*, 1998; Schyns and Rodet, 1997). We call such features *functional* because we wish to highlight the function the features play in category learning.

17.3.2   Task-specific changes

During the course of learning to perform a task, the system can adapt its representations and processes in order to improve performance. We will examine three areas of adaptation. First, we will discuss the importance of similarity and its dependency on the context of comparison. Second, we will address several mechanisms of perceptual learning: attentional weighting, differentiation, and unitization. Third, we will argue that new features can be created from the properties of stimuli when elicited by a given task.

Similarity

Similarity is thought to play a role in many aspects of cognition, such as transfer of learning, memory recall, and categorization. Medin, Goldstone, and Gentner (1993) have suggested that similarity is the result of a comparison of objects based on features and their structural relations. They found that the features listed for a figure (Experiment 1) and for a word (Experiment 2) depended on the figure or word that was paired with them. In Experiment 3, they recorded similarity ratings for words that were presented either together on the screen (same context) or separately (separate context) with other words that were antonymically, metaphorically, or categorically related. They found that similarity of the standard word (e.g. sunrise) and its antonym (sunset) increased when the words were also presented with a categorically related word (sunbeam). In further support of context effects on similarity, Goldstone, Medin, and Halberstadt (1997) showed that the rated similarity of two pictorial faces to a standard face depended on the degree of matching and mismatching features. If similarity is a crucial predictor of categorization and psychological dimensions of stimuli, and similarity itself varies with respect to the aspects of the comparison set, it would seem that the psychological representation of stimuli is not constant with regards to the context of the task. Similarity is not determined solely by comparing existing representations for two entities; rather the comparison process itself affects the representations constructed for the entities, at least during the task.

Perceptual learning

Perceptual learning consists of persistent changes of featural representations and processes. A vast body of research has been associated with perceptual learning mechanisms (see Goldstone, 1998, for a review), but in the present discussion we will only address what is most pertinent to changes in the perception of features and dimensions. Two learning mechanisms, attentional weighting and differentiation of dimensions, operate on features in order to improve performance on tasks such as categorization or identification. Attention weighting allows dimensions that are relevant for categorization to be psychologically separated. Such shifts may be due to strategic choices or involuntary perceptual changes (Goldstone, 1994). Attention may also operate on the level of dimension values, to assist learning the differences between categories (Kersten, Goldstone, and Schaffert, 1998). Attention weighting is applicable when a dimension is already recognized and separable from other dimensions. Another mechanism, feature differentiation, is applicable when two dimensions are originally integrated, but are differentially relevant for a categorization task. In this case, learning can lead to greater isolation of the two dimensions, such that dimensions that once could not be selectively attended to can be separately weighted later. Goldstone (1994) studied the discrimination of integral dimensions (saturation and brightness) when transferred from categorization training. He found that sensitization increased for both the relevant and irrelevant dimensions in the categorization task, but that this effect was greater for the relevant dimension.

Goldstone and Steyvers (2001) studied the effects of training on the classification of face stimuli. The face stimuli were generated by morphing between two pairs of faces. Each face pair constituted the endpoints of a dimension, and a particular face stimulus was defined by its proportion of each of the four faces (Fig. 17.2). The experiments studied the effects of transfer between category learning tasks based on a categorization rule that split the stimulus space in half into two categories (Fig. 17.3). Participants learned to associate each face with one of the two categories through feedback on the correctness of each response. The performance in the training task was equal regardless of the orientation of the

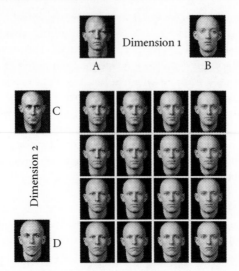

FIG. 17.2. Design of Goldstone and Steyvers (2001) stimuli in the categorization experiments. Two pairs of original faces (A, B and C, D) form the dimensions (1 and 2) of the stimuli. Each face stimulus is a morph created from contributions of the two dimensions.

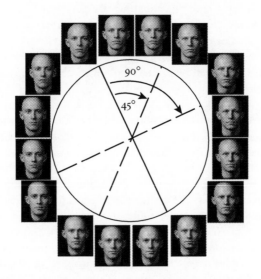

FIG. 17.3. The design of the task stimuli used by Goldstone and Steyvers (2001) in Experiment 3. The solid line represents the initial dividing line for the categorization, although the exact orientation with respect to the original dimensions was varied. Participants were transferred to a categorization that was either a 90° or 45° rotation from the initial task rule.

rule with respect to the original dimensions. They found that a rotational change of the rule in the transfer task of 90° resulted in better performance than a 45° change. In Experiment 1 they demonstrated that a 90° change was also better than a control condition in which participants were trained on two dimensions that were later irrelevant during transfer. They replicated this effect with saturation and brightness. These results are consistent with enhanced processing of the dimensions, but inconsistent with a selective attention account. If selective attention were acting alone, a small change in the relevance of the dimensions, as in the 45° change, should have been easier to detect than a large change, as in the 90° change. However, categorization rules related by 90° degrees encouraged a consistent organization of the set of stimuli into dimensions. Learning that Dimension A is relevant and Dimension B is irrelevant promotes transfer to a task in which Dimension B is relevant and Dimension A is irrelevant. Both tasks encourage isolating Dimensions A and B, albeit for opposite purposes. By contrast, categorization rules separated by 45° are inconsistent because the required dimensions partially cross-cut one another.

The process of integral dimensions becoming more separable can be explained by the differentiation and attention weighting mechanisms. Conversely, initially separable dimensions may be treated more integrally through a process of feature unitization. In general, unitization occurs when several aspects of a stimulus are diagnostic for a task such as categorization. Goldstone (2000) explored unitization using complex stimuli (a continuous line with a jagged profile) composed of components that were conjunctively relevant to the categorization. He found that improvements could be made on this conjunctive categorization task, even when the relevant components were non-contiguous. However, randomizing the left–right ordering of the components interfered with learning. This indicated that the features were combined into a psychological unit based on spatial ordering regardless of spatial contiguity. Furthermore, a higher learning rate (measured in response time) was found as the number of features to be combined increased. These findings could be explained by the unitization of aspects into a single feature, but not by analytic models that treated the aspects separately.

The processes of attentional weighting, differentiation, and unitization allow the system to flexibly use the relevant features. These processes operate on existing features and thereby suggest an even more basic question: How are features determined? Schyns *et al.* (1998) argued that for complex stimuli, a fixed set of features cannot be determined a priori, nor can a fixed set of features account for the variability observed during category learning through a change in attentional weighting. Instead, aspects that are relevant to a categorization can be recognized and represented as distinct features. Schyns and Rodet (1997) called this process *feature creation*. They presented a series of experiments and simulations of the learning of categories using a type of complex stimuli called 'Martian cells'. Exemplars from category X, Y, and XY were defined by features x, y, and xy

(a conjunction of x and y), respectively. In the first phase, the participants were first trained on three tasks in which the 'Martian cells' belonging to the category to be learned had to be distinguished from distractors. One group of participants learned to distinguish instances of X then Y then XY (X→Y→XY); the other group learned XY then X then Y (XY→X→Y). In the second phase, participants categorized new cells consisting of four cells belonging to the X, Y, and XY categories plus four X-Y cells, in which the x and y features were physically separated. The participants were instructed to assign each cell to one of the three previously learned categories. The first group (X→Y→XY) judged X-Y instances as belonging to the XY category on 88 percent of the trials; whereas the second group (XY→X→Y) only judged the same cells as XY on 19 percent of trials. Schyns and Rodet argued that the (XY→X→Y) group formed a unified representation of the features in the XY category that caused them to judge the X-Y instances as either belonging to X or Y, depending on which feature they had attended. Conversely, the (X→Y→XY) group learned the x and y features separately, and then treated the XY category as the conjunction of the x and y features, consequently classifying the separated features in X-Y as belonging to the XY category. In summary, this study and others (Schyns *et al.*, 1998) have shown that category learning can affect which aspects of a stimulus are used as features by the perceptual system.

17.3.3   Developmental changes

In the previous section, we argued for the flexibility of using aspects of a stimulus in response to category learning. This learning takes place in a short amount of time compared to the time course of developmental changes in the perceptual and conceptual systems. During infancy, there is an increasing trend to attend to correlations of features that are initially based on appearance and later on function as well (Madole and Oakes, this volume, Ch. 18). In turn, learning about the functions and actions of objects has an effect on how children perceive shape and categories (Smith, this volume, Ch. 16). The perception of dimensions can also change during development, and word-labels for dimensions can have a strong effect on this process.

Smith and Kemler (1977) first suggested that children process dimensions integrally that are separable for adults. This was based on evidence in a free classification task in which the participants, children in kindergarten, second grade, and fifth grade (approximately 5, 8, and 11 years old), could classify based either on overall similarity (based on size and brightness) or on only a single dimension. They found an increasing trend to use single dimension rules compared to a rule that combined both dimensions with age (Kemler and Smith, 1978). Contrary to the free classification data, *all* children used dimensional terms when justifying their classifications. Smith and Kemler (1978) demonstrated that children are able to recognize the dimensions even though their classification performance does not show a tendency to use single dimension rules. These results suggest that the dimensions that are separable for adults go through a process during development by which they change from being relatively integral to becoming more separable.

A change in features may also contribute to the learning of word meaning. Clark (1983) proposed that 'contrasting conceptual categories can trigger a search for contrasting words and exposure to new words can trigger a search for pertinent conceptual contrasts' (p. 821). This is consistent with the idea that children's semantic and conceptual learning is determined by their recognition of distinct and contrasting features of categories. Smith, Gasser, and Sandhofer (1997) created a connectionist network that modeled the learning of dimensional terms (e.g. red and wet). The model could learn through word-to-property mappings (*red* to red cups), word-to-word mappings (*red, green, blue* to *color*) and property-to-property comparisons (*maroon* and *auburn* to *red*). The model matched empirical evidence that the learning of the dimension word precedes the ability to selectively attend to the dimension. Simulations demonstrated that the network could learn the dimensions only with training on both word-to-property mappings (labeling) and property-to-property comparisons. This suggests that in language acquisition, word labels are necessary in order for the perceptual system to learn the common properties of a dimension. Taken together, Clark and Smith *et al.*'s work implies that learning words and learning contrasting features of categories provide a mutually supporting scaffold upon which language and concepts are built.

17.4   Semantic Features

17.4.1   Is evidence of perceptual feature adaptation relevant to semantic features?

Certainly, in our modern society, a large amount of conceptual information comes through language rather than directly through experience with the physical world. Even so, the cognitive system must find a way to mesh both means of gathering information. Research has exemplified this need in models that seek to represent concepts and semantics in featural terms (McNamara and Miller, 1989). For example, Landauer and Dumais (1997) developed the technique called latent semantic analysis (LSA) that reduces the co-occurrence data derived from a large text corpus to an appropriate number of dimensions. In the previous section, we argued that features are created and adapted based on relevance to an immediate goal (i.e. a categorization task) or over the time course of early childhood. Our evidence for this has largely come from perceptual tasks, with the exceptions of the context effects on word similarity (Goldstone, Medin, and Halberstadt, 1997; Medin *et al.*, 1993) and dimensional word learning (Smith *et al.*,

1997). This raises the question of whether adaptation of perceptual features implies that semantic features are also adaptable.

Starting from a focus on the stimuli themselves, pictures and words allow for different types of processing. An object or picture presents a rich array of information that is immediately available. An aspect must be perceptually available in order to be used adaptively in perceptual learning and feature creation (Goldstone, 1998; Schyns et al., 1998). However, with pictures, some aspects are difficult to describe in words, such as the Martian cells of Schyns and Rodet (1997), the jagged lines of Goldstone (2000), and color dimensions such as saturation, brightness, and hue. Yet, even when stimuli can be easily described in words at a level relevant to the task (e.g. as would be possible for Bruner et al.'s (1956) stimuli), we would expect that linguistic descriptions would require retrieval of information from memory based on the word label alone (e.g. the word square refers to a shape with four equal sides, etc.). In contrast, pictures would allow recognition to be based on features in the stimulus (e.g. the picture is a shape with four equal sides).

Although perceptual and linguistic stimuli provide different information, both could be processed using a common conceptual representational system such as a perceptual symbol system (Barsalou, 1999). Consistent with this idea, a study by Lambon Ralph, Graham, and Patterson (1999) of semantic dementia patients, characterized by a 'progressive loss of conceptual knowledge leading to poor comprehension and pronounced word-finding difficulties' (p. 310), found an overall impairment of feature listing for both words and pictures. Note, however, that this evidence does not rule out the possibility that some part of the perceptual–conceptual system is modality-specific.

The study of the learning of spatial terms and relations provides an interesting point of contact between the perceived, external world and language. Linguistic representations of the world may be biased to describe high-level visual representations (Kasturirangan, this volume, Ch. 5). Clark (1973) described how language maps on to physical characteristics of the world in reference to the symmetries of the body. Spatial language is often egocentric (e.g. the city is ten miles ahead) and Boroditsky (2000) found that spatial terms aid in the understanding of time (e.g. we moved the meeting back two hours). However, the use of spatial terms is influenced by the functional relations of objects in the scene (Carlson-Radvansky and Radvansky, 1996), in particular, based on the features that are critical to its function (Carlson and Covell, this volume, Ch. 12). In summary, spatial language use seems to involve a reference to perceptually identifiable physical attributes, which is further modulated by interpreted relations among the viewer and objects.

In a study by King et al. (1978), featural descriptions of semantic categories exhibited the separability/integrality pattern obtained previously with perceptual dimensions. They asked participants to classify animal names using two dimensions, size and predacity, with two levels each. They found that the stimuli fit the classic pattern of integrality, in that the correlated tasks were easier than the univariate tasks, that, in turn, were easier than the filter tasks. They also gathered similarity ratings for every pair of animal names and generated a multi-dimensional scaling solution. Two of the three dimensions of the space, taken together, fit well with the original dimensions in the classification tasks.

17.4.2 Adaptation of semantic features

In this section, we present evidence of the adaptation of semantic features from an experiment that uses linguistic stimuli in classification tasks, as in King *et al.* (1978), but examines the effects of training (similar to Goldstone and Steyvers, 2001). Our question is: do linguistic stimuli in Garner type classification tasks exhibit transfer effects?

Specifically, we had 116 undergraduate participants perform classification tasks of different types using linguistic stimuli. Three word sets of 40 words each were developed from the superordinate categories: animals, vehicles, and clothing. Each set contained words that varied on two dimensions, forming a 2 × 2 matrix. See Table 17.1 for a description of the stimuli dimensions. The task required the classification of the words into the appropriate category. Using the Garner paradigm, several types of classification tasks were employed. In the filtering condition (Figs 17.1b, 17.4), stimuli from all four cells were used, and the category depended only on the values of one dimension (e.g. fast vs. slow vehicles). The filtering task should facilitate learning the relevant dimension and ignoring the irrelevant dimension. In the correlated condition (Figs 17.1c, 17.4), only two cells were used, and the categories were based on dimensions varying together (e.g. fast and few passengers vs. slow and many passengers). This task should tend to draw attention to the covariance of both dimensions and, in effect, cause them to be represented as a single 'fused' dimension. A new type of task was used called the 'conjunctive' condition (Fig. 17.4). In this task all four cells were used, and the category depended on the co-occurrence of values on both dimensions

TABLE 17.1. *The stimuli classes of the three word sets, the attributes of each word set, and the descriptions of the attribute values used in the current experiment*

Class	Attribute	Value description
Animals	Ferocity	Timid vs. ferocious
	Socialness	Live alone vs. live in groups
Vehicles	Capacity	Only a few passengers vs. many passengers
	Speed	Slow vs. fast
Clothing	Warmth	Little or no warmth vs. much warmth
	Casualness	Formal vs. casual

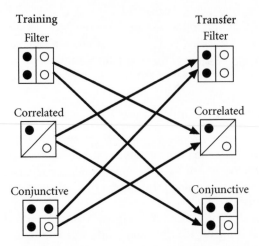

FIG. 17.4. The design of the training and transfer tasks used in the current experiment. Participants were given a different combination of training and testing tasks for each of the three word sets and the task instructions were given in terms of the attribute values of the word set (see Table 17.1).

(e.g. fast and few passengers vs. all others, timid and solitary animals vs. all others). Because the conjunctive task requires attention to two particular values across both dimensions, it should facilitate the fusion of the two values even more strongly than the correlated task.

Each participant performed one task condition during training (randomly selected) and then was transferred to a different task condition for testing (Fig. 17.4). The participant saw three different train-test combinations, one for each word set. At the beginning of each task, the participant was given the definitions and a list of words from the two categories. They were allowed to study this information for as long as they desired. They then proceeded to the categorization trials. On each trial, the participant saw a word displayed on a computer screen, and then selected the correct category for that word. As mentioned above, the correct category depended upon the task condition. Accuracy and response times in the testing task condition were examined as a function of the training condition. We predicted that training in a task that facilitated fusion of the two dimensions (correlated and conjunctive) would have a negative effect on transfer to the filter task, because the filter task required a separation of the dimensions. Similarly, training in the filter task should have negative transfer to the correlated and conjunctive tasks. Positive transfer between the two tasks that encouraged dimension integration might also be predicted.

The data were collapsed over word set for each of nine task conditions (three training conditions and six training-testing combinations). The mean percent correct was above 80 percent for all tasks (Fig. 17.5). The accuracy results

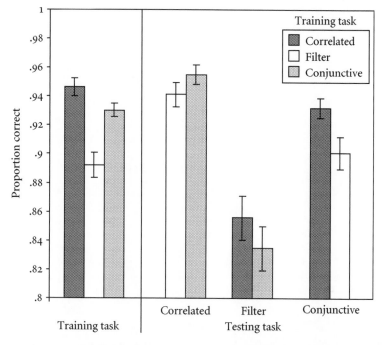

FIG. 17.5. Accuracy data for the current experiment for the initial training tasks and the testing tasks. (Error bars ±1 S.E.)

mirrored the response time results: more accurate performance was associated with fast response times (Fig. 17.6), indicating that there was no speed–accuracy tradeoff.

Planned comparisons were performed to examine the differences between the same tasks during testing as a function of the preceding training tasks. The accuracy and response time performance in training matched the integral pattern: the correlated and conjunctive tasks were performed better than the filter task. King *et al.* (1978) also obtained better performance for the correlated task than the filter task for predacity and size dimensions for animal words.

The conjunctive task was performed with less accuracy and a slower mean response time (both significant) when it was preceded by filter training than by correlated training. The correlated task was performed with significantly slower mean response times when it was preceded by filter training as compared to the initial performance of the correlated task during training. Both of these results can be viewed as a negative transfer effect of filter training. If the correlated and conjunctive tasks benefited from an integral representation of the dimensions, then the filter training seems to have induced a more separated representation of the dimensions that was detrimental to later performance on the correlated and

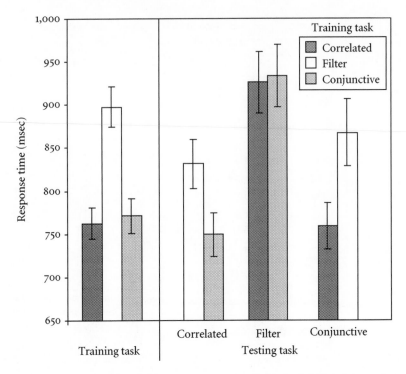

FIG. 17.6. Response time data for the current experiment for the initial training tasks and the testing tasks. (Error bars ±1 S.E.)

conjunctive tasks. By this explanation, we would expect the converse to be true as well, namely, that training in correlated or conjunctive tasks would have a negative effect on later filter testing. This effect was significant in the accuracy data but not the response time data.

An alternative to a dimensional explanation is an attentional weighting hypothesis that would suggest that the effects are due to a change in ideal weights. For example, for the filter task, the weights should be 1 for one dimension and 0 for another. For the correlated and conjunctive tasks, the weights would be 0.5 for both dimensions. Thus, transfer from the filter task to the correlated or conjunctive tasks requires a shift of dimension weighting. Another explanation leaves open the exact weighting of dimensions in the correlated and conjunctive tasks. Because participants could use either dimension (or both) to perform the correlated task, perhaps when participants were transferred to the filter task, they initially used the irrelevant dimension. This would explain the negative trend of correlated training on filter testing. This explanation does not fit the negative effect of filter training, because such training on a single dimension should not hurt performance on the correlated task in which either dimension can be used.

This experiment demonstrates the flexibility of semantic dimensions. Further questions need to be answered to address the adaptation of semantic dimensions. For example, does training on a dimension exhibit the same pattern of effects upon transfer to new words with the same dimensional structure? Some preliminary results indicate that the effects do indeed transfer to new words. Further research could be done to address specific categories and semantic dimensions. We obtained evidence of integrality in only three categories (animals, vehicles, and clothing), and we chose dimensions that we intuited would be relatively integral. We would like to find semantic dimensions that are less integral and study their transfer effects. Finally, we would like to address the duration and extent of the transfer effects. Do these effects produce long-term changes or are they more short-lived and task specific?

17.5 Conclusion

We have argued throughout this chapter that a fixed feature based approach is inadequate. A fixed feature set cannot account for the flexibility with which we learn categories, nor can it account for the changes in processing induced through categorization training. Instead, we have shown evidence that features are dynamically created and processed in ways that are adaptive to task constraints and contexts. We presented new evidence that showed that semantic dimensions are malleable in similar ways as perceptual dimensions. While it is obvious that much work remains to be done, we hope that the technique presented in this study will prove to be useful for studying the flexibility of perceptual and semantic dimensions. One of the unifying themes for this book is captured by Abraham Maslow's quote: 'If the only tool you have is a hammer, you tend to see every problem as a nail.' We seem to have made a new methodological hammer for studying psychological features, and only time and nature will tell if those features are actually nails.

18

Infants' Attention to and Use of Functional Properties in Categorization

KELLY MADOLE and LISA OAKES

Abstract

Function appears to be one of the central features used for categorizing artifacts, but the role of functional properties in early conceptual development remains understudied. In the current chapter we explore the development of infants' attention to object function and how function is used by infants in categorizing objects. According to the developmental progression we propose, infants attend first to the structural properties of objects, then to both structural and functional properties, and finally to the correlation between structural and functional properties. We present data showing that infants are capable of categorizing objects on the basis of structural properties prior to categorizing on the basis of functional properties and that infants treat functional properties of objects as more central to category membership than structural properties. Finally, we review findings that infants' attention to structure–function correlations is initially 'atheoretical' and only later conforms to the kinds of correlations found in the real world. The particular ages at which any change is observed will depend on how categorization is assessed and the kinds of objects that infants are categorizing.

Function

An action upon an object and/or the reaction of an object to an action upon it (see Nelson, 1979). As applied to infants' attention to functional properties, the definition is based more on the information within the perceptual array than on the inferences of the perceiver. Thus, function is how an object is used or its characteristic action.

18.1 Introduction

The emerging ability to divide the world up into meaningful categories of objects is one of the most important developmental changes seen in the first two years of life. Developmentalists have become increasingly interested in understanding the mechanisms underlying the significant and obvious developmental changes in the kinds of categories infants recognize (e.g. Mareschal, French, and Quinn, 2000; Oakes and Madole, 2000). We and others (e.g. Eimas, 1994; Madole and Oakes, 1999; Oakes and Madole, in press; Rakison, in press), have argued that the basic mechanism underlying our ability to categorize objects is a developmentally stable process. That is, the fundamental ability to group discriminably different attributes or objects into categories is present from birth. Developmental changes in the kinds of categories young children form stem from a number of different sources (Madole and Oakes, 1999; Oakes and Madole, in press). One of the most important sources of change for infants' developing categorization abilities is a shift in the kinds of features or attributes infants use in forming categories. To understand this change, we have likened categorization to a process of building new structures (Oakes and Madole, in press). The nature of the structure will depend in part on the building materials that are available. The availability of these materials, in turn, depends on infants' ability to perceive and remember individual features of objects. One important developmental change we propose is that, with increases in infants' motor, linguistic, and information-processing abilities, they become increasingly capable of attending to 'non-obvious' features of objects; features that may not be as readily apparent as are attributes such as shape and color. A second important developmental change is in infants' ability to attend to the relationship among the different features of objects, whether obvious or non-obvious, and to use these relationships in categorizing objects.

One important non-obvious feature of artifacts that is of particular relevance for the current chapter is function. There have been a number of attempts to precisely define what is meant by 'function' (Mervis and Bertrand, 1993; Nelson, 1979, 1991), but these definitions can be distilled into a few basic notions: function is how an object is used, its characteristic action, or the intended purpose of its creator. Function defined in this way appears to be one of the most central features used by adults and older children for categorizing objects, especially artifacts (Lin and Murphy, 1997; Richards and Goldfarb, 1986; Richards, Goldfarb, Richards, and Hassen, 1989; Tversky and Hemenway, 1984). Although it has been argued that functional properties are critically important in early conceptual development (Mervis and Bertrand, 1993; Nelson, 1979, 1991), infants' use of function in forming categories remains understudied.

Nelson (1979) noted three characteristics of functional properties that might be particularly important in understanding how attention to function emerges and develops. First, functional properties encompass dynamic rather than static information. Second, because functional properties are typically dynamic, recognition of functional properties requires integration of information over time. Finally, attention to function enables the individual to predict future actions and changes in an object regardless of the object's present state. Thus, infants' ability to perceive an object's function will be constrained by their ability to perceive and remember dynamic information. As a result, there should be developmental changes in infants' ability to attend to functional features of objects (and consequently, changes in infants' ability to use these features in categorizing objects). In addition, we assume that infants' increasing background knowledge and expectations change the way that they perceive and remember objects. As a result, there should be developmental changes in the kinds of relationships among features to which infants attend.

In the present chapter we outline the development of infants' attention to functional properties, and discuss how those developmental changes influence the categories infants form. First, we review evidence that infants attend to an object's appearance before they attend to an object's function. This developmental progression is consistent with the notion that recognizing function requires sophisticated information processing abilities. Second, we review evidence that infants' recognition of the correlation between appearance and function emerges later than their attention to the individual features. These findings are consistent with the evidence on infants' attention to feature correlations more generally (e.g. Younger, in press). Next, we provide evidence of infants' use of object function in categorization. Specifically, we present findings that infants can use appearance before they can use function to categorize objects. In addition, we review evidence that demonstrates infants' bias to use functional features over non-functional features in forming categories. Finally, we review evidence that infants' growing knowledge and expectations about objects influence the way that they categorize objects and perceive correlations among object features.

18.2 Developmental Changes in Infants' Attention to an Object's Function

During the first year of life, there are important changes in infants' limited memory, attention, and general information-processing abilities (Cohen and Younger, 1983; Rovee-Collier and Hayne, 1987; Ruff and Rothbart, 1996). Thus, the ability to attend to the functions of objects is probably not present early in infancy, but instead emerges as other, more general, cognitive abilities develop. As described above, perceiving an object's function requires that an infant integrates information over space and time, and this ability develops considerably over the first year of life (Arterberry, 1993, 1995; Rose, 1988; Skouteris, McKenzie, and Day, 1992). Although function sometimes is revealed by the object's static appearance, attention to an object's function generally requires that the individual attends to more dynamic information. Hence we should expect to find significant developmental changes in infants' recognition of the functions of objects.

Indeed, we have found that infants' ability to attend to and remember object function changes toward the end of the first year of life (Madole, Oakes, and Cohen, 1993). Specifically, we examined developmental changes in infants' attention to the appearances and functions of individual objects. In this study, infants were presented with actual objects to manipulate and explore and the duration of their clearly focused and concentrated visual attention (*examining*) was measured. First, 10 and 14 month old infants were familiarized with a single novel object constructed from plastic building blocks. For example, infants might be repeatedly presented with a yellow rectangular object that rattled when shaken. Following familiarization with this object, infants' attention to the familiar object and one novel object was assessed. For infants in the *Appearance Novel* condition, the novel object differed from the familiarization object only in appearance (e.g. a red round object that rattled when shaken). For infants in the *Function Novel* condition, the novel object differed only in function (e.g. a yellow rectangular object that rolled when pushed, but that did not rattle when shaken). For infants in the *Appearance and Function Novel* condition, the novel object differed both in appearance and function (a red round object that rolled when pushed).

The goal of this study was to determine whether there were developmental changes in infants' attention to the appearance and function of these objects. Attention to a particular feature would be demonstrated by greater attention to the test object in which that feature was changed than to the familiar object. That is, infants should examine the novel object for longer than the familiar object only when the two objects differ along a dimension to which the infants attend. The results were clear and are shown in Fig. 18.1. The younger infants examined the novel object longer in the two conditions in which that novel object looked different from the familiar object. In the function novel condition, in which the novel object looked exactly the same as the familiar object, 10 month old infants' examining of the novel and familiar objects did not differ. Therefore, 10 month old infants apparently only noticed a change in the appearance of the object. The older infants, in contrast, examined the novel item longer in all three conditions. By 14 months, infants not only noticed a change in the object's appearance, but they also noticed a change in the object's function (in this case what happens when you act on an object). Thus, this study provides support for the notion that attention to the static features of objects (such as color and shape) precedes attention to objects' functional features.

Certainly, the age at which infants attend to particular functions will vary depending on the nature of the function, how much information must be retained and the amount of time and space over which that information must be integrated. Thus, these results provide evidence for the general developmental change that is expected, not the specific age at which infants should recognize any

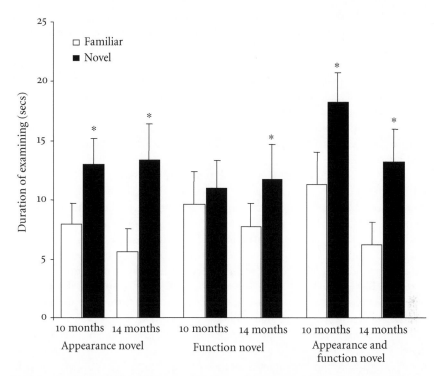

FIG. 18.1. The duration of infants' examining (concentrated visual attention) when presented with novel and familiar exemplars after familiarization in Experiment 1 of Madole *et al.* (1993). Asterisks indicate significant differences in examining within a pair. Error bars represent 1 SE.

function. Indeed, other investigators have found that infants attend to functional properties of objects at even younger ages when function is defined as the simple movement of an object (Nelson, 1979). In general, however, we would predict that before infants are capable of attending to these functional features of objects, infants would attend to and recognize features such as the object's shape and color.

18.3   Developmental Changes in Infants' Attention to Appearance–Function Correlations

One important characteristic of functional properties, as noted above, is that knowledge of an object's function allows an infant to make predictions about how that object will behave in the future. If an infant notices that her rubber ducky has squeaked when it was squeezed the last five times she took a bath, then she can predict that her rubber ducky should squeak when squeezed in the future. However, before such predictions can be made infants must be able to recognize the correlation between an object's appearance and its function. It is certainly possible that infants are capable of recognizing an object's appearance and its function, but are unable to recognize the consistent relationship between these features. Indeed, research on infants' attention to the correlations between different aspects of an object's appearance suggests such a developmental progression—first infants attend to and notice the individual features and only later do they recognize the correlation among those features (Younger, in press; Younger and Cohen, 1986).

Madole, Oakes, and Cohen (1993) explored infants' recognition of appearance–function correlations in a second set of studies with infants at 10, 14, and 18 months of age, using the same basic procedure as before. In these studies, infants were first familiarized with two objects that embodied a particular appearance–function correlation, in that a particular appearance was always associated with a particular function (e.g. a yellow rectangular object that rattled when shaken and a red round object that rolled when pushed). We then tested infants' attention to three objects: (1) a toy from the familiarization set in which the familiar appearance–function relationship was maintained, (2) a 'hybrid' toy in which a familiar appearance and a familiar function were combined in a novel way (e.g. a yellow rectangular object that rolled when pushed), and (3) a completely novel object (e.g. a cylindrical object that 'mooed' when turned over). The notion underlying this design is simple: if infants attended to the relationship between appearance and function that was presented during familiarization, they should increase their attention to the object in which that correlation is violated (the hybrid object).

The results are presented in Fig. 18.2. The 10 and 14 month old infants significantly increased their attention only to the completely novel object. They did not examine the hybrid object significantly longer than they did the familiar object. On the basis of our previous findings, we assume that 10 month old infants in this study attended only to the object's appearance. The 14 month old infants, however, apparently could attend to and recognize an object's function as well its appearance, but they could not recognize the relationship between these two features, at least in the stimuli used here (note that the same stimuli were used in these two studies). The 18 month old infants significantly increased their attention not only to the novel object, but also to the hybrid object in which the familiar correlation was violated. These oldest infants recognized not only the object's appearance and function, but also the combination of these two features. Thus, infants initially attend to appearance and function as independent properties, and it is not until later that they begin to notice the relationship between an object's appearance and its function.

Using a different task and stimuli, Madole and Johnston (1999) reported similar findings. Fourteen and 18 month old infants' attention to the relationship

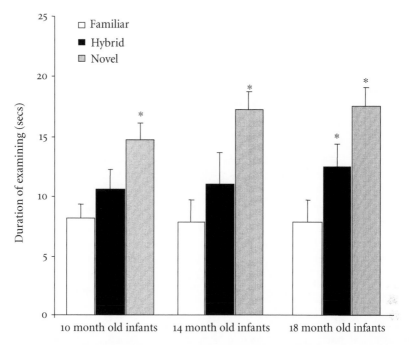

FIG. 18.2. The duration of 10, 14, and 18 month old infants' examining (concentrated visual attention) to correlated, uncorrelated, and novel tests after familiarization in Madole *et al.* (1993). Asterisks indicate significantly greater examining to the novel item than to the familiar item (the open bar). Error bars represent 1 SE.

between appearance and function was assessed by looking at the particular actions they performed on target objects. As in the Madole *et al.* (1993) study, infants were first familiarized with two novel objects in which a particular appearance–function correlation was maintained (e.g. a cube-shaped box that rattled when shaken, and an L-shaped box that beeped when pressed). Madole and Johnston (1999) then evaluated the particular action (e.g. shaking or pressing) infants performed on non-functional objects that were identical in appearance to the familiarization objects. Thus, appearance was the only cue to the test objects' potential function. If infants have learned to predict the object's function from its appearance, then, using the above example, they should direct more shaking actions to the cube-shaped object and more pressing actions to the L-shaped object.

Consistent with the results reported by Madole *et al.* (1993), only the older infants showed recognition of the appearance–function relationship by per-forming the appropriate actions on these test objects. The younger infants were equally likely to perform either action on the test object, regardless of its appearance. In general, therefore, we have evidence that the ability to detect appearance–function correlations emerges relatively late in development—at least later than the ability to attend to the functional properties of objects themselves. Because the functions of objects are often not readily apparent, learning to predict an object's function from its appearance is a crucial step in conceptual development. Moreover, recognition of the relationship between appearance and function allows generalization of this non-obvious property to other similar objects. In other words, recognizing function is important not only for recognizing individual objects, but also for categorizing objects.

18.4   Developmental Changes in Infants' Ability to use Function as a Basis for Categorization

Recognizing the functions of objects and the correlations between appearance and function are fundamentally important for interactions with objects. However, attention to functional information may play a particularly critical role in categorizing objects. The recognition of many object categories, in particular superordinate categories, depends upon categorization of functional properties. For example, the category 'vehicle' is defined less by the similarities in the appearance of the category members than by their common function. In fact, a number of studies with preschool children have tried to determine whether children categorize objects on the basis of appearance or function, with the assumption that categories based on function are more sophisticated (e.g. Corrigan and Schommer, 1984; Gentner, 1978b; Prawat and Wildfon, 1980; Tomikawa and Dodd, 1980). Despite the fact that there has been much recent discussion about the emergence of attention to superordinate or global level categories in infancy (e.g. Mandler and McDonough, 1993; Quinn and Johnson, 2000; Younger and Fearing, 2000), research on infants' categorization has focused almost exclusively on their ability to form categories on the basis of appearance (e.g. shape) (for a review see Quinn and Eimas, 1996). In contrast, there is relatively little evidence about infants' ability to form categories on the basis of functional properties.

Because we believe that categorization is a developmentally stable process, we would predict that once infants have information available about object function, they should use such information to form categories (Madole and Oakes, 1999; Oakes and Madole, 2000). Given the results described above, we expect that infants would first categorize objects on the basis of appearance and later use function to categorize those same objects.

We tested infants' use of appearance and function to categorize objects using a visual habituation task.[1] Infants were shown a series of objects one at a time on a video monitor, and the duration of their looking on each trial was

[1] These data were previously reported in Madole and Cohen (1993) and Madole, Cohen, and Bradley (1994).

recorded. Because we were interested in function, however, these were not static depictions of the objects. Rather, each presentation involved several demonstrations of the particular object's function. As in many studies of infant categorization, infants first were familiarized with several different objects from one category, and then were tested with a new object from the familiar category (within category), and a new object from a different category (out-of-category). Attention to the category presented during familiarization is inferred if infants look longer at the new object from a different category than at the new object from the familiar category.

The design of this experiment is presented in Table 18.1. Ten month old and 14 month old infants were randomly assigned to one of two conditions. During the habituation phase, infants in the *appearance* condition were presented with four objects that were identical in appearance but that performed different functions (e.g. a purple ball that rattled when it was shaken, a purple ball that clicked as it was rolled, a purple ball that squeaked when squeezed, and a purple ball that made a mooing sound when it was inverted). Infants in the *function* condition were presented with four objects that differed in appearance, but all performed the same function (e.g. a purple ball, a yellow cube, a pyramid, a pink tube, and an insect-like object, all of which rattled when shaken). On each trial, the function was demonstrated several times. Infants received habituation trials until the duration of their looking decreased to 50 percent of their initial level of looking or until they had received a maximum number of trials (up to four presentations of each object, or 16 habituation trials).

The questions of interest were whether infants in the appearance condition formed a category based on appearance (e.g. purple balls) despite the fact that all the balls performed different functions, and whether infants in the function condition formed a category based on function (e.g. objects that rattle when shaken) despite the fact that the objects looked different from one another. To answer these questions, we tested all infants with two novel items. One item was a

TABLE 18.1. *Design of Madole (1993)*

	Appearance condition	Function condition
Habituation		
	$Appearance_1-Function_1$	$Function_1-Appearance_1$
	$Appearance_1-Function_2$	$Function_1-Appearance_2$
	$Appearance_1-Function_3$	$Function_1-Appearance_3$
	$Appearance_1-Function_4$	$Function_1-Appearance_4$
Test		
Within category:	$Appearance_{fam}-Function_{nov}$	$Function_{fam}-Appearance_{nov}$
Out of category:	$Appearance_{nov}-Function_{nov}$	$Function_{nov}-Appearance_{nov}$

'within-category' item. For infants in the appearance condition, this item looked like the other objects (e.g. a purple ball) but had a novel function. For infants in the function condition, this item had the same function (e.g. rattled when shaken) but had a novel appearance. The other item was an 'out-of-category' item that was novel in both appearance and function. We reasoned that if infants formed the category in each condition, they should look longer at this out-of-category item than they would to the novel within-category item.

Infants' looking times for these two tests are shown in Fig. 18.3. It can be seen that the younger and older infants responded differently in the two conditions. Specifically, in the appearance condition, infants at both ages looked significantly longer at the out-of-category object than at the within-category object. This pattern suggests that at both ages infants formed a category of the objects based on what the objects looked like. In the function condition, in contrast, only the older

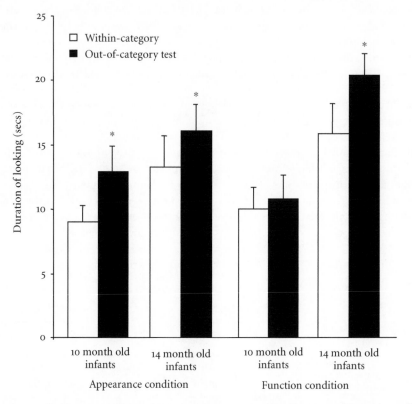

FIG. 18.3. The duration of looking by 10 and 14 month old infants to novel within- and out-of-category exemplars following familiarization with a category of items sharing appearance or function. Asterisks indicate significant differences in examining within a pair. Error bars represent 1 SE.

infants looked significantly longer at the out-of-category object than at the within-category object. The 10 month old infants attended equally to the novel out-of-category and within-category item, suggesting that they included both items in their category. This pattern suggests that 14 month old infants, but not 10 month old infants, formed a category of the objects based on what the objects did.

In other words, both older and younger infants can recognize categories of objects when the category is based on a shared appearance. However, only older infants appeared to recognize categories of objects that are based on shared function. These findings are consistent with our previous findings on developmental changes in infants' attention to appearance and function and correlations between appearance and function. In general, the results described thus far show that there is a developmental shift not only in infants' ability to recognize object functions but also in infants' ability to use these functions to form categories.

However, for adults, function is more than just another feature of objects. Tversky and Hemenway (1984) found that adults do not seem to regard all parts of objects as equally relevant to category membership. Rather, the most prevalent parts listed among category members (the 'essential' parts) seemed to be those that have the greatest functional importance. Richards (Richards and Goldfarb, 1986; Richards *et al.*, 1989) formalized this idea as 'the functionality rule' which states that artifact concepts are typically defined by their functions. Following from this rule, the final determinant of whether a particular feature of an artifact is definitional of the artifact is whether the presence of the feature is necessary for the object's function. Lin and Murphy (1997) also showed that knowledge about the function of an object affects the extent to which a particular feature, or part, of an object is central to categorization judgments, with functional parts being more central than non-functional parts. Adults apparently have a bias, based on their experience with artifacts, to treat functional parts of objects as more essential to category membership than non-functional parts.

The question is, do infants also have such a bias? That is, when categorizing objects do 14 month old infants selectively attend to functional parts of objects over non-functional parts? Such a pattern would suggest that even for infants function is more central than appearance in categorization.

Madole (1993) addressed this question by habituating 14 month old infants to videotaped displays showing a category of objects constructed from plastic building blocks. This set of objects shared two perceptually salient parts, one protruding from the side of the object and one protruding from the top of the object. During habituation, one of the parts was functional (it emitted a noise when turned) and the other part was non-functional (no noise resulted from turning the part). Thus, infants could form a category of objects that shared the functional part, the non-functional part, or both parts. Following habituation, infants were tested with displays of similar objects in which either the functional or the non-functional part was changed. As in the previously described experiment, because infants were habituated to a category of objects, it was assumed that they would increase their attention to the objects that were perceived as non-category members. If infants defined the category presented during familiarization in terms of the functional part, they should increase their attention to the test item in which that part was changed. If they defined the category in terms of the non-functional part, they should increase their attention to the test item in which that part was changed. If both types of features were important in the category they formed, then they should increase their attention to both novel objects. In other words, by assessing which test object or test objects infants preferred, it was possible to determine the nature of the category formed during the habituation phase.

Infants' responding to the familiar item, the test item in which the non-functional part was changed, and the test item in which the functional part was changed is presented in Fig. 18.4. Relative to their looking to the familiar, infants increased their looking to the item in which the functional part was changed but not to the item in which the non-functional part was changed. Thus, the results

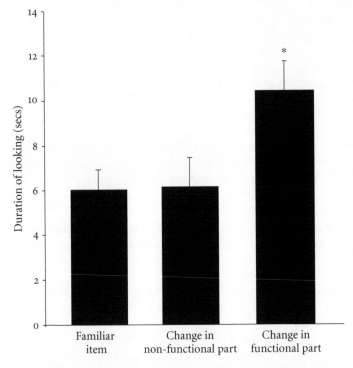

Fig. 18.4. The duration of looking by 14 month old infants in Madole (1993) to a familiar item, an item novel in terms of a non-functional part, and an item novel in terms of a non-functional part following familiarization with a category of items. Asterisk indicates significantly greater examining to the novel item than to the familiar item. Error bars represent 1 SE.

are consistent with the notion that infants formed a category that was based solely on the presence of the functional part. In other words, infants included into the familiarization category objects with novel non-functional parts, but not objects with novel functional parts. Importantly, this pattern of results was obtained only when infants were habituated to a *category* of objects. In a control experiment in which infants were habituated to a single object, infants increased attention both to types of novel objects. That is, infants could notice changes in both functional and non-functional parts, but in the context of a categorization task they showed differential attention to the two types of parts, apparently showing the functional bias present in adults' categorization.

These results are consistent with results obtained by Smith, Jones, and Landau (1996) and Landau, Smith, and Jones (1998) with preschoolers. They found that young children clearly attend to function and, in fact, three year old children's attention was directed toward functionally relevant object parts when making similarity judgments about the objects. Interestingly, however, they found a dissociation between similarity judgments and naming in children: unlike adults, young children fail to use functional information when naming objects, suggesting that the attentional processes that control similarity judgments (and some forms of categorization) are initially separate from the attentional process that control naming and lexical categorization.

Certainly, the depth of infants' understanding of function is not completely clear from this study. Infants may infer that objects with shared functional parts also share a similar internal mechanism, and that a change in a functional part subsequently changes the 'essential nature' of the object. Alternatively, it is possible that infants have a simple attentional bias that guides their attention more to the dynamic parts of objects. The most likely possibility is that both levels of understanding exist at different points in time. Initially, infants' attention may be directed more to parts of objects that move or produce sound, but they may have little understanding of the underlying basis for these properties. As infants' ability to reason causally about non-obvious mechanisms develops, a more theory-like understanding of the shared similarities among objects with shared functional parts may also emerge. The results of a study by Madole and Cohen (1995), described in the next section, provide supporting evidence for this kind of developmental progression.

18.5 Developmental Changes in Background Knowledge Constrain Infants' Attention to Appearance–Function Correlations

The developmental transitions that we have described so far can be described as 'bottom-up' changes. That is, with increasing sophistication in infants' attention, memory, and motor skills, new features (in this case function) become available to use in categorizing objects. However 'top-down' changes also serve to shape infants' attention to and use of functional properties. Specifically, infants' increasing background knowledge and expectations about objects allow them to selectively attend to only the most relevant information when interacting with those objects. In this final section we will describe evidence showing how these expectations about objects influence infants' attention to appearance–function correlations.

For adults and older children, knowledge of the relationship between structure and function is central to concepts (Medin and Ortony, 1989). However, this knowledge goes beyond a simple, passive recognition of the correlation among features. Instead, individuals display an awareness of the *causal* nature of the relationship underlying this correlation (Ahn, Kim, Lassaline, and Dennis, 2000). For example, Spalding and Murphy (1996, 1999) found that adults more easily categorized objects if the features of those objects cohere according to their existing background knowledge (e.g. *arctic vehicles*) than if the features do not cohere according to such knowledge. In other words, their background knowledge influences the kind of relationships they recognize.

In a study designed to determine whether infants' attention to structure–function relationships is similarly influenced by background knowledge, Madole and Cohen (1995) examined infants' attention to 'meaningful' and 'arbitrary' structure–function correlations using a visual habituation task and objects similar to those used by Madole (1993). The meaningful correlations were consistent with the mechanistic behavior of real objects: the structure of one part of the object was correlated with the function of the same part (e.g. the appearance of the wheels was correlated with whether or not the wheels rolled when the object was pushed). The arbitrary correlations, however, were less consistent with the mechanistic behavior of real objects: the structure of one part of the object was correlated with the function of a *different* part of the object (e.g. the appearance of a protrusion on the top of the object was correlated with whether or not the wheels rolled when the object was pushed). Thus, the particular correlations to which they would attend was predicted to change as a function of infants' developing understanding of how objects generally behave and the typical types of correlations between appearance and function that exist in the world. Specifically, younger infants might attend to both arbitrary and meaningful correlations because they do not yet have expectations based on the mechanistic behavior of real objects. Older infants (who have increased background knowledge), in contrast, would selectively attend only to the meaningful correlations because those correlations conform to their understanding of real objects. Madole and Cohen tested this prediction by habituating 14 and 18 month old infants to four objects embodying a set of structure–function correlations. For half of the infants the correlations seen during habituation were meaningful and for half of the infants the correlations were arbitrary. Following habituation, infants were tested with objects that maintained the correlation seen during habituation and with objects that violated it. An increase in attention to the test object in which the correlation was violated shows that infants learned the correlation during habituation.

The data are presented in Fig. 18.5. Both the younger and older infants attended to the meaningful appearance–function correlation. Specifically, both age groups looked approximately equally to a familiar object and a novel object

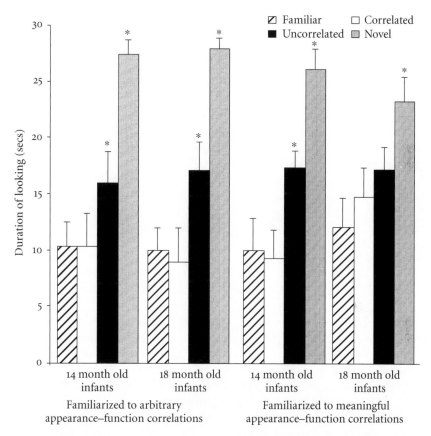

FIG. 18.5. The duration of looking by 14 and 18 month old infants in Madole and Cohen (1995) to a familiar item, a novel correlated item, a novel uncorrelated item, and a completely novel item, following familiarization with items that conformed to an arbitrary correlation (e.g. the appearance of one part was correlated with the function of a different part) or to a meaningful correlation (e.g. the appearance of one part was correlated with the function of that part). Asterisks indicate significantly greater examining to the novel item than to the familiar item (the hatched bar). Error bars represent 1 SE.

that maintained the familiarized correlations, but increased their attention to objects in which the correlation was violated. However, only the younger infants attended to the arbitrary appearance–function correlation. The younger infants, but not the older infants, looked longer at a novel object that violated the familiar correlation. That is, the younger infants seemed to recognize and respond to correlations that were unrecognized by the older infants. The younger infants attended to meaningful correlations as well as to those that were more arbitrary or phenomenalistic, whereas older infants attended only to the meaningful ones. Note that this is the opposite developmental change from that described in previous sections of this chapter. In general, we have shown that with development infants come to attend to *more* features of objects. In the present case, however, we have evidence that with development infants actually attend to *fewer* features of objects. That is, as infants gain knowledge about how objects in the world are typically constructed, this knowledge helps them restrict their attention to the sets of relationships that are most likely, and as a result they are more efficient in their processing of information about objects.

Apparently the older infants in this study have learned something about the way objects behave, knowledge that is shared by older children and adults. For example, if the light on my ceiling fan fails to work, I am unlikely to implicate the structure of the fan blade as the source of the problem. However, younger infants seem to be capable of recognizing the relationships among many different kinds of features, even when these relationships do not 'make sense'.

18.6   Conclusions

The studies described in this chapter provide evidence of a developmental progression that might account for some fundamental changes in the way that infants categorize objects. Infants progress from attending primarily to features that specify the appearance of objects to attending to the functions of objects as well. At this point, infants show the ability to also categorize objects on the basis of these functional properties and in fact, they seem to treat functional parts of objects as more important to category membership than non-functional parts. Later still, infants' attention to the relationship between appearance and function becomes constrained by their background knowledge and by expectations about the way real objects typically behave.

The results described here and the developmental progression we have observed are important for at least two reasons. First, they are consistent with our general framework that the development of categorization stems from developmental changes in the availability of different types of information, rather than from qualitative changes in the nature of the conceptual process. That is, our results do not suggest that with development infants are forming qualitatively different kinds of representations of objects (e.g. *perceptually-based* representations early in infancy and *conceptually-based representations* later in infancy). Rather, our results suggest that the nature of infants' representations need not change; what changes is the kinds of information they use in forming those representations. Clearly, the 10 month old infants in our studies who attended only to appearance and therefore form categories based only on what objects look like are forming quite different sorts of categories than are the 18 month old infants who can selectively attend only to 'meaningful' appearance–function correlations. However, we have shown that this shift can be accounted for by gradual changes in the kinds of information to which infants attend and the biases that emerge with increased knowledge.

Second, these results provide much needed understanding into the role of function in very young children's categorization. Despite the attention of research on the relative roles of appearance and function in preschooler's categorization (e.g. Corrigan and Schommer, 1984; Gentner, 1978; Prawat and Wildfon, 1980; Tomikawa and Dodd, 1980) and the many studies evaluating children's use of appearance and non-obvious information in categorization (e.g. Gelman and Coley, 1990; Gelman and Markman, 1986, 1987), very little research has evaluated young infants' attention to these two types of object properties. The research reviewed here shows that although attention to function emerges later than does attention to appearance, infants can use function to form categories—and seem to have a bias to use functional information—perhaps as soon as that information is available to them. Thus, the present research is consistent with the notion that function (once it is available) plays a central role in infants' category formation.

It is important to point out that we have focused on only one conceptualization of function—an action upon an object and an associated reaction from the object. As pointed out previously, function can be conceptualized in a number of different ways and it remains to be seen whether the developmental changes outlined here generalize to these other conceptualizations. For example, future research might consider the development of attention to functional properties that are less dynamic. For example, Tversky and Hemenway (1984) found that *seat* is treated by adults as a better part of a chair than *stuffing*. Presumably, a chair could not function without a seat, but could without stuffing. However, it is not certain that infants would attend to a seat in the same way they do to the functional parts in these studies. It is probable that for infants, attention to parts like *seats* as functionally significant depends on understanding the causal mechanisms underlying the structure and the function of chairs and on their understanding of physical relationships like support. The point is that our results may depend on developmental changes in attention to dynamic information. Attention to other aspects of function may require developmental changes in attention to other types of information. However, in general we assume that attention to any feature depends on increased information processing abilities and as soon as features become available infants can and will use them to form categories.

In summary, we believe that future research should consider how changes in infants' general cognitive and motor abilities make new pieces of information salient for them and thus available to use as a basis for categorizing objects. In addition, research should examine the ways in which increasing general knowledge serves to shape and constrain this pool of information and allow the infant to form meaningful and useful categories.

19

Developmental Constraints on the Representation of Spatial Relation Information: Evidence from Preverbal Infants

PAUL C. QUINN

Abstract

Research indicates that infants can organize objects into category groupings. This chapter reviews evidence that infants can also form category representations for spatial relations such as ABOVE, BELOW, and BETWEEN. Two developmental changes are discussed. First, category representations for different spatial relations may emerge at different points during development. Infants may initially encode the location of a target relative to a single landmark, and later encode the location of a target in relation to multiple landmarks that define a local spatial framework. Second, category representations of spatial relations may initially be limited to the objects depicting the relations, but later become more abstract so that various objects can be presented in the same relation and the equivalence of the relation is maintained despite this variation. The results are discussed in terms of what versus where processing systems, and the role of language in binding together object and spatial relation information.

Feature

A feature is a component of a visual display that can be used to construct a category representation for a given spatial relation. With respect to the categorization of spatial relation information by infants, candidate features are verticality, place, region, point, line, and plane.

Preparation of this chapter was supported by NSF Grant BCS-0096300 and NIH grant HD-42451. The author thanks Laura Carlson and Emile van der Zee for inviting this contribution and for providing helpful comments on an earlier draft. The author also thanks Jason Parkhill and Ramesh Bhatt for their assistance in creating the figures.

19.1   Introduction

Any informed discussion of the relation between language and space should include an accounting of how young children come to represent the meaning of spatial terms (Bowerman, 1996*a*; Bowerman and Choi, 2001). Evidence on how infants parse space prior to language is essential for understanding the contribution that nonlinguistic spatial cognition makes towards the acquisition of a spatial lexicon (Quinn, 2003). This chapter focuses on the abilities of preverbal infants to represent small-scale spatial relation information.

19.2   Early Category Representations for Objects

My work on how infants structure space is an outgrowth of research on how infants form organized groupings of stimuli in the domain of objects (Quinn, 2002). The internal basis for such early cognitive structure is believed to be a set of *category representations*—mental representations for similar or like entities. Category representations underlie our ability to respond equivalently to discriminably different entities from a common class.

One way to think about category representations is to envision file folders. We use file folders to organize information into meaningful groupings, and we may have mental files or category representations to hold information about various object classes. By developing a storage system in which information about related instances (e.g. dogs) is stored in the same file, and information from related files (e.g. cats) is nested in larger superordinate files (e.g. animal), we enable intellectual functioning to be mediated by a cognitive system in which objects are related to each other through a set of interconnected category representations.[1]

To study the beginnings of object categorization, researchers have utilized a familiarization/novelty-preference procedure that capitalizes on the established finding that infants prefer novel stimuli (Fantz, 1964). First, during a series of familiarization trials, infants are presented with a number of different photographic exemplars, all of which are from the same category. Second, during a novel category preference test, infants are presented with two novel stimuli, one from the familiar category, and the other from a novel category. Infant looking time to the stimuli is recorded throughout the familiarization and preference test trials. Generalization of familiarization to the novel instance from the familiar

[1] The 'file' metaphor used here to refer to category representations should not be confused with the 'object file' metaphor used in the visual attention literature (e.g. Kahneman, Treisman, and Gibbs, 1992; Leslie, Xu, Tremoulet, and Scholl, 1998). Files for category representations are presumed to contain featural information about objects, whereas object files are believed to contain spatio-temporal information that is dissociated from featural information.

category and a preference for the novel instance from the novel category are taken as evidence that the infants have grouped together or categorized the instances from the familiar category and recognized that the novel instance from the novel category does not belong to this grouping (or category representation). This conclusion is also contingent on the results of two control experiments showing that the preference for the novel category is not simply the result of a pre-existing preference or a failure to discriminate among the instances of the familiar category.

Investigations conducted with the familiarization/novelty-preference procedure have revealed that infants are capable of representing a variety of complex object categories at different levels of inclusiveness. For example, three–four month olds have been shown to represent instances of animals and furniture at both general, for example mammal, furniture, and more specific levels, for example cat, dog, horse, chair, table (reviewed in Quinn, 1998, 1999). This early, but nevertheless correct, parsing of the world implies that some of the conceptual representations found in later life are informational enrichments of the perceptual category representations formed by infants (Quinn and Eimas, 1996, 1997, 2000). For example, if infants can represent a perceptual category of horses (e.g. one that is based on body shape, parts, markings, facial information, communicative sounds, and motion) that includes novel horses, but excludes other animal species, as well as members of categories from other domains (e.g. furniture and vehicles), then more abstract information that is learned later through the input system of language (e.g. that horses eat hay, carry heavy loads, possess horse DNA, and give birth to foals) can be incorporated into the original perceptually based representation, thereby enriching the representation, allowing it to become more conceptually based (i.e. attain the cognitive power of a concept). Indeed, it is difficult to imagine how higher-level knowledge processing could proceed without a perceptually based system of object category representations as a foundation. That is, if preverbal infants represented each object as unrelated to every other object on a perceptual basis, it is difficult to envision how names and non-obvious features could be associated with object categories in a rapid and efficient manner. The category representations that infants form for object classes can thus be thought of as perceptual placeholders or anchor points for the accumulation of conceptual knowledge beyond the infancy period (Quinn and Bhatt, 2001; Needham, 2001; Jones and Smith, 1993).

19.3   Early Category Representations for Spatial Relations

19.3.1   *Above* versus *below*

Given the abilities of infants to form category representations of objects, and because even young infants encounter numerous objects in various locations and

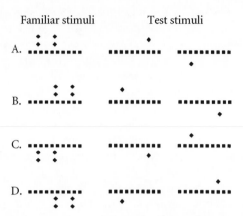

Fig. 19.1. Familiarization exemplars (a composite of the four exemplars) and test exemplars used to determine whether infants could form a category representation for DIAMOND ABOVE BAR (panels A and B) and DIAMOND BELOW BAR (panels C and D) in Quinn, Cummins, Kase, Martin, and Weissman (1996).

in different spatial arrangements, it seemed reasonable to examine whether infants could also parse space into categories defined by the positional arrangements of objects. Experiments were therefore designed to determine whether infants could represent categorical distinctions between spatial relations such as above, below, between, left, and right.

The first question asked was whether three and four month old infants could categorize the ABOVE and BELOW spatial relations between a diamond and a horizontal bar (Quinn, 1994; Quinn, Cummins, Kase, Martin, and Weissman, 1996). Infants in an above familiarization group were familiarized with four exemplars, each depicting a single diamond in a different position above a horizontal bar. As shown in panels A and B of Fig. 19.1, over the course of familiarization with the exemplars, the diamond appeared in the four corner locations of the top left or top right quadrant of the stimulus. The infants were then administered a novel category preference test that paired two novel exemplars, one in which the diamond was located in a novel position above the bar (shifted to the right or left of the familiar exemplars); the other depicted the diamond below the bar (and below the familiar exemplars). The rationale of this test is as follows. If infants form a category representation of DIAMOND ABOVE BAR, then the novel ABOVE exemplar should be recognized as familiar, whereas the novel BELOW exemplar should be perceived as novel, and therefore be preferred. If, however, infants do not form a category representation of DIAMOND ABOVE BAR, and represent only information about the diamond or the bar, or represent information about the diamond and the bar independently of each other, then neither test exemplar should be preferred. Panels C and D

TABLE 19.1. *Summary of major results from experiments investigating categorization of spatial relations by infants*

	Age of infants (months)	Familiarization trials stimuli	Preference test trials		Result
			Familiar category stimulus	vs. Novel category stimulus	
A.	3 to 4	single object in different locations above or below bar	familiar object in familiar relation vs. familiar object in novel relation		preference for novel relation
B.	6 to 7	single object in different locations between bars	familiar object in familiar relation vs. familiar object in novel relation		preference for novel relation
C.	6 to 7	different objects in different locations above or below bar	novel object in familiar relation vs. novel object in novel relation		preference for novel relation
D.	9 to 10	different objects in different locations between bars	novel object in familiar relation vs. novel object in novel relation		preference for novel relation

display how the same procedure was used to test whether infants could also form a category representation of DIAMOND BELOW BAR.[2]

Both the DIAMOND ABOVE BAR and DIAMOND BELOW BAR groups displayed a visual preference for the novel spatial category (see panel A of Table 19.1). This result was computed by taking each infant's looking time to the novel category stimulus, dividing by the looking time to both test stimuli, and converting to a percentage score. The mean preference for the novel spatial relation across the two experimental groups was 59.11 percent, $SD = 11.85$, $N = 24$, t(vs. the chance value of 50 percent) $= 3.77$, $p < .0005$, one-tailed. The finding is consistent with the idea that the infants had formed category representations for

---

[2] It could be argued that the experimental design and form of the preference test places LEFT versus RIGHT information in competition with ABOVE versus BELOW spatial relation information of the object and the bar. For example, in panel A of Fig. 19.1, if infants were representing the object TO THE LEFT versus TO THE RIGHT of the midline of the stimulus display, and this representation was weighted more heavily than any representation of the ABOVE versus BELOW relation information, then one would predict the opposite pattern of preferences during the test trials. However, the results of the experiment render this account unlikely.

the ABOVE and BELOW relations between the diamond and the horizontal bar. It should be noted that this pattern of infant looking could not be attributed to simple generalization based on distance information, because the diamond in the novel category exemplar was moved the same distance away from the familiar diamond locations (either down or up) as the diamond in the novel exemplar of the familiar category (which was moved either to the right or left). It should also be observed that infants in a control experiment were able to discriminate the position changes of the diamond that occurred within the familiar ABOVE and BELOW categories. This finding is important because it indicates that the preference for the novel category exemplar was not simply the result of a failure to discriminate among the familiar category exemplars.

Another informative result is that the preference for the novel spatial relation fell to chance when the ABOVE versus BELOW categorization experiment was repeated, but with stimuli that contained only the diamond, and not the horizontal bar. The stimuli for this control experiment were the same stimuli used in the initial categorization experiment, except that the horizontal bar was removed from the central portion of the stimulus display. The null outcome in this control experiment means that the infants in the initial ABOVE versus BELOW categorization experiment with the bar were not simply responding preferentially to vertical (up–down) as opposed to horizontal (left–right) changes in diamond location. The null categorization result without the bar also implies that the infants in the initial categorization experiment with the bar were not encoding the diamond locations in relation to an internally imposed horizontal midline. In other words, the infants were not spontaneously mentally bisecting the stimulus into top and bottom halves and relating the diamond's position to the line of bisection. The data from the various control conditions, taken together, support the conclusion that the infants in the original experiment had formed category representations for the diamond's ABOVE versus BELOW relations with the horizontal bar.

In unpublished work, we have determined that infants can also form category representations for a diamond appearing either to the left or right of a vertical bar (Burdelski, Rause, Shaffer, and Quinn, 2000; see also Behl-Chadha and Eimas, 1995). A question that arises from the investigations of ABOVE versus BELOW and LEFT versus RIGHT categorization by infants is whether performance might simply reflect sensitivity to a primitive crossing concept. That is, the infants may respond preferentially when they observe that an object has crossed from one side of a bar to another. However, this does not appear to be the case, because when the basic spatial categorization experiment is repeated with a diagonal bar, infants familiarized with stimuli depicting the diamond on one side of the bar do not respond preferentially to a stimulus depicting the diamond on the opposite side of the bar (Adams, Shettler, Wasnik, and Quinn, 2001). Although it could be argued that the null results of this control experiment could be due to the difficulty that infants have with processing diagonal information, there is evidence indicating that under similar experimental conditions, infants in the same age range can distinguish left versus right facing diagonals (Quinn and Bomba, 1986; Quinn, Siqueland, and Bomba, 1985).

A potential objection to the stimulus materials used to study the categorization of ABOVE, BELOW, LEFT, and RIGHT spatial relation information in infants is that the bar, in consisting of little squares, would tend to encourage deployment of Gestalt grouping processes by infants (Quinn, Brown, and Streppa, 1997; Quinn, Burke, and Rush, 1993), which in turn might promote grouping of the entire stimulus display into an abstract configuration. The suggestion is that the infants are engaging in simple pattern discrimination rather than categorization of spatial relations. There are two aspects of the stimulus display that work against this possibility. First, the squares are close to the other squares, but further away from the diamond. Second, although the squares could be said to have the same shape as the diamond, their orientation is different, a factor that impacts on grouping (Wertheimer, 1923/1958). Thus, by virtue of proximity and orientation similarity, the squares would be likely to group with other squares and unlikely to group with the diamond. In addition, it is worth mentioning that Fig. 19.1 displays the stimuli used by Quinn *et al.* (1996). In Quinn (1994) the same experiment was performed with a circle shape and a solid bar (instead of a diamond shape and a bar composed of small squares), and the same results were obtained. A final consideration that supports the idea that infants perceived the stimulus display as two separate entities rather than as a single Gestalt-like entity is the evidence that infants can perceive the numerosity of spatially separated entities (Antell and Keating, 1983; Starkey, Spelke, and Gelman, 1990).

19.3.2   Landmark versus framework representations: the case of *between*

In another investigation of early spatial categorization ability, we examined whether young infants would form a category representation for the spatial relation BETWEEN, depicted by a diamond appearing in distinct locations between two bars (Quinn, Norris, Pasko, Schmader, and Mash, 1999). At the time that we began the study, there was reason to question whether infants would form a representation for BETWEEN as easily as they formed representations for ABOVE versus BELOW (and LEFT versus RIGHT). In particular, in a review of the literature on the encoding of spatial location information by children, Huttenlocher and Newcombe (1984) distinguished between location coding in relation to a single landmark and location coding in relation to a set of landmarks that constitute a local spatial framework. The findings indicated that young children could represent targets in relation to single landmarks before three years of age, but that encoding of targets in relation to multiple landmarks that define a local spatial framework did not appear until five–six years of age. These data led Huttenlocher and Newcombe to propose that children progress from landmark to framework coding during development. Weist and colleagues have made a similar distinction between mono- and bi-referential location in space, and have observed that *above* and *below* are comprehended by two–three year olds, whereas *between* is not comprehended until three to four-and-a-half years (Weist, Lyytinen, Wysocka, and Atanassova, 1997; Weist and Uzunov, 1990; see also, Johnston, 1988). Given these lexical acquisition data, and given that the ABOVE and BELOW categorization task presented to infants requires only the representation of a target object in relation to a single landmark bar, whereas the BETWEEN categorization task requires representation of a target object in relation to multiple landmarks (e.g. two bars) that define a local spatial framework, we sought to determine whether a representation for BETWEEN would be observed as readily as representations for ABOVE versus BELOW.

To investigate whether young infants categorize BETWEEN, two groups of three–four month olds were familiarized with four instances of a diamond appearing between two bars (Quinn *et al.*, 1999). One group was exposed to stimuli in which the bars were horizontal rows. As is shown in the top two panels of Fig. 19.2, for half of the infants in this group, the diamond appeared in each of the four corners in the left half of the space between the rows, whereas for the other half, the diamond appeared in each of the four corners in the right half of the space between the rows. During the novel category preference test, the infants were presented with the diamond appearing in a novel position between the rows paired with a diamond appearing either above or below the rows.

The other group was shown stimuli with vertical columns. As is illustrated in the bottom two panels of Fig. 19.2, for infants in this group, the diamond appeared during familiarization in the corner locations of the top or bottom halves of the area between the columns. During the novel category preference test, the infants were presented with the diamond appearing in a novel position between the columns paired with a diamond appearing either to the left or right of the columns. For both the row and column groups, the prediction is that if infants form a category representation for DIAMOND BETWEEN BARS, then they should display a preference for the novel category exemplar depicting the diamond outside the bars. However, if infants do not form a category representation for DIAMOND BETWEEN BARS, then one would not expect a consistent preference for either text exemplar, since both are novel.

Neither group displayed a preference for the novel category exemplar depicting the diamond outside the bars, indicating that the infants had not formed a category representation for BETWEEN. The same null result was obtained in a follow-up study that provided the infants with double the familiarization time, suggesting that performance was not simply the result of more information for the infants to encode (i.e. two bars instead of one). However, when the original BETWEEN categorization experiment was repeated with a group of six–seven month olds, the older infants were found to prefer the novel category stimulus depicting the diamond outside the bars (see panel B of Table 19.1). The mean preference for the novel spatial relation across the row and column experimental groups was 65.08

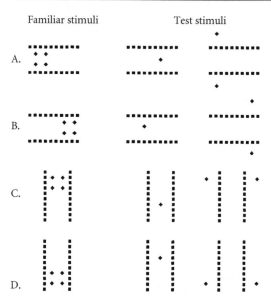

FIG. 19.2. Panels A and B display familiarization stimuli (a composite of the four DIAMOND BETWEEN ROWS exemplars) and test stimuli used to determine whether infants could form a category representation for DIAMOND BETWEEN ROWS. The test stimulus depicted on the far right of each panel is a composite of the two DIAMOND OUTSIDE ROWS exemplars. Panels C and D display familiarization stimuli (a composite of the four DIAMOND BETWEEN COLUMNS exemplars) and test stimuli used to determine whether infants could form a category representation for DIAMOND BETWEEN COLUMNS. The test stimulus depicted on the far right of each panel is a composite of the two DIAMOND OUTSIDE COLUMNS exemplars.

Source: Adapted from Quinn, Norris, Pasko, Schmader, and Mash (1999).

percent, $SD = 15.85$, $N = 16$, t(vs. chance) $= 3.81$, $p < .005$, one-tailed. Control experiments demonstrated that this preference could not be attributed to a spontaneous preference, nor was it the result of a failure to discriminate the location changes of the diamond within the familiar category.

The overall pattern of findings indicates that the older infants had categorically represented BETWEEN. Together with the investigations of ABOVE versus BELOW (Quinn, 1994; Quinn et al., 1996), the BETWEEN studies suggest that representations for different spatial relations emerge at different points during development. The evidence is consistent with the idea that there may be a developmental trend from first encoding the spatial relation of a target and a single landmark to later encoding the spatial relation of a target and multiple landmarks that form a local spatial framework (Huttenlocher and Newcombe, 1994), a trend that may subsequently be reflected in lexical acquisition of the spatial terms *above*, *below*, and *between* (Weist et al., 1997).

19.3.3   Specific versus abstract representations for spatial relation information

A question that arises regarding the spatial categorization of preverbal infants is whether the representations formed for spatial relation information are abstract or specifically tied to the objects depicting the relations. Clearly, to support lexical learning of spatial terms, spatial representations would need to be generalizable across variation in objects. There is evidence that from about the age of two-and-a-half years, children are able to encode the equivalence of a spatial relation across at least some contexts (Deloache, Kolstad, and Anderson, 1991; Uttal, Schreiber, and Deloache, 1995). In our investigations, we examined whether three–four month old infants would form abstract spatial representations that could be maintained independently of the objects depicting the relations. As shown in Fig. 19.3, Quinn *et al.* (1996) repeated the ABOVE versus BELOW experiment, but in this instance with four distinct shapes appearing above or below the bar during familiarization. The shapes were randomly selected for each infant from among seven shapes shown to be discriminably different from each other in a control experiment (i.e. arrow, diamond, dollar sign, dot, letter E, plus sign, triangle). Infants were then preference tested, as in the original ABOVE versus BELOW study, but with the change that a novel shape in the familiar spatial relation was paired with the same shape in the novel spatial relation.

If the infants form category representations for ABOVE and BELOW despite changes in the objects depicting these relations, then they should perform as they did in the original ABOVE versus BELOW experiment conducted without object

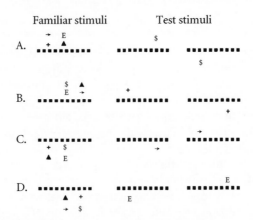

FIG. 19.3. Panels A, B, C, and D display familiarization exemplars (a composite of the four exemplars) and test stimuli used on the object-variation version of the ABOVE versus BELOW categorization task in Quinn *et al.* (1996).

variation. That is, they should prefer the novel spatial relation. Alternatively, if infants do not form category representations for ABOVE and BELOW with object variation, then one would not expect a preference for either test stimulus. The results were that the three–four month olds did not show a preference for the novel category test stimulus, dividing their attention instead across both test stimuli, and this result held true even when the infants were provided with extra familiarization time (Quinn, Polly, Dobson, and Narter, 1998). However, when the object-variation version of the ABOVE versus BELOW categorization task was repeated with a group of six–seven month olds, the older infants responded by preferring the novel spatial relation in the preference test, indicating that they were able to maintain their category representations for ABOVE and BELOW despite changes in the objects from the familiarization phase to the preference test (see panel C of Table 19.1). The mean preference for the novel spatial relation across the ABOVE and BELOW familiarization groups was 58.79 percent, $SD = 15.06$, $N = 24$, t(vs. chance) $= 2.86$, $p < .005$, one-tailed. The findings from the three–four month olds and six–seven month olds support the idea that category representations of spatial relations may initially be limited to objects depicting the relations, but later become more abstract so that various objects can be presented in the same relation, and that the equivalence of the relation is maintained despite this variation.

Given the specific-to-abstract developmental trend observed for representation of ABOVE versus BELOW, it became important to determine whether such a trend would also hold true for representation of BETWEEN. In particular, the six–seven month olds formed a critical age group for investigating an abstract representation of BETWEEN. The Quinn *et al.* (1999) results indicated that this group could form a specific spatial representation for DIAMOND BETWEEN BARS, and the Quinn *et al.* (1996) investigation revealed that these infants could form a more abstract representation for OBJECT ABOVE or BELOW BAR. But how would the six–seven month olds perform on an object-variation version of the BETWEEN categorization task? Would these infants form an abstract representation for OBJECT BETWEEN BARS, or would this ability not appear until later in development (e.g. nine–ten months)? More broadly, does a generalized abstraction ability become functional at six–seven months of age, one that would apply to all spatial relation concepts formed by that age? Or is there a specific-to-abstract developmental trend observed for representation of each spatial relation, such that each representation undergoes its own period of development from specific to abstract?

To address these questions, Quinn, Adams, Kennedy, Shettler, and Wasnik (2003) examined development of an abstract representation for BETWEEN by infants in the age range from six to ten months. In the first experiment, a group of six–seven month olds was familiarized with four exemplars, each depicting a different object in a distinct location between two bars. The objects were shown to be discriminably different in a control experiment. For half of the infants, the

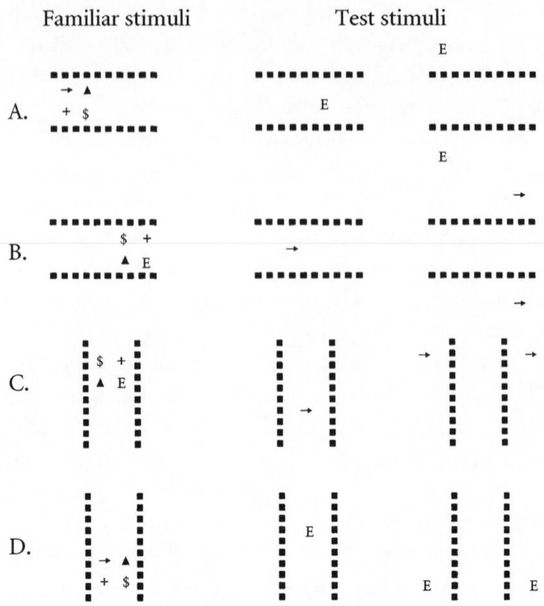

Familiar stimuli   Test stimuli

A.

B.

C.

D.

FIG. 19.4. Panels A and B display familiarization stimuli (a composite of the four OBJECT BETWEEN ROWS exemplars) and test stimuli used in the object-variation version of the BETWEEN categorization task. The novel category test stimulus (depicted on the far right of each panel) is a composite of the two OBJECT OUTSIDE ROWS exemplars. Panels C and D display additional familiarization stimuli (a composite of the four OBJECT BETWEEN COLUMNS exemplars) and test stimuli used in the object-variation version of the BETWEEN categorization task. The novel category test stimulus (depicted on the far right of each panel) is a composite of the two OBJECT OUTSIDE COLUMNS exemplars.

bars were horizontal rows (as shown in the top two panels of Fig. 19.4), and for the other half, the bars were vertical columns (as shown in the bottom two panels of Fig. 19.4). Both groups were then preference tested with a stimulus depicting a novel object in a novel location between the bars, paired with a stimulus in which a novel object was located outside the bars. The infants did not display a preference for the stimulus depicting the object outside the bars, and the same result was obtained when the experiment was conducted with double the familiarization time. However, when the experiment was repeated with nine–ten month olds, the older infants responded with a reliable preference for the stimulus depicting the object outside the bars (see panel D of Table 19.1). The overall findings indicated that nine–ten month olds formed an abstract category representation for BETWEEN, whereas six–seven month olds did not.

Taken together with the findings from the ABOVE versus BELOW studies (Quinn *et al.* 1996), the evidence from the BETWEEN experiments supports the idea that representations for different spatial relations emerge at different points during development, and moreover suggests that each representation undergoes its own period of development from concrete to abstract. Casasola and Cohen (2002) have recently reported experimental results on spatial categorization by infants that are consistent with these developmental trends and also extend them to dynamic events depicted with complex objects. In addition, the fact that a similar specific-to-abstract trend has been reported for infants' representation of other relations between objects (i.e. causality) is suggestive of a more general constraint in the representation of relational information in early cognitive development (Cohen and Oakes, 1993).

19.3.4 Understanding the effect of object variation on spatial categorization

An unresolved issue is why object variation appeared to interfere with the spatial categorization performance of the younger age groups. Consider, for example, the three–four month olds performing in the object-variation version of the ABOVE versus BELOW categorization task. Is it possible that these infants were perceptually or attentionally distracted by the object variation during familiarization, or the object novelty during the preference test? Such a suggestion would be consistent with the idea that separate 'what' and 'where' processing systems may compete for general attentional capacity (Mishkin, Ungerleider, and Macko, 1983; Vecera and Farah, 1994). Quinn, Polly, Furer, Dobson, and Narter (2002) reasoned that if the perceptual-attentional distraction explanation of infant performance in the object-variation version of the ABOVE versus BELOW categorization task is correct, then it should be possible to improve performance by reducing (1) object variation during the familiarization trials, or (2) object novelty during the test trials. To this end, Quinn *et al.* conducted two new twists on the object-variation version of the ABOVE versus BELOW categorization experiment, one in which a consistent object appeared from trial to trial during familiarization (displayed in Fig. 19.5), and another in which the infants were initially administered a single pre-familiarization trial depicting the object to be presented on the test trials. However, in neither experiment did the infants display a preference for the novel spatial relation.

Given these null results and their failure to provide support for the perceptual-attentional distraction account, Quinn *et al.* (2002) alternatively proposed that the difficulty for young infants in the object-variation version of the ABOVE versus BELOW categorization task may arise because of a limitation in conceptually-based generalization. The term 'conceptually-based' refers to a representation that is 'freed' from the perceptual particulars of the category instances. The conceptual limitation hypothesis carries with it the implication that young infants in the object-variation version of the spatial categorization task are representing spatial relation information, but not in an abstract format. That is, the infants may be

Familiar stimuli   Test stimuli

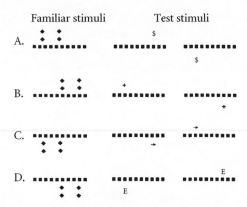

FIG. 19.5. Panels A, B, C, and D display familiarization exemplars (a composite of the four exemplars) and test exemplars used in the modification of the object-variation version of the spatial categorization task in Quinn, Polly, Furer, Dobson, and Narter (2002). Object variation did not occur during the familiarization trials; however, a novel object was presented on the preference test trials.

mapping specific objects into individual spatial representations. On each trial, when a new pair of objects is encountered, a new spatial representation is constructed. Thus, infants presented with the familiarization sequence depicted in Fig. 19.3A may form separate representations for ARROW ABOVE BAR, PLUS SIGN ABOVE BAR, E ABOVE BAR, and TRIANGLE ABOVE BAR, but not join these representations together in a more abstract representation of OBJECT ABOVE BAR or ABOVE. By the same reasoning, during the test trials, DOLLAR SIGN ABOVE BAR would be represented as a novel stimulus, as would DOLLAR SIGN BELOW BAR, and one would not expect a differential preference between them.

The conceptual limitation hypothesis predicts that young infants should perform successfully (with a preference for the novel spatial relation) in a modification of the object-variation version of the ABOVE versus BELOW categorization task—one in which the object–bar relation shown during the preference test trials matches an object–bar relation that appeared during familiarization. The design for this task is shown in Fig. 19.6. For infants shown the familiarization sequence in Fig. 19.6A, the TRIANGLE ABOVE BAR stimulus should match the representation of the TRIANGLE ABOVE BAR stimulus shown during familiarization, whereas the TRIANGLE BELOW BAR stimulus should not match any of the representations constructed during familiarization—thus, it should be preferred. This was the result obtained by Quinn *et al.* (2002). The mean preference for the novel spatial relation across the ABOVE and BELOW familiarization groups was 62.82 percent, $SD = 17.07$, $N = 24$, t(vs. chance) $= 3.68$, $p < .005$, one-tailed.

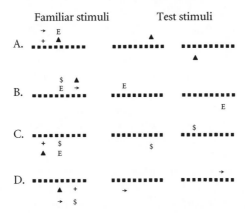

Fig. 19.6. Panels A, B, C, and D display familiarization exemplars (a composite of the four exemplars) and test exemplars used to investigate formation of specific category representations for ABOVE and BELOW in the object-variation version of the spatial categorization task used by Quinn *et al.* (2002).

The overall pattern of findings from Quinn *et al.* (2002) suggests that young infants encode the spatial relations between specific pairs of objects, but do not encode the spatial relations abstracted across a number of different pairs of objects. Although this encoding format is deficient in terms of abstraction, it should facilitate the operation of a young infant's spatial memory system that must remember the location of one specific object relative to another particular object. In this respect, the process of abstract spatial categorization may be secondary to the formation of specific spatial memories during early infancy. That is, the ability to form a specific representation for OBJECT A ABOVE OBJECT Z may have developmental primacy over the ability to maintain a more abstract concept of OBJECTS A, B, C, AND D ABOVE OBJECT Z that can be generalized to OBJECT E ABOVE OBJECT Z.

19.4   Speculations on an Overall Course of Development for the Representation of Objects and Spatial Relations

The findings described in the previous section suggest that object and spatial relational information are tightly bound in young infants. This conclusion needs to be considered in the context of the dissociation between 'what' and 'where' information that has been reported for older infants, not just in the presently described studies, but also by other investigators using different paradigms (Johnson, Mareschal, and Csibra, 2001; Leslie, Xu, Tremoulet, and Scholl, 1998; Xu and Carey, 1996). Tight binding of object and spatial relational information in the early months raises the question of whether the streams for processing 'what and where' information are so neatly segregated in young infants as they are presumed to be in adults (Johnson and Vecera, 1996). In addition, the independence of 'what' and 'where' processing that has been observed for older infants raises the question of how object and spatial relational information are bound together again as development moves toward childhood and adulthood. Some authors have argued that language is the likely mechanism for linking object properties with particular spatial locations (Hermer-Vazquez, Spelke, and Katsnelson, 1999; Xu, 1999), although such a suggestion raises the question of how nonhuman animals bind object properties to spatial locations as observed in their food-finding behavior. An intriguing implication is that if languages differ in the precise way in which they bind together object and spatial relational information, then such differences may contribute to the language-specific conceptualization of space that has been reported by Bowerman, Choi, and colleagues (Choi and Bowerman, 1991; Choi, McDonough, Bowerman, and Mandler, 1999). This research shows that children learning different languages come to classify spatial relations in different ways, and the suggestion offered here is that one of the ways in which languages may differ is in terms of how they conceptually package together object properties with spatial relations. Overall, then, the data reported here and elsewhere are consistent with a kind of U-shaped development for the linkage of object and spatial relational information. Objects and spatial relations may initially be conjoined through an undifferentiated neural processing system, subsequently dissociated via differentiation of separate 'what' and 'where' processing systems, and later reunited through language. Circumstantial evidence for the first two parts of this proposal—that originally the 'what' and 'where' systems may not be dissociated, but that they may become dissociated during the course of development—comes from the computational study of Rueckl, Cave, and Kosslyn (1989). In this study, a connectionist network trained to perform both object identification and object localization starts out with a distributional representation of both object and location information, but gradually develops two separate modular systems for both kinds of information.

19.5   Conclusions

The findings reviewed on the development of spatial categorization indicate that infants younger than one year of age can form category representations for ABOVE, BELOW, and BETWEEN. In addition, there may be a developmental trend from infants first encoding the spatial location of a target relative to a single landmark (i.e. DIAMOND ABOVE vs. BELOW BAR) to later encoding the location of a target in relation to multiple landmarks that define a local spatial framework (i.e. DIAMOND BETWEEN BARS). Moreover, category representations of spatial relations may initially be limited to the objects depicting the relations, but subsequently become more abstract so that various objects can be presented in the same relation and the equivalence of the relation is maintained despite the variation.

The general significance of the studies reported here is that the categorical representation of spatial relation information should allow infants to experience objects in coherent spatial layouts rather than as spatially unrelated entities residing in disconnected locations. As the representations become abstract with development, they may also (1) yield the functional units (e.g. primitives) necessary for the construction of more complex representations of larger scale spaces, and (2) facilitate the ability to use a variety of cognitive skills that operate on spatial relation information (e.g. cognitive map formation, travel map comprehension, object recognition, reading, word recognition).

20

Path Expressions in Finnish and Swedish: The Role of Constructions

URPO NIKANNE

Abstract

This chapter discusses the differences in those Swedish and Finnish path expressions that include more than one instance of a preposition (or locative case) referring to goal-direction without a coordinating conjunction 'and' (e.g. *John ran from home to the supermarket to the bank*). It turns out that these kinds of structures are allowed both in Swedish and in Finnish under certain conditions. However, the same syntactic form refers to different meanings in Swedish and in Finnish. In Swedish (and in English) the consecutive 'to'-phrases refer to a sequence of places along the path ('first to the bank and then to the supermarket') whereas in Finnish the structure refers to places where one is inside the other ('the bank is inside the supermarket').

Functional feature

The semantic feature that is crucial in relating a particular kind of linguistic structure to a particular kind of structure in some other cognitive domain (e.g. the spatial domain).

20.1   Introduction

In this chapter, I will discuss the different restrictions Finnish and Swedish have in their expressions of path. I assume these differences are made possible by certain grammatical differences on one hand and by certain fixed syntactico-semantic mappings (constructions) on the other. I will discuss a description of a construction in the Swedish language.

In this chapter, the term 'functional feature' refers to the semantic feature that is crucial in relating a particular kind of linguistic structure to a particular kind of structure in some other cognitive domain. (Here the other cognitive domain is the spatial domain.)

20.2   Conceptual Structure Representation

According to Jackendoff (1983), PLACEs and PATHs are complex conceptual categories (on the terms simple and complex categories, see Nikanne 1987). This means that a PATH consists of a PATH-function and its argument (the arrow stands for selection):

LANDMARK

FUNCTION

There are several PLACE-functions and five PATH-functions in Jackendoff's (1983, 1990) system. There follows a brief introduction to these functions (see Fig. 20.1).

20.2.1   PLACE-functions

AT   = General place-function, expresses an unspecified location around the Landmark.
ON   = Expresses a location on the surface or on the top of the Landmark.
IN   = Expresses a location inside the Landmark.
UNDER = Expresses a location under the Landmark.

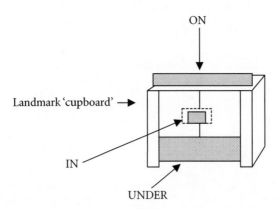

FIG. 20.1. Some place functions (IN, ON, UNDER) and the locations they express (*under the cupboard, on the cupboard,* and *in the cupboard*).

20.2.2   PATH-functions

TO = Bounded path directed toward the Landmark. 'Boundedness' indicates that the path goes all the way to the Landmark.

TOWARD = Unbounded path directed toward the Landmark. (Unboundedness indicates that the path does not go all the way to the Landmark, but, it has such an orientation that if it continued, it would do so.)

FROM = Bounded path directed away from the Landmark. (The path starts at the Landmark.)

AWAY-FROM = Unbounded path directed away from the Landmark. (The path does not start at the Landmark but it has such an orientation that the landmark is on the continuum of the path.)

VIA = Path that goes through or passes by the Landmark.

Nikanne (1990) has suggested that these functions are different combinations of certain hierarchically organized features. Nikanne's hierarchy is shown in Fig. 20.2.

All path functions—by definition—carry the feature [directional] and one of its sub-features. If it doesn't carry the feature directional, then the function is a PLACE-function. (I assume that there is a feature system under the three-dimensional node and, for example, the difference between different English prepositions of PLACE is based on these features. For further discussion on PLACE-functions, see Nikanne (1990).) The feature-combinations of the PATH-functions are as shown in Fig. 20.3. It is not only the PATH-functions that can carry the feature [directional]. Also some SITUATION-functions do that. These are introduced in the following subsection.

20.2.3   SITUATION-*functions*

There are two kinds of function that express the situation type: causative functions and non-causative ones. The non-causative functions are state-functions and

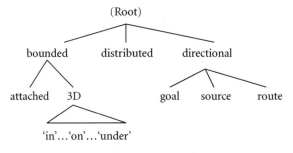

FIG. 20.2. Hierarchy of features.

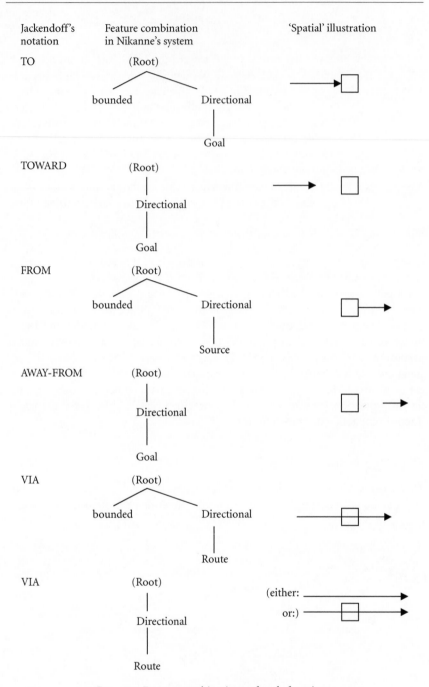

FIG. 20.3 Feature combinations of path functions.

event-functions. Within the non-causative functions there are functions that express direction and those that do not. Both causative and non-causative functions can be divided into monadic (functions that take only one complement) and non-monadic ones (functions that take more than one complement). I use the following abbreviations: causative functions = F3, non-causative Situation-functions = F2, Place- and Path-functions = F1. The motivation for these abbreviations is that the order of the functions in a well-formed function chain (the chain of functions formed by functions selecting other functions) is always the same: F3 → F2 → F1. There must always be one F2 but all well-formed Situations do not need to include any F3 or F1. On the other hand, there may be several F3s or F1s in a well-formed Situation but there cannot be more than one F2.

The functions and their semantics can be expressed as in Table 20.1. The directed non-causative SITUATION-functions (GO, EXT, ORIENT) also carry the feature [directed]. But, unlike the PATH-functions, these functions may have both sub-features [goal], [source], and [route] under the feature [directed]. The PATH-functions may only include one of these sub-features. A directed SITUATION function selects one or more PATH-functions as its complement. It does not have any other possibility (for more details, see Nikanne, 1990). The SITUATION-function and the PATH-functions it selects share the sub-features of the feature [direction]. This leads to a theory of a maximum of three PATH-functions in a conceptual structure representation of PATH. And, what is most important here is that only one function can carry the feature [goal], only one can carry the feature [source], and only one the feature [route]. A non-causative situation-function (F2) with a maximal number of PATH-functions (F1 with feature [directed]) is illustrated in Fig. 20.4. The data collected by Bohnemeyer (2000) supports this theory of PATH formation.

20.3 The Problem

As discussed in the previous section, according to Nikanne (1990, 2000), Finnish and English expressions of Paths are restricted such that only one Goal, only one Route, and only one Source are allowed (ILL = the illative case '(in)to', ELA = the elative case 'from (inside)', and GEN = the genitive case):

(1) a. *Pekka meni Tukholmaan   Göteborgiin
         Pekka went Stockholm+ILL Gothenburg+ILL
     b. *Pekka tuli Tukholmasta   Göteborgista.
         Pekka came Stockholm+ELA Gothenburg+ELA
     c. *Pekka meni Helsingistä   Tukholman   kautta
         Pekka went Helsinki+ELA Stockolm+GEN via
         Oslon   kautta Göteborgiin.
         Oslo+GEN via   Gothenburg+ILL

TABLE 20.1.

Situation	Causative functions (F3)	Non-causative functions (F2)
Monadic	INCH Inchoative function. Takes another situation-function as its complement	MOVE Monadic event-function e.g. in verbs like *laugh, sneeze, wiggle*, etc.
		INCH Monadic state-function
Non-monadic	CAUSE Causative function. Takes the causer as its thematic argument and another situation-function as its other complement	BE Non-directed non-monadic state-function
		STAY Non-directed non-monadic event-function
		GO Directed non-monadic event-function
		ORIENT Directed non-monadic state-function. Expresses orientation. e.g. verbs like *point (to some direction), aim (at something)*, etc.
		EXT Directed non-monadic state-function Expresses extension e.g. verb *extend*

The restriction is not based on syntactic factors, as it is possible to have two illative cases (or other case forms or words indicating Goal) in the same sentence and even in the same path expression if one of the Landmarks is included in the other. The examples in (2) are grammatical because we know that Stockholm is the capital of Sweden:

(2) a. Pekka meni Ruotsiin   Tukholmaan.
       Pekka went Sweden+ILL Stockholm+ILL
       'Pekka went to Sweden and there to Stockholm.'

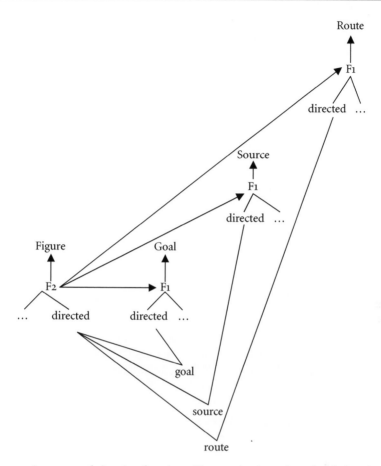

FIG. 20.4. A non-causal situation function with a maximal number of path-functions.

b. Pekka meni Tukholmaan   Ruotsiin.
   Pekka went Stockholm+ILL Sweden+ILL
   'Pekka went to Sweden and there to Stockholm.'

The same holds for the expressions of Source.

(3) a. Pekka tuli   Ruotsista   Tukholmasta.
      Pekka came Sweden+ELA Stockholm+ELA
      'Pekka came from Stockholm, Sweden.'
   b. Pekka tuli   Tukholmasta   Ruotsista.
      Pekka came Stockholm+ELA Sweden+ELA
      'Pekka came from Stockholm, Sweden.'

However, the expressions of Route do not work in this way, perhaps because there is no case form that expresses Route:[1] it must be expressed by the postposition *kautta* 'via':

(4) Pekka tuli   Tukholman   Ruotsin   kautta Helsinkiin.
    Pekka came Stockholm+GEN Sweden+GEN via   Helsinki+ILL
    'Pekka came to Helsinki via Stockholm, Sweden.'

Thus there is an asyndetic coordination of the complements of the postposition *kautta*. (On coordination and Path-formation, see Nikanne, 2000.) In Nikanne (2000), these facts were explained by a constraint operating at the conceptual structure (see Section 20.3).

There are some Swedish data that seem to be problematic for Nikanne's theory. Some speakers of Swedish allow the following types of sentences:

(5) Pekka åkte   (från Åbo   via Tallinn) till Helsingfors till
    Pekka travelled (from Turku via Tallinn) to Helsinki   to
    Stocholm   till Oslo till Göteborg.
    Stockholm to Oslo to Gothenburg
    'Pekka travelled (from Turku via Tallinn) to Helsinki and from there
    to Stockholm and from there to Oslo and from there to Gothenburg.'

Those speakers who accept the sentence, understand it such that Pekka went to Gothenburg via the route Turku → Tallinn → Helsinki → Stockholm → Oslo → Gothenburg. It should be noticed that many Swedish speakers do not accept this kind of structure. However, some do, and in this chapter I try to capture their grammatical understanding.

The structure in (5) is not a coordination—at least not the same as syntactic coordination. Here is an example of coordination, including the conjunction *och* 'and':

(6) Pekka åkte   (från Åbo   via Tallinn) till Helsingfors
    Pekka travelled (from Turku via Tallinn) to Helsinki
    till Stockholm till Oslo och till Göteborg.
    to Stockholm to Oslo and to Gothenburg
    'Pekka travelled (from Turku via Tallinn) to Helsinki, to Stockholm,
    to Oslo, and to Gothenburg.'

Sentence (6) may mean the same as (5), but it is only one reading. The sentence in (6) also allows the reading, according to which Pekka is travelling (from Turku via Tallinn) to Helsinki, Stockholm, Oslo, and Gothenburg in some other order

---

[1] There is, though, the so-called prolative case (ending -*tse*), but it is not productive. One can use the prolative case with certain nouns that express a route, channel, etc. For instance:
meritse (sea+PL+PROLAT),
kiertoteitse (detour+PL+PROLAT),
postitse (post+PROLAT) 'by mail'

than Helsinki→ Stockholm→ Oslo→ Gothenburg. We can even be talking about different trips. (Pekka may for instance come home between his trips to Helsinki and to Stocholm, etc.)

The same pattern is possible in Swedish with the prepositions *via* 'via' and *från* 'from', but the result is not as natural as with *till* 'to':

(7) a. Pekka åkte   från Åbo   från Helsingfors från Stockholm från
       Pekka travelled from Turku to   Helsinki   from Stockholm from
       Oslo till Göteborg.
       Oslo to Gothenburg
       'Pekka travelled from Turku to Helsinki. From there he went to
       Stockholm. From Stockholm to Oslo, and from Oslo to Gothenburg.'

  b. Pekka åkte   från Åbo   från Helsingfors från Stockholm
       Pekka travelled from Turku to   Helsinki   from Stockholm
       och från Oslo till Göteborg.
       and from Oslo to Gothenburg
       'Pekka travelled from both Turku, Helsinki, Stockholm, Stockholm,
       and Oslo to Gothenburg.'

The sentence in (7a) must be interpreted in such a way that the route of the trip was Turku→ Helsinki→ Stockholm→ Oslo→ Gothenburg. The sentence in (7b) indicates that Pekka has made several different trips: he has been going to Gothenburg from different places in different times.

Note that it is only geographical names as Goals that allow this phenomenon.

(8) a. ??Musen sprang till matskåpet   till sitt näste.
       Mouse ran   to food.closet-the to its nest
  b. *Billjardbollen   rullade till kanten till hålet.
       Billiard.ball-the went   to wall-the to hole-the
       'The billiard ball went to the wall and from there to the hole.'

20.4 Different Ways to Analyze the Swedish Construction

The Swedish intransitive sentences in (5) and (7a) seem to be problematic for the theory of PATH-formation. So, what is the correct way to represent the PATH in sentence (9)?

(9) Pekka åkte   från Åbo   till Helsingfors till Stockholm till Oslo
    Pekka traveled from Turku to Helsinki   to Stockholm to Oslo
    till Göteborg.
    to Gothenburg
    'Pekka traveled from Turku to Helsinki and from there to Stockholm
    and from there to Oslo and from there to Gothenburg.'

The spatial interpretation is clear:

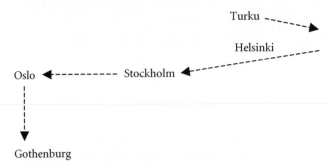

FIG. 20.5. A spatial path representing going from Turku, to Helsinki, to Stockholm, to Oslo, and finally to Gothenburg.

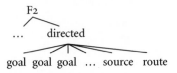

FIG. 20.6. A possible solution with more than one feature [goal] under the feature [direction].

Turku is the Source and Gothenburg is the Goal, but how should we analyze the middle points (Helsinki, Stockholm, Oslo)?

20.4.1   Each of the *till*-phrases stand for a Goal-PATH

This option follows directly the lexical conceptual structure of the preposition *till*. The obvious theoretical problem with this option is that if we accept this analysis, we must also assume that it is possible to have more than one feature [goal] under the feature [direction], at least when it comes to the SITUATION-function, as in Fig. 20.6. This would not be a good solution, as the theory with a maximum of three features is able to explain the productive constraints of path-expressions in many languages. Also in Swedish, we are talking about a very limited construction. It should be emphasized that construction is an exceptional mapping between form and meaning. But I would like to assume that the meanings must be well-formed according to the productive formation principles. (The form, sometimes, may be slightly exceptional as in the English construction *by and large*, in which a preposition and an adjective are coordinated.)

The other problem with this analysis is that on the basis of it, it is not possible to know which one of the Goals actually is the final Goal of the whole PATH. Neither does it indicate the order in which the Theme (*Pekka*) makes his trip. Note that the interpretation of the sentence is clear (see 10).

20.4.2   The middle points are analyzed using the function VIA

This option does make it explicit that Gothenburg is the Goal, the end point of
the PATH. The problem with this formalization is that it does not say anything
about the mutual order of the different Routes. In addition, it is not in accord
with the lexical conceptual structure of the preposition *till*. And theoretically it
suffers from the same problem as the previous option: we should assume that the
sub-features of the feature [direction] are as in Fig. 20.7. This analysis leads, thus,
to as limited a theory of PATH-formation as the first option.

20.4.3   The reference object of each goal may serve as the source
for another Goal-PATH function

This option would look something like that shown in Fig. 20.8 (the parts that are
linked to linguistic material are written in **boldface**). This option does take into
account both the lexical conceptual structure of *till* and it makes the order of the

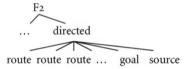

FIG. 20.7. The sub-features of the feature [direction].

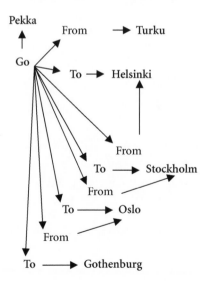

FIG. 20.8. Illustration of the reference object of each goal serving as the source for another
Goal-PATH function.

'middle goals' explicit. The problem with this formalization is that it leads to renovations of the formal account of PATH-functions. In productive cases, they are analyzed successfully as monadic functions. Assuming this option would leave us with difficulties with the most common cases of PATH-expressions. Even though it is inevitable that theories be changed, it is not desirable to radically change a theory that otherwise seems to work well.

20.4.4   The Swedish construction expresses several movements in a fixed order

According to this option the theory in Nikanne (1990, 2000) is correct, and the Swedish expression gives us a fixed set of several movements. By the term *construction*, I refer to a fixed mapping between form and meaning (on this term, see Goldberg, 1995; Fillmore and Kay, 1996; Östman, 2002; etc.). The analysis of the sentence would look as follows. The Greek alphabets indicate binding: X^{α} *binds* α (i.e. α has the same content—X—and same reference as X^{α}). Thus, PEKKA is the Figure (the argument of GO) in each SITUATION. HELSINKI is the Source in the movement in which PEKKA moves to STOCKHOLM. etc., as in Fig. 20.9. I assume that this option is the most promising one. It gives us the correct order of the movement and it does not violate the theoretical assumptions made earlier.

20.5   Differences in Syntactico-conceptual Linking between Finnish and Swedish

In this section, I will discuss some relevant syntactic differences between the Finnish and Swedish expressions of PATH.

20.5.1   Intransitive sentences

The Swedish language does not allow the same inclusion reading as Finnish (see the examples in (10)):

(10)   *Pekka åkte   till Stockholm till Sverige.
       Pekka traveled to   Stockholm to   Sweden.

The sentence in (10) does not mean anything: that is it is not possible to give it any semantic interpretation, according to the syntactico-semantic linking rules of the Swedish language.

In Swedish the inclusion must be expressed by a preposition of Place, for instance *i* 'in':

(11)   Pekka åkte   till Stockholm i   Sverige.
       Pekka traveled to   Stockholm in Sweden.
       'Pekka traveled to Stockholm which is in Sweden.'

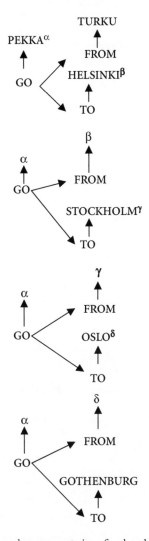

FIG. 20.9. Several movements in a fixed order in Swedish.

In Finnish a corresponding expression is not possible. It is possible to use an expression of place in the same syntactic position as *i* in the Swedish example in (12), but it will modify not only the verb *matkustaa* 'travel' but the whole sentence (INE = the inessive case 'in'):

(12) Pekka matkusti Tukholmaan   Ruotsissa.
     Pekka travelled Stockholm+ILL Sweden+INE
     'In Sweden, Pekka was travelling to Stockholm.'

20.5.2   Transitive sentences

In this subsection we will take a look at transitive sentences. The idea that a whole SITUATION takes place in a PLACE becomes clearer if we talk about sending a letter:

(13)   Finnish:
    a.   #Pekka lähetti   kirjeen   Tukholmaan Suomeen.
        Pekka send+PAST(3SG) letter+ACC Sweden+ILL Finland+ILL
        'Pekka sent a letter to Stockholm, which is in Sweden.'
    b.   Pekka lähetti   kirjeen   Tukholmaan   Suomessa.
        Pekka send+PAST(3SG) letter+ACC Stockholm+ILL Finland+INE
        'As Pekka was in Finland he sent a letter to Stockholm.'

In (13a) the sentence is pragmatically odd (marked with #) if the word in the illative case is *Suomi* 'Finland' (illative *Suomeen*). This is because we know that Stockholm is in Sweden and the only interpretation for the sentence is that Stockholm would be in Finland (or, in principle, *vice versa*). In (13b), the interpretation of the adverb in the inessive case Suomessa 'in Finland' has scope over the whole sentence: the situation 'Pekka sent a letter to Stockholm.' Thus it means that sending the letter takes place in Finland. Here are the same sentences in Swedish:

(14)   Swedish:
    a.   *Pekka skickade   ett brev till Stockholm till Finland.
        Pekka send+PAST a   letter to Stockholm to Finland.
        'Pekka sent a letter . . .
    b.   #Pekka skickade   ett brev till Stockholm i   Finland.
        Pekka send+PAST a   letter to Stockholm in Finland.
        'Pekka sent a letter to Stockholm, which is in Finland.'

Now, in Swedish the PP *i Finland* 'in Finland' can be used to mean the same as the Finnish sentence (14b) if it is placed at the beginning of the sentence:

(15)   I   Finland skickade   Pekka ett brev till Stockholm.
      In Finland send+PAST Pekka a   letter to Stockholm.
      'In Finland, Pekka sent a letter to Stockholm.'

In Finnish, in order to have the inclusion-reading, the PATH-adverbials (adverbials expressing a PATH: 'to X', 'from X', etc.) must be adjacent to each other. A topicalization of one of the PATH-adverbials is not possible.[2]

---

   [2] What topicalization normally does in Finnish is that it marks the topicalized word or phrase with a contrastive focus (see Vilkuna, 1989).

   (i)   Ruotsiin   Pekka lähetti   kirjeen.
      Sweden+ILL Pekka send+PAST(3SG) letter+ACC
      'It was to Sweden where Pekka sent the letter (and not somewhere else).'

In Finnish this kind of topicalization is very productive.

(16) a. *Ruotsiin   Pekka lähetti   kirjeen   Tukholmaan.
           Sweden+ILL Pekka send+PAST(3SG) letter+ACC Stockholm+ILL
      b. *Tukholmaan   Pekka lähetti   kirjeen   Ruotsiin.
           Stockholm+ILL Pekka send+PAST(3SG) letter+ACC Sweden+ILL

The sentence is ungrammatical because it has two separate goals.

20.6 Formulation of the Swedish Construction

In this section, I will outline the construction that licenses the Swedish exceptional PATH expression.

The ingredients for such a construction seem to be as follows:

(a) The Figure is a person.
(b) The Landmarks are geographical places.
(c) The Figure is traveling from one geographical place to another. (i.e. the SITUATION-function must be GO.)
(d) The sentence must be intransitive.
(e) The syntactic structure does not include a coordinative conjunction *och* between the prepositional phrases.
(f) The linear order of the PPs corresponds to the order of the intermediate Goals or Sources.

All these conditions must be mentioned in the construction. It is rather typical that a construction includes some rather specialized information. Nikanne (2001) discusses a set of Finnish constructions in which the elative case may in certain syntactic contexts express an instrument (even though the basic meaning of the elative case is 'from'). The elative does not express just any instrument. It expresses an instrument of quick, hard, and violent hitting. For instance:

(17) Minä sai-n   puuko-sta   maha-a-ni.
      I   got-1.PERS.SG knife-ELATIVE belly-ILLATIVE-POSS.SUFF.(1P.SG)
      'Someone hit me hard in my belly with a knife.'

Figure 20.10 presents the hypothesis for the construction that includes the preposition *till* 'to'. The indices j, k, l, m, n, o, p, q, r indicate the linking between the parts of the syntactic structure and the conceptual structure within the construction. It should be noticed also that the Finnish structures in (2) and (3) are based on construction. The construction must include the following information:

(a) The path expression includes two phrases that express PATHS.
(b) The sub-features of the feature [directional] are the same for both PATHS, either [goal] or [source].

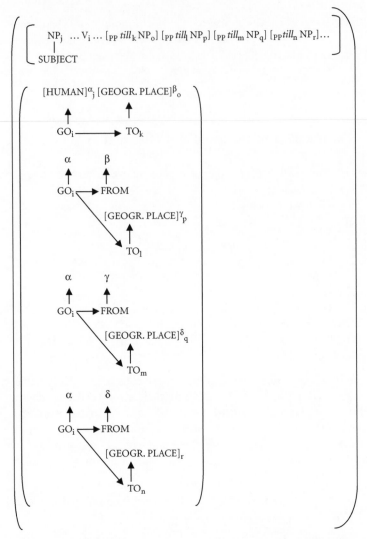

Fig. 20.10. Illustration of the elative case for the preposition *till* 'to'.

(c) The phrases expressing PATHS must be governed by the same verb.
(d) One of the Landmarks of the PATHS is included in the other.

Thus, constructions are a way to make use of such syntactic structures that under productive syntactico-conceptual mapping principles would be ruled out. And, as these constructions often include some rather particular conditions when it comes to the interpretation, these conditions can be understood to be functional ones.

20.7   Conclusion

The exceptional expression of PATH in Swedish can be analyzed as a fixed construction. It is not uncommon that constructions include some rather specialized information, which then could be interpreted as functional. In the Swedish construction, the Landmarks must be geographical places and the Figure must be human. But this kind of functional information is only a part of the construction. Also the form of the syntactic structure is fixed.

Part Four

The Pervasiveness of Functional
Features in Language and Space

21

Form and Function

BARBARA TVERSKY

Abstract

How can we account for spatial language? Perceptual features, functional features, schemas, context, and affordances are among the bases proposed. Here, it is argued that all can be operative. A survey of research from a variety of entity domains, especially natural kinds, artifacts, bodies, scenes, events, abstract categories, and design, and of relational domains, especially spatial relations, shows that perceptual features, especially form or structure, allow inferences to function, forming perceptual–functional units or affordances. Language abets inferences from form to function. These perceptual–functional units account for the coherence of category features and provide the basis for causal reasoning.

21.1 Introduction

When questions in cognition are formulated, 'Is it Theory A or Theory B (think: parallel vs. serial; top-down or bottom-up; prototype vs. central tendency; and here, perceptual vs. functional)?', my usual inclination is to answer: 'Both. And something else we haven't thought of.' Cognition is biological, and biological systems are partially redundant, partially overlapping. Just take the visual system in the brain as an example. To call it 'a' system is to vastly oversimplify; 'it' is a complex of overlapping systems. Even for 'what' and 'where' (e.g. Ungerleider and Mishkin, 1982), or, alternatively, 'what' and 'how' (e.g. Milner and Goodale, 1995), there are many visual and spatial systems in the brain. This is not to say that the various systems are identical; rather like so-called synonyms, they have similarities with differences. And so for functional vs. perceptual in language: both. And more.

This chapter is based in part on collaborations with Kathy Hemenway, Jeff Zacks, Masaki Suwa, Nancy Franklin, David Bryant, Julie Morrison, Holly Taylor, Scott Mainwaring, and Nancy Shayer. I have enjoyed and benefited from their thinking beyond the particular collaborations. Portions of the research and preparation of the manuscript were aided by Office of Naval Research Grants NOOO140PP-1-0649 and NOOO140110717 to Stanford University.

21.2   Accounting for Spatial Language

The challenge we have been given in the workshop is no more nor less than the basis for the meaning of spatial language. Several alternatives were proposed: perceptual features, functional features, schemas, contexts, affordances. What are these, and how are they different? Are they truly alternatives, or might each be operative? Each of these concepts, like most useful concepts, is slippery, hard to pin down. They have meanings that are situated, hence switch with situations; indeed, some of them are used to describe exactly that phenomenon of meanings. Consonant with that view, the uses of these concepts should become clearer as they are analyzed. I believe it is easy to show that all of these alternatives are operative in using spatial language, and not just spatial language.

A priori, spatial language refers to aspects of space. A priori, language serves functions, to inform or affect behavior; language is situated, context bound, dependent on schemas shared by participants. Consider *in*. Of a bowl full of cherries, we can say: 'the cherries are *in* the bowl' when the cherries are contained by the bowl, that is, the cherries have a certain spatial relation with respect to the bowl. So perceptual, spatial properties determine, at least in part, at least sometimes, use of spatial language. Now suppose, to parasketch an example of Garrod and Simon (1988), this is a grand display of cherries, extending above the edge of the bowl, with a sprig of cherry blossoms on top. We can say the sprig of cherry blossoms is in the bowl, as it is supported by the bowl, controlled by the bowl, functionally dependent on the bowl in the sense that the bowl's location determines the sprig's location. So functional properties determine, at least in part, at least sometimes, use of spatial language. In fact, evidence abounds showing that both spatial and functional properties affect comprehension and production of spatial language (e.g. Carlson-Radvansky, Covey, and Lattanzi, 1999; Carlson-Radvansky and Irwin, 1993, 1994; Carlson-Radvansky and Logan, 1997; Carlson-Radvansky and Radvansky, 1996; Coventry, 1998; Coventry, Prat-Sala, and Richards, 2001; Coventry, Carmichael, and Garrod, 1994, Franklin, Henkel, and Zangas, 1995; Franklin and Tversky, 1990; Hayward and Tarr, 1995; Logan and Sadler, 1996; Regier, 1996, 1997). What's more, as will be seen, spatial and functional properties are often not only correlated, but perceived to be causally related, used to make and justify causal inferences.

Schema has been used by Lakoff and his collaborators among others to explicate some spatial language (e.g. Lakoff, 1987). The claim is that terms like *over* have several different senses, each corresponding to a situated set of spatial relations. More generally, *schema* is used to refer to a knowledge structure having certain attributes and values, some of them presupposed or default (e.g. Rumelhart, 1980). People may have schemas not only for senses of words like prepositions but also for the things and situations they experience and talk about. Returning to our example, it would be odd to say, 'the cherries are in the city', even if it were a fact that the city contains the cherries. This is because cherries and cities bear no schematic relations. Indeed, the cherries are technically *in* many containers, a room, a building, a neighborhood, a country, and so on, but these large remote containers are not normally used as reference frames for such small objects as cherries. Unlike bowls, they are not perceived as pertinent. *Context* can change all that. If hidden in this bowl of cherries were a rare diamond, if the bowl had been spirited away, if it were fitted with a GPS locator, then knowing that the bowl of cherries is in this city and not in some other place would be crucial, and make sense as an utterance. Of course, all language is bound to context and shared schemas, not just spatial language (e.g. H. Clark, 1996). Just think about 'here' and 'there', perhaps the most basic spatial terms of all.

What about *affordances*? Affordances are relations between perceptions and actions or potential actions. Actions are frequently enactments of functions, so affordances can link spatial features to functions. To stretch the example that has worked rather well until now, if the bowl were hanging upside down in the air, an art installation perhaps, then it would not afford *in*. A suspended upside down bowl can no longer function as a container. Implicit in this analysis is the idea that spatial features and relations can affect functions so that the spatial and the functional are necessarily intertwined.

It seems the challenge has been answered, and the answer is 'all of the above'. Does this mean an early end to this chapter? Not so fast. It provides an opportunity to explore the relations among these alternatives, especially the relations between perception and potential action, between appearance and function. These considerations will be discussed first for referring to things, then for referring to spatial relations among things. The reciprocal relations will also be examined, that is, the ways referring affects perception, including perceived function.

21.3 Referring to Things

21.3.1 How shall a thing be called? Basic level categories

Half a century ago, Roger Brown (1958) posed a language puzzle, the question that heads this section. Although things may be referred to by many labels, varying in generality, one level seems preferred over a range of contexts. That which we sit on, a *chair*. That which warms our legs, *pants*. That which we eat, a *carrot* or an *apple*. Not *furniture*. Not *easy chair*. Not *clothing* or *khaki pants*. Of course more general and more specific terms exist because they are useful in many contexts. Pippins are better for pies, fujis are better for eating. Dress pants are for job interviews and jeans for weekends. Furniture make us comfortable inside and tools build or repair things, including furniture. Context and schema affect choice of terms referring to spatial entities. Yet one level is the neutral, default, frequent level, the general-purpose way of referring, the *basic level*.

Brown raised the question; one of his students, Eleanor Rosch, along with her collaborators, proposed an answer (Rosch, 1978). This level of reference, the *basic level*, is the level that maximized the tradeoff between the information conveyed at that level of abstraction given the number of category distinctions that have to be kept in mind. The more precise the category, the greater the information conveyed, but also the greater the number of contrast categories. Informativeness was indexed by features people generated to categories at three levels of abstraction. The features people generate to category names are not meant to be taken as an objective catalog of their features, but rather as the features salient to people in thinking about the categories. Notable are the countless features that are not mentioned but that are 'true', that is, that people would agree apply to the categories. Molecules, solid, cells, breathes are but a few examples of features rarely produced. What features are produced depends on many things: on aspects of the world our perceptual systems are tuned to, on aspects context, notably implicit or explicit contrast categories, makes salient, on aspects that are readily named. The number of features generated increased considerably from the level of *furniture* and *fruit*, the superordinate level to the level of *chair* or *apple*, the basic level, but hardly at all from the basic level to the subordinate level, the level of *coffee table* or *fuji apple*. The number of contrast categories, however, increased at both levels, so going from superordinate to basic increases informativeness as well as the number of categories that must be kept in mind, but going from basic to subordinate increases cost in the form of more category contrasts, but offers little benefit of increased informativeness.

Other cognitive operations converge on the basic level. Some of these are about *appearance*. Notably, the basic level is the highest level for which a collective shape can be recognized or an image generated. Other operations are *behavioral* or *function*: behaviors toward all bananas or all grapes are the same, but behaviors toward all fruit are not, so the basic level is the highest level where actions on objects are uniform. Still other operations are *linguistic*; the basic level is the first to enter a new language or a child's vocabulary; it is also the level of preferred reference and fastest naming.

21.3.2   Parts characterize the basic level

The work of the Rosch group emphasized the quantitative differences among the levels, the number of features relative to category distinctions. Their analysis did not consider the qualitative differences in features at different levels of abstraction nor did it analyze the coherence of features within particular categories. Consideration of the features and further research reveals that these issues are related through a special kind of feature, parts (Tversky and Hemenway, 1984 primarily; also Tversky, 1985, 1989, 1990). That work is reviewed below.

At the superordinate level, the level of vehicle and vegetable, features informants regard as characteristic were few in number and primarily functional.

Vehicles are for transporting people and things. Vegetables provide nutrients. Tools are for fixing. The basic level elicited far more features, and these were primarily perceptual; the subordinate level also elicited perceptual features, barely more than the basic level. Within perceptual features there were differences between those elicited by the basic level and those elicited by the subordinate level. One type of perceptual feature was especially prevalent at the basic level: parts (Tversky and Hemenway, 1984). For tables, *legs* and *tops*. For bananas, *peel* and *pulp*. For pants, *legs, zippers, pockets*, and *buttons*. For trees, *trunk, branches*, and *leaves*. Other informants rated parts of objects and living things for goodness. Parts rated as good tend to be perceptually salient; typically, they are discontinuous with the overall shape of the object, that is, they extend from its contour, like arms and legs. Salient parts, in fact, seem to play an important role in object recognition (e.g. Biederman, 1987; Hoffman and Richards, 1984) and parts in their proper configuration determine the shapes of objects, also important in object recognition (Rosch, 1978).

21.3.3 Parts: Features of perception and of function

Parts are not only features of appearance, they are also features of function. It is this duality that seems to privilege parts (Tversky and Hemenway, 1984; see also, Tversky, 1985, 1990). Legs have a certain appearance, they typically come in pairs, they are vertically extended, they are grounded. But they also have a typical function: they support something resting on them. Likewise, a top has a typical appearance, a flat horizontal surface, but it is also at a height and of a strength and an extent to serve certain uses by humans. Part goodness ratings support this correspondence. Parts rated high in goodness tend to be functionally significant as well as perceptually salient. The heads and legs of animals, the trunk of a tree, the wheels of a car, the handle and head of a hammer are rated as relatively good parts. They have distinctive appearances as well as significant functions. Extensions of part names from one object to another illustrate the duality of part names. The head of a committee is the organizer, figuratively at the top, whereas the head of a pin is literally at the top. Both the foot of a bed and the foot of a class are at the bottom; the former correspondence is more spatial and the latter more functional. Different parts have different appearances and different functions. The peel of an apple or peach protects the pulp, the pulp provides nutrients, the seeds germinate and grow into new plants. The table legs support the top and the top supports books, coffee cups, and laptops (which canonically sit on the tops of laps).

21.3.4 Affordances

The form and structure of many parts seem to suggest functions. A case can be made for affordances, as the term has come to be used, though that is probably not the intention Gibson had in mind. Here, the term refers to perceptual–functional units, where form suggests function, or at a minimum, action or interaction. Round things roll, square ones do not. Long, thin things are good for reaching. Squat solid vertically extended things are good for support. Bowl-like things suggest containment. Flat thin horizontally oriented things afford placing smaller objects. Manufactured things, of course, are designed to be functional, likewise their parts, so it is no accident that their parts suggest their functions.

21.3.5   Function for thing and function for user: natural kinds vs. artifacts

Note two different senses of function, one for living things, the other for artifacts. For living things, function means in the service of the things, instrumental to its needs and in some cases wants. The leaves of a tree conduct photosynthesis, the roots bring water and nutrients; both combine to nourish the tree and keep it alive. Thus the separate parts subserve separate behaviors of the organism. Artifacts, by contrast, are created by humans for human use; their origins are to be functional for humans (see also Bloom, 1996, 1998). Their separate parts serve humans in different ways. A hammer's handle is for grasping and its head is for pounding. The seat of a chair supports one part of the human anatomy, the back another part (not by coincidence referred to by the same names); the legs of a chair support the seat and back so they can support the human user. For artifacts, then, the separate parts subserve separate activities or behaviors of the user. People regard and in effect manufacture some living things like artifacts, so that a chicken's legs serve people differently than they serve chickens, banana skins serve people differently than they serve bananas, and tree trunks serve people differently than they serve trees. For living things, function is what they do; for artifacts, it's what we do with them. The Spanish poet, Antonio Machado, expressed the duality of parts elegantly, coming down in favor of function for thing: 'The eye you see is an eye/not because you see it;/ it's an eye because it sees you' (Machado, 1982, p. 177).

Form and function, appearance and use, are correlated for both cases, living things and artifacts, for both senses, function for thing and function for user. Not only are form and function correlated, they can be causally related. Function can often be inferred from form, in part because form can determine function. Tilted surfaces are not as suitable for sitting or putting as horizontal ones. Spheres are not as good for reaching as cylinders. Half spheres with hollow side up allow containment; upside down ones do not. Cylinders of a certain size make good handles. Long things are better for reaching than round things. Small, jointed extended parts like fingers are good for fine manipulations; large, jointed extended parts like arms are good for coarse actions. Round things roll, square things do not. Rough surfaces create more friction than smooth ones, useful for some purposes, a hindrance for others. For these, perception and action are coupled, spatial properties afford, in the recent sense, functions.

21.3.6   Parts promote inferences from structure to function

The dual status of parts, as perceptual and functional features, means that they can serve as a link from appearance to use, that is, they can support inferences from form to function. Perceptual features are relatively immediate, they are apparent from static solo objects. Functional features are relatively less immediate. Some may be inferable from solo static objects in interaction with other objects. Support, containment, and attachment are among them. Of course these inferences may turn out to be mistaken, a table might be built into a wall rather than supported by legs, a bowl may have no bottom. Other functional features seem to be inferred from action, pushing, pulling, lifting, pounding. Still others seem to be knowledge-based, that seeds germinate and produce new plants, that apple peel is edible but banana peel is not, that both peels protect the pulp. Function also seems to require an end, a goal, a purpose, a use. Or that's how we talk about it, rather than in terms of the spatial or action relations (Zacks, Tversky, and Iyer, 2001).

Functional attributes, because they are less immediate, should take longer to learn than attributes based on appearance. This may be the reason that children readily form basic level categories such as apples and cars at a young age, but form superordinate categories such as fruits and vehicles later (Rosch, Mervis, Gray, Johnson, and Boyes-Braem, 1976). Basic level categories can be formed on the basis of appearance, notably shape. Superordinate categories do not share perceptual features; rather, they share function. Consistent with this idea, children tend to form superordinate categories that share parts earlier than superordinates that do not share parts (Tversky, 1989). The shared parts increase perceptual similarity, facilitating grouping. At the same time, they encourage the realization of common function, facilitating the insight that function can underlie useful categorization.

Parts, then, seem to enable the convergence of the multitude of cognitive operations on the basic level. Because they are components of appearance, they account for the operations that depend on appearance. Because they are components of function, they account for the operations that depend on behavior. Breaks in language should follow the natural—and correlated—breaks in appearance and behavior. Categories themselves serve many functions in our lives. Primary among them are *referring* and *inferring*. Referring means identifying category members. Inferring means knowing what to do with them or what they do, that is, what properties they have.

21.3.7   Parts and category coherence: parts are the core of theories, knowledge, and causal reasoning

People do not regard categories as bundles of unrelated features. For one thing, in natural categories, features are correlated; things that have feathers fly and lay eggs, things that have fur bear their young alive (Malt and Smith, 1983; Rosch, 1978). Features are perceived to cohere, to be related in sensible ways. Several accounts for the perceived coherence of attributes for common categories have been proposed. One proposal is that people have theories about categories, albeit not the formal theories of physicists (e.g. Murphy and Medin, 1985), another proposal is 'knowledge' (e.g. Keil, 1989; Murphy, 2000), and a third is causal models (e.g. Ahn, 1998; Rehder, 1999). Significantly, the theories, knowledge, or causal reasoning proposed to support the claims are reasoning about parts, that is, assertions or hypotheses about the different functional roles of different parts, frequently accounting for part function from part form. Wings enable birds to fly, with feathers to augment their aerodynamic function. Wheels, because they are round, enable cars to move. Legs, solid vertical extensions, support tables and horses allowing them to remain upright.

Theory-making and causal reasoning begin by noticing regularities in the world. The regularities that people notice are many; proximity in space or time, and similarity, both observed and conceptual, are but some of them. Noticing regularities promotes a search for explanation, to predict and perhaps to control. Explanations begin by dividing the entities underlying the regularities into parts, in part to simplify reasoning, in part reflecting a belief that different parts have different functions and that the coordinated interaction of the parts yields coherent action. These beliefs or conjectures relating parts to function form the core of the causal theories or knowledge or causal reasoning proposed as underlying the coherence or cognitive glue of categories. They are just that, beliefs and conjectures, they may be correct, they may be erroneous. They serve as initial hypotheses, starting points for scientific investigation. They may later be substantiated or contradicted. Given the inferential power of parts, it is not surprising that parts are the dominant feature of basic level categories and that parts perceived as good are those having perceptual salience and functional significance.

21.3.8   Functional inferences from perception: expertise

If inference from appearance to function is knowledge-based, then just as it characterizes the difference between younger and older children, it should also characterize the difference between novices and experts. Nowhere has more thought been devoted to relations between form and function than in architecture and design. Indeed, form and function can be regarded as the major theme of twentieth-century architecture. Architects use their own sketches to develop and refine design ideas (e.g. Schon, 1983). But sketches are exactly that, schematic, so understanding them requires making inferences from them, about function as well as appearance. Novice and experienced architects differ in the inferences they make from their own sketches (Suwa and Tversky, 1997, 2001). Student and expert architects were asked to design a museum with certain specifications on a particular location. The sketching sessions were videotaped. After the design session, they viewed their own videos while describing the thoughts that motivated each stroke of the pencil. These protocols were analyzed in detail, yielding detailed portraits of the act of design. As hypothesized, experts made more functional inferences from their sketches than novices. Specifically, experts were able to anticipate patterns of circulation and of light from the sketched structure. Notably, these are two of the major concerns of architects and architectural theory. Space syntax, for example, is a research enterprise that predicts circulation patterns of people from grid structures of environments (e.g. Hillier, 1999, 2000). Similarly, formal analyses of building configurations account for the distribution of natural light (Steadman, 2001).

Other novice–expert differences support the idea that with knowledge, people come to make functional inferences from perceptual form. Chess experts can 'see' a history of moves in a mid-game display (Chase and Simon, 1973; De Groot, 1966). Expert sight readers can 'hear' a musical score. Most of us are expert readers; we readily derive sound and meaning from meaningful text, provided it is in an alphabet that we know. These visual symbol systems (see Goodman, 1968) are extreme cases where function or meaning is assigned to visual marks.

21.3.9   Other categories: scenes

The coupling of appearance and function occurs for other categories important in everyday life as well as for objects, notably for environments and events. Like objects, environments, or the settings that objects appear and are used in, have a basic level, the level of school, home, and store for indoor scenes and the level of beach, mountains, and cities for outdoor scenes (Tversky and Hemenway, 1983). Significantly, people regard the different basic level scenes as sharing specifiable features of appearance, notably, parts, as well as allowing specifiable activities. Schools have desks, chairs, and books as well as cafeterias and yards. They permit a variety of educational activities as well as eating and recreation. Stores have merchandise and aisles and cash registers to support purchasing and paying. Schools and stores differ in appearance and in activity, in form and in function.

21.3.10   Other categories: people

Even more than most categories, categories of people can be naturally classified in many ways. Race, gender, and stereotype have been studied by various researchers. Inspired by observations of Brown that the categories of people important for our daily lives are those based on relationships, Shayer and I (unpublished data) asked people to generate categories for two presumed superordinates, people you know and people you don't know. For people you know, informants listed categories such as *friend*, *parent*, and *cousin*; that is, the categories were based on personal, social relations. For people you don't know, informants listed categories such as *lawyer*, *cashier*, and *sales clerk*. These categories were based on services and impersonal social relations. Other informants generated subcategories for each of these. Subcategories for people you know were individuals, particular friends, parents, and other relatives. Subcategories for people you don't know were genuine subcategories, corporate lawyer, supermarket cashier, department store clerk. Notice that these categories, except for the individuals, are nearly purely functional. The categories are based on the roles these people play in our lives, various personal relationships for the known, and various service or economic or other professional relationships for the unknown.

21.3.11   Other categories: events

For events, function plays a role parallel to its role in objects. Events can be regarded as a temporal analog of objects, with parts extended in time rather than space. Like objects, they can form taxonomic hierarchies of kinds, for example, going to entertainment or a health professional or shopping or school (e.g. Morris and Murphy, 1990; Rifkin, 1985; Rosch, 1978). Like objects, events can also form partonomies, hierarchies of part-of relations (e.g. Abbott, Black, and Smith, 1985; Bower, Black, and Turner, 1979; Schank and Abelson, 1977; Tversky and Hemenway, 1984; Zacks, Tversky, and Iyer, 2001; Zacks and Tversky, 2001). Following a procedure developed by Newtson (1973), participants watched videos of mundane events like making a bed or assembling a saxophone, pressing a button every time they thought one event unit ended and another began (Zacks *et al.*, 2001). They did this twice, in counterbalanced order, once for the largest units that made sense and once for the smallest units that made sense. Half the participants described what happened for each segment.

Ninety-five percent of the descriptions of both coarse and fine units of events were actions on objects, for example, putting on the bottom sheet or putting on the mouthpiece. The remaining 5 percent described the entrance or exit of the actor. That is, all of the segments were regarded both perceptually, as specific actions, and functionally, as accomplishing a goal. The coarse level was segmented by higher level goals or functions; the fine level, by lower level goals or functions. The natural parts of events, like the natural parts of objects and scenes, are appearance–function units.

21.3.12   Abstract categories

What about abstract categories, disciplines, such as psychology or linguistics, institutions, such as governments and corporations? These categories also have structure, analogous to appearance in objects, for example, the power and decision-making units and their interrelations in institutions. They have parts that can be identified by 'appearance' and that are differentiated in function. Think of the legislative, executive, and judicial branches of the government. Or perception, memory, and personality in psychology. Think of the uniforms, offices, tools of various branches of the military or an airline or a restaurant or a hospital. Think of the structures of control in corporations and governments. Theories about democracy, flexibility, conflict resolution, and more rest on analyses of the structures of the organizations, for example, hierarchical or distributed. As for objects, scenes, and events, in abstract categories as well, parts promote inferences from structure or appearance to function.

21.3.13   Categories: appearance, function, and affordance

What makes the basic level of reference special, Tversky and Hemenway proposed, is that at the basic level, knowledge about parts is most salient. And what is special about parts is that they connect appearance and function, providing category coherence. This connection accounts for the convergence of the perceptual, behavioral, and linguistic operations on the basic level. The perceptual and behavioral are directly linked to appearance and function. The linguistic operations seem to derive from the others. All other things equal, linguistic distinctions should follow salient perceptual and functional distinctions. The favored names to refer to objects, then, are those that pick out both perceptual and functional features. Basic level names are powerful, maximizing informativeness per distinction, relying on appearance for facile recognition, promoting inferences to function.

For a wide range of categories, living things, artifacts, scenes, and events, appearance and function are inextricably related. This is partly because they are often causally related, form can determine function. By evolution or by design, function can determine form. Together, appearance and function comprise affordances. Many post-Gibsonian examples of affordances are not, as he proposed, immediate. Rather, they depend on knowledge. Appearance, including spatial properties and relations, is more readily perceived than function, as appearance can be perceived from static objects whereas perceiving function typically entails observing or knowing about objects in action or interaction. With increasing experience, developing expertise in a domain, function can be inferred from appearance. Function is not simply activity, action. It is action in the service of a goal, a purpose. The same goal can be attained by different actions.

21.4   **Naming Emphasizes Function**

There are many routes to categories in the mind. Prominent among them are the perception of an object and the name of an object. Object names may bias different aspects of categories. In particular, there is provocative evidence that naming favors functional features of categories (Tversky, Morrison, and Zacks, 2001). This is apparent from our work on the categories of bodies and events.

21.4.1 Bodies

Bodies are a special kind of object; like objects, bodies are experienced from the outside, but unlike objects, bodies are experienced from the inside, known kinesthetically in addition to visually. Biological motion is perceived differently from mechanical motion (Reed and Farah, 1995; Chatterjee, Freyd, and Shiffrar, 1996). Like objects, bodies have parts that vary in size, salience, and function. Which of those factors determines speed of recognizing object parts? Morrison and I (1997) asked this question in two types of task. One task was a perceptual task in which participants viewed pairs of bodies in a variety of poses and positions with a part highlighted; their task was to indicate, as rapidly as possible, whether the parts highlighted were the same. The second task entailed naming. Participants read the name of a body part and viewed a body with a part highlighted; their task was to indicate, as rapidly as possible, whether the named and highlighted parts were the same. We chose the parts widely named across languages: head, feet, arm, hand, leg, chest, and back.

Three theories may account for relative accessibility of body parts. According to an *imagery* account, larger parts should be verified faster, as they are identified faster in imagers (Kosslyn, 1980). According to theories of object recognition based on parts (Biederman, 1987; Hoffman and Richards, 1984), salient parts are those more discontinuous with shape contour, so parts that have greater contour discontinuity should be verified faster. Finally, according to a part significance account (Tversky and Hemenway, 1984), parts that are more significant should be verified faster. Significant parts are those that are perceptually salient, that is, with greater contour discontinuity, and functionally important. Of the three theories of recognition time, size failed miserably, contrary to notions popular in imagery that large parts are identified faster than small ones. In fact, size of part correlated negatively with speed of recognition in both tasks. As the work on part goodness showed, part salience, that is, contour distinctiveness, and functional significance are positively correlated, for bodies just as for objects. In fact, both correlated with recognition speed for both the body–body and name–body tasks. One of the parts considered appears to have functional significance without contour distinctiveness, namely, chest. It is significant because it contains important internal parts; it is the front of the body, the side that engages the world perceptually and behaviorally; it also enjoys a relatively large space in the sensori-motor homunculus in the brain. Indeed, for the name–body task, chest is recognized relatively quickly, but for the body–body task, it is recognized relatively slowly. For the perceptual task, part salience accounted for recognition speed better than part significance, but for the naming task, functional significance accounted for recognition speed better than salience. Naming seems to call attention to functional in addition to perceptual properties, more than the appearance of a body alone.

21.4.2   Events again

Earlier, we described research in which observers segmented mundane events such as making a bed at coarse and fine levels. Some observers described what happened during each segment; others merely segmented (Zacks *et al.*, 2001). The vast majority of descriptions were actions on objects. Another question of interest is whether the segmentation was hierarchical, that is, did the high level boundaries coincide with the low level boundaries greater than chance? It could be that the higher level units were functionally defined, by goals, and the lower level units were perceptually defined, by large changes in activity, and that these might not coincide. In fact, segmentation was hierarchical, both within and across observers. What then is the effect of describing on hierarchical structure? Describing adds another task to segmenting; it could interfere with segmentation, making it more random, hence less hierarchical. On the other hand, describing brings to mind top-down functional information; focusing attention on function could yield more hierarchical segmentation. In fact, the degree of hierarchical coding was considerably greater with concomitant describing than without. It seems that events are segmented on the basis of both bottom-up perceptual information and top-down functional information. For events, language calls attention to top-down, functional processes, reflected in tighter hierarchical organization. Language not only directs attention to functional aspects of events, but semantic access also appears to be necessary for appropriate interaction with objects (Creem and Proffitt, 2001). In the presence of a semantic distractor task, but not in the presence of a visuo-spatial distractor task, participants grasped objects awkwardly, presumably because the distractor task interfered with their ability to access functional information about the object. For events as for bodies, language arouses functional aspects that are not readily in evidence from perception.

21.4.3   Parts, categories, and functions

Categories serve many functions. Primary among them are referring and inferring. Referring picks out objects in the world as category members. Inferring provides information about what the objects can do. Referring depends on identifying instances, on appearance. Inferring supplies functions. Categories are most informative at the basic level of abstraction, the level of chair and pants and car and tree and bird. Parts constitute the vast majority of features people provide for basic level categories. Parts are simultaneously elements of appearance and function. They afford inferences from structure to function, which form the core of the theories or causal reasoning that make categories cohere. Language further facilitates reliance on function as it elicits functional aspects of things in the world.

21.5   Referring to Spatial Relations

So far, we have concentrated on the roles of appearance, function, and affordance on spatial language, reasoning from research on objects, scenes, and events that these are related, in many cases, causally related. These causal relations serve us well, promoting inferences from appearance to function. Now we expand to influences of context and schemas, on using spatial language, drawing on our own research, neglecting other numerous fine studies. We shall first show that use of some of the most basic spatial relation terms, for example, *front* and *back*, depend not just on spatial properties, but on function, context, and schema as well.

21.5.1   Comprehension

Many languages describe the locations of objects in space by using terms that refer to spaces projected from the sides of a body or other object, for example, *front, back, left, right, above, below*. From purely geometric considerations, these directions should be equally accessible, that is, times to comprehend all directions should be the same. They are not. Rather, their accessibility depends on properties of the body as well as properties of the world—both perceptual and functional properties—and the relation of the body to the world, that is, context. When an observer is described as upright, objects in the regions beyond head and feet are most accessible, followed by objects to front and back. Those to left and right are slowest. This pattern changes when an observer is described as reclining. In that case, objects to front and back are more accessible than those to head and feet. Objects to left and right are least accessible as for upright.

The Spatial Framework Theory offers an explanation for this pattern of accessibility (Franklin and Tversky, 1990). In the paradigm situation, participants study narratives describing you, the observer, as situated in an environment such as an opera house or museum or barn, surrounded by objects to head, feet, front, back, left, and right. After learning the situation, participants read that they are turned to face another object. Then they are probed for the objects currently at all sides of their body with the direction terms. According to the Spatial Framework Theory, in order to keep track of the locations of objects around the body, people construct a spatial mental model consisting of extensions of the three body axes, and associate objects to them. The axes of the body vary in accessibility, depending on appearance and function. For an upright observer, the head/foot (or above/below, it makes no difference) axis is fastest because it is an asymmetric axis of the body and because it is correlated with the only asymmetric axis of the world, gravity. In both cases, the asymmetries are perceptual as well as functional. Heads and feet look different and act differently. Gravity causes asymmetries in the way the world appears and in what can be done in the world.

Front/back is next fastest because it has important asymmetries, among them, separating the world that can be viewed and manipulated from the world that is not easily viewed or manipulated. Left/right has no salient asymmetries, and is slowest.

When the observer is described as reclining and turning from side to front to back to side, no axis of the body correlates with gravity, so accessibility depends only on the asymmetries of the body axes. In this case, front/back is faster than head/feet, presumably because its perceptual and functional asymmetries are more important than those of head/feet.

In the original paradigm, the spatial mental models were established as well as tested through language. The basic situation was a person surrounded by objects to the six sides of the body. This situation lends itself to variation, both in the spatial setting and in the medium conveying the information. Many variations have in fact been tested. The spatial array can be in front of the observer rather than surrounding the observer, the external case (Bryant, Tversky, and Franklin, 1992). In the external case, all objects are in front of the observer, including those described as 'front' and 'back'. This contrasts with the internal situation where the 'front' object is in front of the observer, but the 'back' object is behind, in principle, hidden. For the case where the array is external to the observer, times for front and back are about equal, but for the case where the observer is internal to the array, times to front are faster than times to back. This is complemented by a finding of Franklin, Henckel, and Zangas (1995). They asked participants to indicate where 'front' is relative to themselves and relative to a doll. The area for self was much larger than for other. In another variant, narratives described the environment as rotating around the observer, rather than the observer turning in the environment. Although formally the same, the situations differ conceptually. The normal situation in the world is that observers move and environments are stationary. In another variant of the spatial environment that has effects consistent with the spatial framework model, narratives described the environments as rotating around the observer, rather than the observer rotating (Tversky, Kim, and Cohen, 1999).

Other variants have two characters, surrounded by the same or different objects, facing the same or different ways (Franklin, Tversky, and Coon, 1992). Here, too, the spatial context systematically affects retrieval times. When narratives describe the observer as above the environment, viewing both characters, participants' body axes no longer correspond to axes of the characters in the scene, and all directions become equally accessible. When narratives describe each character's viewpoint in turn, participants adopt their viewpoints and the canonical spatial framework pattern emerges. The spatial setting can be conveyed by diagrams or models (Bryant and Tversky, 1999) or by actual perception (Bryant, Tversky, and Lanca, 2001) as well as narrative. For flat diagrams, participants adopt an external viewpoint but for three-dimensional models, participants adopt an internal viewpoint. Instructions to adopt different viewpoints can override the effect of medium and reverse those patterns. Whether the situation is acquired by perception or by description does not lead to changes in the patterns of retrieval times as long as testing is from memory.

All in all, systematic variations in spatial arrangements and in mode of presenting the spatial arrangements yield systematic variations in the patterns of retrieval times for the same basic spatial terms. These variations can be accounted for by variants in the Spatial Framework Theory. These variations illustrate contextual or schematic effects on comprehension of spatial relation terms.

21.5.2   Production: describing complex environments

Clearly, context and schemas affect comprehension of spatial language. They also affect choice of spatial language. When people describe large environments, such as a museum or a town, they typically adopt one of two perspectives, or a combination of both. Perspectives involve reference frames, reference objects, and terms of reference. In a *route* perspective, descriptions take listeners on an imaginary tour of the environment, adopting a viewpoint from within and locating landmarks with respect to the traveler in terms of right, left, front, and back. In a *survey* perspective, descriptions take a viewpoint above the environment, locating landmarks with respect to each other in terms of north, south, east, west. Features of the environment—context—influence the perspective adopted. Route perspectives are relatively more common when the environment has a single path and landmarks on a single size scale (Taylor and Tversky, 1996). For such environments, it is relatively easy to describe all the landmarks by imagining traversing a single route.

21.5.3   Production: which potted palm hides the diamonds?

A simple paradigm developed by Schober (1995) required a speaker to specify one of two identical visible objects to an interlocutor. Speakers normally adopted listeners' perspectives, perhaps from politeness, perhaps to ease cognitive load. We enriched that situation by providing landmarks and/or cardinal directions on some trials and by varying the relative amounts of information speakers and interlocutors had about the spatial situation (Mainwaring, Tversky, Ohgishi, and Schiano, 2003; Tversky, Lee, and Mainwaring, 1999). Participants were told that they were spies, and asked to transmit to their partners which of the identical objects contained the hidden microphone or letter by providing a brief, clear message in a secret tiny communicator. Easing shared cognitive load seemed to motivate most of the choices of spatial relation terms. That in turn depended on both the spatial arrangement of objects and participants and the spatial terms that could specify the target. When the situation allowed it, participants preferred terms like 'near' to projective terms that require computing a direction, like 'right' or 'north'. Participants preferred terms like 'front', that are relatively easy to produce and comprehend because of body asymmetries, to terms like 'left' and 'right', that are relatively hard to produce because of lack of body asymmetries. For some spatial layouts, the target object could be disambiguated only by taking the perspective of one of the spies. When the speaker knew more about the situation, speakers tended to adopt the other's perspective. Alleviating the cognitive load of the interlocutor would presumably increase overall accuracy of communication. When cognitive loads of the conversational parties were equal, there was no preference for others' perspectives. Although Japan is thought to be an especially polite culture, Japanese participants showed exactly the same pattern as Americans; that is, the Japanese did not show a greater tendency to adopt the perspective of the other.

Overall, minimizing joint cognitive load seemed to account for choice of reference frame and reference object. But the determinants of joint cognitive load depend on context and shared schemas and the difficulty of producing and comprehending terms to describe it, which in turn depend on spatial and functional features of the body and the world.

21.5.4   Spatial language and function

Spatial language is used in a variety of contexts, and use of spatial language depends on the context. Context includes more than purely spatial aspects of the setting, but also functional aspects. These functional aspects affect both use and comprehension of spatial language, especially referring expressions.

21.6   **Parting Words**

We are back where we started, having shown some of the ways that terms that refer to entities and spatial relations among entities reflect appearance and function, thus affordances, as well as context and schema. The world we talk about is replete with appearances and functions and contexts and more. Talk necessarily schematizes the world we experience. How simple things would be if we could reduce spatial language to spatial templates. Simpler still if we could do it by merely adding function. Yet such simplicity would just serve simple-minded language and simple-minded theories. It would not account for language use or understanding. Indeed, despite all the nuances and subtleties that our unruly languages provide, we are often at a loss for words.

References

Abbott, V., Black, J. H., and Smith, E. E. (1985). The representation of scripts in memory. *Journal of Memory and Language*, 24, 179–99.

Abkarian, G. G. (1983). More negative findings for positive prepositions. *Journal of Child Language*, 10, 415–29.

Adams, A., Shettler, L., Wasnik, A., and Quinn, P. C. (2001). *Categorization of an arbitrary crossing in 3- to 4-month-old infants?* (Paper presented at the 29th Annual Western Pennsylvania Undergraduate Psychology Conference Penn State-Behrend Erie PA).

Aglioti, S., DSouza, J. F. X., and Goodale, M. A. (1995). Size-contrast illusions deceive the eye but not the hand. *Current Biology*, 5, 679–85.

Aguiar, A., and Baillargeon, R. (1998). Eight-and-a-half-month-old infants' reasoning about containment events. *Child Development*, 69, 636–53.

Ahn, W. (1998). Why are different features central for natural kinds and artifacts? The role of causal status in determining feature centrality. *Cognition*, 69, 135–78.

——, Kim, N. S., Lassaline, M. E., and Dennis, M. J. (2000). Causal status as a determinant of feature centrality. *Cognitive Psychology*, 41, 361–416.

Amorim, M. A., and Stucchi, N. (1997). Viewer- and object-centered mental explorations of an imagined environment are not equivalent. *Cognitive Brain Research*, 5, 229–39.

Antell, S. E. G., and Keating, D. P. (1983). Perception of numerical invariance in neonates. *Child Development*, 54, 695–701.

Arterberry, M. E. (1993). Development of spatiotemporal integration in infancy. *Infant Behavior and Development*, 16, 343–64.

—— (1995). Perception of object number through an aperture by human infants. *Infant Behavior and Development*, 18, 359–62.

Asso, D., and Wyke, M. (1973). Verbal descriptions of spatial relations in line drawings by young children. *British Journal of Psychology*, 64, 233–40.

Baillargeon, R., and Hanko-Summers, S. (1990). Is the top object adequately supported by the bottom object? Young infants' understanding of support relations. *Cognitive Development*, 5, 29–54.

——, Needham, A., and DeVos, J. (1992). The development of young infants' intuitions about support. *Early Development and Parenting*, 1, 69–78.

Barsalou, L. W. (1983). Ad hoc categories. *Memory & Cognition*, 11, 211–27.

—— (1985). Ideals central tendency and frequency of instantiation as determinants of graded structure in categories. *Journal of Experimental Psychology: Learning Memory and Cognition*, 11, 629–54.

—— (1987). The instability of graded structure: Implications for the nature of concepts. In U. Neisser (ed.), *Concepts and conceptual development: Ecological and intellectual factors in categorization* (pp. 101–40). Cambridge: Cambridge University Press.

—— (1989). Intraconcept similarity and its implications for interconcept similarity. In S. Vosniadou and A. Ortony (eds.), *Similarity and analogical reasoning* (pp. 76–121). Cambridge: Cambridge University Press.

—— (1991). Deriving categories to achieve goals. In G. H. Bower (ed.), *The psychology of learning and motivation: Advances in research and theory* (Vol. 27, pp. 1–64). San Diego

CA: Academic Press [Reprinted in A. Ram and D. Leake (eds.), *Goal-driven learning* (1995, pp. 21–176). Cambridge MA: MIT Press/Bradford Books].

Barsalou, L. W. (1992). Frames concepts and conceptual fields. In E. Kittay and A. Lehrer (eds.), *Frames fields and contrasts: New essays in semantic and lexical organization.* Hillsdale, NJ: Lawrence Erlbaum Associates.

—— (1993). Structure flexibility and linguistic vagary in concepts: Manifestations of a compositional system of perceptual symbols. In A. C. Collins, S. E. Gathercole, and M. A. Conway (eds.), *Theories of memory* (pp. 29–101). London: Lawrence Erlbaum Associates.

—— (1999). Perceptual symbol systems. *Behavioral and Brain Sciences*, 22, 577–660.

——, Solomon, K. O., and Wu, L.-L. (1999). Perceptual simulation in conceptual tasks. In M. K. Hiraga, C. Sinha, and S. Wilcox (eds.), *Cultural typological and psychological perspectives in cognitive linguistics: The proceedings of the 4th conference of the International Cognitive Linguistics Association*, 3, 209–28. Amsterdam: John Benjamins.

—— (2003). Situated simulation in the human conceptual system. Language and Cognitive Processes.

Behl-Chadha, G., and Eimas, P. D. (1995). Infant categorization of left–right spatial relations. *British Journal of Developmental Psychology*, 13, 69–79.

Belsky, J., and Most, R. K. (1981). From exploration to play: A cross-sectional study of infant free play behavior. *Developmental Psychology*, 17(5), 630–39.

Bennett, D. C. (1975). *Spatial and temporal uses of English prepositions: An essay in stratifcational semantics.* London: Longman.

Bialystok, E., and Codd, J. (1987). Children's interpretations of ambiguous spatial descriptions. *British Journal of Developmental Psychology*, 5, 205–11.

Biederman, I. (1987). Recognition-by-components: A theory of human image understanding. *Psychological Review*, 94, 115–47.

Bierwisch, M. (1988). Tools and explanations of comparison, Parts 1 & 2, *Journal of Semantics*, 6, 57–93 and 101–46.

—— (1989). Event nominalizations: Proposals and problems. In *Linguistische Studien Reihe A*, 194 (pp. 1–73). Berlin: Akademie Verlag.

—— (1996). How much space gets into language? In P. Bloom, M. A. Peterson, L. Nadel, and M. F. Garrett (eds.), *Language and space* (pp. 31–76). Cambridge, MA: MIT Press.

Bloom, P. (1996). Intention history and artifact concepts. *Cognition*, 60, 1–29.

—— (1998). Theories of artifact categorization. *Cognition*, 66, 87–93.

—— (2000). *How children learn the meanings of words.* Cambridge, MA: MIT Press.

——, Peterson, M. A., Nadel, L., and Garrett, M. F. (eds.), (1996). *Language and space.* Cambridge MA: MIT Press.

Bock, K., Loebell, H., and Morey, R. (1992). From conceptual roles to structural relations: Bridging the syntactic cleft. *Psychological Review*, 99, 150–71.

Bohnemeyer, J. (2000). Constraints on motion event coding: Vectors or path shapes. In E. van der Zee and J. Slack (eds.), *Proceedings of the workshop on axes and vectors in language and space.* Lincoln: University of Lincoln & Humberside.

Boroditsky, L. (2000). Metaphoric structuring: Understanding time through spatial metaphors. *Cognition*, 75, 1–28.

Bower, G. H., Black, J. B., and Turner, T. J. (1979). Scripts in memory for text. *Cognitive Psychology*, 11, 177–220.

Bowerman, M. (1993). Typological perspectives in language acquisition: Do crosslinguistic patterns predict development? In E. Clark (ed.), *Proceedings of the twenty-fifth annual child language research forum* (pp. 7–15). Stanford: CSLI.

—— (1996a). The origins of children's spatial semantic categories: Cognitive versus linguistic determinants. In J. J. Gumperz and S. C. Levinson (eds.), *Rethinking linguistic relativity* (pp. 145–76). Cambridge: Cambridge University Press.

—— (1996b). Learning to structure space for language: A crosslinguistic perspective. In P. Bloom, M. A. Peterson, L. Nadel, and M. F. Garrett (eds.), *Language and space* (pp. 383–435). Cambridge, MA: MIT Press.

—— and Choi, S. (2001). Shaping meanings for language: Universal and language specific in the acquisition of spatial semantic categories. In M. Bowerman & S. C. Levinson (eds.), *Language acquisition and conceptual development* (pp. 475–511). Cambridge: Cambridge University Press.

Bridgeman, B., and Huemer, V. (1998). A spatially oriented decision does not induce consciousness in a motor task. *Consciousness & Cognition: An International Journal*, 7, 454–64.

Brockmole, J. R., and Wang, R. F. (2003). Changing perspective within and across environments. *Cognition*, 87, B59–B67.

Brooks, R. A. (1987). *Intelligence without representation*. MIT Artificial Intelligence Report.

Brown, P., and Levinson, S. C. (1992). 'Left' and 'right' in Tenejapa: Investigating a linguistic and conceptual gap. *Zeitschrift für Phonetik Sprachwissenschaft und Kommunikationsforschung (ZPSK)*, 45, 590–611.

Brown, R. (1958). How shall a thing be called? *Psychological Review*, 65, 14–21.

—— (1973). *A first language: The early stages*. Cambridge, MA: Harvard University Press.

Brugman, C. (1988). *The story of 'over': Polysemy semantics and the structure of the lexicon*. New York: Garland Press.

Bruner, J. S., Goodnow, J. J., and Asutin, G. A. (1956). *A study of thinking*. New Brunswick, NJ: Wiley & Sons.

Bryant, D. J., and Tversky, B. (1992). Assessing spatial frameworks with object and direction probes. *Bulletin of the Psychonomic Society*, 30, 29–32.

—— —— (1999). Mental representations of spatial relations from diagrams and models. *Journal of Experimental Psychology: Learning Memory and Cognition*, 25, 137–56.

—— —— and Franklin, N. (1992). Internal and external spatial frameworks for representing described scenes. *Journal of Memory and Language*, 31, 74–98.

—— —— and Lanca, M. (2001). Retrieving spatial relations from observation and memory. In E. van der Zee and U. Nikanne (eds.), *Conceptual structure and its interfaces with other modules of representation* (pp. 116–39). Oxford: Oxford University Press.

Burdelski, J., Rause, D., Shaffer, J., and Quinn, P. C. (2000). *Categorization of left versus right spatial relations by 3- to 4-month-old infants*. (Unpublished Manuscript. Washington & Jefferson College, Washington, PA).

Burgess, C., and Lund, K. (1997). Modelling parsing constraints with high-dimensional context space. *Language and Cognitive Processes*, 12, 177–210.

Carey, S. (1985). *Conceptual change in childhood*. Cambridge, MA: MIT Press.

Carlson, L. A. (1999). Selecting a reference frame. *Spatial Computation and Cognition*, 1, 365–79.

Carlson, L. A. (2000). Object use and object location: The effects of function on spatial relations. In E. van der Zee and U. Nikanne (eds.), *Cognitive interfaces: Constraints on linking cognitive information.* Oxford: Oxford University Press.

—— and Regier, T. (in preparation). Attention and object use in spatial language.

Carlson-Radvansky, L. A., and Irwin, D. E. (1993). Frames of reference in vision and language: Where is above? *Cognition,* 46, 223–44.

—— —— (1994). Reference frame activation during spatial term assignment. *Journal of Memory and Language,* 33, 646–71.

—— and Jiang, Y. (1998). Inhibition accompanies reference-frame selection. *Psychological Science,* 9, 386–91.

—— and Logan, G. D. (1997). The influence of reference frame selection on spatial template construction. *Journal of Memory and Langauge,* 37, 411–37.

—— and Radvansky, G. A. (1996). The influence of functional relations on spatial term selection. *Psychological Science,* 7, 56–60.

—— and Tang, Z. (2000). Functional influences on orienting a reference frame. *Memory & Cognition,* 28, 812–20.

——, Covey, E. S., and Lattanzi, K. M. (1999). 'What' effects on 'where': Functional influences on spatial relations. *Psychological Science,* 10, 516–21.

Caron, A. J., Caron, R. F., and Antell, S. E. (1988). Infant understanding of containment: An affordance perceived or a relationship conceived? *Developmental Psychology,* 24, 620–27.

Carpenter, P. A., and Just, M. A. (1975). Sentence comprehension: A psycholinguistic processing model of verification. *Psychological Review,* 82, 45–73.

Casad, E. H., and Langacker, R. W. (1985). 'Inside' and 'outside' in Cora grammar. *International Journal of American Language,* 51, 247–81.

Casasola, M., and Cohen, L. B. (2002). Infant categorization of containment support and tight-fit spatial relationships. *Developmental Science,* 5, 247–64.

Chaigneau, S. E. (2002). *Studies in the conceptual structure of object function.* (Doctoral dissertation, Department of Psychology, Emory University, Atlanta, GA).

——, Barsalou, L. W., and Zamani, M. (2004). *Function as a multimodal relational construct.* (Manuscript in preparation).

—— —— and Sloman, S. (2004). *Assessing the casual structure of function.* Under review.

—— —— (in press). The role of function in categorization. *Theoria et Historia Scientiarum* [Reprinted in the Polish journal Kognitywistyka i media w edukacji/ Cognitive Science and Media in Education].

Chase, W. G., and Simon, H. A. (1973). The mind's eye in chess. In W. G. Chase (ed.), *Visual information processing.* New York: Academic Press.

Chatterjee, S. H., Freyd, J. J., and Shiffrar, M. (1996). Configural processing in the perception of apparent biological motion. *Journal of Experimental Psychology: Human Perception and Performance,* 22, 916–29.

Choi, S., and Bowerman, M. (1991). Learning to express motion events in English and Korean: The influence of language-specific lexicalization patterns. *Cognition,* 41, 83–121.

——, McDonough, L., Bowerman, M., and Mandler, J. M. (1999). Early sensitivity to language-specific spatial categories in English and Korean. *Cognitive Development,* 14, 241–68.

Chomsky, N. (1992). Explaining language use. *Philosophical Topics,* 20, 205–31.

Christou, C. G., and Bülthoff, H. H. (1999). View dependence in scene recognition after active learning. *Memory & Cognition*, 27, 996–1007.

Chun, M. M. (2000). Contextual cueing of visual attention. *Trends in Cognitive Sciences*, 4, 170–8.

—— and Jiang, Y. (1998). Contextual cueing: Implicit learning and memory of visual context guides spatial attention. *Cognitive Psychology*, 36, 28–71.

Clark, E. V. (1972). On the child's acquisition of antonyms in two semantic fields. *Journal of Verbal Learning and Verbal Behavior*, 11, 750–8.

—— (1973a). Non-linguistic strategies and the acquisition of word meanings. *Cognition*, 2, 161–82.

—— (1973b). What's in a word? on the child's acquisition of semantics in his first language. In T. E. Moore (ed.), *Cognitive development and the acquisition of language* (pp. 65–110). London: Academic Press.

—— (1983). Meaning and concepts. In P. H. Mussen (Series Ed.), J. H. Flavell, and E. M. Markman (Vol. eds.), *Handbook of child psychology: Vol. III. Cognitive development* (pp. 787–840). New York, NY: Wiley & Sons.

—— and Clark, H. H. (1979). When nouns surface as verbs. *Language*, 55, 767–811.

Clark, H. H. (1973). Space, time, semantics and the child. In T. E. Moore (ed.), *Cognitive development and the acquisition of language*. New York, NY: Academic Press.

—— (1996). *Using language*. Cambridge: Cambridge University Press.

Cohen, L. B., and Oakes, L. M. (1993). How infants perceive a simple causal event. *Developmental Psychology*, 29, 421–33.

—— and Younger, B. A. (1983). Perceptual categorization in the infant. In E. K. Scholnick (ed.), *New trends in conceptual representation: Challenges to Piaget's theory?* (pp. 197–220). Hillsdale, NJ: Erlbaum.

Cohn, A. G., Bennett, B., Gooday, J., and Gotts, N. M. (1997). Qualitative spatial representation and reasoning with the region connection calculus. *Geoinformatica*, 1(3), 1–42.

Cooper, G. S. (1968). A semantic analysis of english locative prepositions. *Bolt, Beranek & Newman Report*, 1587.

Corballis, M. C., and Benle, I. L. (1976). *The psychology of left and right*. Hillsdale, NJ: Erlbaum.

Corrigan, R. (1982). The control of animate and inanimate components in pretend play and language. *Child Development*, 53(5), 1343–53.

—— and Schommer, M. (1984). Form versus function revisited: The role of social input and memory factors. *Child Development*, 55, 1721–6.

Coventry, K. R. (1992). *Spatial prepositions and functional relations: The case for minimally specified lexical entries* (Ph.D. Thesis, University of Edinburgh).

—— (1998). Spatial prepositions, functional relations, and lexical specification. In P. Olivier and K.-P. Gapp (eds.), *Representation and processing of spatial expressions* (pp. 247–62). Mahwah, NJ: Lawrence Erlbaum Associates.

—— (1999). Function geometry and spatial prepositions: Three experiments. *Spatial Cognition and Computation*, 1, 145–54.

—— and Garrod, S. C. (2004). *Saying, seeing and acting: The psychological semantics of spatial prepositions*. Essays in Cognitive Psychology Series. Hove and New York: Psychology Press.

Coventry, K. R., and Mather, G. (2002). The real story of 'over'? In K. R. Coventry and P. Olivier (eds.), *Spatial language: Cognitive and computational aspects.* Dordrecht, The Netherlands: Kluwer Academic Publishers.

—— and Prat-Sala, M. (2001). Object-specific function geometry and the comprehension of 'in' and 'on'. *European Journal of Cognitive Psychology*, 13(4), 509–28.

—— Carmichael, R., and Garrod, S. C. (1994). Spatial prepositions, object specific function and task requirements. *Journal of Semantics*, 11, 289–309.

——, Prat-Sala, M., and Richards, L. (2001). The interplay between geometry and function in the comprehension of 'Over', 'Under', 'Above', and 'Below'. *Journal of Memory and Language*, 44, 376–98.

——, Richards, L. V., Joyce, D., and Cangelosi, A. (in preparation). *Spatial prepositions and the instantiation of object knowledge: The case of 'over' 'under', 'above' and 'below'.*

Cox, M. V. (1979). Young children's understanding of 'in front of' and 'behind' in the placement of objects. *Journal of Child Language*, 6, 371–4.

Creem, S. H., and Proffitt, D. R. (1998). Two memories for geographical slant: Separation and interdependence of action and awareness. *Psychonomic Bulletin & Review*, 5, 22–36.

—— and Proffitt, D. R. (2001). Grasping objects by their handles: A necessary interaction between cognition and action. *Journal of Experimental Psychology: Human Perception and Performance*, 27, 218–28.

de Vega, M. (1994). Characters and their perspectives in narratives describing spatial environments. *Psychological Research*, 56, 116–26.

—— (1995). Backward updating of mental models during continuous reading of narratives. *Journal of Experimental Psychology: Learning Memory and Cognition*, 21, 373–85.

—— and Rodrigo, M. J. (2001). Updating spatial layouts mediated by pointing and labeling under physical and imaginary rotation. *European Journal of Cognitive Psychology*, 13, 369–93.

——, Rodrigo, M. J., and Zimmer, H. (1996). Pointing and labeling directions in egocentric frameworks. *Journal of Memory and Language*, 35, 821–39.

——, Cocude, M., Denis, M., Rodrigo, M. J., and Zimmer, H. D. (2001). The interface between language and visuo-spatial representations. In M. Denis, R. H. Logie, C. Cornoldi, M. de Vega, and J. Engelkamp (eds.), *Imagery, language, and visuo-spatial thinking* (pp. 109–36). Hove and New York: Psychology Press.

——, Rodrigo, M. J., Ato, M., Dehn, D. M., and Barquero, B. (2002). How nouns and prepositions fit together: An exploration of the semantics of locative sentences. *Discourse Processes*, 34, 117–43.

DeGroot, A. D. (1966). Perception and memory versus thought. In B. Kleinmuntz (ed.), *Problem solving.* New York: Wiley.

Deloache, J. S., Kolstad, V., and Anderson, K. (1991). Physical similarity and young children's understanding of scale models. *Child Development*, 62, 111–26.

Denis, M., and Cocude, M. (1992). Structural properties of visual images constructed from poorly or well-structured verbal descriptions. *Memory and Cognition*, 20, 497–506.

Dennett, D. C. (1987). *The intentional stance.* Cambridge, MA: MIT Press.

Downing, C., and Pinker, S. (1985). The spatial structure of visual attention. In M. Posner and O. Marin (eds.), *Attention and Performance XI* (pp. 171–87). Hillsdale, NJ: Erlbaum.

Durkin, K. (1980). The production of locative prepositions by young school children. *Educational Studies*, 6, 9–30.

Duvdevani-Bar, S., and Edelman, S. (1999). Visual recognition and categorization on the basis of similarities to multiple class prototypes. *International Journal of Computer Vision*, 33, 201–28.

Easton, R. D., and Sholl, M. J. (1995). Object-array structure, frames of reference, and retrieval of spatial knowledge. *Journal of Experimental Psychology: Learning, Memory, and Cognition*, 21, 483–500.

Edelman, S. (1995). Representation, similarity, and the chorus of prototypes. *Minds & Machines*, 5(1), 45–68.

—— (1999). *Representation and recognition in vision*. Cambridge, MA: MIT Press.

—— and Duvdevani-Bar, S. (1997). A model of visual recognition and categorization. *Philosophical Transactions of the Royal Society of London*, 352, 1191–202.

Eimas, P. (1994). Categorization in early infancy and the continuity of development. *Cognition*, 50, 83–93.

Ellis, R., and Tucker, M. (2000). Micro-affordance: The potentiation of components of action by seen objects. *British Journal of Psychology*, 91(4), 451–71.

Eschenbach, C. (1995). *Zählangaben—Maßangaben*. Wiesbaden: Deutscher Universitätsverlag.

—— (1999). Geometric structures of frames of reference and natural language semantics. *Spatial Cognition and Computation*, 1, 329–348.

—— and Kulik, L. (1997). An axiomatic approach to the spatial relations underlying 'left'–'right' and 'in front of'–'behind'. In G. Brewka, C. Habel, and B. Nebel (eds.), *KI-97: Advances in artificial intelligence* (pp. 207–18). Berlin: Springer-Verlag.

——, Habel, Ch., and Leßmöllmann, A. (2002). Multiple frames of reference in interpreting complex projective terms. In K. Coventry & P. Olivier (eds.), *Spatial language: Cognitive and computational perspectives* (pp. 209–31). Dordrecht: Kluwer.

——, Tschander, L., Habel, C., and Kulik, L. (2000). Lexical specifications of paths. In C. Freksa, W. Brauer, C. Habel, and K. F. Wender (eds.), *Spatial Cognition II* (pp. 127–44). Berlin: Springer-Verlag.

Fantz, R. L. (1964). Visual experience in infants: Decreased attention to familiar patterns relative to novel ones. *Science*, 164, 668–70.

Farrell, M. J., and Robertson, I. H. (1998). Mental rotation and the automatic updating of body-centered spatial relationships. *Journal of Experimental Psychology: Learning, Memory, and Cognition*, 24, 227–33.

Farrell, Jr., W. S. (1979). Coding left and right. *Journal of Experimental Psychology: Human Perception and Performance*, 5, 42–51.

Feist, M. I., and Gentner, D. (1998). On plates, bowls and dishes: Factors in the use of English 'in' and 'on'. In M. A. Gernsbacher and S. J. Derry (eds.), *Proceedings of the twentieth annual cognitive science society* (pp. 345–49). Mahwah, NJ: Lawrence Erlbaum Associates.

Feldman, J. (1997). The structure of perceptual categories. *Journal of Mathematical Psychology*, 41, 145–70.

Fenson, L., Dale, P. S., Reznick, J. S., Bates, E. *et al.* (1994). Variability in early communicative development. *Monographs of the Society for Research in Child Development*, 59(5), v–173.

Ferenz, K. (2000). *The role of non-geometric information in spatial language.* (Doctoral dissertation. Dartmouth College, Hanover, NH).

Ferrier, G. (1996). *A geometry without angles: The case for a functional geometry of spatial prepositions* (Ph.D. thesis, University of Glasgow).

Fillmore, C. J. (1997). *Lectures on deixis.* Stanford, CA: CSLI Publications (repr. of Lectures given at Santa Cruz, 1971).

Fillmore, C., &, Kay, P. (1996). *Construction grammar* (CSLI Lecture notes. Center for the study of Language and Information. Stanford, CA. Manuscript).

Flores d'Arcais, G. B. (1987). Perceptual factors and word order in event descriptions. In J.G. Kempen (ed.), *Natural Language Generation* (pp. 441–51). Dordrecht: Martinus Nijhoff.

Fodor, J. A., and Pylyshyn, Z. W. (1988). Connectionism and cognitive architecture: A critical analysis. In S. Pinker & J. Mehler (eds.), *Connections and symbols* (pp. 3–71). Cambridge, MA: MIT Press.

Franklin, N., and Tversky, B. (1990). Searching imagined environments. *Journal of Experimental Psychology: General,* 119, 63–76.

——, Henkel, L. A., and Zangas, T. (1995). Parsing surrounding space into regions. *Memory and Cognition,* 23, 397–407.

——, Tversky, B., and Coon, V. (1992). Switching points of view in spatial mental models. *Memory & Cognition,* 20, 507–18.

Freeman, N. H., Lloyd, S., and Sinha, C. G. (1980). Infant search tasks reveal early concepts of containment and canonical use of objects. *Cognition,* 8, 243–62.

Freyd, J. J. (1987). Dynamic mental representations. *Psychological Review,* 94, 427–38.

Friederici, A. D., and W. J. M. Levelt (1990). Spatial reference in weightlessness: Perceptual factors and mental representations. *Perception and Psychophysics,* 47, 253–66.

Gallistel, C. R. (1990). *Organization of learning.* Cambridge, MA: MIT Press.

Gapp, K.-P. (1995). Angle, distance, shape, and their relationship to projective relations. In J. D. Moore & J. F. Lehman (eds.), *Proceedings of the seventeenth annual conference of the cognitive science society* (pp. 112–17). Mahwah, NJ: Lawrence Erlbaum.

Garner, W. R. (1974). *The processing of information and structure.* Potomac, MD: Lawrence Erlbaum.

—— (1976). Interaction of stimulus dimensions in concept and choice processes. *Cognitive Psychology,* 8, 98–123.

—— (1978). Aspects of a stimulus: features, dimensions, and configurations. In E. Rosch and B. B. Lloyd (eds.), *Cognition and categorization.* Hillsdale, NJ: L. Erlbaum Associates.

Garnham, A. (1989). A unified theory of the meaning of some spatial relational terms. *Cognition,* 55, 39–84.

Garrod, S. C., and Sanford, A. J. (1988). Discourse models as interfaces between language and the spatial world. *Journal of Semantics,* 6, 147–60.

——, Ferrier, G., and Campbell, S. (1999). 'In' and 'On': investigating the functional geometry of spatial prepositions. *Cognition,* 72, 167–89.

Gathercole, V. C. M., and Whitfield, L. C. (2001). Function as a criterion for the extension of new words. *Journal of Child Language,* 28(1), 87–125.

——, Cramer, L. J., Somerville, S. C., and Jansen op de Haar, M. (1995). Ontological categories and function: Acquisition of new names. *Cognitive Development,* 10(2), 225–51.

Gelman, R. (1990). First principles organize attention to and learning about relevant data: Number and animate-inanimate distinciton as examples. *Cognitive Science*, 14, 79–106.

—— and Williams, E. (1998). Enabling constraints for cognitive development and learning: Domain specificity and epigenesis. In W. Damon (Series Ed.), D. Kuhn, and R. Siegler (eds.), *Handbook of child psychology: Vol.2. Cognition, perception, and language* (5th edn., pp. 575–630). New York: Wiley.

Gelman, S. A. (1996). Concepts and theories. In R. Gelman and T. Au (eds.), *Perceptual and cognitive development* (Vol. 3, pp. 117–55). San Diego: Academic Press.

—— and Bloom, P. (2000). Young children are sensitive to how an object was created when deciding what to name it. *Cognition*, 76, 91–103.

—— and Coley, J. D. (1990). The importance of knowing a dodo is a bird: Categories and inferences in 2-year-old children. *Developmental Psychology*, 26, 796–804.

—— and Diesendruck, G. (1999). What's in a concept? Context, variability, and psychological essentialism. In I. E. Siegel (ed.), *Theoretical perspectives in the concept of representation* (pp. 87–111). Mahwah, NJ: Erlbaum.

—— and Markman, E. M. (1986). Categories and induction in young children. *Cognition*, 23, 183–209.

—— and Markman, E. M. (1987). Young children's inductions from natural kinds: The role of categories and appearances. *Child Development*, 58, 1532–41.

—— and Wellman, H. M (1991). Insides and essences: Early understandings of the nonobvious. *Cognition*, 38, 213–44.

——, Croft, W., Panfrang, F., Clauser, T., and Gottfried, G. (1998). Why is a pomegranate like an apple? The role of shape, taxonomic relatedness, and prior lexical knowledge in children's overextensions of apple and dog. *Journal of Child Language*, 25, 267–91.

Gentner, D. (1978a). On relational meaning: The acquisition of verb meaning. *Child Development*, 49, 988–98.

—— (1978b). What looks like a jiggy but acts like a zimbo: A study of early word meaning using artificial objects. *Papers and Reports on Language Development*, 15, 137–42.

—— and Boroditsky, L. (2001). Individuation, relativity, and early word learning. In M. Bowerman and S. C. Levinson (eds.), *Language Acquisition and Conceptual Development*. Cambridge: Cambridge University Press.

Georgopoulos, A. P., Schwartz, A. B., and Kettner, R. E. (1986). Neuronal population coding of movement direction. *Science*, 223, 1416–19.

Gibson, J. J. (1979a). *The ecological approach to visual perception*. Boston: Houghton-Mifflin.

—— (1979b). *The perception of the visual world*. Boston: Houghton-Mifflin.

Glenberg, A. M. (1997). What memory is for. *Behavioral and Brain Sciences*, 20, 1–55.

—— and Kaschak, M. P. (2002). Grounding language in action. *Psychonomic Bulletin and Review*, 9, 558–65.

—— and Robertson, D. A. (1999). Indexical understanding of instructions. *Discourse Processes*, 28, 1–26.

—— and Robertson, D. A. (2000). Symbol grounding and meaning: A comparison of high-dimensional and embodied theories of meaning. *Journal of Memory and Language*, 43, 379–401.

——, Robertson, D. A., Jansen, J. L., and Johnson-Glenberg, M. C. (1999). Not propositions. *Journal of Cognitive Systems Research*, 1, 19–33.

Glymour, C. (2001). *The mind's arrows: Bayes nets and graphical causal models in psychology.* Cambridge, MA: MIT Press.

Goldberg, A. E. (1995). *Constructions: A construction grammar approach to argument structure.* Chicago: University of Chicago Press.

Goldstone, R. L. (1994). Influences of categorization on perceptual discrimination. *Journal of Experimental Psychology: General,* 123(2), 178–200.

—— (1998). Perceptual learning. *Annual Review of Psychology,* 49, 585–612.

—— (2000). Unitization during category learning. *Journal of Experimental Psychology: Human Perception and Performance,* 26(1), 86–112.

—— (2003). Learning to perceive while perceiving to learn. In R. Kimchi, M. Behrmann, and C. Olson (eds.), *Perceptual organization in vision: Behavioral and neural perspectives.* Mahwah, NJ: L. Erlbaum Associates.

—— and Barsalou, L. (1998). Reuniting perception and conception. *Cognition,* 65, 231–62.

—— and Steyvers, M. (2001). The sensitization and differentiation of dimensions during category learning. *Journal of Experimental Psychology: General,* 130(1), 116–139.

——, Lippa, Y., and Shiffrin, R. M. (2001). Altering object representations through category learning. *Cognition,* 78(1), 27–43.

——, Medin, D. L., and Halberstadt, J. (1997). Similarity in context. *Memory & Cognition,* 25(2), 237–55.

——, Schyns, P. G., and Medin, M. L. (1997). Learning to bridge perception and cognition. In R. L. Goldstone, P. G. Schyns, and D. L. Medin (eds.), *The psychology of learning and motivation* (Vol. 36, pp. 1–14). San Diego, CA: Academic Press.

——, Steyvers, M., Spencer-Smith, J., and Kersten, A. (2000). Interactions between perceptual and conceptual learning. In E. Diettrich & A. B. Markman (eds.), *Cognitive dynamics: Conceptual change in humans and machines* (pp. 191–228). Mahwah, NJ: Lawrence Erlbaum Associates.

Goodale, M. A., and Humphrey, G. K. (1998). The objects of action and perception. *Cognition. Special Issue: Image-based object recognition in man, monkey and machine,* 67(1–2), 181–207.

—— and Milner, A. D. (1992). Separate visual pathways for perception and action. *Trends in Neurosciences,* 15, 20–5.

Goodman, N. (1968). *Languages of art.* Indianapolis: Bobbs-Merill.

Graham, S. A., Williams, L. D., and Huber, J. F. (1999). Preschoolers' and adults' reliance on object shape and object function for lexical extension. *Journal of Experimental Child Psychology,* 74(2), 128–51.

Grimm, H. (1975). On the child's acquisition of semantic structure underlying the worldfield of prepositions. *Language and Speech,* 18, 97–119.

Habel, Ch. (1989). *Zwischen*-bericht. In Ch. Habel, M. Herweg, and K. Rehkaemper (eds.), *Raumkonzepte in Verstehensprozessen* (pp. 37–69). Tuebingen: Niemeyer.

—— (1999). Drehsinn und Reorientierung. Modus und Richtung beim Bewegungsverb 'drehen'. In G. Rickheit (ed.), *Richtungen im Raum. Interdisziplinäre Perspektiven* (pp. 101–28). Wiesbaden: Deutscher Universitätsverlag.

—— and Eschenbach, C. (1997). Abstract structures in spatial cognition. In C. Freksa, M. Jantzen, and R. Valk (eds.), *Foundations of computer science* (pp. 369–78). Berlin: Springer-Verlag.

Halpern, E., Corrigan, R., and Aviezer, O. (1983). In, on, and under: Examining the relationship between cognitive and language skills. *International Journal of Behavioral Development*, 6, 153–66.

Harnad, S. (1990). The symbol grounding problem. *Physica D*, 42, 335–46.

Hayward, W. G., and Tarr, M. J. (1995). Spatial language and spatial representation. *Cognition*, 55, 39–84.

Hegarty, M. (1992). Mental animation: Inferring motion from static displays of mechanical systems. *Journal of Experiment Psychology: Learning, Memory, and Cognition*, 18, 1084–1102.

Helson, H. (1964). *Adaptation-level theory*. New York: Harper & Row.

Hermer-Vazquez, L., Spelke, E. S., and Katsnelson, A. S. (1999). Sources of flexibility in human cognition: Dual-task studies of space and language. *Cognitive Psychology*, 33, 3–36.

Herskovits, A. (1985). Semantics and pragmatics of locative expressions. *Cognitive Science*, 9, 341–78.

—— (1986). *Language and spatial cognition*. Cambridge: Cambridge University Press.

—— (1998). 'Schematization'. In P. Olivier and K.-P. Gapp, (eds.), *Representation and processing of spatial expressions*. Mahwah, NJ: Lawrence Erlbaum Associates, 149–62.

Herweg, M. (1989). Ansätze zu einer semantischen Beschreibung topologischer Präpositionen. In C. Habel, M. Herweg, and K. Rehkamper (eds.), *Raumkonzepte in Verstehenprozessen* (pp. 99–127). Tübingen: Niemeyer Verlag.

Hespos, S. J., and Baillargeon, R. (2001a). Infants' knowledge about occlusion and containment events: A surprising discrepancy. *Psychological Science*, 121, 141–7.

—— —— (2001b). Reasoning about containment events in very young infants. *Cognition*, 28, 207–45.

Higginbotham, J. (1985). On semantics. *Linguistic Inquiry*, 16, 547–93.

Hill, C. (1982). Up/down, front/back, left/right. A contrastive study of Hausa and English. In J. Weissenborn and W. Klein (eds.), *Here and there. Cross-linguistic studies on deixis and demonstration* (pp. 13–42). Amsterdam: John Benjamin Publ. Company.

Hillier, B. (1999). The hidden geometry of deformed grids: Or, why space syntax works when it looks as though it shouldn't. *Environment and Planning B: Planning and Design*, 26, 169–91.

—— (2000). Centrality as a process: Accounting for attraction inequalities in deformed grids. *Urban Design International*, 3/4, 1007–27.

Hintzman, D. L. (1986). 'Schema abstraction' in a multiple-trace memory model. *Psychological Review*, 93, 411–28.

Hoffman, D. D., and Richards, W. A. (1984). Parts of recognition. *Cognition*, 18, 65–96.

Hofstadter, D. R. (1995). *Fluid concepts and creative analogies: Computer models of the fundamental mechanisms of thought*. NY: Basic Books.

Huttenlocher, J., and Presson, C. C. (1973). Mental rotation and the perspective problem. *Cognitive Psychology*, 4, 277–99.

—— and Presson C. C. (1979). The coding and transformation of spatial information. *Cognitive Psychology*, 11, 375–94.

—— and Newcombe, N. (1984). The child's representation of information about location. In C. Sophian (ed.), *Origins of cognitive skills* (pp. 81–111). Hillsdale, NJ: Erlbaum.

Jackendoff, R. (1972). *Semantic interpretation in generative grammar*. Cambridge, MA: MIT Press.

—— (1976). Towards an explanatory semantic representation. *Linguistic Inquiry*, 7, 89–150.

—— (1983). *Semantics and cognition*. Cambridge, MA: MIT Press.

—— (1990). *Semantic structures*. Cambridge, MA: MIT Press.

—— (1996a). The architecture of the linguistic–spatial interface. In P. Bloom, M. A. Peterson, L. Nadel, and M. F. Garrett (eds.), *Language and space* (pp. 1–30). Cambridge, MA: MIT Press.

—— (1996b). Conceptual semantics and cognitive semantics. *Cognitive Linguistics*, 7, 92–129.

—— (1997). *The architecture of the language faculty*. Cambridge, MA: MIT Press.

Jammers, M. (1957). *Concepts of force*. Cambridge, MA: Harvard University Press.

Jepson, A., and Richards, W. (1993). What makes a good feature? In L. Harris and M. Jenkin (eds.), *Spatial vision in humans and robots*. Cambridge: Cambridge University Press.

Johnson, M. H., and Vecera, S. P. (1996). Cortical differentiation and neurocognitive development: The parcellation conjecture. *Behavioural Processes*, 36, 195–212.

——, Mareschal, D., and Csibra, G. (2001). The functional development and integration of the dorsal and ventral visual pathways: A neurocomputational approach. In C. A. Nelson and M. Luciana (eds.), *Handbook of developmental cognitive neuroscience* (pp. 139–51). Cambridge, MA: MIT Press.

Johnston, J. R. (1984). Acquisition of locative meanings—behind and in front of. *Journal of Child Language*, 11, 407–22.

—— (1988). Children's verbal representation of spatial location. In J. Stiles-Davis, M. Kritchevsky, and U. Bellugi (eds.), *Spatial cognition* (pp. 195–206). Hillsdale, NJ: Erlbaum.

—— and Slobin, D. I. (1979). The development of locative expressions in English, Italian, Serbo-Croation and Turkish. *Journal of Child Language*, 6, 529–45.

Jones, S. S., and Smith, L. B. (1993). The place of perception in children's concepts. *Cognitive Development*, 8, 113–39.

Kahneman, D., Treisman, A., and Gibbs, B. J. (1992). The reviewing of object files: Object-specific integration of information. *Cognitive Psychology*, 24, 175–219.

Kaschak, M. P., and Glenberg, A. M. (2000). Constructing meaning: The role of affordances and grammatical constructions in sentence comprehension. *Journal of Memory and Language*, 43, 508–29.

Kaufmann, I. (1995). *Konzeptuelle Grundlagen semantischer Dekompositionsstrukturen*. Tübingen: Niemeyer (Linguistische Arbeiten 335).

Keil, F. C. (1989). *Concepts, kinds, and cognitive development*. Cambridge, MA: MIT Press.

—— (1994). The birth and nurturance of concepts by domains: The origins of concepts of living things. In L. A. Hirschfeld and S. A. Gelman (eds.), *Mapping the mind: Domain specificity in cognition and culture*, Cambridge: Cambridge University Press.

—— and Wilson, R. A. (2000). *Explanation and cognition*. Cambridge, MA: MIT Press.

Kemler, D. G., and Smith, L. B. (1978). Is there a developmental trend from integrality to separability in perception? *Journal of Experimental Child Psychology*, 26, 498–507.

Kemler Nelson, G. D. (1990). When experimental findings conflict with everyday observations: reflections on children's category learning. *Child Development*, 61, 606–10.

—— (1995). Principle-based inferences in young children's categorization: Revisiting the impact of function on the naming of artifacts. *Cognitive Development*, 10(3), 347–80.

—— (1999). Attention to functional properties in toddler's naming and problem-solving. *Cognitive Development*, 14, 77–100.

——, Russell, R., Duke, N., and Jones, K. (2000). Two-year-olds will name artifacts by their functions. *Child Development*, 71(5), 1271–88.

Kenny, R., and Carlson, L. A. (in preparation). *Contextual influences on defining function: The impact on spatial language.*

Kersten, A. W., Goldstone, R. L., and Schaffert, A. (1998). Two competing attentional mechanisms in category learning. *Journal of Experimental Psychology: Learning, Memory, and Cognition*, 24(6), 1437–58.

King, M. C., Gruenewald, P., and Lockhead, G. R. (1978). Classifying related stimuli. *Journal of Experimental Psychology: Human, Learning and Memory*, 4(5), 417–27.

Kintsch, W. (1988). The role of knowledge in discourse comprehension: A construction-integration model. *Psychological Review*, 95, 163–82.

Klatzky, R. L., and Lederberg, S. J. (2001). Modality specificity in cognition: The case of touch. In H. L. Roediger, III, J. S. Nairne, I. Neath, and A. M. Surprenant (eds.), *The nature of remember* (pp. 233–46). Washington, DC: American Psychological Association.

Kosslyn, S. M. (1980). *Image and mind.* Cambridge, MA: Harvard University Press.

LaBerge, D., and Brown, V. (1989). Theory of attentional operations in shape identification. *Psychological Review*, 96, 101–24.

Lakoff, G. (1987). *Women, fire and dangerous things: What categories reveal about the mind.* Chicago: Chicago University Press.

Lambon Ralph, M. A., Graham, K. S., and Patterson, K. (1999). Is a picture worth a thousand words? Evidence from concept definitions by patients with semantic dementia. *Brain and Language*, 70, 309–35.

Landau, B. (1996). Multiple geometric representations of objects in languages and language learners. In P. Bloom, M. A. Peterson, L. Nadel, and M. F. Garrett (eds.), *Language and space* (pp. 317–65). Cambridge, MA: MIT Press.

—— and Jackendoff, R. (1993). 'What' and 'where' in spatial language and spatial cognition. *Behavioral and Brain Sciences*, 16, 217–65.

——, and Munnich, E. (1998). The representation of space and spatial language: Challenges for cognitive science. In P. Oliver and K. P. Gapp (eds.), *Representation and processing of spatial expressions* (pp. 263–72). Mahwah: Lawrence.

——, Smith, L. B., and Jones, S. S. (1988). The importance of shape in early lexical learning. *Cognitive Development*, 3(3), 299–321.

—— —— —— (1998). Object shape, object function, and object name. *Journal of Memory and Language*, 38(1), 1–27.

Landauer, T. K., and Dumais, S. T. (1997). A solution to Plato's problem: The latent semantic analysis theory of acquisition, induction, and representation of knowledge. *Psychological Review*, 104(2), 211–40.

Lang, E. (1990). Primary perceptual space and inherent proportion schema. *Journal of Semantics*, 5, 121–41.

——, Carstensen, K.-U., and Simmons, G. (1991). *Modelling spatial knowledge on a linguistic basis.* Springer: Berlin.

Langacker, R. W. (1987). *Foundation of cognitive grammar. Vol 1: Theoretical prerequisites.* Stanford, CA: Stanford University Press.

—— (1990). *Concept image and symbol.* New York: Mouton de Gruyter.

Laurence, S., and Margolis, E. (1999). Concepts and cognitive science. In S. Laurence and E. Margolis (eds.), *Concepts: Core readings* (pp. 3–82). Cambridge, MA: MIT Press.

Leech, G. N. (1969). *Towards a semantic description of English.* London: Longman.

Leslie, A. M., Xu, F., Tremoulet, P. D., and Scholl, B. J. (1998). Indexing and the object concept: developing 'what' and 'where' systems. *Trends in Cognitive Sciences*, 2, 10–8.

Lettvin, J. Y., Maturana, H. R., McCollough, W. S., and Pitts, W. H. (1959). What the frog's eye tells the frog's brain. *Proceedings of the Institute of Radio Engineers*, 47, 1940–51.

Levelt, W. J. M. (1996). Perspective taking and ellipsis in spatial descriptions. In P. Bloom, M. A. Peterson, L. Nadel, and M. F. Garrett (eds.), *Language and space* (pp. 77–108). Cambridge, MA: MIT Press.

Levinson, S. C. (1996*a*). Relativity in spatial conception and description. In J. J. Gumperz and S. C. Levinson (eds.), *Rethinking linguistic relativity* (pp. 177–202). Cambridge: Cambridge University Press.

—— (1996*b*). Frames of reference and Molyneux's question: Crosslinguistic evidence. In P. Bloom, M. A. Peterson, L. Nadel, and M. F. Garrett (eds.), *Language and space* (pp. 109–69). Cambridge, MA: MIT Press.

Lhermitte, F., and Serdaru, M. (1993). Unconscious processing in memory recall: A study of three amnesic patients. *Cortex*, 29(1), 25–43.

Lin, E. L., and Murphy, G. L. (1997). Effects of background knowledge on object categorization and part detection. *Journal of Experimental Psychology: Human Perception & Performance*, 23, 1153–69.

Logan, G. D. (1994). Spatial attention and the apprehension of spatial relations. *Journal of Experimental Psychology: Human Perception & Performance*, 20, 1015–36.

—— and Sadler, D. D. (1996). A computational analysis of the apprehension of spatial relations. In P. Bloom, M. A. Peterson, L. Nadel, and M. F. Garrett (eds.), *Language and space* (pp. 493–530). Cambridge, MA: MIT Press.

Loomis, J. M., Da Silva, J. A., Philbeck, J. W., and Fukusima, S. S. (1996). Visual perception of location and distance. *Current Directions in Psychological Science*, 5, 72–7.

Lowe, D. (1985). *Perceptual organization and visual recognition.* Boston, MA: Kluwer Academic.

Machado, A. (1982). *Selected poems.* Translated by A. S. Trueblood. Cambridge, MA: Harvard University Press.

MacLean, D. J., and Schuler, M. (1989). Conceptual development in infancy. *Child Development*, 60, 1126–37.

Macnamara, J. (1982). *Names for things: a study of human learning.* Cambridge, MA: MIT Press.

MacWhinney, B. (1977). Starting points. *Language*, 53, 152–68.

—— (1998). The emergence of language from embodiment. In B. MacWhinney (ed.), *The emergence of language.* Mahwah, NJ: Erlbaum.

Maddox, W. T. (1992). Perceptual and decisional separability. In F. G. Ashby (ed.), *Multidimensional models of perception and cognition: Scientific psychology series* (pp. 147–80). Hillsdale, NJ: Lawrence Erlbaum Associates, Inc.

Madole, K. L. (1993). *The role of functional properties in infants' categorization of objects.* (Poster presented at the Society for Research in Child Development, March, New Orleans, LA).

—— and Cohen, L. B. (1993). *Infants' categorization of form versus function* (Poster presented at the Society for Research in Child Development, March, New Orleans, LA).

—— and Cohen, L. B. (1995). The role of object parts in infants' attention to form–function correlations. *Developmental Psychology,* 31, 317–32.

—— and Johnston, K. E. (1999). *Infants' attention to appearance–function correlations: The role of color, shape, and labels* (Poster presented at the First biennial meeting of the Cognitive Development Society, October).

—— and Oakes, L. M. (1999). Making sense of infant categorization: Stable processes and changing representations. *Developmental Review,* 19, 263–96.

——, Cohen, L. B., and Bradley, K. (1994). *Ten-month-old infants categorize form but not function.* (Poster presented at the Ninth Biennial Conference for Infant Studies, June, Paris, France).

——, Oakes, L. M., and Cohen, L. B. (1993). Developmental changes in infants' attention to function and form–function correlations. *Cognitive Development,* 8, 189–209.

Mainwaring, S. D., Tversky, B., Ohgishi, M., and Schiano, D. J. (2003). Descriptions of simple spatial scenes in English and Japanese. *Spatial Cognition and Computation,* 3, 3–42.

Maki, R. H., and Marek, M. N. (1997). Egocentric spatial framework effects from single and multiple points of view. *Memory and Cognition,* 25, 677–90.

Malt, B. C., and Johnson, E.C. (1992). Do artifact concepts have cores? *Journal of Memory and Language,* 31, 195–217.

—— and Smith, E. E. (1983). Correlated properties in natural categories. *Journal of Verbal Learning and Verbal Behavior,* 23, 250–69.

Mandler, M. J. (1992). How to build a baby: II Conceptual primitives. *Psychological Review,* 99, 587–604.

—— (1994). Precursors of linguistic knowledge. *Phil. Trans. Royal Society London,* 346, 63–9.

—— (1996). Preverbal representation of language. In P. Bloom, M. A. Peterson, L. Nadel, and M. F. Garrett (eds.), *Language and space* (pp. 365–82). Cambridge, MA: MIT Press.

—— (1998). Representation. In D. Kuhn and R. Siegler (eds.), *Cognition, perception, and language,* Vol. 2 of W. Damon (Series Ed.), *Handbook of child psychology.* (pp. 255–308). New York: Wiley.

—— and McDonough, L. (1993). Concept formation in infancy. *Cognitive Development,* 8, 281–318.

Mareschal, D., French, R. M., and Quinn, P. C. (2000). A connectionist account of asymmetric category learning in early infancy. *Developmental Psychology,* 36, 635–45.

Marr, D. (1982). *Vision.* San Fransisco: Freeman.

Masson, M. E. J. (1995). A distributed memory model of semantic priming. *Journal of Experimental Psychology: Learning, Memory, and Cognition,* 21, 3–23.

Matan, A., and Carey, S. (2001). Developmental changes within the core of artifact concepts. *Cognition,* 78, 1–26.

May, M. (1996). Cognitive and embodied modes of spatial imagery. *Psychologische Beitraege,* 38, 418–34.

May, M. (2000). *Imaginal repositioning in space: Transformation versus interference accounts.* Talk at the 41st Annual Meeting of the Psychonomic Society, New Orleans, LA.

McCune-Nicolich, L. (1981*a*). The cognitive bases of relational words in the single word period. *Journal of Child Language,* 8(1), 15–34.

——(1981*b*). Toward symbolic functioning: Structure of early pretend games and potential parallels with language. *Child Development,* 52(3), 785–97.

—— and Carroll, S. (1981). Development of symbolic play: Implications for the language specialist. *Topics in Language Disorders,* 2(1), 1–15.

McDonough, L., Choi, S., Bowerman, M., and Mandler, M. J. (in press). The use of preferential looking as a measure of semantic development. In E. L. Bavin and D. Burnham (eds.), *Advances in infancy research.* Norwood: Ablex Publishing.

McNamara, T. P., and Miller, D. L. (1989). Attributes of theories of meaning. *Psychological Bulletin,* 106, 355–76.

Medin, D. L., and Ortony, A. (1989). Psychological essentialism. In S. Vosniadou and A. Ortony (eds.), *Similarity and analogical reasoning* (pp. 179–95). New York: Cambridge University Press.

——, Goldstone, R. L., and Gentner, D. (1993). Respects for similarity. *Psychological Review,* 100(2), 254–78.

Meints, K., Plunkett, K., Harris, P. L., and Dimmock, D. (2002). What is *on* and *under* for 15-, 18-, and 24-month-olds? Typicality effects in early comprehension of spatial prepositions. *British Journal of Developmental Psychology,* 20(1), 113–30.

Merriman, W. E., Scott, P. D., and Marazita, J. (1993). An appearance–function shift in children's object naming. *Journal of Child Language,* 20, 101–18.

Mervis, C. B. (1987). Child-basic object categories and early lexical development. In U. Neisser (ed.), *Concepts and conceptual development: Ecological and intellectual factors in categorization.* Emory symposia in cognition, 1 (pp. 201–33). New York, NY: Cambridge University Press.

—— and Bertrand, J. (1993). Acquisition of early object labels: The roles of operating principles and input. In A. P. Kaiser and D. B. Gray (eds.), *Enhancing children's communication: Research foundations for intervention* (pp. 287–316). Baltimore, MD: Paul H. Brookes Publishing.

——, Mervis, C. A., Johnson, K. E., and Bertrand, J. (1992). Studying early lexical development: The value of the systematic diary method. *Advances in Infancy Research,* 7, 291–378.

Miller, G., and Johnson-Laird, P. (1976). *Language and perception.* Cambridge, MA: Harvard University Press.

Milner, A. D., and Goodale, M. A. (1995). *The visual brain in action.* Oxford: Oxford University Press.

Mishkin, M., Ungerleider, L., and Macko, K. (1983). Object vision and spatial vision: Two cortical pathways. *Trends in Neuroscience,* 6, 414–17.

Monahan, J. S., and Lockhead, G. R. (1977). Identification of integral stimuli. *Journal of Experimental Psychology: General,* 106(1), 94–110.

Moravscik, J. M. E. (1975). *Aitia* as generative factors in Aristotle's philosophy. *Dialogue,* 14, 622–38.

——(1981). How do words get their meanings? *Journal of Philosophy,* 78, 5–24.

——(1990). *Thought and language.* London: Routledge.

Morris, M. W., and Murphy, G. L. (1990). Converging operations on a basic level in event taxonomies. *Memory and Cognition*, 18, 407–18.

Morrison, J. B., and Tversky, B. (1997). Body schemas. In M. G. Shafto and P. Langley (eds.), *Proceedings of the Meetings of the Cognitive Science Society* (pp. 525–29). Mahwah, NJ: Erlbaum.

Morrow, D. G., Greenspan, S. L., and Bower, G. H. (1987). Accessibility and situation models in narrative comprehension. *Journal of Memory and Language*, 28, 292–312.

Murphy, G. L. (2000). Explanatory concepts. In F. C. Keil and R. A. Wilson (eds.), *Explanation and cognition* (pp. 361–92). Cambridge, MA: MIT Press.

—— and Medin, D. L. (1985). The role of theories in conceptual coherence. *Psychological Review*, 92, 289–316.

Narasimhan, B. (1993). *Spatial frames of reference in the use of length, width, and height.* Unpublished manuscript, Boston University.

Needham, A. (2001). Perceptual, conceptual, and representational processes in infancy. *Journal of Experimental Child Psychology*, 78, 98–106.

—— and Baillargeon, R. (1993). Intuitions about support in 4.5-month-old infants. *Cognition*, 47, 121–48.

Nelson, K. (1974). Concept, word, and sentence: Interrelations in acquisition and development. *Psychological Review*, 81, 267–85.

—— (1979). Explorations in the development of a functional semantic system. In W. A. Collins (ed.), *The Minnesota symposium on child psychology: Children's language and communication* (Vol. 12, pp. 47–81). Hillsdale, NJ: Erlbaum.

—— (1982). The syntagmatics and paradigmatics of conceptual development. In S. A. Kuczaj (ed.), *Language development: Vol. 2, language, thought and culture* (pp. 335–64). Hillsdale, NJ: Lawrence Erlbaum Associates.

—— (1985). *Making sense: The acquisition of shared meaning.* Orlando: Academic Press.

—— (1991). Concept development in the perspective of the recent history of developmental psychology. In F. S. Kessel, M. H. Bornstein, and A. J. Sameraoff (eds.), *Contemporary constructions of the child: Essays in honor of William Kessen* (pp. 93–109). Hillsdale, NJ: Erlbaum.

——, Rescorla, L., Gruendel, J., and Benedict, H. (1978). Early lexicons: What do they mean? *Child Development*, 49, 960–68.

Newcombe, N., and Huttenlocher, J. (1992). Children's early ability to solve perspective-taking problems. *Developmental Psychology*, 28, 635–43.

Newell, A. (1980). Physical symbol systems. *Cognitive Science*, 4, 135–83.

Newton, N. (1996). *Foundations of understanding.* Philadelphia: John Benjamins.

Newtson, D. (1973). Attribution and the unit of perception of ongoing behavior. *Journal of Personality and Social Psychology*, 28, 28–38.

Nikanne, U. (1987). *Rajoittunut Mieli* ['The restricted mind']. Master Thesis, Licentate of Philosophy Thesis, University of Helsinki, Department of Finnish.

—— (1990). *Zones and tiers.* Helsinki: Finnish Literature Society.

—— (1995). Action tier formation and argument linking. *Studia Linguistica*, 49, 1–32.

—— (1997a). Locative case adjuncts in Finnish: Notes on syntactico-semantic interface. *Nordic Journal of Linguistics*, 20, 155–78.

—— (1997b). Lexical conceptual structure and syntactic arguments. *SKY* 1997, 81–118.

Nikanne, U. (2000). Some restrictions in linguistic expressions of spatial movement. In E. van der Zee and U. Nikanne (eds.), *Cognitive interfaces*. Oxford: Oxford University Press.

—— (2001). Constructions in conceptual semantics. In Jan-Ola Östman (ed.), *Construction grammar(s): Cognitive and cross-language dimensions*. Amsterdam/Philadelphia: John Benjamins.

Nosofsky, R. M. (1987). Attention and learning processes in the identification and categorization of integral stimuli. *Journal of Experimental Psychology: Learning, Memory and Cognition*, 13(1), 87–108.

—— and Palmeri, T. J. (1996). Learning to classify integral-dimension stimuli. *Psychonomic Bulletin & Review*, 3(2), 222–26.

Oakes, L. M., and Madole, K. L. (2000). The future of infant categorization research: A process-oriented approach. *Child Development*, 71, 119–26.

—— and Madole, K. L. (in press). Principles of developmental change in infants' category formation. In D. H. Rakison and L. M. Oakes (eds.), *Early category and concept development*. New York: Oxford University Press.

Oestermeier, U., and Hess, F. W. (2000). Verbal and visual causal arguments. *Cognition*, 75, 65–104.

O'Keefe, J. (1996). The spatial prepositions in English, vector grammar, and the cognitive map theory. In P. Bloom, M. A. Peterson, L. Nadel, and M. F. Garrett (eds.), *Language and space* (pp. 277–316). Cambridge, MA: MIT Press.

Olson, R. D., and Bialystok, E. (1983). *Spatial cognition: The structure and development of the mental representation of spatial relations*. Hillsdale, NJ: Erlbaum.

Östman, Jan-Ola (2002). Sulvan kansan wellerismit konstruktiona ('Wellerisms in Solf/Solv as a construction'). In *Äidinkielen merkitykset* ('Senses of the mother-tongue') (For Pentti Leino, April 17, 2002), ed. by Ilona Herlin, Jyrki Kalliokoski, Lari Kotilainen, and Tiina Onikki-Rantajääskö. Helsinki: Suomalaisen Kirjallisuuden Seura (Toimituksia 869), pp. 75–97.

Pearl, J. (1988). *Probabilistic reasoning in intelligent systems: networks of plausible inference*. San Mateo: Morgan Kaufmann.

—— (2000). *Causality: Models, reasoning, and inference*. Cambridge, MA: Cambridge University Press.

Peterson, M. A., Nadel, L., Bloom, P., and Garrett, M. F. (1996). Space and language. In P. Bloom, M. A. Peterson, L. Nadel, and M. F. Garrett (eds.), *Language and space* (pp. 553–77). Cambridge, MA: MIT Press.

Piaget, J., and Inhelder, B. (1956). *The child's conception of space*. London: Routledge & Kegan Paul.

Plumert, J. M., Ewert, K., and Spear, S. J. (1995). The early development of children's communication about nested spatial relations. *Child Development*, 66, 959–69.

Poston, T., and Stewart, I. (1978). *Catastrophe theory and its applications*. London: Pitman Publishing Limited.

Prasada, S. (1999a). Names for things and stuff. In R. Jackendoff, P. Bloom, and K. Wynn (eds.) *Language, Logic, and Concepts* (pp. 119–46). Cambridge, MA: The MIT Press.

—— (1999b). Conceptual representations of exceptions and atypical exemplars: they're not the same thing. In M. Hahn and S. C. Stoness (eds.), *Proc. 21st Annu. Conf. Cognit. Sci. Soc.* (pp. 555–59). Hillsdale, NJ: Erlbaum.

—— (2000). Acquiring generic knowledge. *Trends in Cognitive Sciences*, 4, 66–72.

—— (2003). Conceptual representation of animacy and its perceptual and linguistic reflections. *Developmental Science*, 6, 18–9.

—— and Ferenz, K. (2001). *Is the couch near the television? Functional information and talking about distances* (Unpublished manuscript).

——, Ferenz, K., and Haskell, T. (2002). Conceiving of entities as objects and as stuff. *Cognition*, 83, 141–65.

Prawat, R. S., and Wildfon, S. (1980). The influence of functional context on children's labeling responses. *Child Development*, 51(4), 1057–60.

Presson, C. C. (1980). Spatial egocentrism and the effect of an alternate frame of reference. *Journal of Experimental Child Psychology*, 29, 391–402.

—— (1982). Strategies in spatial reasoning. *Journal of Experimental Psychology: Learning, Memory, and Cognition*, 8, 243–51.

—— and Montello, D. R. (1994). Updating after rotational and translational body movements: Coordinate structure of perspective space. *Perception*, 23, 1447–55.

Proffitt, D. R., Bhalla, M., Gossweiler, R., and Midgett, J. (1995). Perceiving geographical slant. *Psychonomic Bulletin & Review*, 2, 409–28.

Pustejovsky, J. (1991). The syntax of event structures. *Cognition*, 41, 47–81.

—— (1995). *The generative lexicon*. Cambridge, MA: The MIT Press.

Putnam, H. (1981). *Reason, truth, and history*. Cambridge: Cambridge University Press.

Quinn, P. C. (1994). The categorization of above and below spatial relations by young infants. *Child Development*, 65, 58–69.

—— (1998). Object and spatial categorization in young infants: 'What' and 'where' in early visual perception. In A. M. Slater (ed.), *Perceptual development: Visual, auditory, and speech perception in infancy* (pp. 131–65). East Sussex, UK: Psychology Press (Taylor & Francis).

—— (1999). Development of recognition and categorization of objects and their spatial relations in young infants. In C. Tamis-LeMonda and L. Balter (eds.), *Child psychology: A handbook of contemporary issues* (pp. 85–115). Philadelphia: Psychology Press (Taylor & Francis).

—— (2002). Early categorization: A new synthesis. In U. Goswami (ed.), *Blackwell handbook of childhood cognitive development* (pp. 84–101). Oxford: Blackwell.

—— (2003). Concepts are not just for objects: Categorization of spatial relation information by infants. In D. H. Rakison and L. M. Oakes (eds.), *Early category and concept development: Making sense of the blooming, buzzing confusion* (pp. 50–76). Oxford: Oxford University Press.

—— and Bhatt, R. S. (2001). Object recognition and object segregation in infancy: Historical perspective, theoretical significance, 'kinds' of knowledge, and relation to object categorization. *Journal of Experimental Child Psychology*, 78, 25–34.

—— and Bomba, P. C. (1986). Evidence for a general category of oblique orientations in 4-month-old infants. *Journal of Experimental Child Psychology*, 42, 345–54.

—— and Eimas, P. D. (1996). Perceptual organization and categorization in young infants. In C. Rovee-Collier and L. P. Lipsitt (eds.), *Advances in infancy research* (Vol. 10, pp. 1–36). Norwood, NJ: Ablex.

—— and Eimas, P. D. (1997). A reexamination of the perceptual-to-conceptual shift in mental representations. *Review of General Psychology*, 1, 271–87.

Quinn, P. C. and Eimas, P. D. (2000). The emergence of category representations during infancy: Are separate perceptual and conceptual processes required? *Journal of Cognition and Development*, 1, 55–61.

—— and Johnson, M. H. (2000). Global-before-basic object categorization in connectionist networks and 2-month-old infants. *Infancy*, 1, 31–46.

——, Brown, C. R., and Streppa, M. L. (1997). Perceptual organization of complex visual configurations by young infants. *Infant Behavior and Development*, 20, 35–46.

——, Burke, S., and Rush, A. (1993). Part–whole perception in early infancy: Evidence for perceptual grouping produced by lightness similarity. *Infant Behavior and Development*, 16, 19–42.

——, Siqueland, E. R., and Bomba, P. C. (1985). Delayed recognition memory for orientation by human infants. *Journal of Experimental Child Psychology*, 40, 293–303.

——, Adams, A., Kennedy, E., Shettler, L., and Wasnik, A. (2003). Development of an abstract category representation for the spatial relation between in 6- to 10-month-old infants. *Developmental Psychology*, 39, 151–63.

——, Cummins, M., Kase, J., Martin, E., and Weissman, S. (1996). Development of categorical representations for above and below spatial relations in 3- to 7-month-old infants. *Developmental Psychology*, 32, 942–50.

——, Norris, C. M., Pasko, R. N., Schmader, T. M., and Mash, C. (1999). Formation of a categorical representation for the spatial relation between by 6- to 7-month-old infants. *Visual Cognition*, 6, 569–85.

——, Polly, J. L., Dobson, V., and Narter, D. B. (1998). *Categorical representation of specific versus abstract above and below spatial relations in 3- to 4-month-old infants* (Paper presented at the International Conference on Infant Studies, April, Atlanta, GA).

—— ——, Furer, M. J., Dobson, V., and Narter, D. B. (2002). Young infants' performance in the object-variation version of the above versus below categorization task: A result of perceptual distraction or conceptual limitation? *Infancy*, 3, 323–47.

Rakison, D. H. (in press). Parts, categorization, and the development of the animate–inanimate distinction in infancy. In D. H. Rakison and L. M. Oakes (eds.), *Early category and concept development*. New York: Oxford University Press.

Rauh, G. (1997). Lokale Präpositionen und referentielle Argumente. *Linguistische Berichte*, 171, 415–42.

Reed, C. L., and Farah, M. J. (1995). The psychological reality of the body schema: A test with normal participants. *Journal of Experimental Psychology: Human Perception and Performance*, 21, 334–43.

Regier, T. (1996). *The human semantic potential: Spatial language and constrained connectionism*. Cambridge, MA: MIT Press.

—— (1997). Constraints on the learning of spatial terms: A computational investigation. In R. Goldstone, P. Schyns, and D. Medin (eds.), *Psychology of learning and motivation: Mechanisms of perceptual learning*. (Vol. 36, pp. 171–217). San Diego: Academic Press.

—— and Carlson, L. A. (2001). Grounding spatial language in perception: An empirical and computational investigation. *Journal of Experimental Psychology: General*, 130(2), 273–98.

Rehder, B. (1999). A causal model theory of categorization. In *The twenty-first annual conference of the Cognitive Science Society* (pp. 595–600). Vancouver, British Columbia.

—— (2001). *A causal-model theory of conceptual representation and categorization.* (Manuscript submitted for publication).

Richards, D. D., and Goldfarb, J. (1986). The episodic memory model of conceptual development: An integrative viewpoint. *Cognitive Development*, 1, 183–219.

——, Goldfarb, J., Richards, A. L., and Hassen, P. (1989). The role of the functionality rule in the categorization of well-defined concepts. *Journal of Experimental Child Psychology*, 47, 97–115.

Richards, L. V. (2001). *Children's production of locative expressions in English; the influence of geometric and extra-geometric factors* (Unpublished PhD Thesis, University of Plymouth, UK).

—— and Coventry, K. R. (2004). When *above* and *in front of* become *near* and *by*: Functional constraints on how children and adults produce spatial expressions. (Manuscript in submission).

——, ——, and Clibbens, J. (2004). Where's the orange? Geometric and extra-geometric factors in English children's talk of spatial locations, *Journal of Child Languages*, 31, 153–75.

Richards, W. (1988). *Natural computation.* Cambridge, MA: MIT Press.

——, Jepson, A., and Feldman, J. (1996). Priors, preferences and categorical percepts. In W. Richards (ed.), *Perception as Bayesian inference.* Cambridge: Cambridge University Press.

Riddoch, M. J., Humphreys, G. W., and Edwards, M. G. (2000). Neuropsychological evidence distinguishing object selection from action (effector) selection. *Cognitive Neuropsychology*, 17(6), 547–62.

Rieser, J. J. (1989). Access to knowledge of spatial structure at novel points of observation. *Journal of Experimental Psychology: Learning, Memory, and Cognition*, 15, 1157–65.

——, Garing, A. E., and Young, M. F. (1994). Imagery, action, and young children's spatial orientation: It's not being there that counts, it's what one has in mind. *Child Development*, 65, 1262–78.

Rifkin, A. (1985). Evidence for a basic level in event taxonomies. *Memory and Cognition*, 13, 538–56.

Rinck, M., and Bower, G. H. (1995). Anaphora resolution and the focus of attention in situation models. *Journal of Memory and Language*, 34, 110–31.

Rosch, E. (1973). Natural Categories. *Cognitive Psychology*, 4, 328–50.

—— (1978). Principles of categorization. In E. Rosch and B. B. Lloyd (eds.), *Cognition and categorization* (pp. 27–48). Hillsdale, NJ: Erlbaum.

—— and Mervis, B. C. (1975). Family resemblances: Studies in the internal structure of categories. *Cognitive Psychology*, 7, 573–605.

——, Simpson, C., and Miller, R. S. (1976). Structural basis of typicality effects. *Journal of Experimental Psychology: Human Perception and Performance*, 2, 491–502.

——, Mervis, C. B., Gray, W., Johnson, D., and Boyes-Braem, P. (1976). Basic objects in natural categories. *Cognitive Psychology*, 8, 382–439.

Rose, S. A. (1988). Shape recognition in infancy: Visual integration of sequential information. *Child Development*, 59, 1161–76.

Roskos-Ewoldsen, B., McNamara, T. P., Shelton, A. L., and Carr, W. (1998). Mental representations of large and small spatial layouts are orientation dependent. *Journal of Experimental Psychology: Learning, Memory, and Cognition*, 24, 215–26.

Rovee-Collier, C., and Hayne, H. (1987). Reactivation of infant memory: Implications for cognitive development. In H. W. Reese (ed.), *Advances in child development and behavior* (Vol. 20, pp. 185–238). Orlando, FL: Academic Press.

Rueckl, J. G., Cave, K., and Kosslyn, S. (1989). Why are 'what' and 'where' processed by separate cortical systems? A computational investigation. *Journal of Cognitive Neuroscience*, 1, 171–86.

Ruff, H. A., and Rothbart, M. K. (1996). *Attention in early development.* New York: Oxford University Press.

Rumelhart, D. E. (1980). Schemata: The building blocks of cognition. In R. J. Spiro, B. C. Bruce, and W. F. Brewer (eds.), *Theoretical issues in reading comprehension: Perspectives from cognitive psychology, linguistics, artificial intelligence, and education.* Hillsdale, NJ: Erlbaum.

Rumiati, R. J., and Humphreys, G. W. (1998). Recognition by action: Dissociating visual and semantic routes to action in normal observers. *Journal of Experimental Psychology: Human Perception and Performance*, 24(2), 631–47.

Samuelson, L. K., and Smith, L. B. (1999). Early noun vocabularies: Do ontology, category structure and syntax correspond? *Cognition*, 73(1), 1–33.

—— and Smith, L. B. (2002). Shape and early over-generalizations of object names. (In preparation).

Schank, R. (1972). Conceptual dependency: A theory of natural language understanding. *Cognitive Psychology*, 3, 552–631.

—— and Abelson, R. P. (1977). *Scripts, plans, goals, and understanding: an inquiry into human knowledge structures.* Hillsdale, NJ: L. Erlbaum Associates.

Schmidtke, H. R., Tschander, L., Eschenbach, C., and Habel, C. (2003). Change of orientation. In J. Slack and E. van der Zee (eds.), *Representing direction in language and space.* Oxford: Oxford University Press.

Schober, M. F. (1993). Spatial perspective-taking in conversation. *Cognition*, 47, 1–24.

—— (1995). Speakers, addressees, and frames of reference: Whose effort is minimized in conversations about locations. *Discourse Processes*, 20, 219–47.

Schon, D. A. (1983). *The reflective practitioner.* New York: Basic Books.

Schwartz, D., and Black, T. (1999). Inferences through imagined actions: Knowing by simulated doing. *Journal of Experimental Psychology: Learning, Memory, and Cognition*, 25, 116–36.

Schyns, P. G., and Rodet, L. (1997). Categorization creates functional features. *Journal of Experimental Psychology: Learning, Memory and Cognition*, 23(3), 681–96.

Schyns, P., Goldstone, R. L., and Thilbaut, J.-P. (1998). The development of features in object concepts. *Behavioral & Brain Sciences*, 21(1), 1–54.

Searle, J. R. (1980). Minds, brains and programs. *Behavioral and Brain Sciences*, 3, 417–24.

Shelton, A. L., and McNamara, T. P. (1997). Multiple views of spatial memory. *Psychonomic Bulletin & Review*, 4, 102–06.

—— and McNamara, T. P. (2001). Systems of spatial reference in human memory. *Cognitive Psychology*, 43, 274–310.

Sholl, M. J., and Nolin, T. L. (1997). Orientation specificity in representations of place. *Journal of Experimental Psychology: Learning, Memory, and Cognition*, 23, 1494–507.

Shore, C., O'Connell, B., and Bates, E. (1984). First sentences in language and symbolic play. *Developmental Psychology*, 20(5), 872–80.

Simons, D. J., and Wang, R. F. (1998). Perceiving real-world viewpoint changes. *Psychological Science*, 9, 315–20.

Sinha, C. (1982). Representational development and the structure of action. In G. Butterworth and P. Light (eds.), *Social Cognition: Studies in the Development of Understanding* (pp. 137–62). Hassocks: Harvester Press.

——, Thorseng, L. A., Hayashi, M., and Plunkett, K. (1994). Comparative spatial semantics and language acquisition: Evidence from Danish, English, and Japanese. *Journal of Semantics*, 11, 253–87.

Skouteris, H., McKenzie, B. E., and Day, R. H. (1992). Integration of sequential information for shape perception by infants: A developmental study. *Child Development*, 63, 1164–76.

Sloman, S. A., Love, B., and Ahn, W. (1998). Feature centrality and conceptual coherence. *Cognitive Science*, 22, 189–228.

Smith, B. L. (1979). Perceptual development and category generalization. *Child development*, 50, 705–15.

Smith, E. E., Shoben, E. J., and Rips, L. J. (1974). Structure and process in semantic memory: A featural model for semantic decisions. *Psychological Review*, 81(3), 214–41.

Smith, L. B. (1999). Children's noun learning: How general learning processes make specialized learning mechanisms. In B. MacWhinney (ed.), *The emergence of language* (pp. 277–303). Mahwah, NJ: Lawrence Erlbaum Associates, Inc., Publishers.

—— (2003). Learning to recognize objects. *Psychological Science*, 14(3), 244–51.

—— and Kemler, D. B. (1977). Developmental trends in free classification: Evidence for a new conceptualization of perceptual development. *Journal of Experimental Child Psychology*, 24, 279–98.

—— and Kemler, D. B. (1978). Levels of experienced dimensionality in children and adults. *Cognitive Psychology*, 10, 502–32.

——, Jones, S. S., and Landau, B. (1996). Naming in young children: A dumb attentional mechanism? *Cognition*, 60(2), 143–71.

Smith, L. B., Jones, S. S., Landau, B., Gershkoff-Stowe, L., and Samuelson, S. (2002). Early noun learning provides on-the-job training for attention. *Psychological Science*, 13(1), 13–19.

——, Gasser, M., and Sandhofer, C. M. (1997). Learning to talk about properties of objects: A network model of the development of dimensions. In R. L. Goldstone, P. G. Schyns, and D. L. Medin (eds.), *The Psychology of Learning and Motivation* (Vol. 36, pp. 219–55). San Diego, CA: Academic Press.

Sowden, S., and Blades, M. (1996). Children's and adults' understanding of the locative prepositions 'next to' and 'near to'. *First Language*, 16(3), 287–99.

Spalding, T. L., and Murphy, G. L. (1996). Effects of background knowledge on category construction. *Journal of Experimental Psychology: Learning, Memory, and Cognition*, 22, 525–38.

—— and Murphy, G. L. (1999). What is learned in knowledge-related categories? Evidence from typicality and feature frequency judgments. *Memory & Cognition*, 27, 856–67.

Spelke, E. S., Breinlinger, K., Macomber, J., and Jacobson, K. (1992). Origins of knowledge. *Psychological Review*, 99, 605–32.

Stanfield, R. A., and Zwaan, R. A. (2001). The effect of implied orientation derived from verbal context on picture recognition. *Psychological Science*, 12, 153–56.

Starkey, P., Spelke, E. S., and Gelman, R. (1990). Numerical abstraction by human infants. *Cognition*, 36, 97–127.

Steadman, P. (2001). Binary encoding of a class of rectangular built-in forms. In J. Peponis, J. Wineman, and S. Bafna (eds.), *Proceedings of the Third International Space Syntax Symposium.* Ann Arbor: A. Alfred Taubman College of Architecture and Urban Planning.

Suwa, M., and Tversky, B. (1997). What do architects and students perceive in their sketches?: A protocol analysis. *Design Studies*, 18, 385–403.

—— —— (2001). How do designers shift their focus of attention in their own sketches? In M. Anderson, B. Meyer, and P. Olivier (eds.), *Diagrammatic reasoning and representation* (pp. 241–60). Berlin: Springer.

Talmy, L. (1983). How language structures space. In H. Pick and L. Acredolo (eds.), *Spatial orientation: Theory, research, and application* (pp. 225–82). New York: Plenum.

—— (1985). Force dynamics in language and thought. In W. Elfort, P. D. Kroeber, and K. L. Peterson (eds.), Papers from the parasession on causative and agentivity. Chicago: Chicago Linguistic Society.

—— (1987). The relation of grammar to cognition. In B. Rudzka-Ostyn (ed.), *Topics in cognitive linguistics* (pp. 165–205). Amsterdam: John Benjamins Publishing.

—— (1988). Force dynamics in language and cognition. *Cognitive Science*, 12, 49–100.

—— (2000). *Towards a Cognitive Semantics.* Cambridge, MA: MIT Press.

Tarr, M. J. (1995). Rotating objects to recognize them: A case study on the role of viewpoint dependency in the recognition of three-dimensional objects. *Psychonomic Bulletin & Review*, 2(1), 55–82.

Taylor, H. A., and Tversky, B. (1996). Perspective in spatial descriptions. *Journal of Memory and Language*, 35, 371–91.

Thelen, E., and Smith, L. B. (1994). *A dynamic systems approach to the development of cognition and action.* Cambridge, MA: MIT Press.

Tomasello, M. (1987). Learning how to use prepositions: A case study. *Journal of Child Language*, 14, 79–98.

—— (1998). *The new psychology of language.* Mahwah, NJ: Erlbaum.

Tomikawa, S. A., and Dodd, D. H. (1980). Early word meanings: Perceptually or functionally based? *Child Development*, 51, 1103–09.

Treisman, A., and Gelade, G. (1980). A feature-integration theory of attention. *Cognitive Psychology*, 12, 97–135.

—— and Gormican, S. (1988). Feature analysis in early vision: Evidence from search asymmetries. *Psychological Review*, 95, 15–48.

Tversky, B. (1985). Categories and parts. In C. Craig & T. Givon (eds.), *Noun classes and categorization* (pp. 63–75). Philadelphia: John Benjamins Publishing Co.

—— (1989). Parts, partonomies, and taxonomies. *Developmental Psychology*, 25, 983–95.

—— (1990). Where partonomies and taxonomies meet. In S. L. Tsohatzidis (ed.), *Meanings and prototypes: Studies on linguistic categorization* (pp. 334–44). London: Routledge.

—— (1996). Spatial perspective in descriptions. In P. Bloom, M. A. Peterson, L. Nadel, and M. F. Garrett (eds.), *Language and space* (pp. 463–91). Cambridge, MA: MIT-Press.

—— and Hemenway, K. (1983). Categories of scenes. *Cognitive Psychology*, 15, 121–49.

—— —— (1984). Objects, parts, and categories. *Journal of Experimental Psychology: General*, 113, 169–93.

——, Kim, J., and Cohen, A. (1999). Mental models of spatial relations and transformations from language. In C. Habel and G. Rickheit (eds.), *Mental models in discourse processing and reasoning* (pp. 239–58). Amsterdam: North-Holland.

——, Lee, P. U., and Mainwaring, S. (1999). Why speakers mix perspectives. *Journal of Spatial Cognition and Computation*, 1, 399–412.

——, Morrison, J. B., and Zacks, J. (2001). On bodies and events. In A. Meltzoff and W. Prinz (eds.), *The imitative mind*. Cambridge: Cambridge University Press.

——, Zacks, J., Lee, P. U., and Heiser, J. (2000). Lines, blobs, crosses, and arrows: Diagrammatic communication with schematic figures. In M. Anderson, P. Cheng and V. Haarslev (eds.), *Theory and application of diagrams* (pp. 221–30). Berlin: Springer.

Ullman, S. (1984). Visual routines. *Cognition*, 18, 97–159.

—— (1996). *High Level Vision*. Cambridge, MA: MIT Press.

—— (2000). *High-level vision. Object recognition and visual cognition*. Cambridge, MA: MIT Press.

Ullmer-Ehrich, V. (1982). The structure of living space descriptions. In R. J. Jarvella and W. Klein (eds.), *Speech, place and action* (pp. 219–49). Chichester, England: Wiley.

Ungerleider, L. G., and Mishkin, M. (1982). Two cortical systems. In D. J. Ingle, M. A. Goodale, and R. J. W. Mansfeld (eds.), *Analysis of visual behavior* (pp. 549–86). Cambridge, MA: MIT Press.

Uttal, D. H., Schreiber, J. C., and Deloache, J. S. (1995). Waiting to use a symbol: The effects of delay on children's use of models. *Child Development*, 66, 1875–89.

van der Zee, E. (1996). *Spatial knowledge and spatial language: A theoretical and empirical investigation*. Utrecht University, The Netherlands: ISOR Publications.

—— (2000). Why we can talk about bulging barrels and spinning spirals: Curvatur representations in the lexical interface. In E. van der Zee and U. Nikanne (eds.), *Cognitive interfaces. Constraints on linking cognitive information* (pp. 143–82). Oxford: Oxford University Press.

—— and Eshuis, R. (2003). Directions from shape: How spatial features determine reference axis categorization. In E. van der Zee and J. Slack (eds.), *Representing direction in language and space*. Oxford: Oxford University Press.

—— and J. Slack (eds.) (2003). *Representing direction in language and space*. Oxford: Oxford University Press.

——, Watson, M., and Fletcher, K. (submitted). *What does it mean to be between? Is between a function of space, or is there also space for function?*

Vandeloise, C. (1986). *L'espace en français*. Paris: Editions du Seuil.

—— (1987). Complex primitives in language acquisition. *Belgian Journal of Linguistics*, 2, 11–36.

—— (1990). Representation, prototypes and centrality. In S. Tsohatzidis (ed.), *Meanings and prototypes: Studies in linguistic categorization* (pp. 403–37). London & New York: Routledge.

—— (1991). *Spatial prepositions: A case study in French*. Chicago: The University of Chicago Press.

—— (1994). Methodology and analyses of the preposition *in*. *Cognitive Linguistics*, 5(2), 157–85.

—— (1995). Cognitive linguistics and prototypes. In T. A. Sebeok and J. Umiker-Sebeok (eds.), *Advances in visual semiotics: The semiotic web 1992–1993* (pp. 423–42). Berlin: Mouton de Gruyter.

Vecera, S. P., and Farah, M. J. (1994). Does visual attention select objects or locations? *Journal of Experimental Psychology: General*, 123, 146–60.

Vendler, Z. (1957). Verbs and times. *Philosophical Review*, 66, 143–60.

Veneziano, E. (1981). Early language and nonverbal representation: A reassessment. *Journal of Child Language*, 8, 541–63.

Vilkuna, M. (1989). *Free Word Order in Finnish*. Helsinki: Suomalaisen Kirjallisuuden Seura.

Wagemans, J. (1995). Detection of visual symmetries. *Spatial Vision*, 9(1), 9–32.

Wang, R. F., and Simons, D. J. (1999). Active and passive scene recognition across views. *Cognition*, 70, 191–210.

Weist, R. M. (1991). Spatial and temporal location in child language. *First Language*, 11, 253–67.

—— and Uzunov, K. (1990). Spatial location in children's English: On the mono-/bireferential distinction. *Perceptual and Motor Skills*, 71, 1267–74.

——, Lyytinen, P., Wysocka, J., and Atanassova, M. (1997). The interaction of language and thought in children's language acquisition: a crosslinguistic study. *Journal of Child Language*, 24, 81–121.

Werner, S., and Schmidt, K. (1999). Environmental reference systems for large-scale spaces. *Spatial Cognition & Computation*, 1, 447–73.

Wertheimer, M. (1923/1958). Principles of perceptual organization. In. D. C. Beardslee and M. Wertheimer (eds.), *Readings in perception* (pp. 115–35). Princeton, NJ: Van Nostrand.

Wierzbicka, A. (1992). Semantic primitives and semantic fields. In A. Lehrer and E. F. Kittay (eds.), *Frames, fields, and contrasts: New essays in semantic and lexical organization* (pp. 209–28). New Jersey: Erlbaum.

Wilcox, S., and Palermo, D. S. (1975). 'in', 'on', and 'under' revisited. *Cognition*, 3, 245–254.

Wilson, H. R., and Kim, J. (1994). Perceived motion in the vector sum direction. *Vision Research*, 34, 1835–42.

Wilson, R. A., and Keil, F. C. (2000). The shadows and shallows of explanation. In F. C. Keil and R. A. Wilson (eds.), *Explanation and cognition*. Cambridge, MA: The MIT Press.

Wimsatt, W. C. (1972). Teleological and logical structure of function statements. *Studies in History and Philosophy of Science*, 3, 1–80.

Wittgenstein, L. (1953). *Philosophical investigations*. New York: Plenum.

Woodward, A. L., and Hoyne, K. L. (1999). Infants' learning about words and sounds in relation to objects. *Child Development*, 70(1), 65–77.

——, Markman, E. M., and Fitzsimmons, C. M. (1994). Rapid word learning in 13- and 18-month-olds. *Developmental Psychology*, 30(4), 553–66.

Wraga, M., Creem, S. H., and Proffitt, D. R. (1999). The influence of spatial reference frames on imagined object and viewer rotations. *Acta Psychologica*, 102, 247–64.

—— —— —— (2000). Updating displays after imagined object and viewer rotations. *Journal of Experimental Psychology: Learning, Memory, and Cognition*, 26, 151–68.

Wright, L. (1973). Functions. *Philosophical Review*, 82, 139–68.

Wu, L., and Barsalou, L. W. (2004). Perceptual simulation in property generation. Under review.

Wunderlich, D. (1985). Raum, Zeit und das Lexicon. In H. Schweitzer (ed.), *Sprache und Raum: Psychologische und linguistische Aspekte der Aneignung und Verarbeitung von Raumlichkeit* (pp. 66–90). Stuttgart: Metzler.

—— and Herweg, M. (1991). Lokale und Direktionale. In A. V. Stechow and D. Wunderlich (eds.), *Semantik* (pp. 758–85). Berlin, New York: de Gruyter.

Xu, F. (1999). Object individuation and object identity in infancy: The role of spatio-temporal information, object property information, and language. *Acta Psychologica*, 102, 113–36.

—— and Carey, S. (1996). Infants' metaphysics: The case of numerical identity. *Cognitive Psychology*, 30, 111–53.

Younger, B. A. (in press). Parsing objects into categories: Infants' perception and use of correlated attributes. In D. H. Rakison and L. M. Oakes (eds.), *Early category and concept development*. New York: Oxford University Press.

—— and Cohen, L. B. (1986). Developmental changes in infants' perception of correlations among attributes. *Child Development*, 57, 803–15.

—— and Fearing, D. D. (2000). Global-to-basic trend in early categorization: Evidence from a dual-category habituation task. *Infancy*, 1, 47–58.

Zacks, J., and Tversky, B. (2001). Event structure in perception and conception. *Psychological Bulletin*, 127(1), 3–21.

—— —— and Iyer, G. (2001). Perceiving, remembering and communicating structure in events. *Journal of Experimental Psychology: General*, 36, 29–58.

——, Rypma, B., Gabrieli, J. D. E., Tversky, B., and Glover, G. H. (1999). Imagined transformations of bodies: An fMRI investigation. *Neuropsychologia*, 37, 1029–40.

Zimmer, H. D., Speiser, H. R., Baus, J., Blocher, A., and Stopp, E. (1998). The use of locative expressions in dependence of the spatial relation between target and reference object in two-dimensional layouts. In C. Freksa, C. Habel, and K. F. Wender (eds.), *Spatial cognition* (pp. 223–40). Berlin: Springer.

Author index

Index of terms